MODI & INDIA

2024 and the Battle *for* BHARAT

Rahul Shivshankar
Siddhartha Talya

VINTAGE
An imprint of Penguin Random House

VINTAGE

USA | Canada | UK | Ireland | Australia
New Zealand | India | South Africa | China | Singapore

Vintage is part of the Penguin Random House group of companies
whose addresses can be found at global.penguinrandomhouse.com

Published by Penguin Random House India Pvt. Ltd
4th Floor, Capital Tower 1, MG Road,
Gurugram 122 002, Haryana, India

Penguin
Random House
India

First published in Vintage by Penguin Random House India 2023

ISBN 9780670098613

Typeset in Adobe Garamond Pro by Manipal Technologies Limited, Manipal
Printed at Replika Press Pvt. Ltd, India

www.penguin.co.in

Contents

Introduction   vii

1. A Pledge to Bharat Redeemed   1
2. The Hindu Ethos and the Calumny of Communalism   28
3. They Took the Hindu Out of the Indian   44
4. Whither Ganga–Jamuni Tehzeeb?   63
5. A Discriminatory Secularism   79
6. Hindu Raj: A Study of Inclusivity   118
7. Faith in Dharma   132
8. Imagining a Hindu Rashtra   154
9. Can India Be Tolerant without Being 'Secular'?   176
10. 'Yato Dharmastato Jayah'   204

Conclusion   219
Notes   233

Introduction

The 2024 parliamentary election is destined to be discussed long into the future. It has a triggered a debate, with many prompting the question: Will the election be a vote for the establishment of a Hindu Rashtra? [1]

Some have alleged that Narendra Modi's ten-year reign as prime minister has thrived on 'cruelty, fear, division and violence'.[2] Modi's political challengers seem to agree, and to underline this point several Opposition parties have banded together under an umbrella coalition called 'INDIA', or the Indian National Developmental Inclusive Alliance. Tellingly, one 'I' in the acronym stands for 'Inclusive'. The emphasis is deliberate. The use of the word is intended to send a clear message to voters that the 'INDIA' grouping alone can 'safeguard the idea of India as enshrined in the Constitution'.[3]

INDIA resolves to fight 'the systemic conspiracy by the BJP to target, persecute and suppress our fellow Indians. Their poisonous campaign of hate has led to vicious violence against all those opposed to the ruling party and its divisive ideology. These attacks are not just eroding Constitutional rights and freedoms but also eroding the basic values upon which the Republic of India is founded – Liberty, Equality and Fraternity and Justice – Political, Economic and Social. The repeated attempts by the BJP to vitiate public discourse by reinventing and rewriting Indian history are an affront to social harmony.'[4]

Indeed, some have also claimed that the BJP's voters—seduced by a prejudiced, paranoid and parochial Hindutva—are being inexorably primed to vote in a Hindu Rashtra where minorities are reduced to second-class citizens.[5]

The assignation of voters to a political outlook that has nothing to do with their primary identities is a recent trend in the Indian context. A BJP voter is criticized with barbs like 'andhbhakt', 'Godsewadi', 'Hindutvawadi', 'Sanghi',[6] 'Rakshas' (demon).[7] And now there's even 'Musanghi', used often on the social media to shame Muslims sympathetic to the BJP and the RSS or critical of 'secular' parties.[8] The use of the term Musanghi paints a target on the backs of the BJP's Muslim supporters by lumping them with the so-called Hindu fringe.[9]

This trend of using demeaning labels to shame or ridicule voters was observed on a mass scale in the 'world's oldest democracy',[10] when the US Democrat presidential nominee Hillary Clinton chose to describe supporters of her Republican party rival, Donald Trump, as a 'basket of deplorables'.[11] 'You know,' Clinton said to a room full of wealthy donors in 2016, 'to just be grossly generalistic, you could put half of Trump's supporters into what I call the basket of deplorables. Right? The racist, sexist, homophobic, xenophobic, Islamophobic—you name it.'[12]

Clinton's words kicked up a massive storm in the United States. Her rival turned her words into an ad campaign, cornering what he described as her attempt to 'viciously demonize hard-working Americans'.[13] A year later, Clinton acknowledged that her words served as a 'political gift' to Trump, who was able to exploit her remarks to tap into the frustrations of 'millions of White people'.[14]

Clinton admitted one of the reasons for her defeat was that '[Trump] was quite successful in referencing a nostalgia that would give hope, comfort, settle grievances for millions of people who were upset about gains that were made by others . . . I understood that there were many Americans who, because of the financial crash, there was anger. And there was resentment. I knew that. But I believed that it was my responsibility to try to offer answers to it, not to fan it . . .'[15]

Yet, despite Clinton publicly acknowledging the cost of using loaded labels, Indian Opposition leaders, such as those who have compared BJP voters to demons, have had few qualms about adopting the American politician's tactics. It remains to be seen if such remarks will face a backlash from the voter, like Clinton's statements did in America in 2016.

The Congress Party scion, Rahul Gandhi, embarked on a Bharat Jodo Yatra in the latter half of 2022.[16] Over many days and many kilometres, Gandhi never failed to mention how the country was yearning for compassionate leadership, that the need of the hour was to arrest the country's slide into 'hate' and 'divisiveness' propelled by the ideology of the RSS and the BJP.[17] He called upon people to snap out of the dark spell cast on them by Modi and his home minister, Amit Shah, and subscribe to the views of the Congress, which, Gandhi said, is committed to an ideology of 'love and brotherhood'.[18]

In 2023, at least one pejorative attack led by Rahul Gandhi on Modi—dating back to 2019—and allegedly his 'community'[19] caught up with him. A lower court in Surat held him guilty of defamation and handed out a conviction which briefly lost the Congress leader his seat in Parliament. Gandhi, upon appeal, obtained a stay on that conviction from the Supreme Court,[20] paving the way for the restoration of his membership.[21]

At least as of now, Gandhi and many of his political cohorts haven't backed down. They continue to insist without evidence that there is an organized campaign by 'Hindutvawadis' to hijack the Hindu faith, weaponize its symbols and declare war on minorities and those who stand in the way of their project of creating a Hindu Rashtra or even a Hindu Rajya (state) powered by fundamentalism.[22]

Thus the 2024 election is being billed by the Left ecosystem as the last opportunity to stop this alleged mad rush to consecrate the Hindu state—a veritable second republic where the rights of minorities, especially Muslims, are suppressed or even denied by the 'Hindu nationalist'.[23]

Many self-styled secularists believe it might already be too late. The second republic, or the 'Hindu Rashtra', as they call it, is already upon us. They point to the Modi government's scrapping of Article 370;[24] the promulgation of the Citizenship Amendment Act (CAA);[25] the alleged assault on communal amity by some BJP members seeking to repeal the 1991 Places of Worship Act to reclaim sites where Hindus believed temples had been destroyed by colonizers to build mosques or churches;[26] the adoption of 'anti-conversion' or 'anti-love jihad' bills by BJP-ruled state governments; the demand for a reform in Muslim personal law and the endeavour to bring in a uniform civil code.[27] These initiatives, they claim, reek of Hindu supremacism and are aimed at creating an architecture of otherness.

But the BJP and its supporters disagree. Not only were some of these much-derided initiatives at some point supported by the Congress,[28] but, crucially, they all have been pursued through democratic means and institutions. For example, the move to virtually abrogate Article 370 was not outside of the constitutional scheme, because since its inception it was meant to be a temporary provision.[29] The BJP says that the Modi government only fulfilled an obligation bestowed upon it by the framers of the Constitution.[30] The article had been hollowed out by many prior amendments[31] and should have been scrapped long ago but for ritualistic virtue-signalling by governments adept at practising 'pseudo secularism'.[32]

As for the CAA, the BJP never tires of pointing out that it was designed to echo the sentiments of India's first prime minister, Jawaharlal Nehru.[33] Speaking to Parliament in February 2020, Prime Minister Modi referred to a letter Nehru had purportedly written in 1949 to Assam's first chief minister, Gopinath Bordoloi, asking him to 'absorb' refugees from East Pakistan, adding that he would have to 'differentiate' between Hindu refugees and Muslim migrants.[34] Modi said he was astonished that when his government had adopted Nehru's philosophy in letter and spirit, the Congress Party was hypocritically painting the NDA as communal.[35]

But Modi's arguments are brushed aside by some, especially when they see that the backdrop of the BJP's 2024 election campaign is framed against the grand opening of the Ram temple in Ayodhya.[36]

Of course, it can always be asked: Is there ever an ideal time to hand back to Hindus a symbol of their culture and civilization? Even if the inauguration of the Ram temple in Ayodhya were to take place after the 2024 election, the BJP and the NDA, if victorious, would still be accused of saffronizing India's polity.

It never fails to confound one that the construction of the Ram Mandir in Ayodhya is also included in the list of Hindu impositions.[37] Why is it almost always overlooked that the work on the Ram temple began only in earnest after the Supreme Court's unanimous verdict in favour of Hindus,[38] or that even the committee entrusted with the mandir's construction was constituted after the Hindu litigants got possession of the Ram Janmabhoomi through the Supreme Court?[39]

The annexation of the Ram Janmabhoomi and other places of worship has always been symbolic of a violent interruption in the Hindu civilizational journey.

Indeed, the great Hindu civilization has faced an almost unremitting onslaught—first from colonialists and then, after Independence, from the 'rootless anglicized elite', in the words of the author and former diplomat Pavan K. Varma.[40] These inheritors of the colonial mantle have irascibly branded any interest in reclaiming Hindu India as fundamentalism.

Whether it is the Ayodhya movement and its culmination in the construction of the Ram Mandir, the reconstruction of the Somnath temple, the redevelopment of Kashi[41] or the legal attempts being made to restore the birthplace of Lord Krishna in Mathura to the Hindus, the BJP considers these as tributes to an ancient Hindu way that has been almost written out of history.[42]

Yet, despite 'Nehruvian secularists'[43] doing their best to disregard Bharat's Hindu heritage,[44] its emblems feature on most of our modern institutions. Illustrations in the original manuscript of the Constitution also contained pictures of Hindu Gods and Hindu cultural symbols, among others.[45]

Now, as Congress and its allies are under pressure from a politically dominant BJP, the Sangh Parivar and the NDA under Modi are heavily invested in the project of 'decolonizing the Indian mind'.[46] The idea is to go beyond seeing the symbols of Hindu culture as mere decorative art or exotic talismans. The idea is to remake an India inspired by the true meaning these totemic inscriptions and symbols represent. Modi himself has listed this as a priority.

This commitment to decolonization forms one of the main *kartavyas* (duties) of Modi's 'Panch Pran of Amrit Kaal', announced from the ramparts of the Red Fort on Independence Day 2022.[47] Modi said: 'We must take up the responsibility of fulfilling all the dreams of the freedom fighters by embracing those Panch Pran by 2047, when the country celebrates 100 years of independence. The Panch Pran of Amrit Kaal goal of developed India, to remove any trace of colonial mindset, take pride in our roots, unity and sense of duty among citizens . . . Brothers, how long will the world continue to distribute certificates to us? How long will we live on the certificates of the world? Shall we not set our own standards? Can a country of 130 crores not make an effort to exceed its standards? Under no circumstances should we try to look like others. It should be our temperament to grow with our own potential. We want freedom from slavery. The element of slavery should not remain in our mind even under the distant seven seas.'[48]

Using 'Panch Pran' as their inspiration, the NDA and BJP state governments are bringing in hitherto mentioned legislations or policy measures to recast the state and remake Bharat that is India. Almost all of these initiatives are being pursued through Parliament, the legislative assemblies or the courts.[49] This pursuit of ideas through the means of democratic institutions should ordinarily be a source of comfort.

For the BJP, then, victory in 2024 is essential to pivot India to its Hindu past. A past centred on a centuries-old belief in dharma, which is by definition inclusive and secular.[50] Again, there is no logical reason that nostalgia for our roots should be a source of anxiety or shame to some.

Ahead of what was to be a successful G20 summit in Delhi, the Indian President Draupadi Murmu's dinner invitation sent to foreign dignitaries and state chief ministers referred to the

head of state as 'President of Bharat'.[51] The plaque placed before
Prime Minister Modi during the summit read 'Bharat'.[52] And the
venue for the summit was the majestic, newly constructed Bharat
Mandapam, adorned by decorative symbols showcasing the Indic
heritage and tradition in all its glory.[53] For the NDA government,
this pronounced emphasis on Bharat is not a break with modernity
but an assertion of pride in one's traditions and history.

Indeed, mainstream conservative theoreticians, like S.
Gurumurthy, argue with evidence that the NDA is not reordering
the state but merely reconnecting it to the severed threads of our
civilizational past. In an essay in the *New Indian Express* titled
'Recalling the Pre-March 24, 1940 Idea of India', Gurumurthy
writes:[54]

> Just a few examples will demonstrate that the post-
> Independence Idea of India is not the same as the pre-
> Independence Idea of India. Feminist scholar Stephanie Tawa
> Lama, describing how, in India, the feminine force represented
> power, said that the entire Indian freedom movement was
> fought in the name of a woman, Bharatmata. And yet that
> inspiring symbol of Mother India and 'Bharat Mata Ki Jai',
> the war cry of freedom fighters, turned into political liabilities
> post-independence. The mystic song Vande Mataram, which
> inspired the revolutionaries to kiss the gallows and satyagrahis
> to bear lathi blows and jail life, was reduced into a sectarian
> verse post-Independence. Its core content was edited out to
> reduce it to a fourth of its original size.
>
> Before Independence, all those who fought for freedom –
> non-violent satyagrahis or violent revolutionaries, Congressmen,
> communists, socialists, or Hindu Mahasabaites – were revered
> as freedom fighters. But post-Independence, they were all given
> ideological colour; on that basis, they were credited, discredited,

respected, or disrespected. Even the civilisational symbols which, post-1947, ornated the calligraphic Constitution of India signed by all Constituent Assembly members . . . lost legitimacy in secular India. The disconnect from the freedom movement is self-evident.

Modi has obviously zeroed in on and found what has caused the disconnect.

This book—which draws on extensive research and interviews with critical stakeholders—is a provocative and definitive rebuttal to the sustained denigration of the Hindu ethos in ongoing political discourse. By picking on examples both at home and away, it also rebuts the calumny that India cannot be secular if it leverages its civilizational ethos to define its constitutional and governance priorities.

In the chapters that follow we will demonstrate that the 2024 election is not an invitation to some proverbial 'Bajrangis' at the gate who want to mutilate the idea of a tolerant dharmic Hindu culture and carve out a 'Hindu Pakistan'.[55] In fact, the reality is quite the opposite.

1

A Pledge to Bharat Redeemed

'Lockdown'

The state of Jammu and Kashmir felt the full impact of a government-ordered immobilization on 4 August 2019.[1]

Curfew-like restrictions were imposed in various parts of the state.[2] Millions of messages of love, despair, joy, gossip and sorrow had lost their way in the digital fog.[3]

But such restrictions, an exception in the mainland, were not unusual in Kashmir. These are considered by some as 'repression'[4] by the security forces under the guise of combating the swirl of terror that lay waste to whole localities in the Kashmir Valley.

On this occasion, the extremists' plans had been supposedly detected.[5] Just a few days earlier, Governor Satya Pal Malik had warned of a grave terror threat in Kashmir and had even taken the executive decision of issuing a security advisory curtailing the Amarnath Yatra.[6] The advisory cited 'intelligence inputs of terror threats, with specific targeting of the Amarnath Yatra' and the 'prevailing security situation in the Kashmir Valley'.[7]

The same day, Lieutenant General K.J.S. Dhillon, commander
of the XV Corps, and Dilbagh Singh, the J&K Police chief, held
a joint press conference, claiming that they had recovered a huge
cache of arms along the Amarnath Yatra route, which included
sniper rifles.[8] More than ten attempts had been made to trigger
IED blasts in the Valley, in Pulwama and Shopian, but each was
thwarted by security forces.[9] After being informed that there was
a terror threat, the administration told pilgrims to get into buses
and return home.[10]

That was not all. Two former chief ministers were
simultaneously put under house arrest.[11] In the Valley, where being
'alienated' from the state is a mark of one's political credibility,
there had been clampdowns, but this one was unusual.[12]

A series of meetings, on 26 and 27 June 2019, presided over
by the Union home minister Amit Shah in Jammu and Kashmir,
involved discussions on contingency plans to be set in motion if
and when a categorical decision on Article 370 was taken. Lt Gen.
Dhillon (now retired) recalled his '7 a.m. breakfast meeting' with
Shah in his book *Kitne Ghazi Aaye, Kitne Ghazi Gaye*:

> I will not divulge here for obvious reasons but it will suffice
> to say that the issues flagged by Mr Shah included the current
> law-and-order situation, the potential for it to deteriorate
> immediately after any declaration by the government,
> repercussions of the latter on the Line of Control, and the
> pros and cons from the perspective of an anticipated Pakistani
> reaction to the path-breaking declaration that was now certain
> to follow. Ultimately, the home minister was seeking my
> inputs on the likely situation before and after the government
> action, as well as assurances that the Team Security Forces
> would be able to handle any situation that may arise in the

state post the abrogation (which, it was by now clear to me, was in the offing).[13]

Dhillon added, 'I must say that the home minister's knowledge and in-depth assessment of the situation, including the likely fallouts, was exceptional as he had not only covered all bases but was ready with counter-plans for every possible eventuality and contingency.'[14]

Many did not suspect it then, but the life-halting eight-letter word 'lockdown'[15] would become part of the everyday vocabulary of Kashmiris for several weeks after 5 August 2019—way before the first strand of the SARS-CoV-2 virus was sneezed into the air in China's Wuhan.

'Abrogation'

With the stage set in Kashmir on 5 August, Amit Shah trooped into Parliament. Within minutes, word got out that he had something big to announce. Speculation was sparked when an alert photographer posted an image of a sheaf of papers in Shah's hands.[16]

The words—on the top right-hand corner of the first page—heralded the birth of a momentous new order: 'Top Secret'.[17] The rest of the page, it could easily be seen, was divided into three sections: 'Constitutional', 'Political' and 'Law and Order'.[18]

Under each of these headers were action points. Each action had to be triggered with care, and at precisely the right time and in the right sequence. One step too early or too late and the whole scheme could fold upon itself like a piano accordion with punctured bellows.

Under the first section the action points read: 'Inform President, Inform V-P, Cabinet meeting, President's notification, Passage of Bill in Parliament, Security in Rajya Sabha.'[19]

The third section, 'Law and Order', had more unambiguous action points: '. . . send Home Secretary to J&K . . . enhance security measures.'[20]

Was this the government's 'secret plan' to implement new measures for Jammu and Kashmir?

Over the next ninety minutes in the Rajya Sabha, a resolute but visibly pleased Amit Shah revealed the contours of this constitutional revision.[21] It should not be forgotten that up until that moment any talk of changing the status of Jammu and Kashmir had always been mocked by the ideological Left as a grand delusion harboured by saffron fabulists.[22] But here we were, glued to our television screens, hanging on to every word as Amit Shah read out of the Presidential order that revoked Article 35A and nullified Article 370.[23]

Jammu and Kashmir's special constitutional relationship with the Union of India had been unrecognizably altered. The BJP finally redeemed itself in the eyes of the Jan Sangh founder and the party's ideological guiding light, Syama Prasad Mukherjee. The state had stepped out from the old to the new in its own tryst with destiny.[24]

A Waiting Game

The plan to revoke Article 35A and nullify Article 370 had been a closely held secret,[25] but only as closely held as a democracy allows. The truth has a way of trickling out, sometimes at once, sometimes in installments.

In an interview conducted to excavate the truth with an NDA insider we learnt, 'Prime Minister Modi had decided to actively implement the BJP's age-old manifesto pledge about six months earlier, around December–January [2018–2019]. Even the home minister was told two months before August 2019.'[26] That was around the time Amit Shah took over as India's home minister on 1 June 2019.[27]

Fresh from a thumping electoral victory for the BJP in the Lok Sabha election barely a month before, Shah became the principal executor of a strategy conceived by a man with whom he had shared a thirty-two-year-long association.[28]

Shah had first met Narendra Modi in 1987, during the party's preparations for the Ahmedabad Municipal Corporation elections.[29] Dyed in the worldview of the Rashtriya Swayamsevak Sangh (RSS), the duo would form an imperishable bond as mentor and protégé. This bond would strengthen due to the alleged persecution they faced at the hands of a Congress-led United Progressive Alliance (UPA) after the 2002 Gujarat riots.[30]

Since 2014, Shah's elevation to the post of Union home minister had been widely anticipated. Even in his earlier avatar as BJP president and as a member of the Rajya Sabha, Shah had taken the lead in articulating the party's position on national security issues, including terrorism, the National Register for Citizens in Assam[31] and maintaining order in Jammu and Kashmir.[32]

Once a man of few words, in the NDA's first term Shah evolved into a fiery orator who cared little for political niceties. With his polemics against Jawaharlal Nehru, particularly over his handling of Jammu and Kashmir,[33] Shah became the chief spokesperson for the NDA's endeavour to undo Nehru's 'legacy'.[34]

Few realized it then, but when Shah spoke in Parliament during the 2019 Budget session on 28 June,[35] it was the moment when the death knell for Article 370 was first sounded. While appraising the house about the situation in Jammu and Kashmir, Shah caustically recalled Nehru's mistakes, including 'not taking

Sardar Patel into confidence', and the Congress Party's decisions that sowed 'mistrust' among the people of the state. Shah also spoke of why he believed the Modi era heralded a new beginning for Jammu and Kashmir.[36] Crucially, he moved a resolution in the house for an extension of President's rule in Jammu and Kashmir for a further six months, but not before sounding a warning.[37] 'Article 370 is not permanent. We have not changed our stand on it,' Shah said.[38]

The house, dominated by the BJP, assented to this extension. Less than two months later, the President of India (Ram Nath Kovind at the time)—acting on the aid and advice of the council of ministers—would seal Article 370's fate through a Presidential order.[39]

Until then, well into its fourth year, the NDA had only taken incremental steps along the ideological path that the BJP, and its predecessor the Bharatiya Jana Sangh, had set for itself in the 1950s.[40] There was a sense of bewilderment among some within the BJP support base as to why Modi had not acted during his first term to deliver on the promises that were at the core of the saffron fold's Hindutva agenda.[41]

More than that, the Centre's tough talk on security was facing a credibility crisis. The BJP's alliance with Mehbooba Mufti's People's Democratic Party in Jammu and Kashmir had made the BJP cadre uncomfortable.[42] They were unhappy over concessions extended to an alliance partner accused of indulging in 'soft separatism' to appease the separatists in the Valley, something they believed had begun to alienate the party's core voters in Jammu, where the BJP won twenty-five out of the thirty-seven seats it contested in the 2014 state assembly polls.[43]

The common minimum programme of the coalition referred to the secessionists as 'stakeholders',[44] something Chief Minister Mufti repeatedly invoked.[45] The compulsions of coalition politics also prompted the J&K government to grant amnesty to the youths who had pelted stones at India's security forces.[46]

Then, in July 2018, with the alliance creaking under the weight of its contradictions, the BJP pulled the plug.[47] With no common minimum agenda for governance holding the BJP back, it could focus on delivering on its own promise of abrogating Article 370.

Now, Modi could do something decisive about Jammu and Kashmir. As pointed out earlier, this had been a manifesto commitment of the BJP[48] and a principal objective of Syama Prasad Mukherjee.[49]

Rewriting the Rules

A few months later, in early December 2018, Modi summoned his closest confidants in government, including two senior members of the bureaucracy.[50] They were confronted with a leader who talked passionately about the need to undo the mistakes that had shaped India's destiny. The prime minister spoke about the need to be able to come up with strategies of governance that would further the nation along the road to 'Atmanirbharta'.[51]

Modi was determined to insulate India's Kashmir policy from the vicissitudes of external factors. For far too long, he explained, because of errors committed during Nehru's time, Pakistan and its political cohorts had acquired leverage over India in Kashmir. Islamabad exploited these historical missteps to forever bog India down in Kashmir with a wide array of military, diplomatic and political feints. In the meeting Modi reportedly said, 'This was why to outsiders, often, New Delhi's Kashmir policy appeared to be knee-jerk, seemingly contradictory, expeditious, everything but not a sophisticated, enduring doctrine.'[52]

The time had come to develop a Kashmir doctrine.

With the context explained, the group was asked to proceed on two fronts. First, to evolve a legally tenable strategy to alter Jammu and Kashmir's temporary constitutional status.[53] Second, to evolve a model to assess global and regional security as well as the political and diplomatic implications of any prospective move in this regard.[54]

In April–May 2019, there was a general election, which the BJP won with an even bigger mandate than five years earlier. The series of manoeuvres on Article 370 that the government's legal officers had devised over a few months could now be implemented.

The draft presidential order was to follow a legal precedent set in 1954. Back then, Clause 1 of Article 370 had been used to extend some provisions of the Constitution to Jammu and Kashmir. This time, *all* provisions and amendments would apply.[55]

Second, Clause 3 of Article 370 was amended, wherein the words 'Constituent Assembly' of Jammu and Kashmir were replaced with 'Legislative Assembly',[56] through recourse in a rarely used provision in the Constitution, Article 367, 'best understood as a set of legal rules that aid the interpretation of the constitution'.[57]

As the state was under Central rule since December 2018, for all practical purposes the powers of the state were taken over by the President, who then proceeded to render Article 370 ineffective.

But was all this legal? Critics of the way in which Article 370 was nullified feel that the move was both legally and morally wrong. They point out that Article 370 cannot be virtually abrogated without the consent of the people of Jammu and Kashmir through their elected representatives in the state assembly, which, of course, had been dissolved.[58] The Supreme Court held daily hearings in August 2023 over petitions challenging the decisions of four years earlier, before reserving its judgment.[59]

The third significant move was to divide Jammu and Kashmir into two union territories: Jammu and Kashmir, and

Ladakh.[60] In 2002, the RSS had proposed a reorganization of Jammu and Kashmir into three territories—Jammu, Kashmir and Ladakh.[61] The BJP had rejected this then,[62] but the 2019 decision to bifurcate the territory was in keeping with the demands of many Ladakhis.[63] A territory with a large Buddhist presence, Ladakh, which also bordered China, would now be treated as a separate administrative entity. Ladakh had been demanding provincial autonomy since the late 1940s.[64] Now, with Ladakh designated as a separate union territory directly administered by the Centre, another rule had been rewritten. Jammu and Kashmir would also be administered by the Centre as a union territory for a limited time before the restoration of full statehood.

The fourth and final change was a delimitation exercise undertaken by the Delimitation Commission.[65] This increased the number of electoral constituencies in the state from eighty-three to ninety. Jammu was the big gainer. It was to now have forty-three constituencies (up from thirty-seven) and Kashmir would have forty-seven (up from forty-six). Jammu is now not far behind Kashmir in terms of the number of legislators it can send to the state assembly.[66]

These changes, at the time, were largely welcomed by the Hindus of Jammu[67] and the Buddhists of Ladakh,[68] who had long harboured the grouse that their own interests were undermined by what were perceived to be extremely generous concessions granted to the Muslim-majority Valley.[69]

A 'Special' Relationship—Then and Now

'Kashmir is different,' explained Ram Madhav, the RSS impresario who drives the intellectual output of a prominent right-of-centre think tank.[70]

Three years after the abrogation of Article 370, we are meeting him in his cosy office overlooking an inviting patch of lawn in a building complex located on Hailey Road in Lutyens's Delhi.

From this quiet perch, perfect for reflection, Madhav recollects the moment Article 370 was nullified to take away Jammu and Kashmir's special status. Madhav had a ringside view of the political events at play in the state in August 2019. For over two years he served as the architect of the BJP's coalition experiment with the People's Democratic Party.[71]

When, during our interview, we bracketed the decision to scrap Article 370 with 'muscular Hindutva', Madhav plucked a chapter out of India's early medieval history.

'Prime Minister Modi only acted to integrate Kashmir with the mainland as the region was always integral to Bharat's cultural, economic and political life from time immemorial,' he said.[72]

It is well known that Kashmir drew its name from the sage Kashyapa, and the land was even referenced in prayers offered to the Goddess Sharada.[73] Chronicles written by Hsuan-Tsang in 631 CE, when he landed in Kashmir, suggest that the region was a cosmopolitan Shangri-la.[74] Swathed in unearthly beauty, it was ruled by the Karkota dynasty, which, despite its overt Shaivism, was deeply tolerant of the Vaishnava and Buddhist traditions.[75] In fact, some historians believe that Tibetan Buddhism had its origins in Kashmir.[76]

Back then, just as it is today, Kashmir was geopolitically vital. And for the Tang dynasty (618–907 CE) ruling China at the time, Kashmir was one of three influential kingdoms standing in the way of their empire's expansion into the region south of the Hindu Kush.[77] Kashmir was the final frontier that needed to be breached if China was to dominate trade across the Silk Route. For at that time, the Silk Route was China's only connect to the West and the Indian subcontinent, and the Karkota king Lalitaditya (724–760 CE) had a near monopoly over the Silk Route as it passed through his kingdom.[78]

The twelfth-century chronicler Kalhana, in his historical treatise on Kashmir, *Rajataringini*, paints a glorious picture of Lalitaditya's reign, crediting him for heralding Kashmir's Golden Age.[79] The glow of Kashmir's spiritual and intellectual luminescence attracted the gaze of both the malevolent and the benevolent.

An Age of Hindu Ascendance

While the Tang Chinese might have been contained, the danger posed by Islamic invaders constituted an existential threat. Historian Vikram Sampath, in his book *Bravehearts of Bharat: Vignettes from Indian History,* notes that 'in a diplomatic checkmate against the Arabs, Lalitaditya and Yashovarman [of Kannauj] joined hands in a strategic alliance to repel and defeat them', ensuring that the forces led by Junayd-al-Murri of the Umayyad Caliphate, who was also the governor of Sind, could not advance towards central India.[80] But this reprieve from Islamic invaders was temporary.

Nevertheless, till at least the onset of Muslim rule, Kashmir continued to shine as one of the few frontier redoubts of Hindu influence, and its brilliance spurred the imagination of Adi Shankaracharya,[81] the sage who is credited with reviving Sanatana Dharma when he travelled from Kalady, his birthplace in Kerala, to Kedarnath and Kashmir. According to legend, Adi Shankaracharya reached the temple and learning centre Sharda Peeth, in present-day Pakistan Occupied Kashmir, where he held discourses with resident scholars on the Vedas.[82]

Adi Shankaracharya's fabled visit served the added purpose of lending the phrase 'Kashmir to Kanyakumari' to the geographical lexicon of the day. India may not have been a completely unified and clearly defined geographical entity as it is today, but Adi Shankaracharya's visit to Kashmir helped many to imagine its cartographic contours. After Adi Shankaracharya's visit, Bharat's northern border would forever be associated with the geographical limits of Kashmir in the popular imagination.[83]

Article 370: 'Amputating Akhandata'

Self-professed nationalist Indians on the right of the political spectrum often sing hosannas to Kashmir.

The scholar Raghu Vira, who was also a member of the constituent assembly and a one-time president of the Bhartiya Jana Sangh, imbues Kashmir with mythical virtues: '[It] is not only the Switzerland of India . . . not only the paradise of physical delights as Shah Jahan viewed it. It is much more. It is our Punya Bhoomi, where every dale and brook carries within its bosom a hundred mysteries of rishis, sages, divines and nagas. Kashmir is the biggest and most wonderful sanctum in the world that is possessed by any religion . . . Kashmir has once been the brain of India, every *tirtha* is represented here . . .'[84]

It is little wonder, then, that to Hindutva votaries Article 370 had not just prevented Kashmir's constitutional integration with the rest of India, but it had also felt like a surgeon's scalpel that culturally and emotionally amputated Kashmir, weakening an Akhand Bharat.[85]

To the Hindu Right the adoption of Article 370, as BJP MP Rakesh Sinha says, felt like the 'proverbial guillotine had dropped to sever Bharat's head from the rest of its body'.[86]

Sinha is, of course, being theatrical, but he is nevertheless expressing the fear long harboured by the Hindu Right: that

Article 370 played into the hands of those who secretly wish to 'Balkanize' India and turn Kashmir into an Islamic caliphate.[87] Syama Prasad Mukherjee, who had quit Nehru's cabinet in 1950 and became his most vocal ideological adversary, had often warned against Balkanization.[88] Mukherjee went on to form the Bharatiya Jana Sangh,[89] the predecessor of the BJP. In 1953, when he reached Jammu and Kashmir to lead a protest against its 'special status', the crowd greeted his arrival with the slogan: *'Ek desh mein do vidhan, do pradhan aur do nishan nahin chalenge* [One country, two Constitutions, two prime ministers and two symbols won't work].'[90]

This pithy but potent vernacular expression would go on to survive and become, arguably, one of the most durable stump slogans in India's political history. The slogan is effective because it simplifies what was in essence an incredibly privileged constitutional arrangement.

Article 370 (originally Article 306A), at the time of its conception, severely curbed the Centre's writ over the state. For instance, laws passed by India's Parliament could not automatically extend to the state if they hadn't been consented to by Jammu and Kashmir's state government.[91] But in 1953, barely a few years after the adoption of Article 370, a troika of right-of-centre nationalist parties—the Bharatiya Jana Sangh, the Hindu Mahasabha and the Jammu Praja Parishad—launched a large-scale satyagraha in a bid to pressure Nehru to roll back Article 370.[92]

This greatly exercised Nehru, who vociferously condemned the protests.[93] On 5 February 1953, Nehru shot off a letter to Syama Prasad Mukherjee accusing him of harbouring a communal motive: 'According to my thinking, the agitation of the Praja Parishad in Jammu is not only communal but is supported by communal and narrow-minded elements in India. I have not a shadow of a doubt that if that narrow approach was adopted in our country as a whole, it would bring disaster in its train not only for the Jammu and Kashmir State but also the larger interests of India,' he wrote.[94]

Clearly, for Nehru the opposition to Article 370 stemmed from what the Indian National Congress claimed was a worldview comfortable with the two-nation theory. A number of Muslim intellectuals, including Mohammad Ali Jinnah, a fiery orator and founder of the Muslim League, believed that a Muslim-majority state couldn't be reconciled within the geography of India. Nehru's 'idea of India' was an argument against the parochialism of a Muslim Pakistan or even, by extension, a Hindu India, championed by the advocates of a Hindutva worldview.[95]

For Nehru, Kashmir was going to be the idyllic rebuttal. The Indian haven that would showcase to the world the resilience of the unique Indian experiment with 'unity in diversity'. And Nehru wasn't about to let anyone, and most certainly not the 'Hindu Right', saffronize his rainbow nation.

But what Nehru did not understand, or chose to overlook, was that Mukherjee's politics was not founded on promoting an alternative model built exclusively around a Hindu identity; it was the politics of an inclusive Bharat.

In fact, the Bharatiya Jana Sangh's manifesto talked about '. . . building a Bharat on the basis of *Bharatiya Sanskriti* and *maryada* as a political, social and economic democracy granting equal opportunity and liberty to all individuals so as to make her a prosperous, powerful and united nation, progressive, modern and enlightened'.[96]

Challenging the Nehruvian Consensus

The Bharatiya Jana Sangh president Mukherjee was upset with Nehru for linking his party's protest against the special status to Jammu and Kashmir with communalism.[97]

On 8 February 1953, Mukherjee wrote a rejoinder posing some rhetorical questions designed to expose Nehru's hypocrisy:

> Is there anything communal or reactionary or anti-national about it [the agitation]? If India's constitution is good enough for the rest of India, why should it not be acceptable to the state of Jammu and Kashmir? It is amazing how the move for separatism pursued by Sheikh Abdullah and his colleagues is being applauded by you as national and patriotic and the genuine desire on the part of the Praja Parishad to secure the fundamental unity and integrity of India and to be governed as common Indian citizens is being dubbed as treacherous.[98]

Twisting the knife further, Mukherjee went on to chide Nehru for appeasing one community at the expense of others:

> Think in your cool moments how in your life history your failure to stand against Muslim communalism in India has resulted in disastrous consequences. Perhaps you and others followed a policy of concession and appeasement with the highest motive but in ultimate and the country came to be partitioned against your own repeated declarations to the contrary. At that time, a factor of very great importance which worked against us was the existence of an alien power which wanted to function on the policy of divide and rule. If today we want to be cautious and avoid the tragic follies of the past, we do so in the highest interests of the country and not for any narrow communal ends or for any sectarian interest.[99]

The allusion to appeasement by Mukherjee was also a reference to the concessions that Sheikh Abdullah, leader of the Jammu and Kashmir National Conference, had managed to wrest from

Nehru, ensuring a special status for the state distinct from other princely states that had acceded to India.[100]

In fact, even the Constituent Assembly debates testify to Nehru's inexplicable partiality to Sheikh Abdullah. The 'state of Kashmir', as it was originally referred to,[101] was allocated four seats in the Constituent Assembly.[102] Two members were to be nominated by Maharaja Hari Singh and the remaining two from the state legislature, also called the Praja Sabha, that had been constituted after elections in the winter of 1946.[103] A notable absentee from the 1946 Praja Sabha elections in Jammu and Kashmir was Sheikh Abdullah's National Conference, which had launched a 'Quit Kashmir' agitation against the Maharaja.[104]

Interestingly, Nehru refused to go along with this arrangement.[105] He wanted all four representatives from Kashmir to belong to Abdullah's National Conference.[106] This despite him being reminded in the Constituent Assembly by K.T. Shah about Abdullah and his party's role in the Quit Kashmir agitations, as a consequence of which 'events developed and created all the difficulties that have since ensued'. Shah cautioned the assembly that it must not give the impression that its decision was a 'surrender to one man's wishes'.[107] Nehru rejected this.

Invoking his special understanding of Kashmir on account of his ancestry, Nehru justified his decision thus:

> I speak not as the Prime Minister, but as a Kashmiri and an Indian who has been connected with these matters. It amazed me to hear Professor Shah propose that the so-called Praja Sabha of Kashmir should send representatives to this House. If Professor Shah knows anything about Kashmir, he should know that there is nothing more bogus than the Praja Sabha in Kashmir. He ought to know that the whole circumstances under which the last elections were held were fantastic and farcical.

He ought to know that it was boycotted by all decent people in Kashmir. It was held in the depth of winter to avoid people going to the polling booths. And winter in Kashmir is something of which probably Members in this House have no conception of . . . When the National Conference of Kashmir, in spite of difficulties, difficulties including that of their leaders being in prison . . . when they decided to contest these elections, then their candidates were arrested, many of them, and all kinds of obstacles were put in . . . so they decided to boycott it and they did boycott it . . . And it was an amazingly successful boycott.[108]

Nehru had his way. The Praja Sabha was eclipsed; Sheikh Abdullah, together with three other notables from the National Conference—Mirza Afzal Baig, Maulana Masoodi and Moti Ram Baigra—became members of the Constituent Assembly.[109]

In fact, this wasn't the only concession. Other members of the Constituent Assembly also objected to the special status provided to Kashmir when a discussion on Article 306 (A), forerunner of the contentious Article 370, was scheduled.[110]

'Why this discrimination please?' asked Maulana Hasrat Mohani, a member of the Communist Party from Lucknow. He was among the first to challenge the privilege.[111]

'The discrimination is due to the special conditions of Kashmir,' N. Gopalaswami Ayyangar dryly acknowledged as he went on to supply a laborious response to Mohani's pointed question.[112]

Ayyangar was Nehru's point person on Kashmir in the Constituent Assembly.[113] That Ayyangar was especially tasked with handling Kashmir's accession was odd, given that Sardar Patel was the home minister. It was his ministry that was naturally concerned with the accession of more than 500 princely states, provinces and protectorates, including thorny cases like those of Junagadh and Hyderabad.[114]

It is well known that Patel was a recalcitrant backer of Nehru's decision to court Sheikh Abdullah and accept his demand for special status to Kashmir.[115] Suffice to say, Ayyangar's elaborate but not necessarily convincing response to Mohani did not cut much ice.

In the end, the article was included along with a few others in the 'Temporary, Transitional and Special Provisions' part of the Constitution.[116] But it turned out to be anything but temporary and transitional.

Tragedy cut short Mukherjee's exchanges with Nehru. A few months later, on 23 June 1953, Mukherjee died mysteriously in police custody.[117] He had been arrested by the Jammu and Kashmir police upon his arrival in the state, because it was deemed that he 'has acted, is acting or is about to act in a manner prejudicial to public safety and peace'.[118]

But the firebrand's references to concessions and 'appeasement' would go on to form the leitmotif of the BJP's political stance on many issues.

Dismantling the Architecture of Otherness

The BJP views the abrogation of Article 370 and its corollary, 35A,[119] as a legitimate step towards dismantling the 'architecture of otherness'.[120]

The same can be said for its support of a uniform civil code[121] or the backing of some of its members for the legal campaign to reclaim Hindu temples.[122] The othered being those feeling hard done by, victims of the Nehruvian state's political policies dictated by the compulsion of securing the interests of India's Muslims.

Amit Shah and the BJP, more than six decades after Mukherjee's letters to Nehru on Kashmir, fell back on the ideas of their *margdarshak*, Mukherjee, to justify the government's decision.

First, on the issue of the decision's legality, the BJP pointed out that the contentious article was never meant to be a permanent provision.[123] Article 370 (3) in the Constitution clearly states that 'the President may, by public notification, declare that this article shall cease to be operative . . . Provided that the recommendation of the Constituent Assembly of the State . . . shall be necessary before the President issues such a notification.'[124]

It is a fact that the Constituent Assembly of Jammu and Kashmir was disbanded in 1957.[125] But it is also a fact that before dissolution, the state's Constituent Assembly neither recommended the abrogation of Article 370 and nor did it advocate for it to be made a permanent feature of the Constitution.[126]

Notable lawyers like Harish Salve do not believe this is a problem.[127] Salve, who would argue in favour of the decisions of 5 August 2019 in the Supreme Court, told journalist Karan Thapar, in an interview in The Wire, that the method used by the current government to substitute the reference to the Constituent Assembly of the state to 'Legislative Assembly of the State' had a precedent:

> The first time it was done was when Sadar-I-Riyasat was substituted with 'Governor' by amending Article 367 through the mechanism of Article 370 (1) (d) . . . the Supreme Court said that absent that, it would have had to construe whether the governor is the successor to the Sadar-I-Riyasat. If the President has done it by amending Article 367, that's another way of doing it. That is exactly the problem which had come up. The [current] government has traced its steps on precedent.[128]

Furthermore, the Central government, in its defence of its decisions of 5 August 2019, has submitted in the Supreme Court that Presidential orders had been issued on fifty-four occasions to extend the provisions of the Indian Constitution to the state of Jammu and Kashmir.[129] It can be argued that Article 370, as it existed on 5 August 2019, had already been modified so many times that it had perhaps lost its significance as a provision guaranteeing functional autonomy to Jammu and Kashmir, as envisaged by those who advocated it.

Given this, the BJP accused its critics of hypocrisy, wondering why those portending black days for the state remained silent for all those years as Article 370 was watered down.[130]

Second, and perhaps most compellingly, the BJP and its backers turned the secular–liberal argument on its head. They pointed out that Jinnah's two-nation theory clashes with the inherent syncretism of Kashmiriyat.[131]

Why Take Kashmiriyat Out of Kashmir?

Kashmiriyat has evolved from a centuries-old secularism—fortified by the Upanishadic principle of Vasudhaiva Kutumbakam[132] (the world is one family)—dating back to when the region was the seat of monasteries and Hindu ascetics.[133] Even Guru Nanak, it is widely believed, sought out the heavenly abode of Kashmir on his journeys to seek enlightenment.[134] When Islam came to Kashmir it recognized this pastiche of pluralism, and gave space and even patronage to these other philosophical traditions.[135] The Hazratbal Shrine (which houses a relic thought to be the hair of Prophet Muhammad) and the Pas-Pahar, or the Shankaracharya temple, both in Srinagar, were sentinels of this syncretism for centuries.[136]

As pointed out earlier, Sangh ideologues believe that far from tethering Jammu and Kashmir to the mainland, Articles 370 and 35A, in fact, militate against Vasudhaiva Kutumbakam. These provisions accelerate xenophobia, spurring the ghettoization of the Kashmir valley.[137] Only those who see the world through a monochromatic lens or have a vested interest in championing exclusivism could logically back these provisions.

There is much merit in this argument. The provisions of Articles 370 and 35A discriminate between man and woman, as well as insider and outsider.[138] After all, why would anyone create a legal architecture that views with a jaundiced eye the children of Kashmiri women who have married outside the state?[139] Why would such miscegenation be seen as insidious? Why should anyone back a law that denies the offspring of such pan-India unions the right to inherit and, by extension, disincentivize Kashmiri women from marrying an 'outsider' of their choice?

Further, why would anyone deny equal rights to persecuted Hindu refugees fleeing the rapacity of religious persecution in Pakistan?[140] Why would you shackle Valmikis who were brought in 1957 (to work as sweepers) to the pernicious and abhorrent tag of 'untouchability'?[141] Given these facts, can Articles 370 and 35A really be called the keystones of *insaniyat* in a modern democracy?

It is true that guaranteeing Hindus, Sikhs and 'othered' creeds a domicile status, and therefore a ticket to a dignified existence, will undoubtably dilute Kashmiri Muslim influence and interests in the Valley. But as saffron ideologues point out, that's a small price to pay for dismantling the 'architecture of otherness' and furthering the cause of governance as directed by Vasudhaiva Kutumbukam—a defining article of Sanatana Dharma.

'Aap Chronology Samajh Lijiye'

'*Aap chronology samajh lijiye* [Understand the chronology],' shot back Amit Shah at a BJP press conference in April 2019.[142]

Shah was being questioned on the Citizenship Amendment Bill (CAB),[143] which Parliament passed as legislation just a few

months after the nullification of Article 370 and 35A.[144] The
Citizenship Amendment Act (CAA) had been languishing since
2016 in the lower house even as there were concerns over illegal
immigration into India.[145] But many felt that this was a second
legislative strike against Muslims by the Centre.[146]

Shah said, 'First, we will bring the CAB, then the NRC
[National Register of Citizens]. The NRC won't be for Bengal
alone but all India. Infiltrators are a national problem.'[147] Earlier,
he had also said, 'Modiji will bring NRC in Bengal, and every
single infiltrator will be identified and thrown into the Bay of
Bengal . . . The infiltrators are like termites. They are a risk to our
security. They are taking away our jobs and livelihood. It is the
BJP's commitment to drive them out, and we will do so after
coming back to power.'[148]

This rhetoric, aimed essentially at Muslim illegal immigrants
from Bangladesh, struck a chord. The 2019 election marked
the BJP's growth in areas where it had previously struggled
for relevance—it won eighteen out of forty-two seats in
West Bengal, which has witnessed illegal immigration from
Bangladesh.[149]

The CAA fast-tracks citizenship for those who are religious
minorities in Afghanistan, Pakistan and Bangladesh—Hindus,
Sikhs, Jains, Buddhists, Parsis and Christians—and who entered
India before 2014.[150] The Statement of Objects and Reasons
in the CAA states: 'The constitutions of Pakistan, Afghanistan
and Bangladesh provide for a specific state religion. As a result,
many persons belonging to Hindu, Sikh, Buddhist, Jain, Parsi
and Christian communities have faced persecution on grounds
of religion in those countries. Some of them also have fears
about such persecution in their day-to-day life where right to
practice, profess and propagate their religion has been obstructed
and restricted.'[151]

The CAA derives its raison d'être from the Sangh's conception of an Akhand Bharat—a civilizational 'confederation' defined by cultural congruity.[152] Based on such a conception, Bharat is *mata*, mother, forever welcoming her children, providing them succour, even if they were in Pakistan, Bangladesh or Afghanistan.[153] After all, the BJP reasons, how could Bharat Mata accept Partition—a political abomination that snatched her children from her?[154]

However, despite the inherently altruistic ideological motivations of the CAA's conceivers, in the build-up to the 2019 general election, the CAA was deliberately conflated with the National Register for Citizens (NRC).[155] This was an act of pure political opportunism. The NRC, after all, was to be a separate exercise to identify and act against illegal immigrants in India.[156]

Nonetheless, the NDA government reintroduced the CAB in Parliament for passage in November 2019, but its association with the rollout of the NRC was to prove a major public-relations disaster. Massive protests broke out across the nation. Several Opposition politicians and rights activists saw the CAA and a looming national NRC as the first step in stripping Muslims of their citizenship to create an exclusive 'Hindu Rashtra'.[157] Shah's 'chronology samajh lijiye' and the provocative hyphenation of illegal immigrants to 'termites' only added to the ire.[158]

Amid lack of clarity over the contours of the proposed NRC—like the documents that would be needed to prove citizenship—there was a fear that even bona fide Indian Muslims would be rendered stateless if they failed to provide evidence of citizenship.[159] 'If it isn't about excluding Muslims, then why haven't the Ahmaddiyas, who are not even recognized as Muslims in Pakistan and are widely persecuted there, not being denoted as worthy of protection under the CAA?' many would also ask as protestors occupied streets and led marches across many towns and cities.[160]

Clashes with police forces became regular during those fraught winter months of 2019–20.[161] Even Prime Minister Modi could not pacify sentiments when he sought to convince protestors that an NRC, on a national scale, has never been discussed within government circles.[162] Cases were filed in the Supreme Court challenging the 'discriminatory' CAA that the petitioners claimed violated Article 14 of the Indian Constitution, which guarantees the fundamental right to equality.[163]

But the government was confident that it stood on solid legal ground with the CAA, arguing that the classification laid out by the act was rational, that it was not depriving anyone of Indian citizenship but only fast-tracking it for a certain class of people, and that this classification 'is just, fair and reasonable and has a reasonable nexus with the object sought to be achieved by the Act'.[164]

This confidence was perhaps misplaced, given that some within the government had been unsure of the CAA's legality from the beginning.[165]

Inclusive or Exclusive?

From behind his oversized mahogany desk, one of the country's eminent legal minds scrutinized us intently. A mammoth canine lay snoozing at our feet as we sat on a sofa, seeking a perspective on the legal interventions the NDA government had been making to further reaffirm India's identity as a civilizational state.

'The government was told that the CAA falls foul of Article 14,' he informed us solicitously. 'It excludes Ahmaddiyas . . . The Pakistani constitution also does not recognize them as Muslims.

So, in Pakistan they are considered non-Muslims and persecuted even more than the other minorities.'[166]

'So why have they been kept out of the purview of the CAA?' we asked searchingly.

'Because the government did not want the CAA to apply to Muslims, as it drew a distinction between those who cross the border for economic and other reasons and those who flee persecution. But Ahmadiyyas are not considered Muslims in Pakistan, and they are persecuted. The government was advised to include them in the CAA, but they decided not to.'

Even before the words could sink in, the lawyer added that the courts are liable to reject the government's defence of the CAA on the point that it does not violate Article 14.

'There have been legal precedents, in other cases, where the entire act or rule was struck down by the Supreme Court because of an "unreasonable" classification. Today's Supreme Court may not strike down the CAA, but it could read the act down to include Ahmaddiyas.'[167]

The legal ace then cited the Kerala Agrarian Relations Act, which was struck down by the Supreme Court in 1961 as it had exempted plantation crops, such as tea, coffee and rubber, from the purview of certain provisions of the act as opposed to some other crops, such as areca and pepper. This differential treatment for some crops over others in matters of land acquisition and compensation was unacceptable for the top court.[168]

But it isn't as if there's no legal ammunition with the government.

In its submission before the Supreme Court, the government sought to explain the exclusion of groups like the Ahmadiyyas, among others, from the purview of the CAA: 'It is submitted that intra-religious persecutions or sectarian persecution or persecution due to non-recognition of particular sects to be within the fold of majority religion in the said countries, cannot be equated with the persecution of religious minorities admittedly following and practicing a different and completely distinct religion than the majority religion in particular neighbouring countries. It is further submitted that purported persecution arising out of political movement within the recognised border of the particular neighbouring countries cannot be equated with the systematic religious persecution that the CAA seeks to deal with.'[169]

The CAA's supporters could also, in all probability, argue that the Ahmadiyyas played a key role in the movement for the creation of Pakistan.[170] Others may cite the Lautenberg–Specter Amendment in the United States which allowed for Soviet Jews and religious minorities in Iran to qualify for admission as refugees.[171] Additionally, it is also a fact that Muslims from Pakistan, Bangladesh and Afghanistan seeking citizenship for a variety of reasons are still eligible under the Citizenship Act.[172] The government's ministers, including Amit Shah, have also cited data to claim that more than 500 Muslims from these countries have been given citizenship since 2014.[173]

The CAA is inclusive, to the extent that it covers Parsis and Christians, practitioners of religions that trace their origins outside India. But it is also exclusive, as it leaves out certain Muslims who have been banished by their co-religionists as heathens in Pakistan.[174] In fact, the CAA has also been criticized for excluding atheists from its purview.[175] The legislation's constitutionality, or the lack of it, will be determined in the courts.

But it is also true that the proponents of the CAA, in their enlarged embrace of persecuted peoples from India's neighbourhood, absolve themselves of responsibility towards persecuted Muslims in this legislation.[176] In the public eye, this could suggest that Modi's government is not above providing preferential treatment to some religions above others in a secular state.

Is this the first defining feature of a Hindu Rashtra?

2

The Hindu Ethos and the Calumny of Communalism

The Consecration of a Resurrection

For millions of Ram devotees, Ayodhya is, and will perhaps always be, the abode of the most ardent *bhakts*. The ones who never lost faith. Hanuman to Lord Ram, Nandi to Lord Shiva.

Within the dusty confines of the sprawling workshop, scores of devotees, bussed in from all over the country, immediately fall to the ground and scoop up the powdery stone shavings. They chant a mantra and then run the dust-coated tips of their fingers across their foreheads.

Tilak in place, they stare awestruck at the blocks of stone that had been chiselled intricately into highly decorative panels at the Vishwa Hindu Parishad's (World Hindu Council) Ram Sewak Puram *karyashala* (workshop). Each of these panels celebrates a facet of Ram's story. And each of them is an element of design inspired by the works of some of the greatest temple architects of ancient India.

Soon, these decorative panels, which have been meticulously serialized according to a grand design, will adorn the facade of the Ram temple under construction upon the Ram Janmabhoomi just a few hundred meters away.

Once a graveyard of impossible dreams, the Ram Sewak Puram's karyashala is heaving with industriousness, primed as it is to complete work on a 'bhavya' Ram temple by the end of 2023.[1]

Work began soon after the monumental and unanimous Supreme Court verdict on 9 November 2019 that paved the way for the mandir's construction.[2] In August 2020, nine months after the apex court's verdict, Prime Minister Modi took it upon himself to consecrate Lord Ram's birthplace by performing a bhumi pujan for the construction of the temple.[3] But no sooner had the prime minister executed the *dandvat pranam* before the idol of Ram Lalla than the puja attracted controversy.

Purists believed that the puja lacked sanctity. Sharad Pradhan, a long-time commentator on the politics of the Hindi belt, concluded that the prime minister chose to play an 'all-encompassing role during the *bhoomi pujan* in Ayodhya on August 5. He was not only the chief guest but also the master of ceremonies and the official *yajmaan* (patron of a religious ritual) during the ceremony.'[4] In the process, Pradhan notes, several religiously significant formalities were ignored:[5]

> Conventionally, a Prime Minister would attend such an event as the chief guest, while the key rituals would be performed by a religious leader present on the occasion – in Ayodhya, it would be someone like Mahant Nritya Gopaldas, who is not only the head of the old Ram Janmabhoomi Nyas and the newly formed, government-constituted Ram Janmabhoomi Teerth Kshetra Trust but also the senior-most seer in the temple town . . .

The puja could also have been performed by one of the
Shankaracharyas, but they were not present at the ceremony.
As for the 140-odd religious figures who were present at the
venue, they were there only as a token presence and had little
to do with the puja.[6]

Others also believe the event was a meticulous orchestration of
pageantry spun around the prime minister's persona. Modi was
projected as the new 'Hindu Suratrana' (protector of the Gods).
The phrase appears in *The New BJP: Modi and the Making of the
World's Largest Political Party*, a voluminous study by academic
Nalin Mehta, which lays out Modi's blueprint for the saffron party.

On Modi's fronting of the bhumi pujan, Mehta writes,
'Modi was hailed as the Hindu Hriday Samrat when he began
his electoral career in Gujarat. Now, the carefully choreographed
symbolism of the *vedic yajna* in Ayodhya, with him as its *Karta*
(doer), subliminally posited Modi as a new Hindu Suratrana.'[7]

The event may have cast Modi as a catalyst for Hindu
aspirations as he scripted a 'glorious new chapter' in Ayodhya,[8] yet
the prime minister himself was mindful of making any references
in his speech that might have led the public to conclude that the
puja was anything but an ode to Ram and his ideals:

The time has come when a proper temple can be provided to the
deity of Lord Rama by moving it from the makeshift tent and
canopy, where it was kept for decades. A grand temple will now
be built for our Lord Rama . . . Today, the Ram Janmabhoomi
has become free from the centuries-old chain of destruction
and resurrection. Chant with me once again . . . Hail Lord
Ram, Hail Lord Ram. Friends, several generations devoted
themselves completely during our freedom struggle. There was
never a moment during the period of slavery that there was not

a movement for freedom. There was not a place in our country where sacrifices were not made for freedom. 15th August is the embodiment of sacrifices of the lakhs of people and a deep yearning for independence. Similarly, several generations have made selfless sacrifices for several centuries for the construction of the Ram Temple. Today marks the culmination of that centuries-old penance, sacrifices and resolve.[9]

While the homage to Ram is clear in Modi's words, there was also a subliminal message woven into the speech. Modi appeared keen to distance the construction of the temple from the 'cultural nationalism' that undergirded the acrimonious political movement for the reclamation of the Ram Janmabhoomi. He used the language of a lofty universalism and secularism to be found in Lord Ram's invocations to celebrate the inherent diversity that binds the nation state:

I am happy that many historic works are undertaken to enhance glory and divinity of the birthplace of Lord Rama. Friends, it has been mentioned in the scriptures, the holy books that न राम सदृश्यो राजा, प्रतिभ्याम नीतिवान अभूत। – that is there was no ruler who was as virtuous as Lord Rama in the entire world. Lord Rama teaches – 'No one should be sad, no one should remain poor.' Lord Rama gives [the] social message that all the people, both men and women should be equally happy. Lord Rama gives [the] message, 'Farmers, cowherds should always remain happy.' Lord Rama orders, 'the old, the children and the doctors should always be protected.' Lord Rama calls for protecting the one who seeks refuge is the responsibility of all. The slogan of Lord Rama is 'our motherland is superior than heaven also'.

And brothers and sisters, Lord Rama's principle is भयबिनु होइ नप्रीति i.e. 'There is no love in absence of fear.' Therefore, India would be peaceful and happy as long as it continues to grow stronger.

The same policy and practice of Lord Rama has been guiding India for many years. The father of [the] nation, Mahatma Gandhi, envisioned Rama Rajya with reference to these formulae and principles. The life and conduct of Lord Rama inspired Gandhiji's vision of 'Rama Rajya' . . . Lord Rama is the advocate of change and modernity. India is moving ahead today profoundly with these inspirations, these ideals of Lord Rama. Friends, Lord Rama has taught us how to fulfil our duties. He also taught us how to face challenges and how to seek and attain knowledge. The Ram Mandir should be built with bricks of love, respect and brotherhood. We need to respect the sentiments of all. We need to be together, progress together and trust one another.[10]

Cutting through the prose, it was clear that for Modi the massive silver brick dropped into the soil to serve as a ceremonial foundation stone was not the first building block of a Hindu Rashtra. For Modi, the ceremony was the consecration of a new Bharat that would draw its sustenance from the all-embracing, genteel humanism of Lord Ram. A philosophy that had even inspired Mahatma Gandhi to advocate for a Ram Rajya in India.[11]

A Requiem for a Secular India?

The consecration of a resurrection was broadcast to millions of viewers across the length and breadth of India. Those glued to their television sets watched commentators and *purohits* sitting in studios that were designed to appear like the inner sanctum of the putative Ram temple.

Ram had lost none of his appeal. Thirty years earlier he had drawn the faithful, like moths, to the flickering incandescence of a Televista TV set.[12] There he appeared larger than life, as the telegenic Maryada Purushottam[13] played by Arun Govil. The actor became an instant celebrity when he was picked by celebrated storyteller Ramanand Sagar to play the lead role in his evocative TV dramatization of the Ramayana.[14]

History would, of course, go on to note that Ramanand Sagar played as much of a critical role during the schismatic Ram Janmabhoomi movement as the RSS, VHP and BJP's stalwarts did.[15] The weekly serial undeniably amplified the Sangh Parivar's objective of reclaiming and then resurrecting the legacy of Ram to galvanize Hindus to a more political and spiritual end.

It surprised no one then that some saw the carefully choreographed liturgical iconography of the Ram Janmabhoomi puja—with the PM as acting 'pontiff'—as a cynical attempt at reinforcing the political message. It didn't take long for some to script a requiem for a secular India.

In fact, a day before the bhumi pujan, the equivalent of a dirge appeared in the press, penned by political scientist Suhas Palshikar. His ominous op-ed predicted at Ayodhya the 'dismantling of the old and the *Bhoomi Pujan* of the new republic . . .'[16]

Palshikar went on to write that the bhumi pujan was 'also dismantling another relic of the first republic – interfaith accommodation. The Supreme Court ruling in the Ayodhya case, ordering that Muslims be given an "alternative" site, formalised the peripheralisation of the Muslims both spatially and politically, while the celebrations openly involving state machinery underscore the officialisation of the status of Hindu religion as the basis of the new republic.'[17]

Is Palshikar so convinced of his thesis that he is ready to attribute motives to even the judiciary? In his mind's eye, are the supreme priests of the bar equally complicit in creating the legal framework for the new republic? He wrote, 'This political transformation would not have been so easy without the willingness of the judiciary to look the other way, and occasionally join in the project. In the Ayodhya dispute, the court validated the basic premises propounded by the Ram Janmabhoomi agitation. That ruling did not merely give the disputed land to one set of litigants, it facilitated a historic space legally and ideologically to the project behind the agitation.'[18]

Whether the judiciary is so jaundiced and whether it can even provide legislative ballast to the alleged democratic barbarism of the NDA dispensation supposedly engaged in creating an exclusivist state will be discussed in a later chapter. But Palshikar's proclamations portending the rise of a new exclusivist Hindu republic from the bhumi pujan at Ayodhya were echoed by many others.

Political scientist Pratap Bhanu Mehta wrote of his anguish over witnessing the bhumi pujan before claiming that 'Ayodhya's Ram temple is the first real colonisation of Hinduism by political power'.[19]

Mehta observed that the construction of the temple would not be a tribute to Ram but would instead make his name 'synonymous with revenge, with an insecure pride, with a blood curdling aggression, violence towards others, a coarsening of culture, and the erasure of every last shred of genuine piety in public devotion and public life'.[20]

Mehta is essentially arguing that a temple built on the detritus of a vengeful 'brute majoritarianism subordinating others' diminishes the meaning of Ram, who 'redeemed' even his opponents.[21]

So for some, far from the Ram Mandir being a symbol of Hindu pride, it is an epitaph for the secular republic that is destined to end with, as Suhas Palshikar writes, the phrase 'Hey Ram'.[22]

No one can, of course, find fault with the argument that the demolition of the Babri Masjid was an egregious assault on constitutionalism. Moreover, it undermined the *maryada* of Ram, in whose name the case for the reclamation of the Ram Janmabhoomi was built both in court and outside.

Thankfully, even the people Mehta and Palshikar have accused of 'waging war' in Ram's name had the sense to express regret.[23] In his autobiography, L.K. Advani—BJP veteran, mass leader and spearhead of the Ram Janmabhoomi agitation—writes, '. . . I could not share the sense of elation that some leaders of the movement exhibited. "It was the saddest day in my life," I wrote: "I have seldom felt as dejected and downcast as I felt that day."'[24]

Advani also went on to chastise those involved in the demolition because it had dealt a blow to the credibility of the movement. 'Why the demolition of the disputed structure pained me was because it severely dented our credibility in the eyes of the people. We in the BJP had all along declared that our goal was to construct the Ram temple at the Ram Janmabhoomi after respectfully relocating the mosque structure, and that we would like to achieve this either by a due process of law or through an amicable settlement between the Hindu and Muslim communities. However, as it turned out, we could not live by our word.'[25]

The loss of credibility prevented the BJP from deriving electoral benefits solely from the Ram Janmabhoomi issue.[26] Left stranded at the ballot and very far from where it needed to be to stake power in Delhi, the 'politically untouchable'[27] BJP consciously embarked upon an era of blunting the jagged edges of its Hindutva outreach.

One of the most noticeable steps the BJP took was to quickly renounce the use of any extra-judicial means to complete the political mission of galvanizing Hindus around the Ram Mandir.[28] The 1989 Palampur resolution was effectively dead in the water.[29]

A lot of time and energy was devoted by the Sangh Parivar, and those loosely adjunct to the movement, to engage in many rounds of mediation designed to arrive at a settlement with the Muslim parties in the dispute.[30] But it was not as if the BJP suddenly became apologetic about the events of 6 December 1992. It took on those who condemned the demolition as a 'national shame'.[31]

Though he had expressed his sadness in his autobiography, Advani was also clear that for him and the party, 'December 6 represented an epoch-making day in the life of India and also of Hindus.'[32] He wrote:

> It was the clearest signal in modern India's history that the Hindu community would not forever tolerate denial of and disrespect towards its legitimate sentiments. Those who took Hindu concerns and aspirations for granted and tried to thwart them through an endless process of political machinations and judicial delays, got an answer which they will hopefully not forget. As I have said earlier, mass movements sometimes acquire an inner dynamic of their own which even its leaders cannot always comprehend and fully control. Thus, through an action that neither the leaders of the temple movement nor the leaders of the central government could control or prevent, a group of *Kar Sewaks* delivered their own verdict on some of the seminal questions of Indian history, both medieval and modern. Ram or Babar? Genuine secularism or pseudo secularism? Justice for all or always appeasement of some? Are Hindus to perpetually remain divided on caste, regional and linguistic lines or should they unite when fundamental challenges confront faith and nationalism? It is not my claim that 6th December answered all these questions in the most

satisfactory manner. But it did mark a day of Hindu awakening of truly historic import.[33]

Advani, could well have been addressing these questions to Suhas Palshikar and Pratap Bhanu Mehta. For a section of India's intelligentsia, any inquiry into these questions or into India's Hindu past is driven by an exclusivist mindset fuelled by a narrow religious fanaticism. For years, there has been a concerted attempt by the 'rootless anglicised elite', as writer–diplomat Pavan K. Varma describes them, to de-hyphenate Bharat's Hindu roots from our civilizational history.[34]

Varma observes, 'The ingrained hostility to India's Hindu civilization also stems from the ill-informed claim that this is essential to preserve the nation's secular fabric.'[35]

He even puts a name to the face of such an outlook: 'Amartya Sen, the noble laureate, is an ardent votary of this school of thought. In his book *The Argumentative Indian*, he argues that those who speak of a Hindu civilization "are the promoters of a narrowly Hindu view of civilization."'[36]

Of course, Sen is not the only one. The Nobel Prize-winning litterateur V.S. Naipaul had this to say about celebrated historian Romila Thapar, in an interview to Dilip Padgaonkar, then editor of the *Times of India*:

Romila Thapar's book on Indian history is a Marxist attitude to history, which in substance says: there is a higher truth behind the invasions – feudalism and all that. The correct truth is the way the invaders looked at their actions. They were conquering, they were subjugating. And they were in a country where people never understood this. Only now are the people beginning to understand that there has been a great vandalizing of India. Because of the nature of the conquest and the nature of Hindu society, such understanding had eluded Indians before. What is happening in India is a mighty creative process. Indian intellectuals, who want to be secure in their liberal beliefs, may not understand what is going on, especially if these intellectuals happen to be in the United States. But every other Indian knows precisely what is happening: Deep down he knows that a larger response is emerging even if at times this response appears in his eyes to be threatening.[37]

'A larger response is emerging', but threatening it isn't.

The Calumny of Communalism

The construction of the Ram Mandir is not the denouement of a project to build a Hindu Rashtra but, as Advani said, the beginning of an 'integral part of the historical process of Hindu self-renewal and self-affirmation'.[38]

As we will more than amply demonstrate in subsequent chapters, what is being sought to be renewed was not, by any stretch of the imagination, an 'othering' or 'majoritarian' way of being. Much like after the completion of the construction of the Somnath temple in 1951, even the Hinduism actualized today through the construction of the Ram temple remains very much in sync with the syncretism that is at its civilizational core. It isn't, as Pratap Bhanu Mehta puts it, 'brute majoritarianism subordinating others'.[39]

It is easy to overlook that the construction of the Ram temple has been complemented by the grant of land measuring 5 acres within the city of Ayodhya to the Muslim community.[40] This compensation is an acknowledgement of the wrong committed upon Muslims.[41] No subordinating state machinery with a revanchist predilection would ever acquiesce in any gesture that seeks to make amends for a wrong done to the supposed other.

This is not to say that the temptation to exact revenge doesn't exist. Awakened Hindus know that the construction of mosques over centuries under Muslim conquest, either through demolitions of temples or building structures over their ruins, was an insult and more than that an act of effacement—an attempt to erase any trace of an ancient Hindu civilization, to erase an idea.[42] The idea of a universalist Hindu epitomized by Ram.

In an interview to the daily *Panchajanya*, RSS chief Mohan Bhagwat said, 'Hindu society has been at war for over 1000 years—this fight has been going on against foreign aggressions, foreign influence and foreign conspiracies. The Sangh has offered its support to this cause, so have others. There are many who have spoken about it. And it is because of all these that the Hindu society has awakened. It is but natural for people, those at war, to be aggressive.'[43]

But in the same interview Bhagwat also cautions against untrammelled misdirected aggression. He, in fact, spreads the onus of keeping the peace across people of all stripes—Hindus, Muslims and even Communists—by asking them to shun the 'logic' of 'supremacism':[44]

From the earliest point in recorded history, Bharat has been 'Akhand', undivided. Islam's devastating invasion ended in a hundred years. How come the country got suddenly divided later? I see only one reason – हिंदू भाव को जब-जब भूले आई विपद महान, भाई टूटे . . . धरती खोई . . . मिटे धर्म संस्थान (whenever we have forgotten the core Hindu sense, we have faced great calamity, brothers got separated . . . land is lost and religious institutions were ruined). Hindu is our identity, our nationality, our civilisational trait – a trait that considers everyone as ours; that takes everyone along. We never say, mine is only true and yours is false. You are right at your place, I am right at mine; why to fight, let us move together – this is Hindutva. If adherents of this value stay in [the] majority, Bharat remains united. There is no harm to the Muslims living today in Bharat. If they wish to stick to their faith, they can. If they wish to return to their ancestors, they may. It is entirely their choice. There is no such stubbornness in Hindus. Islam has nothing to fear. But at the same time, Muslims must abandon the boisterous rhetoric of supremacy. 'We are of an exalted race; we once ruled over this land and shall rule it again; only our path is right, rest everyone is wrong; we are different, therefore we'll continue to be so; we cannot live together' – they must abandon this narrative. In fact, all those who live here – whether a Hindu or a communist – must give up this logic.[45]

Bhagwat makes it clear that awakened Hindus, who are alive to the history of their civilizational values, will find it hard to ignore the tolerance that is rooted in its traditions. That is perhaps why, even today, when the executive is under the sway of a saffron party, the state continues to be guided by the Hindu philosophical credo *sarva dharma sambhava* (equal respect for all religions or peaceful co-existence of all religions).

While some have alluded to the Indian state's complicity in the act of 'brute majoritarian'[46] subordination of Muslims, the fact is that the Supreme Court was very critical of the demolition of the Babri Masjid in its judgment. The judges noted that it was an 'egregious violation of the rule of law'.[47] Not just that, but the five judges unanimously championed the need to compensate Muslims:

Allotment of land to the Muslims is necessary because, though on a balance of probabilities, the evidence in respect of the possessory claim of the Hindus to the composite whole of the disputed property stands on a better footing than the evidence adduced by the Muslims, the Muslims were dispossessed upon the desecration of the mosque . . . This Court in the exercise of its powers under Article 142 of the Constitution must ensure that a wrong committed must be remedied. Justice would not prevail if the Court were to overlook the entitlement of the Muslims who have been deprived of the structure of the mosque through means which should not have been employed in a secular nation committed to the rule of law. The Constitution postulates the equality of all faiths. Tolerance and mutual co-existence nourish the secular commitment of our nation and its people.[48]

Later, donations for the construction of the mosque were made tax-free.[49] In fact, Hindus have been shouldering a significant share of the costs for constructing a mosque in Ayodhya through donations.[50]

In Spain, many mosques in the Al-Andalus—the name given to the medieval Muslim-ruled region of the Iberian Peninsula—were destroyed or reclaimed and reconverted into churches and cathedrals.[51] Did Spain's rulers ever compensate their Muslim minorities by building alternative places of worship? And the Turks, too, did not when they converted the church of Santa Sophia into a mosque.[52]

However, those who are anxious about the state dispossessing and marginalizing Muslims will rightly point out that for all the outrage it expressed over the demolition, the judicial system also failed[53] to punish the vandals behind the 'egregious violation'.[54] While this is truly an appalling omission, the Supreme Court in its judgment on the Ayodhya Ram Janmabhoomi title dispute has reminded the executive that it has an obligation towards ensuring that a repeat of a Babri Masjid-like demolition at other contested sites never happens.[55] The Supreme Court did this by invoking the instrumentality of a law passed by Parliament in 1991. The law freezes the character of religious buildings as they existed on 15 August 1947.[56] The bench noted:

> The Places of Worship Act is intrinsically related to the obligations of a secular state. It reflects the commitment of India to the equality of all religions. Above all, the Places of Worship Act is an affirmation of the solemn duty which was cast upon the State to preserve and protect the equality of all faiths as an essential constitutional value, a norm which has the status of being a basic feature of the Constitution. There is a purpose underlying the enactment of the Places of Worship Act. The law speaks to our history and to the future of the nation. Cognizant as we are of our history and of the need for the nation to confront it, Independence was a watershed moment to heal the wounds of the past. Historical wrongs cannot be remedied by the people taking the law in their own hands. In preserving the character of places of public worship, Parliament has mandated in no uncertain terms that history and its wrongs shall not be used as instruments to oppress the present and the future.[57]

As we write the Places of Worship Act, 1991, is being challenged in the Supreme Court on the grounds that it places an illegal and arbitrary restriction on the rights of communities to reclaim, through the courts, places of worship that have either been demolished or were converted before 1947.[58] Some view the legal challenges of a piece with majoritarian vengefulness that led to the destruction of the Babri Masjid.[59] While this opinion is held by one section, it must also be noted that those associated with the Ayodhya movement have themselves urged caution.

As Hindu groups have moved court seeking to reclaim the Gyanvapi mosque site in Kashi, RSS chief Bhagwat chimed in with some advice. Drawing a line in the ground, Bhagwat said:

> The Gyanvapi issue is on. Gyanvapi has a history which we cannot change now. We did not create that history. Not today's Hindus, not Muslims. It happened then. Islam came here with the invaders. In these attacks, temples were destroyed to subdue the morale of those seeking freedom for this country. There are thousands of such temples. Issues of temples, which hold special significance in the hearts of Hindus, are now being raised. Hindus are not opposed to Muslims. The ancestors of Muslims were Hindus. Many feel that what was done (the demolition of temples) was done to break the morale of Hindus. A section of Hindus now feels that these temples need to be reconstructed. One should not raise a new issue every day. Why escalate fights? On Gyanvapi, our faith has been there for generations. What we are doing is fine. But why look for a Shivling in every mosque? . . . We participated in the Ram Janmabhoomi movement contrary to our nature, due to historical reasons and the needs of the time. We completed that task. We do not want to launch any other movement.[60]

Bhagwat's comments here are a reminder that confronting the past need not translate into an exercise in vengefully dispossessing the Muslims of today who cannot be held guilty for the crimes of invaders from the past. The sage exhortation is very much in step with the Upanishadic credo Vasudhaiva Kutumbakam—the world is one family.

The question that arises is this: If the tenets of the faith itself discourage any lurch towards exclusivism, why are many so quick to link any historical inquiry into the past or its celebration to an exercise of othering others?[61]

3

They Took the Hindu Out of the Indian

One for All, All for One?

In cricket it is often said, 'One run can change your day.' In football just one goal 'kicked off' a war.[1] One week is a long time in politics. One 'thin red line' can change the fortunes of a war and thus the course of civilization. The power of one cannot be emphasized enough.

And so it came as no surprise that in 2017, 'one mark'[2] not only cost an examinee the chance of reimagining his life but also sparked a nationwide debate on the essence of the Indian civilization.

K. Veeramani ended up with 70 marks in the Tamil Nadu Teacher's Recruitment Board (TRB) exam, one short of the cut-off needed to qualify.[3] He had made the mistake of selecting Bengali among the options provided to describe the language in which the national song 'Vande Mataram' was written first.[4] The four options provided were (a) Bengali, (b) Urdu, (c) Marathi and (d) Sanskrit. The Tamil Nadu government believed that the song was written in Sanskrit and therefore Veeramani was wrong.[5]

Despondent but determined to disprove what he believed was a mistake on the part of the Tamil Nadu government, Veeramani moved court.[6] After a few rounds of litigation, the Tamil Nadu government admitted its mistake and acknowledged that the song was written in Bengali but that some of the phrases, in particular 'Vande Mataram', were in Sanskrit.[7] The Madras High Court ruled in favour of Veeramani, restoring the one wrongly deducted mark and thereby allowing the aspiring teacher to make the cut and realize his life's ambition.[8]

The story would have faded away from the headlines had Justice M.V. Muralidharan not been appalled by the shocking lack of awareness about India's national song.[9] To rekindle a sense of patriotism, reflect on the sacrifices made and develop our sense of nationhood, the judge directed that the song be played in all government offices and institutions, private companies, factories and industries once a month, either on a Monday or a Friday.[10] Justice Muralidharan wrote:

> Patriotism is an essential ingredient for every citizen . . . The fact that this country is our motherland should always be remembered by every citizen . . . Several people have sacrificed their lives and families to the independence struggle . . . In these tough times, it was songs like our national song 'Vande Mataram' which created a sense of belief and confidence in the people . . . Perhaps in today's modern era where we have marched ahead with technology, our lives have changed a lot. We have become [so] busy with our own lives that sometimes we forget our nation.[11]

Though the singing of the song wasn't compulsory, the move immediately elicited a welter of protests, particularly from members of the Muslim community.[12] Many believe that 'Vande

Mataram' contains stanzas that are deemed to conflict with the monotheistic fundamentals of Islam.[13] The Muslim faith, according to Islamic researcher A Faizur Rahman, forbids the apotheosis of any deity (animate or inanimate) except Allah.[14] Even Prophet Muhammad, Rahman writes, cannot be ascribed any divinity, as that would create a dualism in a religion where there is only one supreme God.[15]

The fourth stanza of the national song is therefore deemed especially problematic. Singing 'Thou art Durga, lady and queen, with her hands that strike and her swords of sheen, thou art Lakshmi lotus-throned . . .' a Muslim is forced to equate his country with Hindu goddesses, constituting apostasy.[16] For, it is said, the tenets of the religion don't allow anyone to equate the nation with God. In 2016, the Darul Ifta at the Islamic seminary Darul Uloom in Deoband, claimed that even chanting 'Bharat Mata Ki Jai' (Hail Mother India) is unacceptable for Muslims. 'Bharat Mata, according to a section of Hindus, is a goddess and they worship her. For Muslims, participating in the worship of that goddess would be apostasy and against Islam.' It added, 'India is without doubt our country. We and our ancestors were born here. We love our country, but we do not think it is our God.'[17] The assumption being that in Islam, according to the seminary's interpretation, God is above everything else, even allegiance to the nation.

Before Independence, Bankim Chandra Chattopadhyay's 'Vande Mataram', this great, unabashed ode to nationalism, was shot down by the Muslim League.[18] Its leader Muhammad Ali Jinnah wrote an article in 1938 for the *New Times of Lahore* to distance Muslims from Chattopadhyay's exhortation. 'Muslims all over India have refused to accept "Vande Mataram" or any expurgated edition of the anti-Muslim song as a binding national anthem.'[19]

Jinnah expressed his disdain for what is today our national song despite Jawaharlal Nehru making a major concession to Muslims over the song in October 1937.[20] Bowing to Muslim sentiments, the Congress Working Committee met in Kolkata under his presidentship and resolved to sing only the first two stanzas of the song:[21] 'Wherever "Vande Mataram" is sung at national gatherings, only the first two stanzas should be sung, with perfect freedom to the organisers to sing any other song of an unobjectionable character, in addition to, or in the place of, the "Vande Mataram" song.'[22]

But Muslim leaders like Jinnah were still not satisfied, believing that the first two stanzas couldn't be seen in isolation, since 'motherland' was clearly depicted as one with the Hindu pantheon of deities elsewhere too.[23] Indeed, Bharat Mata is often depicted as a goddess in Indian iconography dressed in a sari holding a red flag.[24]

But it is not as if all Muslims oppose 'Vande Mataram'. In recent times, the governor of Kerala, Arif Mohammad Khan, who had quit the Rajiv Gandhi government in the 1980s over the then prime minister's decision to upend the Supreme Court's Shah Bano verdict,[25] has criticized those Muslims who oppose the national song.[26] In a 2006 article published in *Outlook*, Khan wrote:

It is true that in the 1930s, there were differing opinions. The Congress Working Committee after lengthy deliberations took a view in 1937 to adopt first two stanzas as National Song. It is also true that the Muslim League persisted in its opposition till the country was divided. But the Constituent Assembly adopted *Vande Mataram* as National Song ('the song *Vande Mataram*, which has played a historic part in the struggle for Indian freedom, shall be honoured equally with Jana Gana Mana and shall have equal status with it'). Those who persist in their opposition are actually negating a

constitutional ideal. After all, the Constitution is not merely
an exercise in semantics but expression of the people's national
faith. *Vande Mataram* was composed in 1870s and was made
part of the *Anandamath* in 1881. In the Calcutta session of the
Congress, the song was sung by Rabindranath Tagore, who
had composed music for the song as well. This session was
attended by a good number of Muslim delegates and nobody
had objected to the song. In fact, since 1896, the song had
become permanent part of the proceedings of Congress sessions
held in various cities of India. It is important to remember
that when Maulana Abul Kalam Azad was the president of
the Congress, *Vande Mataram* was sung in all party sessions.
In fact, Mr Rafi Ahmad Kidwai in his statement that was
published in *The Pioneer* on October 19, 1937, observed: 'For
years the song was sung at the beginning of Congress sessions
and Muslims including Jinnah began to object only in the late
1930s. Jinnah left Congress not because he thought *Vande
Mataram* was an anti-Islamic song but because he had found
the idea of swaraj unacceptable.'[27]

Khan recalled what a leading litterateur of Bengal, Reyazul Karim,
who wrote a critique of 'Vande Mataram' had said: 'The main
purpose of opposition to *Vande Mataram* was to bring Muslims
out of the freedom struggle.'[28] Karim, according to Khan, said
that the song gave language to the dumb and courage to the faint-
hearted, and this remains Bankim Chandra Chattopadhyay's
lasting gift to the country.[29]

In the article, Khan even elaborates on why the opposition
to 'Vande Mataram' on religious grounds doesn't hold water:

From the Islamic viewpoint, the basic yardstick of an action
is Innamal Aamalu Binnyat (action depends on intention).

Hailing or saluting [the] Motherland or singing its beauty and beneficence is not sajda. Maulana Azad was a great Islamic scholar, but he found nothing anti-religion about this song. Rafi Ahmad Kidwai strongly defended *Vande Mataram*. Moreover, we must remember the words of the Prophet: 'The whole earth has been made mosque for me.' Now, nobody would dispute that [the] mosque deserves reverence. More so the piece of earth where we are born and brought up, the piece of earth that God has blessed us with to enjoy its beneficence. And if we join our compatriots to revere that piece of earth as our motherland, can this be anti religious? Certainly not.[30]

Machinations of the Marxist Mind

But despite Muslim intellectuals like Khan exposing the political agenda behind the opposition to 'Vande Mataram', several Muslims and secular liberals were incensed with the Madras High Court order.[31] Was Justice Muralidharan—whose order would be modified by another bench of the Madras High Court, leaving it to the state government to decide on a policy on the playing of the song—really seeking to resurrect Hindu civilizational iconography?

Not that Justice Muralidharan's motives could be deemed communal either. Precedent exists. If not in India, then at least in the United States, the self-professed guardian angel of freedom and secularism. There, the Pledge of Allegiance, which includes the phrase 'one nation, under God', considered by some to be derogatory to atheists and polytheists, is routinely recited in schools.[32] In fact, in the face of legal challenges, the US Senate and House of Representatives took a bipartisan view and reaffirmed the words 'under God' in the pledge.[33]

But the reflexive outrage against a directive to make 'Vande Mataram' a more regular part of our national life wasn't surprising. It is symptomatic of a barely disguised contempt towards Hindu civilizational iconography and especially its identification with Indian nationalism. The Left has gone to the irrational length of even taking the Hindu out of the Indian.

In his book *The Great Hindu Civilization*, Pavan K. Varma challenged, for instance, historian Romila Thapar's attempt to describe historical inquiries into the Hinduness of the Indian civilization as 'communal' and that which 'excludes the study of others'. He asked: 'Why should the study of religion, if it has played a dominant role in influencing the world view of a historical period, be communal?'[34]

Thapar's proposition ignores the evidence that has now been dredged to the surface through more objective research on India's ancient civilizational past.[35] These studies have amply demonstrated that Hinduism itself is the best disincentive against majoritarianism. Wasn't that the reason Mahatma Gandhi invoked Ram—the embodiment of our civilization's tolerant spiritual and moral value system?[36]

Girilal Jain, the celebrated former editor of the *Times of India*, wasn't surprised by the Left's position, observing:

When a historic change of this magnitude takes place [the Ram Janamabhoomi movement], intellectual confusion is generally unavoidable. The human mind, as a rule, trails behind events; it is not capable of anticipating them. But it should be possible to cut through the mass of confusion and get to the heart of the matter. The heart of the matter is that if India's vast spiritual (psychic in modern parlance) energy, largely dormant for centuries, had to be tapped, Hindus had to be aroused; they could be aroused only by the use of a powerful symbol; that symbol could only be Ram, as was evident in the twenties when the Mahatma moved millions by his talk of Ram Rajya; once the symbol takes hold of the popular mind, as Ram did in the twenties and as it has done now, opposition to it generally adds to its appeal.[37]

If the truth and confronting the truth is a path to reconciliation, then why do 'secularists' go to such great lengths to stigmatize anyone concerned with the excavation of it? What is it that a section of the intelligentsia does not want us to unearth? Various attempts have been made to answer this question. The most eloquent responses have settled on identifying a sleight of hand. A Marxist machination—the discovery of which could upend years spent constructing a secular historiography centred on extirpating the Hindu from India's civilizational history.

In *The Great Hindu Civilization*, Varma focused on this tendency of historian Sanjay Subrahmanyam, noting:

Historian Sanjay Subrahmanyam examines two conceptions of India. The first, which for some inexplicable reason he calls the 'constructivist approach,' believes that 'India as we know it was invented in not too distant a past, probably by the British, or perhaps by Indians and Britons acting together in the period of Colonial rule.' The second view is that some very stable and automatic notion of India has been around for a very long time, indeed from the time when a classical Indian civilization put down its roots in the Indo-Gangetic plain. His contemptuous conclusion is that 'we need to see India not as a civilization but as a crossroads, as a space open for external influences.' What was before medieval India was only 'intellectual constructions and wishful thinking', and thus, 'ancient India is not a reality for us in the same way as medieval India, and it can never achieve the same state.' Ancient Indian civilization then is 'just a hybrid, a crossroads, a mixture of elements derived from chance encounters and unforeseen consequences' and anyone who contests this is taking 'the path to xenophobia and cultural paranoia' . . . To admit that there could have been an identifiable civilization where Hinduism was dominant, is to unleash forces of 'cultural paranoia'. Why is this automatic conflation made ignoring historical objectivity? The approach of the naysayers is not to examine the possibility of an ancient Indian civilization, but to immediately conclude that to even essay such a possibility is a conspiracy of Hindu fanatics.[38]

The answer to the question asked by Varma is that Subrahmanyam's postulations are part of a project aimed at evolving a contrived narrative of a 'composite culture'.[39] How this was to be done was also defined in the recommendations of the Committee on School Textbooks of the Government of India after Independence. One such committee that submitted its recommendations in 1969 called for 'a creative and purposeful reinterpretation of history and a judicious selection of historical truths'.[40]

The problematic part in these recommendations is not that they were issued at a time when there was a need to further the interests of national unity but that the stress was on 'reinterpretation' and 'judicious selection'. In practice, this took the form of reinterpreting history so as to de-hyphenate the Hindu from the Indian while simultaneously cherry-picking facts. For instance, downplaying bigotry associated with Muslim invaders, more on which will follow in a later chapter.

Is it this pedagogic machination that certain historians want to shield from intellectual scrutiny?

Perhaps the integrationists in the early decades after Independence took Lenin at face value and believed that all truth is partisan.[41] But as the rise and fall of the Soviet Union has shown, Lenin was wrong. The conclusions drawn on the back of 'partisan' truth are usually wrong and are easy to pick apart—especially in the long run—built as they are on the falsification of demonstrable facts. The advocates of the so-called 'Ganga–Jamuni Tehzeeb'[42] here in India unfortunately have not been able to resist the same temptation.

Even an intellect of the eminence of Nehru, ostensibly to preserve secularism, downplayed the fact that an ancient Indian civilization was dominantly Hindu.[43] Yet, as the minute hand moved closer to the momentous 'midnight hour' on 15 August 1947, even Nehru was hard-pressed to acknowledge that India's civilizational past was going to have a huge influence in shaping its future. The not-so-tacit acknowledgement came when Nehru conceded to participate in a ceremony, arguably, conducted to signal the 'transfer of power' from the British to the Indians.[44] The ceremony was centred on the ancient Hindu ritual of the Raj Purohit handing 'a sacred Sengol' (staff or sceptre) to the newly anointed king.

The Sengol is a visual metaphor for righteousness. It obliges the bearer of the Sengol to uphold Dharma, to dispense equal justice throughout the realm.[45] The Sengol that was gifted to Nehru was a replica of the kind used in Chola-era coronation ceremonies. In fact, the one handed to Nehru was made by the priests of one of India's oldest Adheenams.[46]

The handover ceremony was evocatively relived in the pages of *Time* magazine of 25 August 1947:[47]

When at last they reached Nehru's house, the flutist played while the sannyasis awaited an invitation from Nehru.

Then they entered the house in dignity, fanned by two boys with special fans of deer hair. One sannyasi carried a

scepter of gold, five feet long, two inches thick. He sprinkled
Nehru with holy water from Tanjore and drew a streak in
sacred ash across Nehru's forehead. Then he wrapped Nehru
in the pithambaram and handed him the golden scepter. He
also gave Nehru some cooked rice which had been offered that
very morning to the dancing god Nataraja in south India, then
flown by plane to Delhi.

Later that evening Nehru, and other men who would
be India's new rulers on the morrow, went to the home of
Rajendra Prasad, president of the Constituent Assembly. On
his back lawn four plantain trees served as pillars for a temporary
miniature temple. A roof of fresh green leaves sheltered a holy
fire attended by a Brahman priest. There, while several thousand
women chanted hymns, the ministers-to-be and constitution-
makers passed in front of the priest, who sprinkled holy water
on them. The oldest woman placed dots of red powder (for
luck) on each man's forehead.

. . . Thus dedicated, India's rulers turned to the secular
business of the evening. At 11 o'clock they gathered in the
Constituent Assembly Hall, ablaze with the colors of India's
new tricolor flag—orange, white and green. Nehru made an
inspired speech: 'Long years ago we made a tryst with destiny,
and now the time comes when we shall redeem our pledge . . .
At the stroke of midnight hour, when the world sleeps, India
will awake to life and freedom.'

The religious connotations of the ceremony were not lost even
on a devout secularist like Nehru. Dominique Lapierre and Larry
Collins wrote in *Freedom at Midnight*:

They sprinkled Jawaharlal Nehru with holy water, smeared
his forehead with sacred ash, laid their scepter on his arms

and draped him in the Cloth of God. To the man who had never ceased to proclaim the horror the word 'religion' inspired in him, their rite was a tiresome manifestation of all he deplored in his nation. Yet he submitted to it with almost cheerful humility. It was almost as if that proud rationalist had instinctively understood that in the awesome tasks awaiting him no possible source of aid, not even the occult that he so scornfully dismissed, was to be totally ignored.[48]

In an article, Girilal Jain noted, 'Nehru also wrote and spoke [before Independence] of the spirit of India asserting itself again and again. Surely, that spirit could not be a composite affair.'[49]

De-hyphenation a Stepping Stone to Denial

Not satisfied with burying the Hindu roots of India's ancient civilization, some 'secularists' went to the absurd length of denying the existence of Hinduism itself. For instance, possibly driven by fears that the idea of linking the word 'Hindu' with India's civilizational roots could get hijacked by Hindu revivalists, Romila Thapar went on to question what she described as a 'modern search for an imagined Hindu identity from the past . . .'[50]

Thapar does not at all appear coy about the motive for such a denial, which she admits clearly stems from her suspicion of Hindu revivalists. In *The Penguin History of Early India*, Thapar explains, 'Nationalism seeks legitimacy from the past and history, therefore, becomes a sensitive subject.'[51]

One can see how an attempt at stripping crores of Indians of their religious identity can induce a backlash. Especially, when the brazen denial of the existence of a Hindu view on life itself flies in the face of the lived rituals that inform the daily lives of the majority.

It is interesting to note that several of the framers of the Indian Constitution were reluctant to posit the word 'secularism' in the Preamble. As author Ashwin Sanghi remarks: 'By leaving the word out of the Preamble, the fathers of the Constitution were making it incumbent on Hindus to remember their commitment to the Upanishadic ideal of "*Vasudhaiva Kutumbakam*". That the world is one family. The framers of the Constitution were subtly saying that the Indian ethos was essentially Hindu in character but that ethos implied an ingrained respect for and tolerance of all faiths.'[52]

Indeed, H.V. Kamath, a member of the Constituent Assembly from Madhya Pradesh, stated that a secular state for him was not a godless or an irreligious state. Articulating his own idea of a secular state alive to its spiritual roots, Kamath said, 'If we have to make this disunited Nations [*sic*] really united, if we have got to convert this Insecurity Council into a real Security Council, we have to go back to the values of the spirit, we have to go back to God in spirit and truth, and India has stood for these eternal values of the spirit from time immemorial.'[53]

Ram Madhav, in *The Hindutva Paradigm*, persuasively counters historians like Thapar and Subrahmanyam, attempting to provide a philosophical and spiritual framework for this pluralism. Madhav talks about a uniquely Indian, all-inclusive concept of nationhood, he calls this the 'Rashtram', which flows from the Rig Veda, the foundational texts of Hindu philosophy: 'The Indian word for denoting this eternal emotional and spiritual idea of nationhood, as distinct from the European racial, political and geographical idea of nation, is Rashtram.'[54]

> . . . Rashtram is etymologically explained as a firm, enlightened path for the welfare of a community. The word is derived as a combination of two roots: *ras'mi*—'the sun' and *sTha*—'firm,

placed in'. This led to an extraordinary evocation in the Vedas: rashtram me datta (Give me that lighted path). In India, the concept of nation existed in the form of a pan-Indian, spiritual-emotional identity since millennia. References to Rashtram can be found in many places in ancient Indian literature. In the *Rig Veda*, the most ancient work of Hindu seers, the word 'Rashtram' was used to describe the national identity of the people of the land called Bharatavarsha.[55]

By invoking this concept, Madhav not just proves that Hinduism is yoked to India's ancient civilization but also establishes that there always existed an incipient indigenous sense of nationalism. The Rashtram conceived by the ancients, Madhav emphasises, is a 'unifying and development-oriented (*Abhyudayam*) . . . invested with divinity and motherhood in the vedas . . .'[56] In essence, a motherly, nurturing entity and not mean-spirited, insular or exclusivist.

Madhav writes: 'Sage Vak, one of the many women composers of hymns in the Vedas, said in Pratham Mandala of the Rig Veda, "*Aham rashtri sangamani vasunam chikitushi prathama yagyiyanam* (I am the beholder of this rashtra, benefactor of the gods and first among the worshipped)."'

Thus, an effort was made to infuse a sense of divinity, sacredness and motherhood in 'Rashtram' from the times of the Rig Veda. The nation is a feminine entity in India in contrast to the common Western masculine understanding of the country as fatherland. This vedic hymn, is in a sense, the origin of the concept of Bharat mata – the motherland. Sri Aurobindo described her as, '*Jagajjanani* – the mother of all mothers – the Universal Mother.'[57]

Readers will agree that historical evidence of India's Hindu civilizational past, when so apparent, is hard to suppress.

The Politics of History

For the BJP and the RSS, this course-correction of history was long overdue.

With just months to the 2024 election, the government appears to be keen on addressing concerns raised by many in the saffron fold that it hasn't done enough to correct the narrative in favour of the so-called Hindu Right when it has the mandate to do so.[58]

The RSS and its supporters don't want to miss out, as they did in 1977, when the Bharatiya Jana Sangh merged with the Janata coalition. At that time, elements in the Sangh wanted to scrub out textbooks written by left-leaning historians Bipan Chandra and Romila Thapar, but failed to do so because of an 'outcry'.[59]

Now, with a clear majority in government, the NDA is fast-tracking its 'rationalization' of curricula.[60] In early 2023, barely a year ahead of the Lok Sabha elections, the National Council for Educational and Research Training (NCERT) began the textbook 'rationalization exercise'.[61] What immediately caught the eye was the pruning of 'achievements' of the Mughal age and, in general, references to Islamic rulers.[62] There were also reports that the NCERT had removed references to the first education minister of India, Maulana Abul Kalam Azad, from its textbooks as well.[63]

When accused of scrubbing out the references to the Mughals, to India's Islamic history and to other leading Muslim notables, the NCERT chairman, Dinesh Saklani, spoke in a Times Now interview to set the context.[64] Saklani said:

> The rationalization process took place due to the Covid-19 pandemic. Students lost a lot of time, and therefore to reduce their content load, a committee of experts was constituted to rationalize content. The committee felt that wherever chapters

are repetitive, or less significant, deletions can be done. In so far as Mughal history is concerned, it's a lie that their history is being erased. Our textbooks have retained chapters about agrarian policies introduced by Mughals, for example. The experts felt that it was important to retain content about Mughal policies as opposed to simply a chapter that named each ruler and mentioned the duration of his rule, his birth and death.[65]

On the even more controversial alleged 'deletion' with respect to Maulana Abul Kalam Azad, the government's managers circulated 'notes' among journalists to distance the NCERT from talk of blacking out Muslims. The Congress Party, in April 2023, held a press conference condemning this 'deletion' as 'absolutely shameful' and adding, 'Nobody is safe from the pace of rewriting history this government is undertaking.'[66]

But the NCERT's note clarified, 'While exploring the matter in earlier editions of the textbook, it was found that from 2014–15 onwards the name of Maulana Azad was not there in the referred para. This textbook for the session 2014–15 was finalized for printing in October 2013 as per the record of the Publication Division.'[67] In October 2013, the UPA was still in power.

The record shows that the Congress, in its time in government, was not above politicizing history. Saiyid Nurul Hasan, a Congress MP from Uttar Pradesh, had been India's education minister between 1972 and 1977. He was identified as one of those who 'happily arranged the marriage between Marxist social science and state patronage'.[68] As a 2001 article in *India Today*, by journalists Laskhmi Iyer and Ashok Malik, notes, 'The Marxist school of history controlled institutions, scholarships, key jobs. It arrogated unto itself the power to write textbooks. Hasan's historians were hardly democratic. Worse, they were terribly poor writers. The books they wrote bored a generation.'[69]

When the BJP was dislodged from power in the 2004 Lok Sabha election, the UPA government began its own purge, withdrawing, for instance, a recommendation for a book on early medieval history written by historian Meenakshi Jain, known for her critical views on Islamic rule in India.[70]

Despite this and many more examples of selectiveness and partisanship in the retelling of history by the Left, doesn't it seem hypocritical on the part of the same Left to subject the NDA to higher scrutiny?

One former bureaucrat, who served in the HRD ministry during the UPA era, told us, on condition of anonymity, that 'it's one thing to make additions to bring a sense of balance but quite another to use history as a tool to redeem the sins of the Hindu Right. Why else would anyone, erase the "extremism" of Mahatma Gandhi's assassin, Nathuram Godse? Why would references to the ban on the RSS after Gandhi's assassination, or to the 2002 Gujarat riots be expunged?'[71]

Of course, the question can be turned on its head. And insiders in the NDA's intellectual circles asked us to ponder why references to riots in one state and not others were included in textbooks in the first place.[72] Why was the evil of caste only alluded to in Hindu society and not in other denominations? Why was the student taught to believe that 'religious or cultural minorities' would be vulnerable if a 'majority community were to capture political power'?[73]

In the din of the culture war that broke out in early 2023, what was drowned out was that the pruning exercise by the NDA involved deleting chunks of chapters dealing with the worst excesses of the Emergency, including mass arrests, custodial deaths, forced sterilizations and censorship of the press.[74] If this entire exercise of revising textbooks was driven purely by partisan considerations, why was this gory chapter of our modern history, scripted entirely by Indira Gandhi, deleted? It isn't as if the present BJP dispensation tires of reminding its critics that between 1975 and 1977, many among them were complicit in 'rationalizing' the arbitrary incarcerations of Opposition leaders and several others serving today in the NDA.[75]

Celebrated Hindutva ideologue and editor of the iconic *Tughlaq*, S. Gurumurthy said on Times Now's *Converse* that not just the BJP and RSS, but some like him too were intellectually battling a 'post-colonial Indian establishment which never allowed colonial theories to be verified, tested, proved or disproved'.[76]

This battle, which one suspects is part of the larger political project, is not going to end with the conclusion of the 2024 election, as it is not confined to textbooks or history but covers 'the entire range of Indian thought, philosophy, culture, model and way of life'.[77]

Gurumurthy, rued that the 1852 book *India in Greece*, by Edward Pococke, was 'never allowed to be circulated' in British India because it undermined their case for colonizing India, '. . . a land that had to be civilized'.[78] Gurumurthy said that Pococke was able to put forth a theory that is 'not rebutted even today', that

the 'Pelasgians' who colonized Greece came from India, because their philosophy, poetry, culture and history of the 'Pelasgi' constitutes the philosophy of Greece. 'Pelasgi' means a wandering people. It is immigration from India westward that is being evidenced by a lot of Indian names, including those from the Mahabharata, tribes, the Ganga . . . and he [Pococke] said that without studying Indian civilization, Greek civilization doesn't have a mother home. In fact, historians have said that the history and origin of Ancient

Greece was not written down by the Greeks themselves, and that without the Indian Puranas, Mahabharata and Rajput genealogies, they may not be able to have the key to understand their own civilization.[79]

Gurumurthy made it a point to highlight that he was only going to cite 'foreign sources' to add to this thesis,[80] perhaps due to the credibility they have in the eyes of an academic elite sceptical, to put it mildly, of the claims of Indian 'nationalist' historians.

Referring to *The Shape of Ancient Thought,* by Thomas McEvilley, published in 2001, Gurumurthy said, 'He came to the conclusion that pre-Hellenistic Greece imported from India and Hellenistic Greece exported to India, and he put it so beautifully that the entire Socrates idea of Atman has no laboratory in Greece, its laboratory was only in India. You know this is a much larger issue than writing the history of kings, what they did and did not do, because this will put India in a very different position.'[81]

Gurumurthy believes that a study of the indigenous antecedents of Indian civilization holds the key to decoding the origin of Western philosophical ideas that have gone global today. 'Once the truth emerges, it will lead to a better appreciation of India's place in the world because India's role has been that of a thought-giver to the world.'[82]

The BJP has been calling upon the electorate to vote it back in 2024 to enable India to evolve into a 'Vishwa Guru'.[83] It's for this reason that the G20 summit hosted in New Delhi under India's presidency has become a vital spoke in the BJP's ever-turning electoral wheel.[84] With the NDA seemingly committed to positioning the Second Republic as a spiritual, moral and industrious Vishwa Guru, it also means that it is now more crucial than ever for Hindutva nationalism to shed its truculence.

4

Whither Ganga–Jamuni Tehzeeb?

A Secularized Encounter

In 1001 AD, Yamin al-Dawlah Abu al-Qasim Mahmud ibn Sebuktigin, also known as Mahmud of Ghazni, arrived in the Punjab at the head of 15,000 horse troops.[1] He was finally on the cusp of redeeming his vow: to invade India once a year.[2] But if he were to get further into the heartland, he knew he would need to subdue his arch-nemesis, Jaipal, the ruler of Punjab.

Jaipal was ready, waiting near Peshawar (now in Pakistan). Though superior in number, his troops, as the *Encyclopaedia Britannica* notes, 'Fell back under the onslaught of the Muslim horsemen, leaving behind 15,000 dead. After falling into the hands of the victors, Jaipal, with 15 of his relatives and officers, was finally released. But the raja could not bear his defeat, and, after abdicating in favour of his son, Anandpal, he mounted his own funeral pyre and perished in the flames.'[3]

But the Indian resistance to Ghazni rose from the ashes to challenge the invader. Anandpal assembled a formidable army conscripted from the forces of equally anxious regional potentates

63

who feared that they would be next. The finances to feed and pay this enormous army were raised from the sale of jewellery by Hindu women.[4]

It is said that for forty days the two armies squared off, sizing each other up between Und and Peshawar, until Ghazni succeeded in enticing Anandpal to attack.[5] It was a mistake. At least it appeared that way for one moment.

As *Encyclopaedia Brittanica* goes on to describe, 'A force of 30,000 fierce Khokar tribesmen charged both flanks of the sultan's army with such ferocity that Maḥmūd was about to call a retreat. But at that critical moment Anandpal's elephant became panic-stricken and took flight. The Indians, believing that their leader was turning tail, fled from the battlefield strewn with their dead and dying.'[6]

Thus began the Islamic invasion of India.

These invasions were brutish. The Iranian scholar, Alberuni, who accompanied Ghazni, chronicled his rapacious pillaging and utter disregard for human life. But since he was an embedded chronicler, Alberuni's prose often exalted the subjugation of the Hindus. 'Mahmud utterly ruined the prosperity of the country, and performed these wonderful exploits, by which Hindus became like atoms of dust scattered in all directions.'[7]

Ghazni's last foray into India was marked by the destruction of the Somnath temple in Gujarat. The evisceration of one of the twelve Jyotirlinga shrines of Shiva is described by some as an enduring act of asserting Islamic supremacy.[8]

Others followed Ghazni. The intensity of their chauvinism did not lack any of Ghazni's fanaticism. The destruction of the universities of Nalanda, Odantapuri and Vikramshila in Bihar—at the hands of Bakhtiyar Khilji—and the mass murder of students and teachers in the thirteenth century were aimed at striking at the very roots of the Indic faiths.[9]

In the years that followed, especially after Independence, the fanaticism that accompanied the invasions was glossed over with hoary and accommodating historical accounts. There were many examples. Pavan Varma has exposed the selective emphasis on certain facts to posit the 'Ganga–Jamuni Tehzeeb'—a synthesis of Hindu and Muslim culture.[10] Varma recalls how some historians built up Amir Khusrau's 'invention' of the sitar, tabla, the qawwali and his mastery of the Braj language as an example of cultural synthesis. But what they conveniently ignored, Varma also points out, were Khusrau's celebration of the desecration of the Shiva temple in Chidambaram by Malik Kafur under another monarch Allaudin Khilji.[11]

Varma has even critically examined the attempt to project Mughal emperor Akbar as a beacon of Hindu–Muslim amity. Here, too, historians ignored that Akbar's syncretic invention of 'Din-e-Ilahi'—divine faith, as in considering all sects as one—was not widely accepted.[12] In fact, Akbar's liberalism clashed with an extremely conservative and intolerant ulema, or clergy, that even declared a fatwa against him.[13]

That Akbar's reign was the exception to the rule was proved when his son Jehangir revived the fanaticism that underpinned Mughal rule in India. Jehangir oversaw the vandalism of temples in Kangra and Ajmer,[14] while his son Shah Jahan—even as he commissioned the architectural marvel Taj Mahal—presided over the obliteration of temples in Anantnag, Kashmir, and built the Jama Masjid in Delhi that 'included a rather miscellaneous arcade made of disparate columns from twenty-seven demolished Hindu temples'.[15]

In fact, Shah Jahan appointed a superintendent to 'make more converts', remitting sentences of prisoners of war and granting daily allowances if they embraced Islam.[16] Apostasy, or conversion to another faith from Islam, was punishable by death.[17]

One may ask: What about Hindu kings and the way they treated Muslim subjects?

As Varma writes, '. . . for Muslim rulers to pursue a policy of violent religious tolerance towards the Hindu faith was more a matter of norm than an exception. By contrast, in the Hindu civilisation that preceded their coming, and in the action of Hindu rulers who survived their onslaught, this kind of destruction of religious sites was more an exception than the norm.'[18]

To illustrate his point Varma cites the conduct of Krishnadevaraya in the sixteenth century in Vijayanagar.[19] The Portuguese traveller Duarte Barbosa described Krishnadevaraya as, 'The king who allows such freedom that every man may come and go and live according to his own creed, without suffering any annoyance and without enquiry whether he is a Christian, Jew, Moor or heathen.'[20]

Donald Eugene Smith, an authority on South Asian studies, in his seminal book *India as a Secular State,* is more generous about Akbar's contribution to religious tolerance[21] and takes a critical view of the inequality perpetuated under the law along the lines of caste in ancient India.[22] But while doing so, he writes, '. . . religious liberty which prevailed in ancient India, however, does represent one essential character of the secular state. Government never sought to impose a particular creed upon the people. Various schools of thought propounded the doctrines of agnosticism, atheism, and materialism. Jainism, Buddhism, and later Judaism, Christianity, Zoroastrianism, and Islam were permitted to propagate their teachings, build their places of worship, and establish their respective ways of life. The struggle for freedom of conscience in Europe and America, stretching over many centuries, has no counterpart in Indian history.'[23]

In the face of Islamic repression there were the odd instances of reprisals. As historian Vikram Sampath writes in

Bravehearts of Bharat, Rana Kumbha of Mewar's invasion of Nagaur in the fifteenth century 'was perhaps one of the rarest of cases when a Hindu monarch adopted the same policy as the Muslim conquerors or rulers and demolished the latter's place of worship, the mosque, quite like how countless temples had been desecrated'.[24]

There is, however, near unanimity over the legacy of one man, Aurangzeb. His fanatical hatred brought on a juggernaut of forced conversions of Hindus, the imposition of *jizya*[25] (tax paid by non-Muslims) and the murder of the Sikh leader Guru Teg Bahadur.[26]

Aurangzeb caparisoned his zealotry, literally, by constructing mosques atop some of Hinduism's most revered sites in Kashi and Mathura.[27]

The Secularization of History

The Germans call it *Vergangenheitsaufarbeitung*[28]—coming to terms with the past, specifically with the historical memory of National Socialism, the Nazis, the Second World War and the Holocaust. The de-Nazification of Germany after its defeat triggered a larger, societal introspection—in politics, culture, cinema and education—about the trauma inflicted in Europe and beyond by the Nazis and their spiteful allies. Though Germany was itself divided after the war, both East and West Germany approached this confrontation of their history as essential to shaping a new future.[29]

India could have had its own version of Vergangenheitsaufarbeitung. After all, in his stirring 'Tryst with Destiny' speech in the Constituent Assembly at that epochal 'midnight hour', Jawaharlal Nehru spoke of the 'soul of a nation, long suppressed', finding utterance as it 'stepped out from the old to the new'.[30]

This soul, however, was not allowed to step out of the shadows cast by the ravages of an extremely dark era of colonization— Islamic, British and Portuguese (in Goa). But it is in facing the impact and legacy of Islamic-settler colonization that independent India has had the greatest difficulty. One of the reasons for this was that it could not decide upon the approach.

Any meaningful endeavour had to, and ought to, steer clear of holding the current generation of Muslims responsible for the deeds of some of their co-religionists in the past. But since there was little political will in evolving the means, we weren't able to accomplish the ends (exorcizing the demons of the past). Unfortunately, even the most elementary step, that is truthfully documenting the past, was not taken.

The classroom is perhaps the only setting where this could have been done without the fear of politics or dogma adulterating the message. Instead, the Indian state, immediately after Independence, adopted a policy of secularizing history. And so evolved a sanitized version of history that romanticized inter-faith relations of the past without acknowledging the existence of a collective memory that believed in a different truth.

Sample this report of the University Education Commission, led by Constituent Assembly member Sarvepalli Radhakrishnan in 1948, regarding the aims of university education in India under the section titled 'The Spread of Islam':[31]

> From very ancient times India had intimate relations with the Arabs, especially in commerce and trade, and there were land and sea routes established between the two countries. The Muslims were welcomed in India by the Hindu rulers, who permitted them to build mosques and spread their teachings. Indian culture did not believe in compelling people to choose its way of life. It encouraged each group that found its home

in India [to] live by its own conception of the good life . . .
With the advent of the Moghuls, the imperial court became
the meeting ground of Hindu and Muslim scholars who
made themselves familiar with each other's cultures. In the
eleventh century, the great Muslim scholar, Alberuni, mastered
the Sanskrit language and left us an impressive and critical
account of the achievements of the Hindus in sciences and
philosophy. India's spirit of comprehension and forbearance
influenced the Moghuls and the cultural activities of India
between the fourteenth and the nineteenth centuries illustrate
Hindu–Muslim collaboration. In science and literature, music
and architecture, in painting and dancing, there was a notable
synthesis of Hindu and Muslim ideas.[32]

It could be argued that at Independence the wounds of Partition
were still raw, and it was best not to scratch at them. But could the
whole truth remain shrouded in perpetuity?

Over two decades later, the Committee on School Textbooks
of the Government of India in 1969 continued with the project
of secularizing history.[33] While paying lip service to the idea that
'There can be no compromise with truth', the committee went on
to recommend:

In view of the fact in teaching Indian history in the past, during
British rule, stress has often been laid on religious differences
and conflict, it is necessary that we should now highlight those
situations – and they are legion where people of all religious
faiths have worked together in unity and co-operation. Where
certain facts of history are important in themselves and
cannot – and, indeed, should not – be ignored, they should
be used wisely to show how ugly these episodes of the past are
things of which all of us should be ashamed and everything

should be done to avoid them in the future. This would, obviously, involve a creative and purposeful reinterpretation of history and judicious selection of historical truths. The interests of national unity and the needs of a modernizing society should be the primary considerations in our choice and presentation of material.[34]

On the other hand, one of the principal architects of the Indian Constitution was also a serious sceptic when it came to the notion that Hindu–Muslim relations were underpinned by any deep sense of collective belonging to India.

Dr B.R. Ambedkar, in his book *Pakistan or the Partition of India*, responds to the arguments that champion 'composite culture'—the prevalence of Hindu customs in Muslim practices, the idea that 'Muslim pirs had Hindu disciples', that 'Hindu yogis had Muslim chelas', or that saints or prominent religious figures from both communities sometimes shared the closest of bonds.[35]

While acknowledging that both Hindus and Muslims were of the same race, Ambedkar wondered if this facet alone was enough for scholars to conclude that the two communities 'long to belong to each other'.[36] Ambedkar argued that these 'common features' were less an outcome of any genuine attempt to 'adapt to or adopt' another's practices than a result of 'incomplete conversions'.[37]

'In a land like India, where a majority of the Muslim population has been recruited from caste and out-caste Hindus, the Muslimization of the convert was neither complete nor effectual, either from fear of revolt or because the method of persuasion or insufficiency of preaching due to insufficiency of priests,' Ambedkar wrote.[38]

He also claimed, 'Political and religious antagonisms divide Hindus and Musalmans far more deeply than the so-called common things are able to bind them together.'[39] He believed that a history of mutual animosities in the political and religious realms was a serious obstacle.[40]

The Roots of Muslim Separatism

It is likely Ambedkar came across literature from more than two centuries earlier, when there existed advocates for the preservation of Islamic purity. Many then lamented the decline of 'Islamic supremacy' in India as the Mughal Empire dwindled after Aurangzeb.[41]

The author and advocate J. Sai Deepak comprehensively documents the roots of the Pakistan movement in his book *India, Bharat and Pakistan: The Constitutional Journey of a Sandwiched Civilization.*[42] He traces the movement back to the notion of Muslim 'separateness' preached by Shah Waliullah Dehlawi. Born in India, Dehlawi emerged as an influential voice among these purists. Sai Deepak quotes Dehlawi in his book:

> I hail from a foreign country. My forebears came to India as emigrants. I am proud of my Arab origin and my knowledge of Arabic, for both bring a person close to 'the ayyid (master) of the Ancients and the Moderns,' 'the most excellent of the prophets sent by God' and 'the pride of the whole creation.' In gratitude for this great favour I ought to conform to the habits and customs of the early Arabs and the Prophet himself as much as I can, and to abstain from the customs of the Turks ('ajam') and the habits of the Indians.[43]

Dehlawi appealed to several Muslim rulers of the time to restore the 'supremacy of Islam', even inviting the Afghan Ahmad Shah Abdali to invade and dislodge the Marathas, while pleading that the lives of Muslims in areas with mixed populations should be spared and secured.[44]

Dehlawi's spiritual successor, Syed Ahmad Barelvi, a flagbearer of Wahabi Islam in India, recruited 'one lakh soldiers committed to the cause of Jihad'.[45] But they couldn't achieve much. On 6 May 1831, their leader Barelvi was beheaded, at the Battle of Balakot, in a clash with the Sikh forces of Maharaja Ranjit Singh.[46]

Interestingly, this is the same Balakot that is in today's Khyber Pakhtunkhwa in Pakistan, which is now dubbed the 'the epicentre of Jihad in South Asia'.[47] It is well established that Balakot serves as the largest training centre for new recruits to the Islamist revanchist terror group Jaish-e-Mohammed.[48] Balakot, of course, dominated the news cycle in 2019, when it was targeted by the Indian Air Force in retaliation for the deadly terror attack in Pulwama, Jammu and Kashmir, earlier that year.[49]

By citing these examples of Muslim separatism, Sai Deepak argues persuasively that there existed, well before the nineteenth century, a spirit of pan-Islamic solidarity powered by the message of religious purity. The policy of divide and rule under the British was perhaps only taking advantage of a fault line that already existed and was ripe for exploitation.

It is curious that Hindutva icon Vinayak Damodar Savarkar, who is reviled today[50] by many 'secularists' and 'integrationists', chose not to dwell much on the roots of 'Muslim separateness' in his assessment of the revolt of 1857 against the British. Savarkar viewed the revolt as an example of Hindus and Muslims uniting for a common cause.[51]

Though aware of the bloodstained legacy of Islamic invasions in India, Savarkar waxed lyrical about Hindus and Muslims joining forces against the British.[52] For instance, he said of the initial successes in Delhi by the rebels:

The five days will be ever memorable in the history of Hindusthan! Because these five days proclaimed by beat of drum the end of the continuous fight between the Hindus and Mahomedans dating from the invasion of Mahmud of Ghazni and on these days it was proclaimed first that the Hindus and the Mahomedans are not rivals, not conquerors and conquered, but brethren . . . Bharatmata pronounced the sacred spell of these days. Hence forward you are equal and brothers. I am equally the mother of you both!

But perhaps Savarkar's motivations were wholly political. At that time, perhaps, Savarkar saw the British as the greater threat to the idea of Bharat. Is this the reason why he continued to build upon his brotherhood thesis?

Whatever his motivations, Savarkar remained committed to his view, observing that 'The Eastern mind has maintained that there are no vast barriers between heaven and earth but the two are ends of one and the same thing. Our idea of *swadharma* is not contradictory to that of *swaraj* . . . The sepoys would take the water of the Ganges or would swear by the Koran that they would live only to achieve the destruction of the English rule.'[53]

The revolt of 1857 ended in defeat. Realizing that the military superiority of the British was, at that stage, impossible to overcome, some Muslim purists adopted a more pragmatic approach.[54] The pioneer of this strategy was that other so-called ambassador of Hindu–Muslim unity[55], Syed Ahmed Khan, who established the Aligarh Muslim University.

For the 'atrocity' committed in 1857–58, Khan blamed 'Ramdin and Matadin', a reference to Hindus. He distanced himself from the Muslims who participated in the revolt but never quite abandoned the path of Dehlawi and Barelvi.[56] Khan's disguised motives were purely tactical. If he couldn't beat the British and the Christians, he would, in a manner of speaking, join hands with them to advance Muslim interests ahead of Hindu interests.[57]

Sai Deepak writes that even before the establishment of the Indian National Congress, Khan 'expressed detailed and vehement opposition to the introduction of representative institutions based on simple elections since he felt "the larger community would totally override the interest of the smaller community"'.[58]

More than two decades before the scourge of separate electorates would set in motion the chain of events that would lead to Partition, Khan had already articulated a view that Pakistan's founders would incorporate in arguing for a separate nation. Khan even saw the emergence of the Congress Party (which went on to become the most potent vehicle for the aspirations of India's freedom fighters) as a threat to Muslims.[59] Khan remarked:

> The aims and objects of the Indian National Congress are based upon an ignorance of history and present-day realities; they do not take into consideration that India is inhabited by different nationalities . . . I consider the experiment which the Indian National Congress wants to make fraught with dangers and suffering for all the nationalities of India, especially for the Muslims. The Muslims are in a minority, but they are a highly united minority. At least traditionally, they are prone to take the sword in hand when the majority oppresses them. If this happens, it will bring about disasters greater than the ones which came in the wake of the happenings of 1857. The Congress cannot rationally prove its claim to represent the opinions, ideals, and aspirations of the Muslims.[60]

Entrenched Hindu–Muslim fault lines and a historical memory clouded by deep resentment culminated in the British-abetted first partition of Bengal in 1905 and the emergence of

Muhammad Ali Jinnah, who founded the Muslim League. The anglicized Savile Row-suited barrister, who 'spoke English as a first language and profoundly disagreed with Hindu Mahatma Gandhi's Indian peasant garb',[61] would go on to become the founder of Pakistan.

As India approached Independence and the movement for Pakistan intensified, the Muslim League began to present the 1946 provincial assembly election as a virtual plebiscite for Pakistan. On the occasion of Eid on 8 September 1945, Jinnah declared, 'There is only one solution of the problem of this great sub-continent, and that is that we should be free to establish Pakistan in our homelands in all Provinces where Muslims are dominant . . . The election will be fought on the issue of Pakistan or Akhand Hindustan.'[62]

The results of the election were an eye-opener. Even among many Muslims who were to stay back in India there was widespread yearning for a separate Muslim state. Of course, there was no universal adult suffrage at the time and the franchise for Muslim seats was limited to 15 per cent of the Muslim population based on 'property' and 'educational qualifications' among other considerations.[63]

In Punjab, Bengal and Sind, the Muslim League swept the Muslim seats. But it also did the same in Assam, Bihar, Bombay, Central Provinces, Madras, United Provinces and Orissa—territories that would remain in India. Across all these regions the Muslim League walked away with 93 per cent of the Muslim seats.[64]

Venkat Dhulipala, author of *Creating a New Medina: State Power, Islam, and the Quest for Pakistan in Late Colonial North India*, believes that in the context of some territories, 'the hostage population theory' might have been at work.[65] He said in an interview to Scroll.in:

If you looked at the map of India and its demography, you had substantial non-Muslim populations in the east and the west [which subsequently became Pakistan], just as you had substantial Muslim minority population in Hindustan . . . The Muslim League put out that in case Muslims were harassed or oppressed or deprived of their rights, retributive violence could visit the non-Muslim minorities in Pakistan. Balance of terror was therefore portrayed as the best guarantee for the security of minorities in both countries.[66]

Dhulipala added, 'The Muslim League emphasised the hostage population theory quite a lot in UP. It also assured supporters that there would be a *treaty* between the two sovereign states as far as the security and rights of the minorities on both sides was concerned. And that despite Partition, life would go on as usual. As a local functionary of the League in Bareilly said, the creation of Pakistan did not mean someone in Allahabad couldn't take the Frontier Mail to Peshawar anymore.'[67]

And there was a direct appeal about the creation of an Islamic state. 'However,' Dhulipala said, 'there was also the Muslim League propaganda that it was trying to create Pakistan as the first Islamic state in history after the Prophet's creation of Medina 1300 years ago. Wouldn't you want to participate in the creation of that Islamic State, the Leaguers asked their supporters.'[68]

The endeavour here is to not question the loyalty of Muslims and their contribution to the freedom struggle. The examples of their commitment to the fight for independence are numerous—from their involvement in the revolt of 1857[69], the non-cooperation movement[70] and the resistance to the British in Punjab before and after the Jallianwala Bagh massacre[71] to their role in the Indian National Army[72] and the naval mutiny of 1946.[73]

Indeed, many Muslims spoke out against Partition.[74] Muslims who chose to remain in India have accepted the secular embrace of India's Constitution, but many among them have also expected concessions. In the 1960s, after Nehru's demise, some continued to cling to an outdated exceptionalism. The Muslim Majlis-i-Mushawarat in Uttar Pradesh and Bihar was constituted to be a vehicle for Muslim aspirations that underlined this exceptionalism.[75]

Then, in 1988, barely two years after outrage among conservative Muslims had forced the Rajiv Gandhi government to overturn the Supreme Court verdict in the Shah Bano case (more on this in the next chapter), historian Mushirul Hasan saw in this disillusionment with the Congress Party worrying parallels with the discourse in the build-up to Partition. Hasan noted in an essay in the *Economic and Political Weekly*:

In the 1940s the phenomenal success of the Muslim League and its allies was, in some measure, linked with the fact of Muslim alienation from the Congress after the 1942 Quit India movement. Capitalising on the 'wrongs' done by the Congress ministries of 1937–39, the League propaganda machine was able to persuade splinter Muslim groups to join its bandwagon. Nearly three decades later, Muslim organisations of different shades of opinion were able to broaden their base of support by harping on the Congress failure to stem the communal tide and its inability to assuage the fears of the minorities. The rise of the Itehadul Muslimeen in Hyderabad, the active political intervention of the Jamaat-i Islami in Kashmir, and the increased support enjoyed by the Muslim League in Kerala must be seen against this background. They remain, as always, the principal force behind Muslim conservatism and political reaction.[76]

Hasan frowned upon this conservatism, remarking that 'its more tangible manifestation was in the resistance to modern education, opposition to the composite and syncretic trends in Indian Islam, and a tendency to thwart reformist initiatives'. This, Hasan said, insulated the community from the 'process of social change and modernisation', and resisted the 'secularising tendencies generated during and after colonial rule'. Indian Islam was an outlier in this aspect, Hasan writes, as 'reformist ideas and movements were not inconsequential in Muslim countries like Egypt, Turkey and Iran'.[77]

Three and a half decades ago, Hasan wrote that the Muslim conservative response had been 'most pronounced in opposing the demand for a uniform civil code'.[78] As we shall see in the next few chapters, this notion of exceptionalism continues to have implications for Indian politics.

5

A Discriminatory Secularism

Rahul Gandhi's Bharat Jodo Yatra[1] arguably captured the public imagination in Karnataka, where the Congress won a decisive mandate in the assembly election of May 2023. But it remains to be seen if the Bharat Jodo Yatra has galvanized the Congress into a unified fighting force that can defeat the NDA at the national level. Nevertheless, ahead of the 2024 parliamentary election, the yatra has certainly sparked a conversation about the perceived religious polarization in society.

Commenting on the need for a Bharat Jodo Yatra, acclaimed academic-turned-politician Yogendra Yadav noted, '. . . never before have hate, division and exclusion been unleashed on us with such impunity and never before have we seen an exclusion of the farmers, Dalits and Adivasis, women and religious minorities in shaping the nation's future.'[2]

In the build-up to the 2024 election, the BJP is working overtime to combat the Opposition's charge that it is the party of discord and discrimination. It is now almost a matter of routine for the NDA's top guns and the BJP's media managers to be challenged on alleged complicity in marginalizing minorities of all stripes. Foreign media and, at times, even foreign-rights watchdogs are quick to flag crimes of a communal nature committed by Hindu reactionaries.[3]

This has forced the NDA to undertake a damage-control exercise to convey its disapproval of communalism. The BJP removed two of its spokespersons, Nupur Sharma and Naveen Kumar Jindal, for their controversial remarks on Prophet Muhammad.[4] It initiated an outreach towards Pasmanda Muslims (the marginalized sections among the Muslim community)[5] and fielded almost twice the number of Muslim candidates in urban body elections in Uttar Pradesh in 2023 than it had done the previous time.[6]

Even in the *Bharatiya Nyaya Sanhita*, the proposed overhaul of the Indian Penal Code, the Central government has strengthened laws against hate speech. If adopted, questioning the loyalty of any individual to the Constitution or to the nation on the grounds of his or her religion would qualify as a crime.[7]

The NDA's keenness to underline its commitment to multiculturalism also finds expression in the choice of the motto adopted for the G20 summit, Vasudhaiva Kutumbakam (one earth, one family, one future).[8]

The prime minister himself is the most aggressive publicist for the inclusionary nature of the NDA's governance record in its time in office. In February 2023, with one eye on a series of crucial elections in states where minorities are in numbers that can influence the outcome, Modi said in Parliament:

> . . . to ensure that cent percent beneficiaries avail welfare schemes and the cent percent benefit reaches we chose a path of 'saturation' our government marches on such a past of honesty that 'saturation' is the true secularism. Achieving 'saturation'

means no discrimination whatsoever as discrimination breeds corruption. We have committed to 'saturation' where we want the benefits of every scheme to reach 100 per cent of the beneficiaries. This is true 'secularism' and we are working honestly to achieve it.[9]

The reference to 'true secularism' is not accidental. The BJP has long accused its opponents of practising 'pseudo secularism'.[10] Sample this from another speech by Modi from four years earlier. 'In this election not even one political party has the guts to wear the mask of secularism to fool the country,' he said on 26 May 2019, after the results of the Lok Sabha elections were declared and the BJP won an even bigger mandate than in 2014. 'They have been unmasked.'[11]

At other times, the BJP has pointed to its own constitution to stress upon its secular DNA.[12] Indeed, the BJP's constitution calls upon every one of its members to take an oath upholding a 'secular state and nation not based on religion'.[13]

The BJP may not be too off the mark in apportioning blame for the practice of what it describes as 'pseudo-secularism' on its biggest political opponent. If secularism has acquired a pejorative connotation in India today, it is largely due to how it has been practised by one of its principal advocates, the Congress Party. The state under Congress rule drifted from maintaining neutrality in matters of religion. The grand old party's secularism is synonymous with the 'politics of appeasement'.[14]

It need not have turned out this way.

'Path of Wisdom for Minorities to Trust the Majority'

Right from the Constituent Assembly debates, there was an overwhelming consensus to maintain neutrality towards all faiths. In July 1947, based on the recommendations of the Minorities Sub-Committee of the Constituent Assembly, another larger advisory committee, led by Sardar Vallabhbhai Patel, noted that separate electorates had 'in the past sharpened communal differences to a dangerous extent' and had 'proved one of the main stumbling blocks to the development of a healthy national life'.[15]

Nevertheless, the advisory committee backed reservations on the grounds of religion, stating that 'seats for different recognised minorities shall be reserved in the various legislatures on the basis of their population'.[16]

But, importantly, in the deliberations that took place in the advisory committee over the next year and a half, this view changed. The committee members rightly apprehended that reservations along religious lines 'would lead to a certain degree of separatism' and would be 'contrary to the conception of a secular democratic state'.[17]

As lawyer and author Abhinav Chandrachud writes in *Republic of Religion: The Rise and Fall of Colonial Secularism in India*, Muslim opinion within this advisory committee was divided, with Maulana Hafizur Rehman in favour of religious reservations, while Tajamul Hossain, among others, against them.[18] When the committee met again in May 1949 a consensus seemed to have emerged, wherein, apparently on the instructions of Maulana Abul Kalam Azad, those Muslims who had earlier been in favour of reservations did not press their case.[19] Eventually, Begum Aizaz Rasul, a Muslim League member who had stayed back in India and was one of fifteen women in a Constituent Assembly of 299, settled the matter in favour of doing away with reservations in legislatures on religious grounds.[20]

She reasoned that such reservations would

'. . . [keep] up the spirit of separatism and communalism. The Muslims comprise a large part of the population in this country . . . I don't think any political party can ever ignore them. To my mind reservation is a self-destructive weapon which separates the minorities from the majority for all time. It gives no chance to the minorities to win the good-will of the majority. It keeps up the spirit of separatism and communalism alive which should be done away once and for all . . . The second ground on which I support it [abolition of religion-based reservations] is that there is still a feeling of separatism prevalent amongst the communities in India today. That must go. I feel that it is in the interests of the minorities to try to merge themselves into the majority community. It is not going to be harmful to the minorities I can assure them, because in the long run it will be in their interests to win the goodwill of the majority. To my mind it is very necessary that the Muslim living in this country should throw themselves entirely upon the good-will of the majority community, should give up separatist tendencies and throw their full weight in building up a truly secular state.[21]

H.C. Mookherjee, a Christian, backed Aizaz Rasul, saying it was 'the path of wisdom for minorities to trust the majority'.[22] Sardar Hukam Singh, a Sikh from the Akali Dal, also felt reservations were counterproductive: 'When you are reserving, say 30 per cent, for the minorities, indirectly you are reserving 70 per cent for the majority.'[23]

Ironically, most members of the Constituent Assembly had been indirectly elected[24] by legislators who had been voted in during the Provincial Assembly elections prior to Independence, which had been conducted on the basis of separate electorates.[25] However, the assembly evolved a consensus to not only abolish separate electorates but also dismiss the idea of reservations in legislatures for religious minorities.

The consensus also encouraged the erosion of a majority–minority binary over the course of time. Sardar Patel summarized the efforts thus:

> It is not our intention to commit the minorities to a particular position in a hurry. If they really have come honestly to the conclusion that in the changed conditions of this country, it is in the interest of all to lay down real and genuine foundations of a secular State, then nothing is better for the minorities than to trust the good-sense and sense of fairness of the majority, and to place confidence in them. So also, it is for us who happen to be in a majority to think about what the minorities feel, and how we in their position would feel if we were treated in the manner in which they are treated. But in the long run, it would be in the interest of all to forget that there is anything like majority or minority in this country and that in India there is only one community.[26]

While the framers of our Constitution were clear in this regard, Sardar Patel's hopes are yet to be realized. Far from suffering an erosion, the majority–minority binary was kept alive through the adoption of a myriad of different political strategies.

Minority-ism

On 3 October 2022, the Press Information Bureau put out a 'fact check' against a news item[27] claiming that the Central government was considering scrapping the Ministry of Minority Affairs. Its activities would continue but under the aegis of the social justice ministry, the report suggested. The government promptly debunked the report.[28]

The news, had it been true, would have been a step, even if incremental, towards redeeming the legacy of a flawed secularism still in practice in India. Had the government taken the small but symbolic step, it would have been consistent with a promise made by the BJP in its 1998 manifesto, where it had stated that, if voted to power, it would 'Entrust the responsibilities of the Minorities Commission to the Human Rights Commission, thus providing greater protection to members of minority communities'.[29] Twenty-four years later, however, the same party, more dominant than ever, was eager to put any speculation along similar grounds to rest.

The Ministry of Minority Affairs was created in January 2006.[30] The Congress-led UPA government carved it out of the Ministry of Social Justice 'to ensure a more focused approach towards issues relating to the notified minority communities namely Muslim, Christian, Buddhist, Sikhs, Parsis, and Jain'.[31]

This was an exercise in superfluity and excess symbolism, when the Constitution itself guarantees the protection of minorities. For instance, Article 30 pertains to rights of minorities, linguistic or religious, to establish and administer educational institutions.[32] Article 29, which relates to the protection of the 'interests of minorities', states that any section of citizens residing in India who have a distinct language, culture or script of its own shall have the right to conserve the same.[33] But vote-bank considerations meant that the political class would not be stopped from perpetuating religious 'separateness' at an institutional level. All this was done in the name of accommodative secularism.

Interestingly, even the forerunner of the BJP, the Jan Sangh, was not above this. In 1978, as part of Prime Minister Morarji

Desai's coalition government, it was party to the setting up of a
Minorities Commission.[34]

At the height of the Ayodhya Ram Janmabhoomi movement
in 1992, the Central government, led by the Congress, gave
the then Minorities Commission an elevated status through the
National Commission for Minorities Act.[35] With the eventual
establishment of ministries for minority affairs, not just at the
Centre but also in state governments, a significant sum in state and
union budgets was allocated for welfare initiatives, scholarships
and the modernization of madrasas, among other measures.[36] But
this do-gooding came with its own set of problems.

The national majority, comprising the Hindus, is also
a minority population in several states in the country: Jammu
and Kashmir (now a union territory), Punjab, Arunachal Pradesh,
Nagaland, Meghalaya and Mizoram.[37] This prompted the
question: If six nationally recognized minorities were beneficiaries
of welfare initiatives from the Ministry of Minority Affairs, wasn't
it only fair for Hindus to be accorded a similar status in states
where they are in minority?

Why should Hindus be discriminated against? Was it even
legal? According to the Supreme Court judgment in 'TMA Pai
Foundation and Others vs State of Karnataka', 2002, it was
held, 'If, therefore, the state has to be regarded as the unit for
determining "linguistic minority" vis-à-vis Article 30, then
with "religious minority" being on the same footing, it is the
state in relation to which the majority or minority status will
have to be determined.'[38]

To date, the non-Hindu majority states of Arunachal Pradesh
(Buddhist majority), Meghalaya, Mizoram and Nagaland
(Christian majorities), and the union territory of Jammu and
Kashmir (Muslim majority) do not accord this minority status
to Hindus.[39]

This discrimination is being challenged in the Supreme Court. On 25 March 2022, when the Central government was asked to respond by the Supreme Court, it seemed more interested in washing its hands of the entire issue.[40] It told the court that the matter was in the domain of the states, as the states were empowered to classify a group as minorities.[41] The Centre also, interestingly, called on the Supreme Court to dismiss the challenge, saying that it was not in the larger public or national interest.[42]

But in May 2022, the Central government appeared to do a volte-face. The Ministry of Minority Affairs submitted an affidavit in the top court, claiming that the issue had far-reaching ramifications, and that more meetings with stakeholders and state governments were necessary.[43] As of April 2023, Muslim-majority Jammu and Kashmir, currently administered by the Centre, and Hindu-majority Rajasthan and Telangana, both ruled by Opposition parties, the Congress and the Bharatiya Rashtra Samithi respectively, hadn't submitted their full replies.[44] The prevarication of the administration in charge of Jammu and Kashmir is particularly curious, amid a spate of targeted killings and a sordid history of ethnic cleansing of Hindus in the late 1980s and early '90s.

Whatever the ultimate outcome of the hearings in this matter, the attempt to woo non-Hindus through the establishment of institutional superstructures—like minority commissions and ministries—ended up privileging one set of people over another.

Secularism = State's Right to Regulate Religion?

Of the 3.6 million words spoken in the Constituent Assembly debates held at the birth of the nation for 165 days, over three years and accounting for some 8000 pages of written documents, the word 'secular' was used around 300 times.[45]

There were almost 800 references to 'God' and the terms 'Hindu' and 'Muslim' were used close to 2000 times. The word used most often, understandably dominating the discourse, was 'rights', which was iterated more than 8000 times.[46]

That the words pertaining to religion and issues related to religion were uttered less frequently than those related to one's rights doesn't mean that the former were less important to the framers of the Constitution. There were heated debates on whether the original Preamble to the Indian Constitution should include the word 'secular'. And if it did not, what would be the implications.

Between the undeniably religious nature of Indians (including many of the framers of the Constitution) on the one hand and the state's own agnosticism on the other, there was still a diverse range of suggestions about how India ought to define herself. Some members—H.V. Kamath, Govind Malaviya and S.L. Saxena—proposed that the Preamble should begin by invoking God or a supreme being.[47] At least two other members sought to introduce the word 'secular' in the Preamble. One was K.T. Shah, who proposed that the Preamble should include this line, 'The State in India being secular shall have no concern with any religion, creed or profession of faith.'[48]

Another member, Brajeshwar Prasad, suggested, 'We the people of India, having [sic] resolved to constitute India into a secular co-operative commonwealth to establish socialist order.'[49]

These suggestions were, of course, rejected at that time.

The Congress stalwart K.M. Munshi felt that even though the state may not necessarily espouse a religion, it should not be completely divorced from matters of religion either. Munshi said:

> The non-establishment clause [of the US Constitution] was inappropriate to Indian conditions and we had to evolve a characteristically Indian secularism . . . We are a people with deeply religious moorings. At the same time, we have a living tradition of religious tolerance – the results of the broad outlook of Hinduism that all religions lead to the same god . . . In view of this situation, our state could not possibly have a state religion, nor could a rigid line be drawn between the state and the church as in the US.[50]

This was an important intervention, and B.R. Ambedkar, chairman of the Drafting Committee of the Indian Constitution, was alive to it. After all, as author and lawyer Abhinav Chandrachud writes, Ambedkar had inserted an Establishment Clause for the Indian Constitution in March 1947 as part of his draft on Fundamental Rights.[51] It said, 'The State shall not recognize any religion as State religion.' Other proposals for an Establishment Clause included 'neutrality' of the state in matters of religion.[52]

Curiously, Chandrachud notes, in 1947, when the subcommittee on fundamental rights submitted its report to a larger advisory committee, the Establishment Clause was mysteriously missing.[53] Ambedkar, who had originally envisioned an Establishment Clause, did not dissent at this deletion.[54]

If the Constitution was to be a vehicle for social change, as many members of the Constituent Assembly hoped it would be, this wall between 'church and state' would have to be brought down—not for identifying the country with any one religion but for effecting religious reforms, including taking steps to end caste discrimination. Indian secularism would be interventionist, to enable the state to step in, where and when necessary, particularly in matters involving Hindus to facilitate social inclusion and equality. This, however, would assume an outright, discriminatory edge over time and work against Hindu interests.

So, after much debate in the Constituent Assembly, the Indian Constitution guaranteed the fundamental right to practise and propagate religion, as stated in Article 25, 'subject to public order, morality, and health'.[55] It also does not prevent the state from 'regulating or restricting any economic, financial, political or other secular activity which may be associated with religious practice'.[56] And, it allows the state a hand in 'providing for social welfare and reform or throwing open Hindu religious institutions of a public character to all classes and sections of Hindus' (taken to mean Jains, Sikhs and Buddhists too).[57]

Article 17 abolished untouchability, and several states subsequently passed the Devadasi Abolition Acts to end the practice of 'dedicating' women to temples that had left them vulnerable, in many cases, to sexual exploitation.[58] The caveats of 'public order, morality and health' were also added to Article 26, which allows every religious denomination to manage its own religious affairs.[59]

But in practice, the rights that flow under Article 26 do not, strangely, fully apply to Hindus. They have had to endure decades of state control over their places of worship.[60]

The Temple 'Liberation' Movement

A true secularist would argue that the administration of, according to some estimates, more than 1,00,000 temples in India[61] by state governments militates against the fundamental principle of separation of church and state. And it does.

The administration of Hindu temples by the Indian state amounts to a total usurpation of Hindu rights by those entrusted to protect them.

State patronage to religious institutions, especially temples, was the norm before the advent of British rule, with kings investing significantly in their maintenance, upkeep and practices. The British continued the practice through a formal takeover by way of the enactment of rules, but over time they withdrew. Chiefly because Christian missionaries opposed Christian 'entanglement' in the faith of people they believed were heathens.[62]

But a new political class of Indians, who were in positions of power in provincial governments, were keen to bring places of worship under the purview of the state,[63] though the extent of control exercised over temple administration varies from state to state.

The Madras Hindu Religious Endowments Act of 1926, for instance, allowed the government to appoint a board to run the affairs of temples.[64] After Independence, several other states would adopt laws to govern Hindu temples (only four states, by 1960, did not have them).[65]

The Government of Andhra Pradesh, as per its own Charitable and Hindu Religious Endowments Act of 1987, appoints an executive officer to, among a whole list of responsibilities, 'Foster faith, devotion and ethical conduct in the society, by facilitating [the] formation of a *Bhaktha Samajam* attached to each Institution, on [a] voluntary basis, consisting of the devotees thereof in order to periodically organize Bhajans, Religious discourses, devotional and other Religious programmes such as Nagara *Sankeertans* etc., appropriate to the Custom, Usage, Tradition and *Sampradayams* of the Institution concerned'.[66]

Initially, a commissioner appointed under the Madras Hindu Religious and Charitable Endowments Act, 1951, several of whose sections were struck down later by the Supreme Court,[67] had a lot of say in the administration of temples under his jurisdiction. From the unfettered right to enter the premises of a religious institution to approving the annual budget of the trustees, providing and withholding permissions for the sale of immovable property belonging to the temple by a trustee, and deciding how surplus funds of the temple ought to be spent, the sweep of powers was vast.[68]

In his 1963 book *India as a Secular State,* Donald Eugene Smith states: 'It is no exaggeration to assert that the commissioner for Hindu religious endowments, a public servant of a secular state, today exercises far greater authority over Hindu religion in Madras state than the Archbishop of Canterbury does over the Church of England.'[69]

The rationale for such authority, its defenders argued, flowed from Article 25 (2)(a), which, as mentioned earlier, pertained to 'regulating or restricting any economic, financial, political or other secular activity which may be associated with religious practice'.[70]

But as Smith contends, 'When a deputy commissioner sanctions the expenditure of surplus temple funds for the establishment of orphanages rather than for the propagation of the religious tenets of the institution, he is dealing as much with religion as he is with finances. Behind this preference lies a whole set of religious assumptions which are in effect being imposed on the temple trustees.'[71]

Over time, some of these legislations were challenged. Many of these provisions of the Madras Hindu Religious and Charitable Endowments Act, 1951, were struck down in 1954 by the Supreme Court on the grounds of interference.[72] However, the act itself remained. In fact, the Tamil Nadu government in 1959 revived, with some modifications, according to petitioners who have challenged this act in the Supreme Court, several provisions that had been struck down 'under the guise of better management and regulation'.[73, 74]

The petition filed by the Sri Subramanyaswamikoil Swathanthra Paripalana Sthalathargal Sabhai seeks the quashing of several provisions of the act on the grounds of arbitrary encroachment into the domain of religion, and seeks to highlight how, despite sweeping powers, the administration has left the temples in Tamil Nadu in a pitiable state.[75] The petition states:

> Post the promulgation of the 1959 Act, till date, close to 44,121 temples in Tamil Nadu have been taken over by the state government, out of which approximately 85 per cent of the Temples receive INR 10,000 or less in contributions from devotees [annually]. In other words, Temples with a monthly income of less than INR 1,000 are under state control, which defies logic and reasonableness. Since [they were] taken over by Government, there have been no poojas in 16,000 temples due to the alienation of the local communities from the temple administration and care by Government. State appointees, who go by the title of 'executive officers' and 'fit persons', are appointed to Temple administrations without there being a due cause and for indefinite periods. In most instances, there is no written order pursuant to which these appointments have been made, which violates the fundamental requirements of natural justice. Once appointed, the executive officers stay put for good and effectively take control of the administration of temples in all respects, secular and religious. From the approval of budgets for performance of daily rituals in the temple to the appointment of key functionaries to the temple administration, the executive officer has the last word.[76]

The problem, as the petition notes, was not confined to Tamil Nadu. Temples in Karnataka and Andhra Pradesh, too, face the same concerns.[77] It is estimated that more than 1,00,000 acres of temple lands in three states have been 'under encroachment or hostile occupation'.[78]

In another case, as the petition notes, this time in the state of Kerala, the high court in 1990 came down hard on the Travancore Dewaswom Board and Cochin Dewaswom Board for 'innumerable illegalities, misappropriation of funds ... mismanagement, incompetence, and indiscipline'.[79]

One might ask: How is this any different from the administration of places of worship in other faiths? In the case of Muslims, the Waqf Act of 1995 is a Central law that in each state places considerable powers in the hands of a board that is not entirely state-controlled, to ensure the maintenance, control and administration of 8,33,558 Waqf properties.[80] Waqf properties may also include mosques. By definition, they are movable or immovable properties dedicated for permanent use for Islamic religious, or charitable, purposes.[81] The board scrutinizes the budgets, has the last word over the sale or lease of immovable properties, and can appoint as well as remove *muttawalis* (overseers or managers of the Waqf land).[82] Waqf boards retain a sense of autonomy, as the law mandates that the elected members in the board outnumber those nominated by the state government.[83] Moreover, the surplus income of the Waqf is to be used to meet the 'objects of the Waqf'.[84]

On the other hand, under the 1959 act in Tamil Nadu pertaining to Hindu temples, a state-appointed official can determine if the temple funds can be reallotted to any '*other* [emphasis ours] religious institution' which is 'poor and in needy circumstances'.[85] The petitioners who've challenged the act claim that such a provision, allowing temple funds to be transferred to non-Hindu institutions, clearly violates the fundamental right to equality guaranteed by Article 14.[86]

In the neighbouring state of Karnataka, there has been a limited course-correction. The Muzrai department, which controls more than 34,000 temples in the state,[87] issued a formal order preventing the diversion of temple funds to institutions of other religions.[88]

This battle for the control of temples has played out in the courts for decades, but the BJP has only recently shown the slightest signs of willingness to divest control. In 2021, when one of its own chief ministers, Trivendra Singh Rawat in Uttarakhand, tried to bring the Char Dham shrines under government control and was met with serious resistance on the ground, the party decided to replace him.[89]

The movement to 'liberate' temples from government control, or even significantly reduce the extent of government interference in temple administration, has not acquired a mass character, and this perhaps explains the BJP's own tepid response. However, those defending state control of places of worship argue that these laws have been an instrument of reform.

Writing in *The Hindu*, Manuraj Shanmugasundaram, a lawyer and spokesperson for the Dravida Munnetra Kazhagam, the ruling party in Tamil Nadu, says:

> Early interventions of the Dravidian movement ensured that people belonging to backward classes were given the right to walk on the roads adjoining the Shiva temple in Vaikom and resulted in the promulgation of the Travancore Temple Entry Proclamation of 1936. In the subsequent decades, Kerala and Tamil Nadu, especially, have seen significant reforms within Hindu temples that have culminated in the appointment of persons belonging to backward classes as *archakas* (priests) through government action. In August 2021, the DMK made 208 appointments under the TNHR&CE Act which included *archakas* from all castes and a woman *odhuvar* (singer of hymns) . . .
>
> The Supreme Court has upheld laws such as the TNHR&CE Act and found them to operate within the constitutionally

permissible framework of regulating the secular aspects of the Hindu religion. The framers of our Constitution emphasised the need for social reform in religion. And so, any effort to 'free Hindu temples' can only be regarded as an attempt to redefine secularism and ultimately rewrite the fundamentals of our Constitution.[90]

But the lines have been blurred between the 'secular' and 'religious' aspects of Hinduism by these laws. The state must be equidistant from all places of worship cutting across faiths.

The Personal Law Distortion

It took an hour and a half during peak-hour evening traffic to reach Govindpuram in Ghaziabad. We were late for our appointment, but lawyer Ashwini Upadhyay was understanding. 'This is the only time you'll get with me. I'm off to Deoghar tomorrow, and then to Hazaribagh the day after. I have to deliver lectures on "Ram Rajya Aur Samvidhan [Constitution]".'[91]

Upadhyaya, once a founding member of the Aam Aadmi Party,[92] joined the BJP in 2014.[93] He is an advocate, and the court of law and the instrument of public interest litigation (PIL) are the medium for his activism. A serial litigator, Upadhyaya has made it his mission to use the courts to rectify the discriminatory nature of our secularism, which, he is convinced, has worked against Hindu interests.

A few days before we met him, the Supreme Court had chastised Upadhyaya for his petition that had sought the establishment of a 'Renaming Commission' to 'find out original names of ancient, historical, cultural, religious places named after barbaric foreign invaders'.[94] Upadhayay argued that the retention of the names of 'brutal invaders' was a violation of the right to dignity under Article 21 of the Constitution, and the right to conserve and protect ancient culture.[95] In its oral observations, the court criticized Upadhyaya: 'You want to keep this as a live issue and keep the country on a boil? Fingers are pointed at a particular community. You run down a particular section of society. India is a secular state, this is a secular forum.'[96] The petition was dismissed, but Upadhyaya was undeterred. His demand for a fair and honest inquiry into the past was a valid one, he said, and his efforts would persist.[97]

In several other instances, his efforts have paid off. His petition demanding minority status for Hindus in predominantly non-Hindu states continues to be heard,[98] as does his demand for the revocation of the Places of Worship Act.[99] The Delhi High Court has sought responses from the government on Upadhyaya's petition, demanding a uniform banking code for foreign exchange transactions.[100] Upadhyaya believes such a code is the need of the hour to control the flow of 'black money' that he believes is being diverted to fund Maoists and even religious conversions.[101]

Upadhyaya's petitions are intended to serve another purpose: keep the government of the day, even if it is led by the party he belongs to, on its toes regarding a host of unresolved issues that the equation between the Indian state and religion have birthed. In essence, he is filing PILs against the silence or inaction of the NDA. We asked him if he was 'deployed' to test the water on a contentious issue in court before his party or government takes a stand. He said:

> There is no truth to this. I am proud of the fact that if an issue is for the greater good of the nation, the BJP will never hinder the process of raising that issue. Tell me if there is a single *karyakarta* of any other party who files PILs making his own party's government as a respondent.

I have filed a PIL demanding a population control law. I challenged Article 35A of the Constitution about Jammu and Kashmir. After I challenged it, people got to know about it. The government moved to remove it. Similarly, on the issue of uniform age of marriage for men and women, which I had raised, the government formed a committee and came out with a bill that is now being discussed. I live by my own rules, I never ask the party about this. I do this independently.[102]

On 29 March 2023, the Supreme Court dismissed Upadhyaya's petition seeking gender-neutral and religion-neutral legislations in matters of divorce, adoption and inheritance—essentially a uniform civil code.[103] The Central government insisted that this was for the legislature to decide, and the Supreme Court agreed.[104] In 2022, another such petition filed by Upadhayaya had met with the same response in the Delhi High Court.[105] Upadhyaya's objective is to make the Indian state realize the urgent need for bringing in a truly secular legislation. If the state is entitled to step in and use legislation as a means to initiate reform within religion, like it has done with Hindu customs and practices, it is equally entitled to harmonize the personal laws of all faiths into a uniform code applicable to all Indian citizens.

Not only is a uniform civil code part of the Directive Principles of State Policy under Article 44,[106] it has also been a long-standing manifesto promise of the BJP,[107] Upadhyaya's own party.

Suitably chastised by the likes of Upadhyaya, who form the core of the BJP's voter base, and with little time to placate them before the 2024 election, several BJP governments at the state level are drafting a uniform civil code within their territories.[108] Some Central BJP leaders and NDA union ministers have also vowed that the BJP will bring about a uniform civil code nationally.[109]

Of course, no debate on the uniform civil code can be complete without reference to the iconic fight of a divorced Muslim woman who challenged Muslim patriarchs but was betrayed at the altar of political expediency. Shah Bano's case exemplifies all that is wrong with secularism in India.[110]

Shah Bano had married a lawyer, Mohammad Ahmad Khan, in 1932 in Indore. The couple had five children. Forty-two years after the marriage, in 1975, Shah Bano was 'driven out' of her matrimonial home.[111] During this time, Khan married again—polygamy being allowed under Islamic law in India. Three years later, in April 1978, Shah Bano approached the courts seeking a maintenance of Rs 500 per month from her husband, who was earning an income of Rs 60,000 a year. In November 1978, Khan divorced Shah Bano by an 'irrevocable talaq'[112] and said that he was under no obligation to provide any maintenance to his wife. He claimed that he had already paid her Rs 200 a month for two years and had deposited a sum of Rs 3000 in the court as money meant for her during the *iddat*, or a waiting time after divorce that can vary based on circumstances.[113] The Madhya Pradesh High Court ordered that a maintenance amount of Rs 179 continue to be paid,[114] and Khan challenged this order in the Supreme Court, claiming that Muslim personal law, as it stood in India, did not oblige him to do so.[115] In this, he was backed by the All India Muslim Personal Law Board (AIMPLB), the self-proclaimed custodian of Muslim personal law in India.[116]

Formed in 1972, the AIMPLB is an NGO whose single biggest objective is to protect the applicability of Sharia, or Islamic law, on Indian Muslims in matters of marriage, inheritance and adoption.[117] Indeed, it views the uniform civil code as a 'conspiracy'[118] and has impleaded itself in multiple cases to protect the Sharia when the patriarchy in the implementation of Islamic laws and practices was challenged by Muslim women themselves—be it over the practice of instant divorce, triple talaq, or polygamy.[119]

In 1985, the Supreme Court ruled in favour of Shah Bano.[120] It delivered its verdict through an examination of Muslim personal law and concluded that there was no conflict between what the Quran prescribed for divorced women by way of maintenance and Section 125 of the CrPC, which empowered a magistrate to direct a divorced husband to pay his former wife a monthly sum if she was unable to provide for herself.[121] While delivering this judgment, the court lambasted the AIMPLB for taking an 'extreme position by displaying an unwarranted zeal to defeat the right to maintenance of women who are unable to maintain themselves'.[122] It also lamented the absence of a uniform civil code in the country.[123]

But in a bid to placate conservative Muslims outraged by what they regarded as interference in their personal law, the Congress-led government (under Prime Minister Rajiv Gandhi) overturned the Supreme Court verdict.[124]

The bill passed in Parliament, labelled 'Muslim Women (Protection of Rights on Divorce Act), 1986', placed an obligation upon the husband to pay 'a reasonable and fair provision and maintenance within three months' or the iddat period.[125]

The defenders of this law claim that this was an improvement on what the Supreme Court itself had prescribed, as the act provided for a fixed amount as maintenance—which could even mean for a lifetime—to be paid by the former husband *within* a span of three months.[126] However, it still represented a submission to conservative Muslim sentiments and the AIMPLB, which had held multiple meetings with Rajiv Gandhi.[127] And that was because the Congress government, through this act, privileged Muslim personal law and the Shariat over common law. What's more, the AIMPLB was allowed by the government to be a part of the process of drafting the bill.[128]

In Indore, Shah Bano had been labelled an 'infidel'[129] and was sadly 'ostracized'[130] even by her neighbours. In a final act aimed at sending a message to those who challenged the hegemony of Muslim personal law in India, the hapless woman was made to swallow her pride and issue a statement 'saying that she disavowed the Supreme Court verdict, that she would donate the maintenance money to charity, and that she opposed any judicial interference in Muslim personal law'.[131] Her thumbprint will forever blot the report card of liberalism in India.

Very few backed Shah Bano. Even the minister of state Arif Mohammad Khan, now the governor of Kerala, who had resigned from Rajiv Gandhi's council of ministers in disgust, was rebuked and ostracized. 'He [Arif Mohammad Khan] is one of the third-class, *sarkari* Muslims, like Rafiq Zakaria,' said Ahmed Ali Qasmi, general secretary of the All India Muslim Majlis-e-Mashwrat, in 1986.[132]

Ironically, a few months earlier, Rajiv Gandhi had backed Khan for opposing a private member's bill that had sought to exempt Muslims from Section 125 of the CrPC—essentially undoing the Shah Bano judgment.[133] Rajiv Gandhi's 'first and last instinct', as Khan said in an interview many years later, was to oppose such a bill.[134] Little did he know then that Gandhi was no less an opportunist than the next politician.

An *India Today* article, published on 31 March 1986, suggests that Rajiv Gandhi had decided to appease Muslim conservatives after he received intelligence reports alerting him that the 'overwhelming feeling in the community was against the Shah Bano judgement'.[135]

As senior journalist Neerja Chowdhury writes in her book *How Prime Ministers Decide*, 'The Muslim Women's Bill was deliberately drafted by Law Minister Ashoke Sen in such a way that it would undo the Shah Bano judgement, satisfy an irate Muslim community, but not fall foul of the courts in the future.'[136] Sen was instructed in Parliament to take a firm position against the Supreme Court ruling. He saw the surrender as a celebration of India's 'secular' mosaic:[137]

> It [Indian secularism] flourishes on an acknowledgement of the different cultures of the various communities and religions which have come to stay in this great country. It is a combined strength that has made Indian democracy and culture and civilisation so great in the past, now, and forever. If we start on a fine mosaic and try to draw one single pattern all over the country, then we shall be playing absolutely against the very foundation of our philosophy.[138]

The decision to overturn the SC verdict was textbook 'selective secularism'. The state would bend over backwards to protect the supremacy of Muslim personal law in its applicability for the Muslim community.[139]

Worse, the decision to overturn the Supreme Court ruling on Shah Bano was in total contradiction to what an elected government was expected to do in the interests of national unity. In fact, in multiple judgments since, Indian courts have urged the legislature and executive to promulgate a uniform civil code.[140] The Allahabad High Court reminded the government in 2021 of what the top court had told the Centre in the Shah Bano case in 1985:

> A belief seems to have gained ground that it is for the minority community to take a lead in the matter of reforms of their personal law. That has been the consistent official stand of the Government within the country and in international forums. A common civil code will help the cause of national integration

by removing disparate loyalties to laws that have conflicting ideologies. No community is likely to bell the cat by making gratuitous concessions on this issue. It is the State which is charged with the duty of securing a uniform civil code for the citizens of the country and, unquestionably, it has the legislative competence to do so.[141]

Almost four decades ago, when the Shah Bano judgment was being overturned in Parliament, it took K.P. Unnikrishnan, member of Parliament from the Congress Socialist Party, representing Vatakara in Kerala, to remind Rajiv Gandhi of his own family's commitment to social reform. Unnikrishnan urged the Congress to consider the example of Jawaharlal Nehru.[142] At the time of Nehru's prime ministership in the 1950s, the Congress frowned upon the resistance by 'obscurantists'[143] opposing socio-cultural reforms being initiated by Parliament. Unnikrishnan contrasted that unambiguity with how the Rajiv Gandhi government had 'surrendered to the dark forces of fundamentalism of the type that are posing a grave challenge to the very forces of integration in the country'.[144]

Indeed, despite active resistance from within the Hindu community,[145] including the RSS,[146] Nehru had determinedly proceeded to codify, through Parliament, Hindu personal laws pertaining to marriage, guardianship, adoption and inheritance. Though in time the RSS and the BJP grew to publicly reconcile themselves to reforms of Hindu customs and practices, the saffron fold, an insider told us, 'never forgave Nehru for not pursuing reform on the Muslim side of the fence'.[147]

The Bharatiya Jana Sangh's Syama Prasad Mukherjee would maintain that while 'It is nobody's case that monogamy is good for Hindus alone or for Buddhists alone or Sikhs alone . . . I am not going to tread on this question because I know the weakness of the promoters of this Bill. They dare not touch the Muslim community. There will be so much opposition coming from throughout India that Government will not dare to proceed with it. But of course, you can proceed with the Hindu community in any way you like and whatever the consequences may be.'[148]

Nehru, when pushing for the codification of Hindu personal laws, said of the uniform civil code that though he had 'extreme sympathy' for the idea, he did not think 'the present moment was ripe in India for me to try to push it through. I want to prepare the ground for it and this kind of thing is one method of preparing the ground.'[149]

It was also deemed, during the Constituent Assembly debates, that perhaps the time was not right to embrace a uniform civil code, amid large-scale opposition from the Muslim members.[150] Only two Muslims, Naziruddin Ahmad and Hussain Imam, had said that the implementation should be gradual.[151]

Ambedkar, too, proceeded cautiously but emphasized that until 1937 many Muslims in India, in the Central Provinces, United Provinces and Bombay, were governed by laws of Hindu succession, and that, in Malabar, the matriarchal 'Maummakathayam law applied to both Hindus and Muslims'.[152] He also said that certain portions of Hindu law applied to all communities in India, not because of their Hindu origin but because the laws were 'most suitable'.[153]

But with the adoption of the Shariat Act of 1937, which gave Sharia Law pride of place in the determination of Muslim personal law, Muslim law became homogenized.[154] Hari Vinayak Pataskar had replaced B.R. Ambedkar as union law minister when the Hindu Code Bill was passed in installments in Parliament through the early 1950s. He took a practical view at the time, saying that the bills covered 85 per cent of the population, and he was confident that the 'rest of the 15 percent population without any compulsion on our part, without any force, may in time, which will shortly come, fall in line'.[155] But most of those 15 per cent—primarily Muslims—have not done so.

The overturning of the Shah Bano verdict in 1986 represented the third missed opportunity by India's elected representatives to push for a uniform civil code.[156] Rajiv Gandhi had the mandate he needed but sacrificed true reform at the altar of vote-bank considerations. Today, Hindu (including Jain, Sikh and Buddhist) and Christian personal laws are, by and large, codified and scrutinized by the courts.[157]

On the other hand, the self-appointed guardians of Muslim personal law, like the All India Muslim Personal Law Board, have been resistant to change.[158] Polygamy is legal. Laws pertaining to inheritance and marriageable age are not favourably disposed towards women.[159] Even challenges to regressive practices, such as instant triple talaq, were opposed for decades, until, in 2017, the Supreme Court ruled that the practice was illegal and also not in conformity with the prescriptions of the Quran and Islamic law.[160]

The case of Shayara Bano and her challenge against the practice of instant triple talaq is instructive in conveying the contrasting approaches adopted by two different governments in dealing with Muslim personal law.

A resident of Kashipur in Uttarakhand, Shayara Bano had married Rizwan Ahmed in 2001 and had two children. She claimed she was abused, harassed for dowry and suffered domestic violence.[161] In October 2015, Ahmed divorced her through the pronouncement of the word 'talaq' thrice in the presence of two witnesses, and retained the custody of their children.[162] Shayara Bano challenged this, saying such a practice had no sanctity in the Islamic religion and had even been outlawed in several Muslim countries.[163] The Supreme Court, in a majority judgment, held: '. . . it is clear that this form of talaq is manifestly arbitrary in the sense that the marital tie can be broken capriciously and whimsically by a Muslim man without any attempt at reconciliation so as to save it. This form of talaq must therefore be held to be violative of the fundamental right contained under Article 14 (Right to Equality) of the Constitution of India.'[164]

Far from seeking to overturn the judgment of the court, as Rajiv Gandhi's government had done more than three decades ago, the NDA government proceeded to pass a law in Parliament criminalizing the practice of instant triple talaq to safeguard the rights of Muslim women.[165]

The Sangh Parivar has made it a point to strike a progressive posture, especially post 2014, on issues regarding Muslim women. In fact, on numerous occasions, the BJP's spokespersons have aggressively defended the right of Muslim women to approach the courts to seek redress from what they deem are oppressive patriarchal practices.[166]

Ahead of the 2024 election, there are at least two other practices, polygamy and 'nikah halala', that are being challenged in court.[167] Opposition politicians like Asaduddin Owaisi, member of Parliament and All India Majlis-e-Ittehadul Muslimeen (AIMIM) chief, claim that the NDA's championing of Muslim women's rights is a design to drive a wedge into the Muslim fold.[168]

Whether the BJP is, in fact, looking to further its appeal among Muslim women by championing their fight for equal rights is anyone's guess. But there is no denying that the BJP is certainly well disposed towards the idea of gender equality under the law.

The Law Commission in 2016 put forth a questionnaire in the public domain to seek feedback on personal laws that needed reform, and it received 75,378 responses. After wide-ranging consultations, the Commission prepared a consultation paper,[169] which spoke of a gamut of laws that needed to be re-examined before proceeding towards any move to adopt a uniform civil code:

The sixth schedule of the constitution of India provides certain protections to several states. While some tribal laws in fact protect matriarchal systems of family organisations some of these also preserve provisions which are not in the interest of women. There are further provisions that allow for complete autonomy on matter of family law which can also be adjudicated by the local panchayats which once again, follow their own procedures. Thus, while framing a law it has to be borne in mind and cultural diversity cannot be compromised to the extent that our urge for uniformity itself becomes a reason for threat to the territorial integrity of the nation.[170]

The Commission also said: 'While diversity of Indian culture can and should be celebrated, specific groups, or weaker sections of the society must not be dis-privileged in the process. Resolution of this conflict does not mean abolition of difference. This Commission has therefore dealt with laws that are discriminatory rather than providing a uniform civil code which is neither necessary nor desirable at this stage.'[171]

The BJP's endeavour to bring a uniform civil code faces resistance in some of the predominantly tribal states in the Northeast, and is also being opposed among a significant section of the scheduled tribes elsewhere that the party is assimilating into the larger Hindu fold. Some of the BJP's own allies have spoken out against interference with indigenous traditions and practices that enjoy constitutional protection.[172]

Scheduled Tribes constitute 9 per cent of India's population, and the BJP has been keen to highlight its outreach, including welfare programmes, to empower them. However, the BJP should be mindful that any exceptions made for a section of the population by excluding it from the ambit of a uniform civil code would defeat the purpose of such a legislation. After all, the BJP's advocacy of a uniform civil code has been couched in the language of gender justice and national unity. Exceptions would invite the charge of appeasement.

The NDA, while committed to a uniform civil code, bought time by asking the Law Commission to continue its consultative exercise. This time around, following another process that ended in July 2023, the Law Commission had received almost 8 million suggestions.[173]

Reclaiming Secularism

On 13 December 2021, Prime Minister Narendra Modi inaugurated the Kashi Vishwanath corridor that connects Varanasi's iconic Shiva temple, one of the twelve Jyotirlingas, to the banks of the Ganga.[174]

This temple was built in the late eighteenth century by the Maratha queen Ahilyabai Holkar, following Aurangzeb's 1669 demolition of the Vishwanath temple, upon the ruins of which he had built the Gyanvapi mosque.[175]

That site today is the subject of what will likely be a protracted legal battle. Hindu Shiv bhakts have moved court to stake claim to the entire Gyanvapi mosque complex.[176] This is very much a repeat of the civil suits filed before Independence for the reclamation of the Ram Janmabhoomi.

In the Gyanvapi case too, the Shiv bhakts claim that since the site is one among the twelve where the Jyotirlingas were installed, or had manifested, the denial of access would violate their fundamental right to practise their faith under Article 25 of the Constitution.[177]

But such suits face a potential roadblock. In 1991, a year ahead of the demolition of the Babri Masjid, Parliament passed the Places of Worship (Special Provisions) Act, which put paid to legal proceedings that sought to change the character of a place of worship in India after 15 August 1947.[178] In essence, a temple would remain a temple, and a mosque would remain a mosque, even if there was a dispute over its ownership. A major exception to this act was the Ram Janmabhoomi in Ayodhya,[179] because the legal challenge in this case predated Independence. But the constitutionality of the Places of Worship Act has now been challenged in the Supreme Court on the grounds that it violates the fundamental right to freely practise one's faith.[180]

Deliberations in Parliament in September 1991, before the act was passed, capture the bitterness among the champions of Hindu rights in regard to the Congress Party's 'selective appeasement'. The then home minister, S.B. Chavan, introduced the bill in Parliament saying, 'It is considered necessary to adopt these measures in view of the controversies arising from time to time with regard to conversion of places of worship which tend to vitiate the communal atmosphere.'[181]

The opposition to the bill was led by the BJP's Uma Bharti, then a member of Parliament from Khajuraho.[182] She recalled her first visit to Gyanvapi the previous month:

Even when completely drenched I saw the mosque built on the remnants of the temple, some sort of current of anger ran through my body. I felt disgraced at the fate of my ancestors, who I think were challenging my womanhood and asking me, whether the intention of Aurangzeb was merely to build a mosque, then why were remnants of the temple left. Was not the intention of Aurangzeb behind leaving remnants of temple at the site of mosque, to keep reminding Hindus of their historical fate and to remind coming generations of Muslims of their past glory and power? . . .

I would like to know from the movers of the Bill, the Congress (I) Government, why do they want to preserve and protect the wrong done by Aurangzeb and Britishers. Why are they keeping the bone of contention alive? . . . With a view to keep the issue alive, efforts are again being made to maintain status-quo of 1947. If the intentions are not bad, then this is not the correct way of finding out the solution of dispute. The best way of finding solution of disputes in respect of all the disputed religious places, whether it be temples or mosques, is to restore the old traditional glory of all the religious places.[183]

Bharti said that the bill, instead of securing peace, would deepen the divide between Hindus and Muslims. She proposed an alternative legislation that would restore religious shrines to their original status.[184] The Congress, Bharti claimed, was indulging in appeasement:

Owners of bullock carts in villages, create a wound on the back of the ox and when they want their bullock carts to move faster they strike at the wound. Similarly, these disputes are wounds and marks of slavery on our 'Bharat Mata.' So long as 'Gyan Vapi' continues in its present condition at Banaras and a grave remains in a temple at Pavagarh, it will remind us of the atrocities perpetrated by Aurangzeb including his efforts to convert Hindus to Islam and this would be very painful.

I am aware of the feelings of all honourable Members present in the House. All of them feel that this Bill will not provide a permanent solution to the problem. But as in the Mahabharata, Bhisma Pitamah, Dronacharya, Dhritrashtra and even the Pandavas knew that Draupadi's 'Chirharan' was wrong but certain reasons made them keep quiet. The move to restore the status of religious shrines as in 1947 shown [sic] that efforts are being made to denigrate the country's position. All these mute spectators are behaving like Bhishma Pitamah, Dronacharya, Dhritrashtra and the Pandavas did in Mahabharata when Duryodhana proceeded to disrobe

Draupadi. I want all honourable Members to come out in the open and oppose this Bill.[185]

Several members of the Congress rose to defend the bill, but Mani Shankar Aiyar, then a member of Parliament from Mayiladuthurai, chose to directly address the concern raised by Bharti.[186] A self-proclaimed 'secular fundamentalist',[187] Aiyar, educated at the best residential schools in India and subsequently at the University of Cambridge, began by mocking Bharti's lack of academic credentials: 'Chairman, Sir, whenever Km. Uma Bharati speaks in the House, she says that she is not educated. Through you, I would like to request her that she need not say it because whenever she speaks, one can find it out easily.'[188]

Aiyar then sought to address the crux of the matter as he saw it: 'Uma Bharti told us that when she had visited Varanasi and saw a temple and a mosque together, a feeling came to her that the temple had been demolished. She considered it to be a disgrace to Hinduism. According to her a Muslim king had built a mosque there. *There is only one difference between her and myself, to what she thinks a sign of servility, I take that thing as a symbol of secularism* [emphasis ours].'[189]

Aiyar continued:

The differences between Bhartiya Janata Party and myself is that it understands the last thousand years were the years of slavery, but I think that in these thousand years a new culture, a new religion, new feelings and new ideas have entered into our country. These influenced and attracted us. I say that if India is the first Hindu country in the world, I also say that India is the second Muslim country in the world. After Indonesia, the Muslim population in our country is far more than their population in any other country which include all the Gulf countries from Iran to Morocco – Iraq, Saudi Arabia, Turkey, Egypt, Libya, Algeria, Morocco, etc.[190]

Aiyar went on to speak of the influence that bhajans sung in temples had on Muslims, who took the qawwali to the dargahs; of Ustad Asad Ali Khan's mastery of the rudra veena, an instrument held by Goddess Saraswati; of Hazrat Amir Khusrau being the greatest Hindi poet.[191] Aiyar spoke of how Hinduism survived with the Bhakti movement:

> It was from the Muslims from who we learned how to pray collectively to God and they too learned some things from us . . . Our Hindu society was deficient in the feeling of equality. The Brahmin priests used to perform their religious rites in the temples in a unique language Sanskrit. Acharya Ramanujam came out of the temples and he acquainted people with Sanskrit spoken hitherto in ritual rites. We learned from them that when one went to a mosque, he might find that the poorest of the poor and the Sultan sit together at the same place and wash their hands and mouth with the same water and perform their namaj together.[192]

He concluded by saying the time was right for secular forces to take on the forces of communalism as represented, presumably, in the eyes of Aiyar, by the likes of Uma Bharti.[193]

The bill was backed by the Left parties; by the AIMIM, which was represented by Sultan Salahuddin Owaisi; and by Ram Vilas Paswan of the Janta Party, among others, while the BJP walked out.[194] Ghulam Nabi Azad, the then parliamentary affairs minister, said the bill was essential to 'impose some check on political parties which adopt religion as a means to win elections'.[195] The bill was passed a day later, on 10 September.[196]

To many Hindus, Aiyar's rambling rant and the passage of the bill signalled that the Indian state was ready to impose heavy costs on Hindus—in this case, an arguably arbitrary and illegal cut-off date on Hindu interests and aspirations.[197] The BJP had another reason to remind Hindus that 'pseudo secularists' had, for vote-bank considerations, once again deftly shifted the burden upon Hindus to prove their secular credentials.

Let's not forget that this was all happening within a year of the 'genocide'[198] of Hindus in Kashmir that had been glossed over.[199] The Places of Worship Act, 1991, remains suspended in a legal morass, and the NDA government has still not made its stand clear to the Supreme Court on the issue.[200] Some believe that the BJP will only unleash this 'Bhramastra' tactically, to polarize the electorate, if and only if the going gets tough ahead of the 2024 election.[201]

But at his Lodhi Estate residence, the chief information commissioner of India, Uday Mahurkar, who reportedly has the prime minister's ear, disagrees with this view.[202]

While Mahrukar does concede that Muslim control of Hindu places of worship is an emotive issue for the BJP, as the Places of Worship Act, 1991, is 'highly unjust to Hindus',[203] it cannot be deployed as some sort of weapon of mass assertion:

At least these three places [Ayodhya, Kashi and Mathura] should have come to the Hindus. That was a big mistake on the part of Jawaharlal Nehru. Lord Ram, whose name a Hindu takes when somebody dies, when somebody is born . . . you can't have a temple to him? What kind of secularism is this? So . . . I am not a supporter of people who say all 33,000 desecrated places should be returned to Hindus . . . The act should be revoked with the rider that so many places will come back, the number could be ten or fifteen, not more than that. Some leader has to take a call. There can be a consultative committee where even some Muslim leaders can be included, even if they are opposing. There should be a considered process to give effect to this. But I certainly feel that this Places of Worship Act, 1991, even today, is very unjust to Hindus. Highly unjust!

Many within the BJP have told us that this issue has now reached a point of criticality, and many among the BJP's Hindu supporters are looking to Prime Minister Modi to be the leader who addresses this issue.[204] Whether the prime minister will make an open declaration of support to this project before the 2024 general election is perhaps the most anticipated question.

The Rancour of Collective Memory

Right from the epochal 'midnight hour' to today, this judicious selection and purposeful reinterpretation aimed at advancing the notion of a 'composite culture' of India has not served the cause of national unity. All it has done is invite a backlash.

The rancour of 'collective memory' has proven too strong. It spawned the Ayodhya movement, which was as much about the symbolic restoration of Hinduness—in all its civilizational glory—as it was about justice.

Justice was delayed, and we can be grateful to the virtues of our vibrant democracy that when it was ultimately delivered it was done through the judicious proclamations of gavel-wielding judges. And the principal reason for the ultimately lawful resolution of the Ram Janmabhoomi dispute was that Hindus had found a democratic vehicle for their aspirations in the shape of the BJP.

Uma Bharti may not have been able to convince Aiyar, but her party was able to convince a vast mass of Hindus that 'secularism'—as it was being practised after the demise of Sardar Patel and Mahatma Gandhi by the so-called secular parties, namely Congress—had come to mean an aversion to Hinduism. And that perhaps switching allegiance to the BJP was their best hope at deliverance from institutionalized bias.

L.K. Advani was the first to catch on to this when he was a member of the Bharatiya Jana Sangh, the predecessor of the BJP. As a young Hindu man who had witnessed the furies of Partition and the cruelties of the Raj, he became aware of a tug from the past that many Hindus like him felt: '. . . that 1947 should signify not only freedom from British rule but also a clean break from those aspects of the pre-British history that were identified with subjugation, assaults on Hindu temples, vandalizing idols and erosion of our noble cultural traditions. Further, since India's independence was accompanied by blood-soaked partition on the basis of a communal demand by the Muslim League, it was only natural that the cultural reformation of India's national spirit would come out to some extent, to seek appropriate Hindu idioms and symbols to articulate itself.'[205]

The most accessible and most visible of these Hindu idioms of India's national spirit were its temples.

Even Swami Vivekananda, philosopher and one of Hinduism's most renowned thinkers, was clear that the 'regeneration' of temples ravaged by medieval iconoclasm was inextricably linked to the reawakening of the 'national mind' and the rejuvenation of the 'national life current':

> Temple after temple was broken down by the foreign conquerors but no sooner had the wave pass [sic] than the spire of the temple rose up again. Some of these old temples of South India, and those like Somnath in Gujarat, will teach you volumes of wisdom, which will give you a keener insight

into the history of the race than any amount of books. Mark
how these temples bear the marks of a hundred attacks and a
hundred regenerations, continually destroyed and continually
springing up out of the ruins, rejuvenated and strong as ever!
That is the national mind, that is the national life current.
Follow it and it leads to glory.[206]

Is it any wonder, then, that the rancour of the collective Hindu
memory has been channelled through sometimes trenchant
temple reclamation or rejuvenation movements beginning from
the Somnath temple in Gujarat? And is it at all surprising that the
discriminatory secularism that perceptibly othered Hindus from
their constitutional rights has fuelled Hindu reassertion?

One would have thought that after the movement for the
restoration of Hindu pride and cultural traditions was blessed by
staunch integrationists like Mahatma Gandhi, Sardar Patel, K.M.
Munshi and India's first President, Rajendra Prasad, the state
would have been less averse to Hindus and their sense of collective
consciousness.

But this was not to be.

Indrajit Gupta, who went on to become home minister of
India in the United Front governments in the mid- to late 1990s,
epitomized those who equated a burgeoning Hindu sense of self
with majoritarianism.

In Parliament, Gupta chastised the BJP and others who talked
of a 'Hindu Rashtra' and blamed them for fanning the flames of
Hindu separatism: 'The Hindu Rashtra slogan is a slogan which
goes directly against the integrity and the unity of this country. If
a Hindu Rashtra means a Hindu State, if that is a slogan which
is permissible and acceptable, then so is Khalistan. How can you
combat the people who are propagating Khalistan if you go on
talking here about Hindu Rashtra?'[207]

Gupta was strongly rebutted by Ram Naik, then BJP MP from Mumbai North: 'There is a substantial difference between the concept of a nation and a state. We are not saying that this is a Hindu State. Hindu Rashtra is a cultural concept. Nobody has said that in this Hindu State means only Hindus can stay here.'[208]

Naik's sentiments are often echoed these days by the likes of RSS chief Mohan Bhagwat, who responds to the same ecosystem of 'secular sainiks' as they continue to raise the bogey of an othering Hindu cultural nationalism.[209]

It is trite to say that for India to remain a unified political entity the debate must end on whether a Hindu Rashtra is, or can ever be, inclusive. Crucially, how will our courts respond if a demand for a Hindu Rashtra does gain currency?

6

Hindu Raj: A Study of Inclusivity

King Shibi's Sacrifice

There is a famous story from our Puranas about the mythical king Shibi that has been used to teach morality and dharma for centuries.[1] The story goes that King Shibi is widely known for being a staunch upholder of dharma. So the Gods decide to assess this for themselves and set out to test him. One day, the king is accosted by a dove, who is really the fire-God Agni. The dove is seeking refuge from a kite, who is the God Indra, the king of the *devas*, in disguise. King Shibi's advisers tell him that it is his dharma to protect the dove—a metaphor for life.

But as he goes about fulfilling his duty towards the dove, the kite appears and chastises the king for interfering in the order of nature. The king is reminded that it is the kite's prerogative to hunt its natural food. By protecting the dove, the king has arbitrarily discriminated against the kite's rights. The kite demands that the king provide him with food to compensate for what he has taken from him.

Caught in a bind, the king offers a compromise. He promises to give the kite a bit of his own flesh, equal in weight to that of the dove, so as to satiate the winged predator's hunger. The dove is placed on one of the two pans of a measuring scale. The king then begins to cut away pieces of his flesh and places them on the corresponding pan of the weighing scale. But soon, to his horror, the king realizes that no matter how much he carves out from his own body and places on the scale, the dove's weight turns out to be more. There's just no balancing the scale to feed the kite's bottomless desire for food.

Eventually, the king is forced to mount the scale himself—to sacrifice himself entirely to fulfil his promise and uphold dharma. The story ends with the devas hailing the king for his sacrifice in the interest of providing equal justice, which is the king's dharma.[2]

But the story has an important lesson for rulers that goes deeper. In the Puranas, the story is told to the Pandavas—the five legendary brothers and central characters of the Mahabharata—when they are in exile and being schooled by the sages. The sages hope the Pandavas will think twice about taking any decision aimed at gratifying the unquenchable human need for accumulating material wealth.[3]

Devdutt Pattanaik, the celebrated author who writes on the relevance of mythology in modern times, provides an insight into the moral lesson of the story about upholding dharma: 'The story [of Shibi] ends with everybody celebrating the great sacrifice of the king. But what is often overlooked is the attention drawn to the weight of the eagle's hunger that is greater than the weight of the flesh offered. The eagle does not value the flesh being given, as it is not enough for all his meals. Did the king not promise to satisfy all his hunger, not just the hunger of a single meal?'[4]

King Shibi, of course, could have chosen to deny the kite. After all, it is his dharma to protect the meek from the mighty. Doesn't he, then, stand guilty of dispensing *matsya nyaya* or the 'law of fish'—a form of *adharma*, the antithesis of dharma, the Hindu version of 'jungle law' where might prevails?[5]

Pattanaik cites the 'mythological story of Manu saving the "small fish from the big fish" and later the "big fish" saving Manu from the flood. Dharma, Pattanaik writes, 'thus clearly means when the mighty care for the meek. In a feudal system, it means the rich minority taking care of the poor majority. In a democracy it means, where the majority protect the minority.'[6]

That King Shibi could have taken two divergent pathways to upholding dharma is a lesson in the dangers of absolutism. Dharma is a totally unique Hindu civilizational concept much removed from the strict codes of conduct laid down by the Abrahamic faiths.[7] It is also this moral elasticity that confuses Western scholars and their ideological flagbearers here in India. But more on this later.

The story of King Shibi's fidelity to dharma also establishes that Hindu rulers had evolved not just a moral framework but also understood sophisticated politico–philosophical ideas.

It is striking that the Pandavas were retold a fable where the king is forced to contemplate the ultimate sacrifice—give up his life at the altar of expediency to uphold dharma. It is clear that both the dove and the kite submitted themselves to a higher arbitrator in the hope that their rights would be equally protected. In the end, when the king couldn't resolve which path would best serve the purpose of upholding dharma, he contemplates a third way. This he does in the interest of preserving the integrity of the social contract, which was necessary to ensure the greater good. Doesn't the concept of a 'social contract', with citizens willing to surrender their autonomy in favour of a higher authority to maintain equilibrium in society, undergird every modern-day electoral democracy?

This perspicacity and the existence of a sophisticated political philosophy—much before the West stumbled upon it—expose the fallacious propaganda dispensed by colonial theorists that Indian rulers were all despotic.[8] In fact, the colonial project has been described as a civilizing one, where the indigenes had to be freed from the dark ages, ruled by savages who had no concept of rights, ethics or justice.[9]

Dharma: Hindu Rajya's Unique Organizing Principle

Dharma is a complex and important organizing principle of Hindu life. It is a code governing human conduct that can't be summed up in one word but encompasses a variety of attributes: piety, duty, goodness, virtue and righteousness, to name just a few. And as King Shibi's fable makes apparent, there are no prescribed means or rules towards upholding dharma.

While there is consensus in academia that the word 'dharma' first appeared in the even more ancient Rig Veda a few times, there are differences as to its importance to Hindus of that time.[10]

But what is certain is that just before the Common Era, dharma acquired a salience, along with artha, kama and moksha, as a key organizing principle of the Hindu view of life.[11]

Texts like the *Dharmashastras* and *Dharmasutras* describe at great length that which is at the core of dharma to shed light on its defining principles.[12] In *The Great Hindu Civilisation*, author Pavan K. Varma attempts to put the concept of dharma into a more relatable context:

Dharma is at the core of the Hindu notion of ethics. What is right conduct? Is there an infallible touchstone to judge what is right? Who has the authority to pronounce what is correct behaviour? Is there a set of unchanging rules which are universally applicable? Does ethical conduct vary with context and circumstance, or is it absolute for all situations? Most civilizations have chosen to believe that certain things are absolutely right or absolutely wrong . . . The Hindu approach, on the other hand, is highly nuanced and complex, both emphasizing certain virtues which should be followed, and simultaneously providing derogations from that ideal, based on context, situation in circumstance. Many observers have inferred from this calibrated ambiguity a debilitating moral relativism. Hindu society, they argue, was tainted by the absence of an iron cast moral framework and a clear and prescriptive set of dos and don'ts, while accommodating a convenient set of alibis to avoid moral responsibility. The truth is that Hinduism hesitates to endorse certitudes which are not universally validated. What is right in one set of circumstances may be wrong in another. The purposes of morality are best served by an indicative framework of ethical conduct without the rigid and absolute condemnation of all deviations.[13]

In ancient India the state, as Varma writes, manifested itself in different forms—the autocratic monarch, hereditary king and even republics—where an assembly of elders took decisions by consensus.[14] Since monarchies were the most prevalent among these, elaborate works were written to advise kings on the best course of action to adopt, to govern or even defend their realms. Upholding dharma was at the heart of all these prescriptions. Just like Gods could not absolve themselves of serving the ends of dharma, neither could rulers.

Chanakya (375–283 BCE) was an ancient Indian polymath who, when wearing the hat of a political scientist, authored the *Arthashastra*. This tome talks about dharma at length as one of the more prominent organizing principles of kingship. By some estimates, the word is used about 150 times in this treatise on realpolitik.[15] Apart from laying down the precepts of governance, the *Arthashastra* also concerns itself with the ingredients required for the making of a perfect leader, 'a dharmic raja or rajarishi'.[16]

Chanakya, by his own admission, was not by any means the first to contribute to the art of statecraft.[17] The Hindu view on dharma, as Varma writes, had evolved along two diametrically opposite lines. On the one hand, it went to great lengths prescribing the dharma that must be adopted to strengthen the rule of the king, preserve the state, defend it from its enemies. But on the other hand, it discussed how to limit the powers of the state and the king, so that they don't become instruments of tyranny.[18]

The Mahabharata illustrates this best: 'Let the king first discipline himself. Only then must he discipline his subordinates and his subjects, for that is the proper order of discipline. The king who tries to discipline his subjects without first disciplining himself becomes an object of ridicule in not being able to see his own defects. The interest of his subjects is his sole interest, their well-being his well-being, what is pleasing to them is pleasing to him, and in their good lies his own good. Everything that he has is for their sake, for his own sake he has nothing.'[19]

And here's the *Arthashastra* on the subject: 'The king's pious vow is readiness in action, his sacrifice, the discharge of his duty. In the happiness of his subjects lies the king's happiness, in the welfare of his subjects, his welfare. The king's good is not that which pleases him, but that which pleases his subjects.'[20]

This lesson, of course, was felicitously conveyed by apocryphal fables like the story of King Shibi. But there were other stories too.

Ram Madhav, member of the RSS's National Executive, suggests in *The Hindutva Paradigm* that a king, in ancient times, was made aware of the limits of his power on coronation day itself.[21] Madhav recollects how the Bhartiya Jana Sangh stalwart

Deendayal Upadhyaya would retell a colourful story to emphasize how the king would be made aware of the constraints of his powers through a fairly elaborate ritual: 'In older times, during the coronation ceremony, the king would declare: "*adandosmi, adandosmi,*" meaning no one can punish me. Then, the royal priest would raise his staff and gently hit the king on the back, saying, "*Dharma Dandyosi*" – meaning, *Dharma*, the rule of law will punish you. The king would run around the sacred fire and the priest would follow him with the staff. Thus, after completing three rounds, the ceremony would come to an end, wherein the king would be unambiguously told that not he, but Dharma would be the absolute sovereign.'[22]

'Ekam Sat, Vipra Bahudha Vadanti'

Rule by Hindu dharma may have been a king's sacred duty, but a 'dharma rajya' itself was not a theocratic state. A king may have been a devout Hindu, Jain or Buddhist, but the state was not allowed to privilege any religion or subscribe to any one denomination.

King Asoka (c. 268–232 BCE), the third emperor of the great Mauryan Empire, was a devoutly Buddhist neo-convert.[23] But in elaborate rock edicts strewn across his realm, he spelt out his dharma (Dhamma) and established himself as a pillar of tolerance.[24]

Rubert Gethin, professor of Buddhist studies at the University of Bristol, cites an inscription on one of Asoka's rock edicts to underline this divergence between the propensity of a king to follow one faith even as the state he governed advocated a dharma for the welfare of all.[25] The inscription reads:

> The king . . . honours all religious sects . . . with gifts and with honours of various kinds. But he does not value gifts or honour as

much as the promotion of the essentials of all religious sects. The root of this is guarding one's speech so that neither praising one's own sect nor blaming others' sects should occur on improper occasions; and it should be moderate on every occasion. And others' sects should be honoured on every occasion. Acting thus, one both promotes one's own sect and benefits others' sects. Acting otherwise, one both harms one's own sect and wrongs others' sects. For whoever praises their own sect or blames another's sect out of devotion to their own sect with a view to showing it in a good light, instead severely damages their own sect. Coming together is good, so that people should both hear and appreciate each other's teaching.[26]

Dharma, unlike religion, then, is not just a guiding light stipulating a view on life and governance but is also a unifying universally applicable value system. It emphasizes *Ekam sat, vipra bahudha vadanti*, a Sanskrit phrase which means, 'That which exists is One, Sages call it by various names.'[27]

Philosopher Sri Aurobindo's words set the context: 'Hinduism gave itself no name, because it set itself no sectarian limits; it claimed no universal adhesion; asserted no sole infallible dogma; set up no single narrow path or gate of salvation: it was less a creed or cult than a continuously enlarging tradition of the God-ward endeavour of the Human spirit. An immense, many-sided and many-staged provision for a spiritual self-building and self-finding, it had some right to speak of itself by the only name it knew, the eternal religion, Sanatana Dharma.'[28]

And so, it follows that a Hindu dharmic king ruling over a realm, could not have been anything but accommodating.

In an interview with us, the historian and author Meenakshi Jain said that the tolerance of Hindu rulers, influenced by their Hindu dharma, never withered—even after encountering the proselytizers and missionaries among Muslims and Christians.[29] Jain said that in the period marking the decline of the Mughal Empire, during the 'repositioning' of Hinduism in the eighteenth and nineteenth centuries, Hindu kings advocated an 'integrative kingship'.[30]

By way of example, Jain pointed us in the direction of the Marathas. She cited historian Christopher Bayly, who wrote that the Marathas 'espoused an integrative kingship, insisting not on the exclusivity but the primacy – or merely the equality – of their form of worship'.[31] Indeed, Jain provides historical accounts of Marathas providing full protection to Muslim shrines under their control, continuing the practice of Chhatrapati Shivaji Maharaj (reign c. 1674–80 CE), who, while battling Emperor Aurangzeb for decades, never vandalized a mosque in his realm and also appointed several Muslims to important posts.[32] This integrative approach also included extending due courtesies to Muslim holy men.[33]

Other Maratha monarchs, like Mahadji Sindhia (c. 1730– 94 CE), 'showed deference to the saint Mansur Shah and his successor, Daulat Rao Sindhia (c. 1789–1827 CE), to Bala Qadir, son of Mansur Shah. While actively sponsoring the construction of ghats at Banaras, the Sindhias and Holkars donated generously to the Pirzadas of Moin-ud-Din Chishti at Ajmer,' Jain added.[34]

The all-embracing nature of 'integrative kingship' is illustrated beautifully in *Letters from a Mahratta Camp* by T.D. Broughton (1778–1835), who was an English soldier posted to India.[35]

Broughton observes in 1809, while accompanying Daulat Rao Sindhia (c. 1779–1827 CE), the maharaja of Gwalior state in central India: 'Seendhiya, whose devotion to Moohumedan saints and religious customs I have more than once had occasion to mention, has given this favourite entertainment three times since our arrival (the filling of the enormous copper boilers with *maunds* of rice, sugar, butter, sweetmeats etc., which after being cooked the whole night were distributed among devotees the following day, "an extraordinary spectacle"); he has also bestowed a superb pall and canopy of cloth of gold upon the tomb; and even the *Peer-zadus* seem to be pretty well satisfied with his pecuniary donations.'[36]

Broughton was also taken by the large proportion of Muslims at the camp and the 'universal ardour' with which the Marathas commemorated Muharram.[37]

In one letter, he writes of the maharaj:

At the Durbar the other day he was dressed entirely in green, the mourning of the Moosulmans, with no other ornament than eight or nine strings of beautiful emeralds round his neck. In this garb, accompanied by a few of his confidential servants, he roams about at night, and visits the different *Taziyas* throughout the camp.[38]

There are some, of course, who have sought to divorce the 'integrative' aspects of Hindu kingship from their dharmic roots, suggesting that expediency might be why Hindu kings displayed an 'ardour' for heterogeneity in the name of self-preservation. Hindu kings, after all, did take in Muslim mercenaries or allied with Muslim rulers and had to keep them happy.[39]

But to solely attribute the open-mindedness of Hindu kings to the tug of a king's own interest is to be unfair to the historical record. Their counterparts among different faiths the world over had already launched brutal inquisitions or waged jihad against 'infidels and heretics'. The persecution of Jews and Muslims in Granada during the Spanish Inquisition is illustrative of this.

Simon Jenkins, in his book *A Short History of Europe: From Pericles to Putin,* writes: 'Spain now saw a campaign of conversion, expulsion or execution, first of Jews then of Muslims. Evidence would be collected of suspect practices by supposed converts, with tortures and burnings at the stake . . . The Alhambra Decree of 1492 demanded the conversion or expulsion of all non-Catholics from Granada, as from the rest of Spain. Some 40,000 Jews converted and more than 100,000 fled into exile, most of them initially to Portugal. The great library of Granada, some 5000 Islamic books, went up in flames. It is believed that 2000 Jews died at the Inquisition's hands.'[40]

During these baleful, bigoted, desecrating campaigns, everything was fair game to expunge—religious places, educational institutions, libraries, music, dance, clothes, food—any cultural facet that spoke for the hapless who professed a different faith. The Islamic conquest of India had set its own gory example.

The dharmic kindliness of spirit among Hindu rulers in India was a contrast. Others among the overarching dharmic tradition were also exhibiting a similar spirit of religious accommodation.

Once again, let's turn to Meenakshi Jain. She cites the example of Sikh ruler Ranjit Singh (1780–1839) who, 'While identifying with the Khalsa tradition, issuing coins in the name of the Gurumutta (the general council of Sikh leaders), banning cow slaughter in his domains and azan (Muslim call to prayers) in the holy city in Amritsar (his only recorded act which could be considered "anti-Muslim"), did not endeavour to curb the practice of Islam in his kingdom.'[41]

In fact, Jain explains that Ranjit Singh invited learned Muslim men to his court when the Sikh warrior first assumed royal title in 1801. 'Ranjit Singh also appointed Nizamuddin *qazi* and head of the Muslims of the Lahore region, thereby fulfilling an important requirement for Punjab to be regarded Dar-ul-Islam, a land where Islam could be freely practised. In a public gesture of respect, Ranjit Singh visited the mausoleums of Data Ganj Bakhsh and Shah Abul Maali, and made offerings. He contributed to the repair of mosques in his kingdom, besides granting land for the upkeep of several Muslim shrines.'[42]

In the interview to us, Jain talked about the case of Sonahri Masjid, which she has documented in her own writings.[43] Here is an excerpt from a fascinating story:

The incident regarding the Sonahri Masjid in Lahore was illustrative of Ranjit Singh's approach. The fifth Guru, Arjan, had dug a *baoli* (well) in the area in memory of his father. Following the Guru's execution on the orders of Emperor Jahangir (c. 1569–1627 CE), the baoli was taken over by the Mughal state. In 1753, an officer, Nawab Bhikari Khan, built a mosque near the baoli. When Ranjit Singh captured Lahore in 1799, the baoli was re-occupied by the Akalis and the mosque converted into a gurudwara. In the late 1820s, however, the Muslims appealed to Faqirs Aziz-ud-Din and Nur-ud-din, to intercede with the Maharaja and have the mosque returned to them. The Maharaja acceded to the request. It is pertinent to recall that Lahore, termed Dar-us-Sultanat during the period of Muslim rule in Punjab, boasted of no architecturally significant temple or gurudwara in the year 1799, when Ranjit Singh occupied the city. A list of such structures in 1892 listed thirty-one important *shivalas* or Hindu temples, thirteen from the time of Ranjit Singh, two from the years 1839–49, seven from the period of British rule, while the remaining bore no specific dates, though some very small ones were identified as 'very ancient'.[44]

Ranjit Singh was not just righting historical wrongs, but actively seeking to keep the Islamic religion alive in his domains by ensuring there were no curbs on religious education.

The nineteenth-century British orientalist Gottlieb Wilhelm Leitner wrote a report on indigenous education in Punjab and placed the number of Quran schools at 1766[45]. And Charles Masson, who was a British East India Company soldier, independent explorer and pioneering archaeologist, also documented how Ranjit Singh ruled 'with an equal hand for both Mussulman and Hindu. The only hardship of which the former complains is the interdiction of the *azan* ... Although himself illiterate, he has a respect for acquirements in others, and when occasion presented itself, during his first visit to Peshawar, of showing his esteem for literature, he did not neglect it, and issued positive orders for the preservation of the extensive library of the Mussulman saint at Chamkanni. He must be deemed charitable, if we may judge from the large sums daily lavished upon *faquirs* and others, and his bounty extends to the Mahomedan as well as the Hindu. He is undoubtedly gifted with liberality of mind, as evinced in his deportment to his Mahomedan subjects, who are admitted to all posts and ranks.'[46]

There is also the story of Ranjit Singh's particular fondness for the Faqir brothers. As Meenakshi Jain has documented:

Over a dozen Muslims were appointed at the highest level of the political hierarchy, the most important being the Faqir Brothers from Lahore. Faqir Aziz-ud-Din was the Maharaja's trusted minister and physician. Baron Hugel, on a visit to Punjab in 1835–1836, described him as 'Ranjit's confidential secretary, through whom all business is transacted. He is a prudent, sagacious Muhammedan, who is employed by him in all difficult affairs.'[47]

Jain adds: 'Charles Masson confirmed that "No man perhaps is more trusted by him".[48] Two brothers of Faqir Aziz-ud-Din were also entrusted with key positions. Nur-ud-din received several important state guests on behalf of the maharaja and was appointed governor, while Imam-ud-din held the post of *qiladar* of Gobindgarh Fort at Amritsar, where the state jewels were housed.'[49]

These episodes from history are particularly striking as they speak of a universal generosity of spirit. An undying dharmic commitment, if you will, to not just displaying an appreciation for the ethical but also empathy.

As pointed out earlier, this commitment has been enjoined by the Shastras upon rulers from ancient times. Nevertheless, had this spirit of accommodation been a feature among rulers of other faiths, it is quite possible that thorny issues like the Babri Masjid–Ram Janmabhoomi dispute could have been resolved through dialogue, if not earlier then at least in independent India.

7

Faith in Dharma

The Unbridled and Universal Sanatana

History has delivered a more or less unanimous verdict: Hindu Raj, guided by dharma, cannot be anything but plural. The problem is that over the ages Hindu dharma, or *sanatana* (eternal) dharma, has been confused with religion.[1]

When Islamic and Western colonizers encountered Indian civilization, they came across the word 'dharma'. Since dharma is an organizing principle of the Hindu view of life, followers of Abrahamic traditions would have logically assumed that any concept prescribing an order to life would have been revealed by God Himself. Understandably, they confused dharma with religion[2]—for there was no equivalent word for a non-religious philosophy and morality in their vocabulary.

What was easily overlooked was that inhabitants of India also took great care to differentiate dharma from religion. Even in modern times, this view has prevailed among ardent Hindus.

For Mahatma Gandhi, dharma existed first as an idea—a pure form of 'religion' or moral belief—and then as an organized religion or a practised sect (*panth*): 'It is not the Hindu religion, which I certainly prize above all other religions, but the religion which transcends Hinduism, which changes one's very nature, which binds one indissolubly to the truth within and whichever purifies.'[3]

He also said, 'Religion must pervade every one of our actions. Here religion doesn't mean sectarianism (*panth*). It means a belief in ordered moral government of the universe. It (dharma) is not real because it is not seen. This religion transcends Hinduism, Islam, Christianity, etc. It doesn't supersede them. It harmonises them and gives them reality.'[4]

Rajiv Malhotra, author and ideologue, elaborates on this doctrinal difference between a formal sect, or a religion as an institution, and dharma as an idea:

> Hindu dharma has the Sanskrit root *dhri,* which means 'that which upholds' or 'that without which nothing can stand' or 'that which maintains the stability and harmony of the universe . . .'[5]
>
> Dharma encompasses the natural, innate behaviour of things, duty, law, ethics, virtue, etc. Every entity in the cosmos has its particular dharma – from the electron, which has the dharma to move in a certain manner, to the clouds, galaxies, plants, insects, and of course, man. But dharma is not limited to a particular creed or specific form of worship. To the Westerner, an 'atheistic religion' would be a contradiction in terms, but in Buddhism, Jainism and *Charvaka* dharma, there is no place for God as conventionally defined. In some Hindu systems the exact status of God is debatable. Nor is there only a single standard deity, and one may worship one's own *ishta-devata*, or chosen deity. Dharma provides the principles for

the harmonious fulfilment of all aspects of life, namely, the acquisition of wealth and power (*artha*), fulfilment of desires (*kama*), and liberation (*moksha*). Religion, then, is only one subset of dharma's scope.[6]

Malhotra then goes on to hold dharma as distinct from religious laws. He cites the Roman emperor Constantine, who began the system of 'canon laws', which were determined and enforced by the church.[7] This is true also of Islam and Judaism, which are governed by their own set of laws derived from their own scriptures.[8]

As Malhotra points out:

> In contrast with this, there is no record of any sovereign promulgating the various *dharma-shastras* (texts of dharma for society) for any specific territory at any specific time, nor any claim that God revealed such 'social laws,' or that they should be enforced by a ruler.
>
> The *dharma-shastras* did not create an enforced practice but recorded existing practices. The smritis do not claim to prescribe an orthodox view from the pulpit, as it were, and it was not until the 19th century, under British colonial rule, that the smritis were turned into 'law' enforced by the state.[9]

Secularism in the West evolved from a backlash to the stranglehold of the church on the affairs of the state.[10] In India, the concept of dharma militated against theocratic imposition. For the state to uphold dharma meant that it was duty-bound to treat all religions equally. The phrase *sarva panth samadar* (equal respect to all religions) neatly summed up the state's approach to religion.

India could be *panth nirpeksh* but never dharma nirpeksh.

Panth and Prejudice

The framers of our Constitution grappled with the civilizational primacy given to dharma in governing the affairs of the state. Some in the Constituent Assembly believed that the modern Indian state must also be guided by the universalism of dharma.[11]

H.V. Kamath, representing the Central Provinces and Berar, addressed the assembly and agreed that India should not be identified with any one religion. But he had a crucial caveat:

> Let me not be misunderstood. When I say that a state should not identify itself with any religion, I do not mean to say that a state should be anti-religious or irreligious. We have certainly declared that India would be a secular state. But to my mind a secular state is neither a God-less state nor an irreligious nor an anti-religious state . . .
>
> Coming to the real meaning of this word 'religion,' I assert that 'dharma' in the most comprehensive sense should be interpreted to mean the true values of religion or of the spirit. 'Dharma,' which we have adopted in the crest or the seal of our Constituent Assembly and which you will find on the printed proceedings of our debates: 'Dharma Chakra Pravartanaya' – that spirit, Sir, to my mind, should be inculcated in the citizens of the Indian Union. If honourable Members will care to go just outside this Assembly hall and look at the dome above, they will see a sloka in Sanskrit: 'Na sa Sabha yatra na santi vriddha Vriddha na te ye na vadanti dharmam.' That 'dharma,' Sir, must be our religion. 'Dharma' of which the poet has said: Yenedam dharyate jagat (that by which this world is supported).[12]

To Kamath, dharma was akin to a higher religion, a higher discipline, represented by a set of values. In fact, he was an advocate of spiritual training or instruction by the state, and the discipline of yoga was part of this. He recalled how these had been passed down from the rishis and seers of the Upanishads to the icons of the freedom movement, including Mahatma Gandhi and Subhas Chandra Bose. In fact, Kamath drew the assembly's notice to the curriculum of the Azad Hind Fauj (the Indian National Army founded by Subhas Chandra Bose), which included spiritual instruction to soldiers.[13]

Indeed, the aim of Kamath's submissions was to highlight the need to tap into the reservoir of ancient wisdom and thought that had formed the bedrock of India's civilizational continuity, to set an example in a 'war-torn, war-weary world, where the values of the spirit are at a low ebb, or at a discount'.[14]

A secular state, to Kamath, was in perfect harmony with spirituality. Though he may not have used the expression, Kamath was in effect making a case for India to assume the mantle of a 'Vishwa Guru', identified by a uniquely Indic spiritual philosophy as opposed to the Western or Sinitic model.

Deep into its second term, the Modi administration is now giving shape to what it often refers to as a 'spiritual democracy'.[15] In fact, the BJP has made this a national talking point, with a view to winning wide public endorsement for this project. The repeated references to Ram Rajya that are heard in stump speeches by BJP campaigners are just the beginning.[16]

Vinay Sahasrabuddhe, president of the Indian Council for Cultural Relations, explained to us why the BJP and the RSS are steadfastly attached to this idea. He spoke to us in his capacious office in Delhi, where three sizeable picture portraits of President Draupadi Murmu, Swami Vivekananda and Prime Minster Modi arrest the gaze.

'Hindutva is the other name for large-heartedness,' he said. 'And when we say Hindutva, we outline and communicate our commitment to what I describe as spiritual democracy. Hindutva or Hinduness is something that teaches me that *ekam sat vipra bahudha vadhanti* is the ultimate truth. Everybody must understand that the truth is one. The ways to approach that truth could be different. Therefore (on this basis), a theocratic outlook is incompatible with Hindutva.'[17]

But what does a 'spiritual democracy' actually entail? Sahasrabuddhe said, 'Democracy is where there is equality. Everybody is a voter of a particular age. And he or she has only one vote, and he or she can become the king or the kingmaker. Likewise, in Hindutva, or from our ideological point of view, we never allow any kind of monopoly. It is equality of respect and worship for all religions, all belief systems, all gods for that matter. We never say that Mhasoba, who is worshipped in some remote villages of Maharashtra, is not equally worthy of worship as the idol of Ram in Ayodhya. For all gods we have the same kind of reverence. So, in that sense, it is a democracy. There is neither monopoly nor hegemony. Why should there be?'[18]

When we specifically asked him if the NDA government had any plans to introduce the words 'Ram Rajya' or 'Dharma Rajya' in the Preamble to the Constitution, Sahasrabuddhe stated that he was not authorized to comment on the matter. But he was convinced that the 2024 election would be a reaffirmation of the irreversible nature of this Indic reawakening.

'Even before secularism was there in our Constitution's Preamble, we were equally or perhaps more secular,' he said. 'But we were shy about using the words "Ram Rajya" or "Dharma Rajya", which is not going to happen at any point of time in the future. It's a changed India, post the renaissance, if I may use that word. In that sense, the 2024 election is a watershed election. That obligation to be apologetic—that was wantonly thrust upon Hindus—will now be a thing of the past.'[19]

Indeed, according to Sahasrabuddhe, who is part of the brain trust of the BJP and NDA government, the 2024 mandate will have a potent message for the rest of the world. 'The elite in India, as well as the Western opinion-makers whom they emulate, they all tried to, and have been trying to, impose their ideas and their worldview on those who are "desis". This is not going to happen in the future.

'People should, and I hope they would, think twice before describing Ganpati as just an "Elephant God", or before denying that it's Kolkata and not Calcutta. All these are symptoms of a colonial mindset refusing to go away. The prime minister clearly mentioned this in his "Panch Pran" [speech]. We have to do away with it. And it's not just us, but all former colonies will have to resolve this matter. It has been happening. We're seeing that with the South–South dialogue. Culturally, the southern hemisphere has had a lot in common. Why should we have the White man as our burden?'[20]

Secular, but Not by the Book?

For those who might chafe at the idea that the word 'secular' did not feature in the original Preamble, let us remind you that even Nehru, an avowed secularist in the Western sense of the term, and B.R. Ambedkar were reluctant to insert the word into the Preamble.[21]

It was K.T. Shah who had intervened during the Constituent Assembly debates, demanding the inclusion of 'secular' in the Preamble: 'Sir, I beg to move, that in clause (1) of article 1, after the words "shall be a" the words "Secular, Federalist, Socialist" be included. The amended article or clause shall read as follows: "India shall be a Secular, Federalist, Socialist, Union of States."'[22]

Historian Ian Copland explained why Nehru and Ambedkar might have balked at this: '"Enlightenment Secularism", with its core principle of separation, founded on the Protestant conception of religion as essentially a private concern with which states had no legitimate business, was never going to work in a country where rulers and religious publics had been interacting from time immemorial, it was better not to use the term at all, than to use it fraudulently.'[23]

Consequently, to strengthen the commitment to religious freedom, Articles 25, 26 and 27 were inserted into the Constitution.[24] These articles guaranteed every person the right to freedom of conscience and the right to freely profess, practise and propagate religion subject to public order, morality and health. They also gave all religions the right to manage their own affairs in matters of religion. That this right came to be bestowed selectively is, of course, a travesty that has already been discussed in preceding chapters.

As is clear, secularism, though not formally written into the Constitution, became a defining feature of India's constitutional bedrock.[25]

The decision to not include the word 'secular' in the Preamble also paid off politically, as it allowed the state to make appeasing concessions. Had the framers, including B.R. Ambedkar, incorporated the word in the Preamble, the Indian state would not have been able to justify protecting Muslim personal laws or include cow protection (which was also a dharmic concept)[26] as an objective to strive for in the Directive Principles of State Policy.[27]

But as we know, in 1976, the then prime minister, Indira Gandhi, in a populist measure, inserted the words 'secular' and 'socialist' into the Preamble of the Constitution through an amendment.[28] But even Indira Gandhi was advised against using the term 'dharma nirpeksh' (dharma neutral) in the Constitution.[29]

In fact, the Hindi version of the Preamble carried the term 'panth nirpeksh' after L.M. Singhvi, the jurist, parliamentarian and diplomat, was invited by Gandhi's administration to comment on what exact term needed to be used.[30]

Singhvi opined: 'If you want to express neutrality between different faiths and religions, *dharma nirpeksh* is not the right word. Dharma stands for morality and ethical conduct. If ever a question of ethics arises, one should never be neutral *(nirpeksh)*. What you have in mind are the different faiths distinguished by their rituals, mythologies and beliefs. If you want to be neutral between them, then the correct expression is *panth nirpeksh*.'[31]

As such, a 'rashtra' enlightened by Sanatana Dharma could not be anything but a universal torchbearer of tolerance. But, references to the terms 'Hindu' or 'Hindu Rashtra' in public life, especially at the hustings, elicit shrill condemnation from self-proclaimed integrationists.[32]

As Rajiv Malhotra writes: 'The result of equating Hindu dharma with religion in India has been disastrous: in the name of secularism, dharma has been subjected to the same limits as Christianity in Europe. A non-religious society may still be ethical without belief in God, but an a-dharmic society loses its ethical compass and falls into corruption and decadence.'[33]

Sin of Omission

On a warm day in October 2022, Lalit and Nisha, who run a milk dairy in Ghaziabad, made their way to Delhi with their three children.[34] It wasn't just another outing. This was their journey out of Hinduism.

'Those who say that caste-based discrimination doesn't happen anymore should come and visit our society,' Nisha told The Quint. 'Children from our caste are not allowed to sit on chairs.

Even though my children have not faced it, I see it happening around me all the time. We are here because we don't want our children to be treated that way.'[35]

On that day, 7000 others followed Lalit and Nisha out of the Hindu fold at a mass-conversion event organized by Mission Jai Bheem at Ambedkar Bhavan in Jhandewalan (where, coincidentally, the RSS is also headquartered) in the national capital.[36]

Mission Jai Bheem is an organization founded by Rajendra Pal Gautam of the Aam Aadmi Party. Incidentally, Gautam had to tender his resignation as minister in the Arvind Kejriwal cabinet following outrage over the incident.[37]

This outrage was on account of the vitriolic nature of the oath that the converts took. Penned by Dr Ambedkar, the words capture the contempt he had for his upper-caste Hindu oppressors:[38] 'I shall have no faith in Brahma, Vishnu and Mahesh nor shall I worship them. I shall have no faith in Rama and Krishna, who are believed to be incarnations of God, nor shall I worship them. I shall have no faith in "Gauri", Ganapati and other gods and goddesses of Hindus nor shall I worship them. I do not believe in the incarnation of God. I do not and shall not believe that Lord Buddha was the incarnation of Vishnu. I believe this to be sheer madness and false propaganda.'[39]

Mass conversion events are quite routine.[40] But they never fail to make the votaries of Hindu solidarity anxious. They are, after all, a grim reminder of the unaddressed caste fault lines that prevent Hindus from speaking and acting as one.

* * *

Any debate on the accommodative spirit of Sanatana Dharma will be incomplete without a reference to caste. For caste is an inescapable scar that has left a permanent imprint on Hindu society. It has spawned incalculable prejudice that even the most vociferous defenders of Hinduness have struggled to play down. If dharma is elementally inclusive, why did it cast out so many from the Hindu fold and discriminate against so many within?

There are several views on this. For some, the immediate reference point about the origins of a social hierarchy in Hindu society is the Purusha Suktam of the Rig Veda, a dedication to the *purusha* or the cosmic being.[41] An often-quoted verse from the Purusha Suktam, to refer to the roots of the caste system, is: 'From His face (or the mouth) came the *brahmanas*. From His two arms came the *rajanya* (the Kshatriyas). From His two thighs came the *vaishyas*. From His two feet came the *shudras*.'[42]

But as author and scholar Pavan R. Varma has argued, this was neither prescriptive nor meant to be exclusive.[43] However, Varma writes, this changed around the first century CE, when social hierarchies not only ossified but also acquired an oppressive edge. This was done through the misuse of the Dharmashastras by 'vested interests' and by adopting a dogmatic approach to the interpretation of the *Manusmriti*.[44]

Subsequently, be it through the teachings of Adi Shankaracharya, the great eighth-century Vedic scholar and thinker, or the message of reform carried through the Bhakti movement, Hinduism evolved its own resistance to this oppression.[45] Centuries down the line, this was carried forward by modern-day reformers, including those who resisted British colonialism. Vinayak Damodar Savarkar, one of Hindutva's and the Sangh Parivar movement's most revered icons, was among them.[46]

Savarkar, who also led the Hindu Mahasabha, was a strong campaigner for the eradication of untouchability.[47] And, though he was known to be an atheist,[48] he invoked Hindu scriptures to endorse inter-caste marriages, inter-caste dining and the throwing open of temple doors for all Hindus. He wrote:

> Some of us were Aryans and some Anaryans; but Ayars and Nayars – we were all Hindus and own a common blood. Some of us are Brahmans and some Namashudras or Panchamas; but Brahmans or Chandalas – we are all Hindus and own a common blood. Some of us are Daxinatyas and some Gauds; but Gauds or Saraswatas – we are all Hindus and own a common blood. Some of us were Rakshasas and some Yakshas; but Rakshasas or Yakshas – we are all Hindus and own a common blood. Some of us were Vanaras and some Kinnaras; but Vanaras or Naras – we are all Hindus and own a common blood.[49]

Indeed, upon his release from prison in 1924—following more than a dozen brutal years of incarceration on sedition charges by the British—Savarkar's desire to achieve Hindu unity through the abolition of untouchability and the breaking of caste barriers became his single-biggest endeavour. While lodged in jail, Savarkar had been witness to these cleavages in Hindu society. He began a campaign against the conversions of Hindu prisoners to Islam. In fact, he was ridiculed by Hindu wardens and prisoners, and called a 'Bhangi Babu' or 'someone who had lost his caste and become "untouchable"' after he encouraged converts to return to the Hindu fold.[50]

Once out of prison, he redoubled his efforts at ending untouchability. In 1924, at a public gathering in Bhagur in Nashik, Maharashtra, Savarkar said, 'When I die, I want Hindus from all castes – a Mahar, a Maratha, a Brahmin and a Mang – to shoulder my dead body.'[51]

The emphasis on abolishing caste discrimination was also meant to incentivize Shuddhi, a movement that Savarkar

championed for the reconversion to Hinduism of those who had
left the Hindu fold.[52] For Savarkar, this Hindu solidarity was
essential to countering conversions to Islam and Christianity, and
for protecting Hindus at a time when the Khilafat movement—
aimed at achieving Hindu–Muslim unity against the British
through the restoration of the Caliphate in Turkey—had short-
changed Hindu interests.[53] The need for Hindus to organize
themselves, by burying all their differences, was also all the more
necessary after the brutality they had been subjected to by Islamists
during the Moplah riots in Kerala in 1921.[54]

But B.R. Ambedkar took another view. He believed that the
scourge of caste discrimination, of which he was a victim as a
member of the scheduled castes, emanated from Hindu scriptures.
He publicly renounced Hinduism and converted to Buddhism
in 1956 in a mass ceremony in Nagpur—the gathering included
more than 3.6 lakh people.[55] He believed that the destruction of
caste as a reform was linked to the destruction of the 'authority
of the Shastras and the Vedas'. Ambedkar was categorical[56] about
this. He wrote:

> Caste is the natural outcome of certain religious beliefs which
> have the sanction of the Shastras, which are believed to contain
> the command of divinely inspired sages who were endowed with
> a supernatural wisdom and whose commands, therefore, cannot
> be disobeyed without committing a sin . . . The Hindus hold to
> the sacredness of the social order. Caste has a divine basis. You
> must therefore destroy the sacredness and divinity with which
> Caste has become invested. In the last analysis, this means you
> must destroy the authority of the Shastras and the Vedas.[57]

Ambedkar was also critical of Savarkar and the Hindu
Mahasabha's approach towards eradicating caste discrimination.

Writing in April 1929, Ambedkar said, 'The Hindu Mahasabha movement is contrived, narrow-visioned, lacking in an ideal and divorced from principles. The leaders of the movement do not have a genuine concern for the Untouchables. They have taken up the issue of eradication of untouchability only to ensure that the Untouchables do not convert, and thereby the population of Hindus does not decrease.'[58]

In other words, for Ambedkar, a true Hindu organization actually 'retards the progress of Hindu society and incapacitates it'.[59]

Others have argued that caste is alien to Hinduism and that the existence of a social structure did not automatically translate into discrimination based on prejudice.

Rajiv Malhotra and Vijaya Vishwanathan, in their book *Varna Jati Caste*, write that there were merits to the *varna* and *jati* systems—of social structures—including the ability to 'integrate the various diverse social groups into one ecosystem in which communities cooperate, transact, negotiate, evolve and adapt', and 'yet maintain an open architecture that resists centralized authoritarianism'.[60]

Malhotra and Vishwanathan posit that it was because of the onset of Islamic rule in India, and the economic deprivation it wrought, that increasingly 'occupations became hereditary'[61] and the jatis that had evolved from the parent varna system became more 'rigid in matters of marriage and sharing food and disintegrated into opportunism and social stratification'.[62]

With the arrival of the Portuguese and then the British, the *jati* system became equated with caste, as derived from the Portuguese word *casta*, to denote 'tribe, clan or race', and then a 'caste system' was formalized.[63]

Still, whatever the origins of this social structure, the oppression and inequality it has yielded are real. Those at the receiving end of this historical injustice have rightly demanded an equal footing in society after Independence.

In September this year, Udhyanidhi Stalin, son of the Tamil Nadu chief minister M.K. Stalin, spoke at a 'Sanatana Abolition Conference' and advocated exactly that, even likening it to diseases like dengue and malaria.[64] The junior Stalin sought to clarify these remarks by citing B.R. Ambedkar and E.V. Ramasamy's (also known as Periyar) resistance to caste discrimination. This discrimination was among the social evils, Stalin said, that Sanatan Dharma was 'responsible' for.[65]

The BJP hit back at what they said was another assault on Hindu sentiments by constituents of the INDIA bloc. And a few days later, the response provided by Prime Minister Narendra Modi during a poll rally in Madhya Pradesh was a strong indication that the BJP was not going to hold back from making this 'slander' an election issue.[66]

Modi said, 'This *ghamandiya* alliance has come with the intention of ending Sanatan values and traditions which inspired Devi Ahilyabai Holkar, who worked for social causes, leading a campaign for women's upliftment . . . It was the strength of this tradition that enabled Rani Lakshmi Bai of Jhansi to boldly declare to the British, "I will not give up my Jhansi." It was Sanatan that Mahatma Gandhi embraced throughout his life, inspired by Lord Shri Ram, and those became his final words— Hey Ram. Sanatan inspired him [Gandhi] to start a movement against untouchability . . . It is the Sanatan tradition from which Swami Vivekananda drew strength to awaken people about various societal shortcomings. The INDIA alliance seeks to end that Sanatan tradition.'[67]

The caste system and its outcomes continue to influence the debate on Sanatan Dharma.

'Caste' in Politics

The framers of the Constitution decided that one way of empowering the marginalized communities was through providing reservations in government jobs and education as a form of affirmative action.[68]

But despite almost seven decades of state-mandated affirmative action—expanded to now include other backward classes, apart from the scheduled castes and scheduled tribes—caste remains a burden, and many are still imprisoned by their identity.

The RSS, like Savarkar, believes that the caste system has rendered Hindu society vulnerable and seeks that caste differences would eventually evaporate.[69] A case in point is PM Modi, who belongs to the OBC community. At an early age and after visiting RSS *shakhas*, Modi became very active in the anti-corruption agitations in Gujarat in the 1970s and was promoted to the position of a full-time RSS *pracharak* (activist), eventually joining the BJP in 1987, where he clawed his way to the top as a consequence of his superior organizational skills, growing mass support and reputation as an efficient administrator.[70]

But the RSS and the BJP's approaches to caste sometimes represent a contradiction. Like the RSS, the BJP has also spoken in favour of a casteless society.[71] If for no other reason than to create a consolidated Hindu vote bank. But, given that it is in the game of competitive politics, it has found little success in changing the rules.

In fact, it has even managed to use caste politics to its advantage. In Uttar Pradesh, for instance, it has successfully cultivated support among the marginalized sections within the OBC and SC communities—something that caste-based parties in the state, like the Samajwadi Party (relying mainly on OBCs of the Yadav caste) or the Bahujan Samaj Party (relying mainly on the Jatav scheduled castes) could not do.[72]

This has not merely been achieved through the successful delivery of economic welfare measures, the creation of a loyal class of beneficiaries or *labhartis*,[73] but also through genuine political empowerment from the grassroots up.

As political analyst and academic Nalin Mehta writes in *The New BJP: Modi and the Making of the World's Largest Political Party*, 'OBCs and SCs accounted for as many as 57.5% of the BJP's UP Lok Sabha candidates in the 2019 elections, 52.8% of its candidates in the 2017 assembly poll that it swept, 50% of its office-bearers in the state in 2020, 48.1% of Chief Minister Yogi Adityanath's council of ministers and 35.6% of BJP's district-level presidents.'[74]

In the 2022 assembly election in Uttar Pradesh, as the Centre for the Study of Developing Societies (CSDS)–Lokniti numbers show,[75] the BJP captured almost 60 per cent of the vote among non-Yadav OBCs and 41 per cent of the vote among non-Jatav scheduled castes, while retaining its upper-caste base. Even among the Yadavs and the Jatavs, the BJP increased its vote share from the previous state elections in 2017, by 2 per cent and 13 per cent respectively.

Crucially, this rainbow coalition has been constructed through a combination of an appeal to Hindu identity and the promise of inclusive development.

As Badri Narayan, director at the Govind Ballabh Pant Social Science Institute and author of *Republic of Hindutva: How the Sangh is Reshaping Indian Democracy*, told us, 'Today, the Hindutva movement is also being led by OBCs and Dalits. Development and governance have reached them, and there is an aspiration to become part of the Hindutva fold.'[76]

Barely a few weeks before we met Narayan, Swami Prasad Maurya, the prominent OBC leader belonging to the Maurya sub-caste who had defected from the BJP to the Samajwadi Party before the 2022 Uttar Pradesh election, had called for the 'deletion' of certain verses from the *Ramcharitramanas* (the sixteenth-century retelling of the Ramayana by saint and poet Tulsidas) that he deemed 'insulting' to the backward castes.[77] Some of his supporters even burnt the sacred text as a mark of protest.[78]

But this, Narayan told us, was not a mainstream view within the marginalized sections of the Hindu fold: 'Some of the strongest followers of the Ramayana are among the Dalit and OBC communities. Many OBC and Dalit groups may not relate to Maurya's protest.'[79]

While there is anxiety within the saffron *parivar* about the continued marginalization of these communities prompting conversions out of Hinduism,[80] the RSS and the BJP have been equally responsive to the urge of these groups to remain Hindu. It is this urge to be part of the larger Hindu identity that the RSS has harnessed.

As Professor Narayan tells us, 'In Uttar Pradesh, most Dalits are Kabirpanthis [a denomination whose members follow the teachings of the fifteenth-century saint Kabir] and Ravidasis [followers of the fifteenth-century saint Ravidas], very few of them are Buddhists. That's the reason why Kanshi Ram [founder of the Bahujan Samaj Party] did not convert to Buddhism. There is a larger section of Dalits who have an inclination towards Hindutva arguments. They desire greater importance within the larger Hindutva fold, which will provide them with greater social respect and dignity. The Hindutva movement is telling them, "You're part of our bigger history, you've made many sacrifices and we acknowledge this." In Bundelkhand, for instance, tribal groups, which are now scheduled castes, began placing idols and deities of their communities under trees. As their aspirations grew in society, they also began to demand a temple for their own deity. So, while the Ram temple is fine, they also want their own temple. Who understands this desire? The Hindutva movement is responding to this. Non-Hindutva movements talk about socio-economic equality but not religious equality, and religious equality is very important for Dalits and marginalized communities.'[81]

Another prominent example shared by Professor Narayan is of the Nishads, a marginalized caste among the OBCs who changed their loyalties from the Samajwadi Party and Bahujan Samaj Party to the BJP. During the Ram Janmabhoomi agitations in 1990, when the then UP chief minister, Mulayam Singh Yadav, had ring-fenced the disputed site with an elaborate security cordon, it was the Nishads, traditionally boatmen, who helped many karsevaks reach the area by ferrying them across the Sarayu (according to folklore, the Nishads helped Lord Ram, Lakshman and Sita cross the Ganga when they were in exile.)[82] The BJP was able to use this episode from the Ramayana to integrate the Nishads within the larger narrative of the Hindu civilizational reclamation that the construction of a Ram Mandir represented.[83]

Equally, through the abrogation of the contentious Article 35A in Jammu and Kashmir in August 2019, the BJP-led NDA enabled the Valmiki community, part of the Dalit fold, to acquire domicile certificates and permanent resident status in a state where they had, until then, been deprived of equal rights, despite having lived there for generations.[84]

The BJP has constantly made efforts to undo the fragmentation of the Indian polity and society that the emergence of political parties catering to the interests of certain caste groups, and even specific sub-castes, had intensified. In Karnataka, a more dominant Congress, under Devraj Urs, had devised the AHINDA (a Kannada acronym for Alpasankhyataru, or minorities, Hindulidavaru, or backward classes, and Dalitaru, or Dalits) model—bringing together a consolidated vote bank of Muslims, backward classes and Dalits.[85]

The BJP's electoral strategy in each of these states had to be a response to the caste coalitions that other parties had built. In Uttar Pradesh and Bihar, as discussed earlier, the BJP has successfully built its own coalition of non-Yadav OBCs, scheduled castes and upper castes.

In the run-up to the May 2023 assembly election in Karnataka, the BJP continued to focus on wooing the Lingayats, but also the Vokkaligas and the non-Kuruba OBC castes, realizing that the Kurubas have traditionally thrown in their lot behind Siddaramaiah, a Congress stalwart and the current chief minister who belongs to this caste.[86] While the BJP retained the Lingayat vote to a large extent, the party's experiment to fracture the AHINDA vote of the Congress didn't quite succeed.[87]

The BJP's ploy in the 2023 assembly election was to isolate this alliance by rallying the rest of the communities around the party. One way of trying to achieve this was by scrapping the reservations for Muslims (classified in its entirety in Karnataka as a backward community in one category) in state government jobs and education, and redistributing that quota equally between the politically influential Vokkaligas and Lingayats (who together form 30 per cent of Karnataka's population and already enjoyed the perks of reservations).[88]

This evoked outrage from the 'secular' parties, who alleged this was a deliberate attempt to further alienate and marginalize Muslims.[89] The then BJP government justified the decision by arguing that reservations based on religion are unconstitutional in a secular polity.[90] Its critics cited their own set of judicial precedents that allowed for an entire community to be classified as backward.[91] The move, nevertheless, appeared to suggest that the BJP would not mind risking losing the Muslim vote if the 'goodwill' showed to certain caste groups was repaid at the ballot. Though the move to consolidate non-Muslim votes did not quite deliver the result for the BJP in the May 2023 Karnataka election, it is unlikely to abandon this strategy.

The BJP has had to play its own caste card by uniting those caste groups that other political parties and formations had excluded. It has also meant that on the contentious issue of caste-based reservations, which were extended to the other backward classes through the implementation of the Mandal Commission report in 1990, it had to shed its initial reluctance. The BJP had to eventually submit to political compulsions and go with the dominant view within these caste groups that such quotas are necessary.[92]

'It's a tightrope walk for any party that wants to unite society,' Vinay Sahasrabuddhe told us when we asked him about the BJP's reliance on caste politics.[93] 'We have to look at the fact that in our society, although we want to unite it, the abolition or annihilation of caste—or if annihilation is a distant dream, then trying to have the caste identities less sharpened than they are today—is also a very difficult thing.

'Identity, though not primordial, is an important part of your social being. Caste won't go simply because you don't want it to be there. To move beyond that will take Herculean efforts. That is what we are attempting to do. At times, we may be seen as using caste as a ladder, or providing it as a ladder to someone, but that is not the objective. The objective is to bring equality of opportunity, security and respect.'[94]

Sahasrabuddhe acknowledged that the unanimous political backing of caste-based reservations has conveyed an impression that caste identities, far from being erased, are only crystallizing.

But, he added, 'After all, whether you belong to a particular caste or not, the conflict you see everywhere is between the more fortunate and less fortunate. If the more fortunate understand that we can have a peaceful life thanks to the less fortunate . . . if the less fortunate hoist a flag of reward and make life for you difficult, we are all going to perish. The more fortunate will always have to be grateful to the less fortunate. The quota-reservation system is one way of recognizing this fact that we have to care for the less fortunate. It is part of a correction being introduced into the idea of social justice.'[95]

For the RSS, which aspires to achieve Hindu unity through a casteless society,[96] the hardening of caste-based identities is worrying. Mohan Bhagwat, the RSS chief, acknowledged as much in a speech in 2018 when he said, 'The ethical practices of the society are reflected in the politics of the country. For example, I don't want to use caste politics, but I am compelled to use it because the society votes based on caste. If I stay in power, only then can I change the system. So if the society changes, the politics of the country will also change, not vice versa.'[97]

The BJP and the RSS appear to realize that dismantling caste is a Sisyphean task, but they do believe that the bigger project of cultivating a larger Hindu consciousness among all caste groups is an attainable goal.

Whether this consciousness emerges out of empowerment, or through the 'othering' of non-Hindus, or both, remains to be seen.

8

Imagining a Hindu Rashtra

The Anxious Hindu

V Kalathur, a village in the Perambalur district of Tamil Nadu, shot into the national limelight in 2018.[1] Since 2012, Muslim residents there had objected to the 'sin' of an annual Hindu temple procession passing through areas where Hindus were in the minority.[2] After a stand-off, the matter reached the Madras High Court, which ruled against the stance taken by the Muslim community.

Warning against intolerance, the court said that if the Muslim side were to have its way, 'It would create a situation in which minority people cannot conduct any festival or procession in most of the areas in India' and that the resulting bad blood would damage the 'secular character of our country'.[3]

While the dispute in V Kalathur was decided by the courts, there are several similar conflicts that continue to afflict the peace. Nuh in Haryana was witness to a major conflagration in August 2023 that once again served as a grim reminder that changing demographics in villages, and also in some states, never fails to ignite passionate talk about the perils posed by population replacement.[4]

Union minister Amit Shah played on such insecurities when he addressed a Vijay Sankalp Maha Rally in Jharkhand in February 2023.[5] Shah was in Deoghar, part of the Santhal Parganas division, where the demographic change in this once-tribal-dominated region of erstwhile Bihar, now Jharkhand, is evident.[6]

Shah ominously intoned, 'Illegal immigrants are settling here, and the population of tribals and backward classes is decreasing. These infiltrators are taking over Adivasi lands, committing atrocities on Adivasi girls . . .'[7]

The 'infiltrators' Shah was presumably referring to, without naming them, were Muslims of Bangladeshi origin who began arriving in Santhal Parganas through the 1980s,[8] having made their way into India during the 1971 war. The resulting population 'imbalance', according to BJP leaders in the state, is a threat to both tribals and non-tribal Hindus and their traditions.[9] The BJP appeals to non-Muslims in the region to support it in the larger interest of restoring Hindu and Adivasi *asmita* (pride). It is a strategy that is finding traction among voters.[10]

The BJP's leaders in the state, according to a report in *Swarajya*, have also accused the local administration in Jharkhand, under a state government led by the Jharkhand Mukti Morcha and the Congress in a coalition, of changing traditional routes of processions during Sarhul (a three-day spring festival celebrated by tribals), so that they don't pass through areas which have a significant Muslim presence.[11]

There is no denying that demographic change is also altering the social landscape of several regions of Assam and West Bengal abutting Bangladesh. In sixty years between 1951 to 2011, the Muslim population in Assam has grown from 24.8 per cent to 34.2 per cent.[12] In West Bengal, in the same duration, the Muslim population share has jumped from 19.4 per cent to 27 per cent.[13] In some districts, Muslims are in an overwhelming majority.[14]

What's more, the replacement level fertility—the rate at which the population replaces itself from one generation to the next—still remains high for Muslims. This agitates many Hindus,[15] especially as these anxieties over population replacement, which were thus far described as an irrational preoccupation of conspiracy theorists on the Far Right,[16] begin to be expressed in the mainstream.

Here is author and journalist R. Jagannathan: 'Muslims are the only community still above replacement levels of Total Fertility Rate or TFR 2.36 versus Hindu levels of 1.94, against replacement levels of 2.1 live births per woman). In comparative terms, Muslims will keep raising their share of population for at least one or two decades. Hindu growth rates will shrink, while Muslim ones will expand in the foreseeable future.'[17]

The numbers, as per the latest National Family Health Survey, stand at 1.88 for Christians and 1.61 for Sikhs.[18] Jagannathan explains his concerns in more detail in his book *Dharmic Nation: Freeing Bharat, Remaking India*, where he writes that simply dwelling on the fact that Muslim birth rates are falling faster than those of Hindus—46.5 per cent since 1992–93 as opposed to 41.2 per cent for Hindus—is misleading. About the 'data-illiterate' media highlighting these numbers, he says, 'What they miss out is a simple statistical fact: when the base is high, percentage changes tend to get exaggerated. Muslim TFRs were super high at 4.41 in NFHS-1, while the Hindu TFR was 3.3.'[19] And despite a 'sharp' fall, the Muslim TFR was not below the threshold of 2.1.

The numbers, Jagannathan believes, are worrying because 'the partition of India on religious lines is proof that whenever Hindu demography deteriorates in any region, it impacts Hindu rights and prompts Hindu migration away from that region. We have seen this happening not only in Pakistan and Bangladesh but also in India itself, in Kashmir; and this may be quietly happening in other districts which have seen increases in Muslim populations. These include districts in north Kerala, Assam, West Bengal and parts of Bihar and Uttar Pradesh, among others. Hindu concerns are valid if demography is adversely affected in any state or district of India. One cannot use data for the whole of India to invalidate Hindu concerns.'[20]

* * *

Taha al-Jumailly had no courage to face the public when he reached a court in Frankfurt in 2021.[21] Barely a few years ago, he had been forcing women to don the veil in Syria and then in Iraq as a member of the ISIS.[22] But in court, while being tried and convicted for enslaving and killing a five-year-old Yezidi girl, as part of a genocide against this Kurdish-speaking minority, al-Jumailly would bury his own head in a veil of shame.

The Yezidi religion has Pagan roots. As economist and popular historian Sanjeev Sanyal writes, 'Interestingly, their beliefs have many similarities with Hinduism—for example, they believe in reincarnation, say their prayers facing the sun at sunrise and sunset, and even have a system of castes. They also worship Tawûsê-Melek, the peacock angel—a bird that is found in the Indian subcontinent but not in Yezidi lands.'[23]

Sanyal even speculates that, based on cultural and genetic evidence, the Yezidis may trace their origin to 'Indian tribes that migrated West in the second millennium BC'.[24] The Yezidis were then subjected to persecution by both Christians and Muslims, who labelled them 'devil worshippers'.[25] The Ottoman Turks, who were especially brutal, and the ruthless fanatics of the Islamic State saw Yezidi annihilation necessary to achieve their puritanical objectives.[26]

The Christian destruction of Pagan belief systems preceded Islam. Indeed, the word Pagan was used pejoratively by Christians.[27]

'It was also a Christian innovation: before Christianity's ascendancy few people would have thought to describe themselves by their religion at all,' writes Catherine Nixey in her book *The Darkening Age: The Christian Destruction of the Classical World*. 'After Christianity, the world became split, forevermore, along religious boundaries; and words appeared to demarcate these divisions. One of the most common was "pagan".'[28]

Nixey documents the widespread persecution comprehensively, including the extermination of the literary culture of the pre-Christian age. 'It has been estimated that less than 10% of all classical literature has survived into the modern era. For Latin, the figure is even worse: it is estimated that only one-hundredth of all Latin literature remains. If this was "preservation" – as it is often claimed to be – then it was astonishingly incompetent. If it was censorship, it was brilliantly effective. The ebullient, argumentative classical world was, quite literally, being erased.'[29]

Writer George Thundiparambil, in an article in *Swarajya*, describes Hindus as the 'last polytheistic Pagans that remain on earth'.[30] The interaction between Abrahamic dogma and polytheism has, for a significant part of our history, been fraught with conflict.

In India's north-eastern states of Meghalaya, Mizoram and Nagaland, Christianity has been supplanting mostly tribal and pagan traditions. From the early to mid-twentieth century, British and American missionary activity in this region was so extensive that (excluding Tripura and Assam) Christians, according to the Centre for Policy Studies, now form 68.4 per cent of the population of the North-east as opposed to 2.1 per cent in 1901.[31]

In more recent times, the doctrinaire revulsion towards Hinduism has manifested itself in Kashmir. Since the 1980s,

Islamists there have been persecuting Hindus.[32] The words 'ethnic cleansing' and 'Hindu Holocaust' are being used most often now to describe this declared war on the state's unique multicultural legacy—Kashmiriyat.

In the face of this broad 'assault', how does an anxious Hindu protect his or her identity?

The Hindutva Lifeline?

For some on the Hindu Right, the solution for the anxieties many Hindus feel has been, and remains, the establishment of a Hindu Rashtra.

As we've already pointed out, many adherents of Hindutva— let's call them political Hindus—believe that secularism, as it is practised today by the Indian state, is perhaps not equipped to protect Hindu interests. The adoption of Hindutva is seen as an essential prerequisite to the survival of Hinduism. Loosely, it is also seen as a coalescing political doctrine with a set of features and principles designed to bridge the many fault lines that prevent Hindus from presenting a united face.

But Hindu Rashtra and Hindutva are not current-day concepts and date back to well before Independence. And they are just as controversial as the word 'secularism'. They are abused, misused, misunderstood, largely because secularists believe that Hindutva is cut from the same cloth of zealotry that binds some practitioners of the Abrahamic traditions and gives them a parochial outlook.

If secularism has come to be euphemistically used by the Hindu Right to define preferential treatment for Muslims at the expense of Hindus, then a Hindu Rashtra to its harshest critics is the graveyard of a plural India.[33] In this version of Hindu Rashtra, its main champion, the RSS, seeks to reduce religious minorities, in particular Muslims, to the status of second-class citizens.[34]

Furthermore, the 'threat' from Hindutva to Hinduism is routinely served up by the Congress in its bid to urge voters to unseat the BJP and unshackle India and her institutions from the communal stranglehold of the RSS.[35] However, the Supreme Court, for reasons briefly explained later in the book, did not recognize this distinction between Hinduism and Hindutva.[36]

Without, for the moment, getting into the Supreme Court's reasoning, it is sufficient to say at this point that treating Hindutva as distinct from Hinduism seems illogical. If Hinduism is a big-tent tradition, then it would be churlish to suggest that after accommodating so many *prathas* (traditions) it would turn its back on only one specific variant called Hindutva. Never mind that Hindutva, as contemplated by many of its proposers, is in sync with the tenets of the larger Dharmic Hindu tradition and is therefore unlikely to be exclusivist.

A Graveyard of Pluralism?

London-based journalist Hasan Suroor believes that another idea is at play here—that this 'failed secularism' is not the result of the Hindu desire to even the scales tilted against them. Instead, as he wrote in his column for the *Times of India*, 'The idea that Hindus have a first claim over India has become deeply ingrained, even among many liberals.'[37]

Suroor suggests recognizing this as the only way forward. 'Any sustainable solution will require the recognition of de facto Hinduisation of India over the past decade.' A workable idea, Suroor writes, is a 'Hindu Democratic Republic of India' that does not discriminate against its citizens.[38]

To quote Suroor:

There's a mistaken notion that the only alternative to a secular state is a theocracy. It is not. A state can have an officially recognised religion—in India's case, it will be Hinduism—and yet remain secular in practice by treating all citizens as equal and making sure that their religious and civil rights are protected by law—as in many western liberal democracies including Britain where the State is Christian, but government practices are secular. There is a robust and strictly enforced equality law which ensures that nobody is discriminated against because of their religion or ethnicity. As a British citizen, I can vouchsafe that it's working.[39]

Suroor's solution leads us to ask: Can a Hindu Rashtra be open and tolerant? To answer this, let's first examine how it was defined by its proponents.

Savarkar's Hindu Rashtra

On 26 February 2003, President A.P.J. Abdul Kalam unveiled the portrait of Vinayak Damodar Savarkar in the Central Hall of Parliament.[40] A day earlier, Sonia Gandhi, president of the Congress Party, had written to Kalam explaining the Opposition's decision to boycott the ceremony.[41] While Savarkar is an object of veneration for the Hindu Right, he is utterly loathed by the Left, whose proponents see him as the lynchpin of a divisive ideology that spawned Hindu majoritarianism.[42]

An unabashed champion of Hindutva, Savarkar popularized the terms Hindutva and Hindu Rashtra. His views were influenced by his own experiences during his incarceration for anti-British activities in the infamous Cellular Jail, where he had survived years of torture and abuse.[43] He was disillusioned with Mahatma Gandhi's support for a pan-Islamist Khilafat movement,[44] outraged by the brutal Moplah massacre of Hindus in the Malabar region[45] and expressed growing concern over repeated concessions granted to the Muslim League, including separate electorates that he believed only weakened the nationalist movement.[46]

Savarkar was also an advocate of the Shuddhi movement,[47] or reconversions to Hinduism, and was terribly pained by the assassination of Swami Shraddhanand,[48] chief campaigner for Shuddhi, by one Abdul Rashid, whom Mahatma Gandhi would refer to as a 'dear brother'.[49]

These factors, as Savarkar's biographer Vikram Sampath suggests, likely shaped Savarkar's understanding and definition of Hindutva. Said to be an atheist,[50] Savarkar's determinant of who was a Hindu transcended religion. Sampath writes: 'The factors that bonded this group despite their geographical separation in this vast tract of land were those of common blood, common culture, common epics, common laws and rites, the Sanskrit language, common feasts and festivals, and the shared works of art and literature. Thus, a nationalism led by cultural integration was another essential component of this "Hindu-ness" that had run unbroken over millennia.'[51]

These views are summed up by Savarkar thus:

These are the essentials of Hindutva—a common nation (Rashtra), a common race (Jati) and a common civilisation (Sanskriti). All these essentials could best be summed up by stating in brief that *he is a Hindu to whom Sindhusthan is not only a Pitribhu (Fatherland) but also a Punyabhu (Holyland)*. For the first two essentials of Hindutva—nation and Jati— are clearly devoted and connoted by the word Pitribhu while the third essential of Sanskriti is pre-eminently implied by the word Punyabhu (Holyland), *it is precisely Sanskriti including Sanskartas, i.e. rites and rituals, ceremonies and sacraments* that make a land a Holyland.'[52]

So, Savarkar's Hindutva was inclusive to the extent that it considered Jains, Buddhists and Sikhs as Hindus, since the birthplace of their religion (Holy Land) was India. But did it automatically exclude Muslims, Christians, Jews and Parsis?

Savarkar saw their 'divided love' as an obstacle for integration. He wrote:

> For though Hindustan to them is Fatherland as to any other Hindu, yet it is not to them a Holy land too. Their holy land is far off in Arabia or Palestine. Their mythology and Godmen, ideas and heroes are not the children of this soil. Consequently, their names and their outlook smacks of a foreign origin. Their love is divided. Nay, if some of them be really believing what they profess to do, then there can be no choice—they must, to a man, set their Holy land above their father land [*sic*] in their love and allegiance. That is but natural. We are not condemning nor are we lamenting. We are simply telling the facts as they stand.[53]

Savarkar called on non-Hindus to become part of the 'Hindu fold' by voluntarily pledging their 'love' to a 'common Mother' and recognize India not only as Pitribhu but also as Punyabhu (holy land[54]). He cited the examples of Sister Nivedita and Annie Besant, who had devoted themselves to the cause of India's freedom, as those whose Christian birth did not disqualify them from being considered as Hindus.[55]

But did Savarkar's seemingly exclusionary idea of nationhood influence his vision of what the Indian state ought to be? Not quite. Consider Savarkar's public address as president of the Hindu Mahasabha in 1937:[56]

> Let the Indian State be purely Indian. Let it not recognize any invidious distinctions whatsoever as regards the franchise, public services, offices, taxation on the grounds of religion and race. Let no cognizance be taken whatsoever of man being Hindu or Mohammedan, Christian or Jew. Let all citizens of that Indian State be treated according to their individual worth irrespective of their religious or racial percentage in the general population. Let that language and script be the national language and script of that Indian state which are understood by the overwhelming majority of the people as happens in every other state in the world i.e. England or the United States of America and let no religious bias be allowed to tamper with that language and script with an enforced and perverse hybridism whatsoever. Let 'one man one vote' be the general rule irrespective of caste or creed, race or religion.[57]

Seven years later, many of these ideas formed the core of the constitution of the Hindusthan Free State—'the name of the free country to be Hindusthan and not India'—put together by the Hindu Mahasabha.[58] While guaranteeing the fundamental right to equality and free expression, and to propagate and practise one's religion under a democratic government elected by universal adult franchise, this constitution categorically ruled out any state religion for the Hindusthan Free State or any of its provinces.[59] In other words, by inference, it was secular in its outlook.

While Savarkar's 'Hindusthan' was essentially secular, the RSS's longest-serving sarsanghchalak, Madhav Sadashivrao Golwalkar, would come across as an exclusivist.

Golwalkar's Hindu Rashtra

Golwalkar, who served as the RSS's second chief between 1940 and 1973, is most often credited with 'presenting the academic and intellectual arguments that formed the [Sangh's] worldview'.[60] And yet, today, the Sangh is diffident about associating itself with many of Golwalkar's extreme pronouncements.[61]

The RSS today talks about a Bharat where its citizens share a common DNA[62] and not Golwalkar's initial concept of a Hindu nation predicated on a distinction between races where one would dominate. As Golwalkar had said in his book *We or Our Nationhood Defined*: 'A Race is a hereditary society having common customs, common language, common memories of glory and disaster; in short it is a population with common origin under one culture . . . Race is the body of the Nation, and that with its fall, the Nation ceases to exist.'[63]

And what of non-Hindus? Golwalkar was unambiguous. 'The foreign races in Hindusthan must either adopt the Hindu culture and language, must learn to respect and hold in reverence the Hindu religion, must entertain no idea but those of the glorification of the Hindu race and culture i.e. of the Hindu nation and must lose their separate existence to merge in the Hindu race, or may stay in the country, wholly subordinated to the Hindu nation, claiming nothing, deserving no privileges, far less any preferential treatment – not even citizen's rights.'[64]

In 2006, the RSS officially disowned Golwalkar's entire book as 'neither representing the views of the grown Guruji nor of the RSS'.[65] It was even suggested then by RSS ideologue Rakesh Sinha, now a BJP MP, that the book did not carry Golwalkar's own views but was an 'abridged version of GD Savarkar's [V.D. Savarkar's brother] Rashtra Mimansa'.[66] M.G. Vaidya, former RSS spokesperson, had then said that the book that is 'central to us is Golwalkar's *Bunch of Thoughts* since it consists of his views after he became Sarsanghchalak on June 21, 1940'.[67]

But even in *Bunch of Thoughts*, which is a collection of Golwalkar's speeches and writings at different times, he is again suspicious about Muslims and Christians, and their compatibility with India's national life:

> They are born in this land, no doubt. But are they true to their salt? Are they grateful to this land which has brought them up? Do they feel that they are the children of this land and its tradition, and that to serve it is their great good fortune? Do they feel it a duty to serve her? No! Together with the change in their faith, gone is the spirit of love and devotion for the nation.
>
> Nor does it end there. They have also developed a feeling of identification with the enemies of this land. They call themselves 'Sheikhs' and 'Syeds.' Sheikhs and Syeds are certain clans in Arabia. How then did these people come to feel that they are their descendants? That is because they have cut off their ancestral national moorings of this land and mentally merged themselves with the aggressors. They still think that they have come here only to conquer and establish their kingdoms. So we see that it is not merely a case of change of faith, but a change even in national identity. What else is it, if not treason, to join the camp of the enemy leaving their mother-nation in the lurch?[68]

For a non-Hindu to 'assimilate' and be one with the 'national current',[69] Golwalkar affixed certain conditions: a *rashtra* dharma, or national responsibility; a *samaj* dharma, or duty to society; a *kula* dharma, or duty to ancestors; and only in his *vyakti* dharma, or personal faith, 'can he choose any path which satisfies his spiritual urge'.[70]

Several decades later, the current chief of the RSS, Mohan Bhagwat, would distance his organization from even these comments as well. When specifically asked about *Bunch of Thoughts* and Golwalkar's references to Muslims as enemies, Bhagwat did not defend his predecessor. Instead, he said that Golwalkar's writings should be reviewed keeping in mind certain circumstances and context.[71]

For a proper perspective, Bhagwat recommended reading another book brought out by the RSS, *M.S. Golwalkar: His Mission and Vision*, a compilation of Golwalkar's thoughts. But in this book, only those thoughts with 'eternal relevance' have been retained, while his views that were 'contemporary in nature' were omitted.[72]

For all his prejudices, however, during the establishment of the Bharatiya Jana Sangh in 1951, Golwalkar backed its founder Shyama Prasad Mukherjee's policy of accepting people of all faiths into the party.[73] He is also said to have told Mukherjee to avoid the use of the word 'Hindu' in the party name to distinguish the Bharatiya Jana Sangh from the Hindu Mahasabha, once led by the other towering champion of Hindutva, Savarkar.[74]

The Sangh evolved its own understanding of Hindutva and Hindu Rashtra to suit the demands of time and circumstance.

The Sangh's Hindu Rashtra

In September 2018, Bhagwat held a three-day lecture series in Delhi titled The Future of Bharat.[75] It marked a first for an organization that otherwise prefers to shun the limelight. Bhagwat dwelt on a myriad of issues, from the Sangh's economic outlook to its views on homosexuality, but most crucially on the Constitution and the idea of a Hindu Rashtra.

A member of the RSS's national executive, Ram Madhav, in his column in the *Indian Express*, described these interactions as a 'Glasnost' moment for the Sangh. Bhagwat came across as a latter-day Mikhail Gorbachev—the former president of the USSR whose political movement for reform, known as Perestroika, evolved an open society, Glasnost, and contributed to the end of the Cold War—keen to present the RSS as a socially and culturally progressive organization.[76] So, over the course of a few days, Bhagwat went about setting the record straight on commonly held misconceptions about the Sangh.

The exercise was a refreshing change. The RSS chief engaged with his audience, taking questions transparently and answering them sincerely.

Bhagwat spoke of the RSS's acceptance of, and allegiance to, the Indian Constitution and its Preamble, which he read out, including the word 'secular'[77] (introduced in 1976), before adding: 'Dr Ambedkar had said in the Constituent Assembly that it was because of our internecine fighting that the foreigners won and made us their slaves. I am only giving the gist of what he had said. You can very well read the details of it in his words. He [Ambedkar] said: "We are sitting in warring camps as mutual enemies. And the limitation of our system should be blamed for it. If we fail to create such a fraternal feeling, I can't say what sort of fate awaits us."'[78]

Acknowledging the truth in Ambedkar's assessment and their implication for India's unity, Bhagwat went about reassuring his listeners while simultaneously positing a formulation to uphold fraternity:

> The Sangh is engaged in creating this fraternity and only unity in diversity can be the basis of this fraternity. This thought process that has come down to us by tradition is called Hindutva. Hence, we say that ours is a Hindu Rashtra.

This does not mean that there should be no Muslims here. The day we say Muslims are not required here Hindutva will be lost.

Hindutva speaks about viewing the entire world as a family. So, the moment we say only the Vedas are acceptable and the Buddhists, who do not recognize the Vedas, are not acceptable, Hindutva will be lost. Because, in our nation, we have incessantly been in the pursuit of truth and all these spiritual systems have arisen out of this process. So, all these are respectable and deserve to be respected. This is the conviction of all of us and it should be so. As Hindutva is the only source that provides the feeling of fraternity with an ideological foundation, we have been following it.[79]

Bhagwat also sought to dispel any notion that there was an attempt to impose a larger Hindu identity on non-Hindus. He said that they were free to refer to themselves as 'Bharatiya' if they so wished.[80] But he did say that the RSS would not hold back from referring to Indians as Hindus, as 'We feel, Hindu is the only word useful in creating the culture of our imagination and, hence, we are sticking to that word. Even if it proves a losing proposition, we are ready to bear it. Because we believe that till this word continues to exist, this nature of Bharat will never become moribund. And the people of Bharat will move forward, taking all along with them.'[81]

And this shared Hindu identity, according to Bhagwat, was divorced from the concept of race and, most importantly, from Punyabhuu, or Holy Land. The shared Hindu identity was instead premised on four principal meeting grounds: 'By tradition, by nationality (Rashtriyata), by our motherland and by our common ancestors, we say, we are all Hindus, and we will continue to say so. However, that does not mean that we don't treat you as our own. On the contrary, we are saying it so that we can claim you as our own. We cannot claim you as our own based on your religion, sect, language, caste, etc. It is only possible on the basis of the motherland, the culture and the ancestors. And so, we insist on that. We consider them as the organs of our Rashtriyata (nation).'[82]

To further allay the apprehensions of secularists and minorities, Sunil Ambekar, among the senior-most pracharaks of the RSS, has elaborated upon the Sangh's understanding of a Hindu Rashtra: 'It is the imagination of a contemporary, non-violent nation where peace and prosperity prevail, which promotes freedom of worship and equality of women.'[83] The attention, once again, is to the concept of a nation (rashtra) as opposed to a state (rajya).

Armed with a Hindu dharmic calling card, the RSS, led by Bhagwat, has embarked on a period of active Muslim outreach. Bhagwat visited a mosque and a madrasa in Delhi in September 2022.[84] This was on an invitation from the All India Imam Organization. He has also engaged with prominent members of the Muslim community, including the former Delhi lieutenant governor Najeeb Jung and former chief election commissioner S.Y. Quraishi, in what is widely seen as an effort to pitch Hindutva as an inclusive doctrine.[85]

Bhagwat is said to have emphasized for his Muslim audiences that the Indian Constitution is 'sacrosanct' (perhaps implying that the word 'secular' was here to stay) and that Hindutva is an 'inclusive concept' where 'all communities have equal room'.[86]

The last phrase is an important one. Bhagwat was keen to underline that this kind of social accommodation needs to be a two-way street. He was keen to impress upon Muslims that in states where cow slaughter is not banned, they should 'voluntarily shun beef'. He encourages his Muslim interlocutors to call upon their community to stop using phrases like *kafir*, or non-believers, so that Hindus do not feel 'othered'. For his part, Bhagwat agreed that equally offensive terms like 'jihadi' and 'Pakistani', used by some to malign Indian Muslims, should be done away with.[87]

These meetings have been hailed for their lack of rancour, and the mature acknowledgement that Hindus and minorities need to talk to each other and continue the *samvad* in the national interest.[88] Whether this yields results and a favourable impact in the long term remains to be seen. But one must also acknowledge that Bhagwat's samvad with minorities would not have happened had the RSS championed a Hindu theocratic state.

The more fluid Hindutva being patented under Bhagwat is a 'dynamic and continuing process' resting on three pillars: 'patriotism, respect for ancestors and culture', which have contributed to the growing acceptance of the RSS. It has found the doctrinal elbow room to proclaim that, 'Our call is rooted in *Rashtriyata*. It is about the tradition of the Muslims, the tradition of the Christians, and of all others in Bharat.'[89]

It also helps that Bhagwat is the first sarsanghchalak born after Independence, someone who was not witness to the upheavals of Partition and the acrimony that characterized Hindu–Muslim relations at the time.

Another factor here, which isn't talked about much, is that the RSS had to tone down because of expediency. The RSS's political 'special purpose vehicle' is the Bharatiya Janta Party. As the world's largest political party, it has come to represent several caste and community interests. Some have even compared it to the once-catch-all Congress. The Sangh's leadership is aware that the BJP's continued electoral successes depend solely on its ability to carry as many people along as it possibly can.

The BJP's Bharat

For all the vitriol that some BJP leaders heap on the word 'secular', the party's own constitution makes more references to it than the Congress Party's guiding document.[90]

Even Yogi Adityanath, the chief minister of Uttar Pradesh, who said the word 'secularism is the biggest threat to develop India's prosperous traditions',[91] would have had to swear by the party's constitution.

This document promotes 'integral humanism' as the party's basic philosophy. It also asks its cadres to swear to uphold 'Nationalism and National Integration, Democracy, Gandhian Socialism, Positive Secularism, (Sarva Dharma Sama Bhava) and Value-based politics . . . [in a] Secular State and Nation not based on religion'.[92]

The opponents of the BJP who apprehend that the party secretly aspires to remove the word 'secular' from the Preamble of the Constitution[93] forget that in order to do so it would first have to amend its own party's constitution.

Interestingly, as author Vinay Sitapati writes in *Jugalbandi: The BJP before Modi*, in the late 1970s, while drafting the document, the party's stalwarts quarrelled not so much over secularism as the suitability of including the term 'Gandhian Socialism' in the party's constitution.[94] Of course, lofty declarations made in a party constitution aren't necessarily sacrosanct. But the BJP's founding document does provide a useful starting point for any serious analysis of that party's view on what ideals our nation's constitution ought to edify.

In 2015, following the publication of a government advertisement that carried the original Preamble to the Constitution without the words 'socialist' and 'secular', the Opposition was up in arms. Several critics of the Modi administration became convinced that moves were afoot to strip India of its secular identity.[95] The government was quick to douse the fire, with the then parliamentary affairs minister, Venkaiah Naidu, declaring that 'secularism is there in the blood of the Indian people, that's part of our culture. It was not there in the original Preamble and was inserted during the Emergency. But the government advertisement was about the original Preamble. We are committed to secularism, and we don't have any idea to drop it.'[96]

The BJP idolizes Savarkar and is an ideological descendant of the RSS, which it looks up to as a paternal guide. But, as a political entity in the business of governance and fighting elections, its senior leadership has been guarded about overtly describing India as a Hindu Rashtra. Even when prompted to specifically discuss Savarkar's views describing India as a Hindu Rashtra, and whether the BJP and the Modi government saw India as one, the Union home minister, Amit Shah, in a 2019 interview, was categorical: 'Absolutely not. We believe in the Constitution, and we accept the Constitution in its spirit. In this country, all sects have complete freedom. The government has only one religion and that's the Constitution and nothing else.'[97]

The NDA, at least for now, believes that the Preamble to our Constitution is sacrosanct. But does this also mean that a Hindu Rashtra, in a cultural sense, would never find constitutional expression under the current government?

Today, the BJP is electorally at its strongest following two successive mandates, giving it an outright majority in the Lok Sabha. Significantly, it has ninety-four out of 245 seats in the upper house.[98] This gives Modi's NDA far greater freedom to pursue its stated goals through Parliament.

But even so, aside from virtually abrogating Article 370, it is yet to use its majority to bring legislation in line with its core objectives. For instance, it resisted pressure to enact a Central law to introduce a uniform civil code so far or construct a Ram Mandir in Ayodhya. And there has never even been a hint from its highest leadership pulpit about tinkering with the Constitution's Preamble to eject the word 'secularism'.

In fact, the NDA has sought to dispel fears from secular quarters over legislation and policy that have been criticised as steps being taken by the BJP towards turning India into a Hindu Rashtra. In the one reference Modi as prime minister has made to a Hindu Rashtra,[99] he did so in the context of the CAA in Parliament, when he chose to remind agitated Congress MPs of Jawaharlal Nehru's own commitment to protect minorities in Pakistan. Modi invoked the Nehru–Liaquat pact in 1950: 'For them [Opposition], they are Muslims. For us, they are all Indians. The act does not affect any Indian. I want to clearly state that with the CAA coming, there will be no impact on citizens of India, practising any faith. The CAA does not affect any Indian, it doesn't harm minority interests. Pandit Nehru himself was in favour of protecting minorities in Pakistan. I want to ask Congress, was Pandit Nehru communal? Did he want a Hindu Rashtra?'[100]

Indeed, the NDA government has been keen to counter any claim that Muslims in India are living in fear. Especially in a year in which India has assumed the mantle of the G20 presidency, its representatives in government have gone to some lengths to allay such concerns.

Sample this response from the country's finance minister, Nirmala Sitharaman, in Washington, DC, in April 2023: 'India has the second-largest Muslim population in the world, and that population is only growing in numbers. If there is a perception, or if there's in reality, their lives are difficult or made difficult with the support of the state, which is what is implied in most of these write-ups, I would ask, will this happen in India in the sense, will the Muslim population be growing than what it was in 1947?'

Sitharaman drew attention to the contrasting situation in Pakistan. 'Violence prevails against Muhajirs, Shia and every other group you can name which is not accepted by the mainstream . . . whereas in India you would find every strand of Muslims doing their business, their children getting educated. Fellowships are being given by the government.'[101]

Rajeev Mantri, who has co-authored *A New Idea of India: Individual Rights in a Civilisational State*, is of the view that those who continue to think that the 2024 election will see the BJP pursuing a more militant line are being alarmist. Mantri believes that the BJP is not about to shoot itself in the foot. If anything, he believes that the BJP may be more inclined to push a harder secularism:

> Any other course of action [modifying the Constitution to describe India as a Hindu Rashtra], while doable will be prone to misrepresentation . . . and frankly, my fear is that we will see a good idea getting hamstrung or diluted because of overwhelming pushback with people projecting it to be something which it is not, similar to what happened with CAA . . . Ultimately, being a secular republic means to me having the same/equally applicable laws to all citizens of India, so that is what we should aspire towards . . . let's become truly secular.[102]

9

Can India Be Tolerant without Being 'Secular'?

How To Be Both

Let's say, sometime in the future, a government, through an amendment, were to remove the word 'secularism' from the Preamble to the Indian Constitution and replace it with the word 'Hindu'.

What if, hypothetically, the Preamble were to then read 'We, the people of India, having solemnly resolved to constitute India into a sovereign, socialist, Hindu democratic republic and to secure to all its citizens . . .'? Could such a putative Indian state have a Hindu identity and still be a plural Mecca for minorities?

As we have demonstrated, a Hindu Rashtra driven by an inherently plural, variegated, non-proselytizing dharma can hardly pose a threat to other more organized religions and denominations. If anything, we've shown that Hindus, even in the face of existential threats, are vulnerable to bouts of fractious infighting enabled by Hinduism's own inherent elasticity.

Moreover, Hindus—prisoners of a seemingly unyielding caste system and therefore more gullible to believe that all faiths are equal—are forever vulnerable to the guiles of conversion. Hinduism is, after all, up against creeds that are sworn to spread the word and some of their practitioners have, in the past, overwhelmed many faiths and traditions, especially the unorganized.

This last point feeds into a Hindu sense of being under siege. A comprehensive 2015 Pew Research Center survey[1] on religions and their spread globally set off alarm bells when it was first published in India. It predicted that by 2050, while India will retain a Hindu majority, it will also have the largest Muslim population of any country in the world, surpassing Indonesia.

While anxieties over population replacement are often dismissed as the preoccupations of conspiracy theorists,[2] it bears mentioning that aside from Hinduism, the other great traditions of the East—Buddhism, Shinto and native Shamanic practices—are all, by and large, losing ground.

In South Korea, according to a 2014 Pew survey, the fastest-growing religion is Christianity at almost 30 per cent of the population.[3] Interestingly, while there are hundreds of thousands of Buddhist temples, 46 per cent of South Koreans prefer to classify themselves as having 'no religious affiliation'. In Japan too, Buddhism and Shinto are on a decline.[4] Coincidentally, both South Korea and Japan declare themselves as secular nations with no state religion. Only Thailand bucks the trend.[5] Is it because its constitution requires the king to be Buddhist, an 'upholder of religions', and mandates that the 'State should support and protect Buddhism and other religions'?[6]

With no recourse to conversions and the wide legal room given to Muslims and Christians to proselytize,[7] what if a government in the future is compelled to declare India a Hindu Rashtra?

We already know what the usual suspects, who also happen to be the most influential opinion makers, will say. Because they continue to yoke the idea of a Hindu India with brute majoritarianism, a Hindu Rashtra for them will always be synonymous with a 'Hindu Pakistan'.[8]

Shashi Tharoor, member of Parliament from the Congress Party and easily one of the most influential figures among liberals, invoked the term in a speech in Kerala in 2018, when he was warning voters against the perils of voting the BJP back into power. Tharoor said: 'If they [the BJP] win a repeat in the Lok Sabha, our democratic constitution as we understand it will not survive as they will have all the elements they need to tear apart the constitution of India and write a new one. That new one will be the one which will enshrine principles of Hindu Rashtra, that will remove equality for minorities, that will create a Hindu Pakistan and that isn't what Mahatma Gandhi, Nehru, Sardar Patel, Maulana Azad and great heroes of freedom struggle fought for.'[9]

But all this talk about 'Hindu Pakistan' is masterful subterfuge. Tharoor builds his case not on the utterances of the moderate principals of the BJP and the RSS, but on the preposterous militant fringe among Hindus. The idea seems to be fear-mongering among the Congress Party's Muslim constituents. Making Muslims feel insecure about their survival as a culture in order to consolidate them into a vote bank is an old political trick.

Muslim separatists in the pre-Independence era used it to devastating effect when they were building a case for separate electorates. Muhammad Iqbal, a leading Muslim philosopher of his era and president of the Muslim League in 1930, warned that in any putative democratic set-up in an independent India minorities would be reduced to the status of second-class citizens.[10]

Tripurdaman Singh and Adeel Hussain, authors of *Nehru: The Debates That Defined India*, even write about Iqbal's proposal to group Muslim-majority provinces in India's north-west together, an idea they observe 'was later spun forward, albeit in very different shape and form, by proponents of the Pakistan movement'.[11] Significantly at the time, Iqbal did not just fear oppression from Savarkarites but also from the bigwigs of Nehru's Congress Party.

Singh and Hussain capture a spat between Nehru and Iqbal to illustrate the point: 'In 1933, during their first brief spat, Iqbal had sharply criticized Nehru in a public statement for ascribing the failure of the Round Table Conferences, where India's constitutional future was discussed, to the conservative political outlook of the Muslim delegation and their lack of nationalism. Partly embracing this criticism, Iqbal retorted that "If by nationalism he [Nehru] means a fusion of the communities in a biological sense, I should personally plead guilty to the charge of anti-nationalism".'[12]

The authors add:

In Iqbal's understanding of nationalism, rejecting the fusion of communities into a single nation was not anti-national. Nationalism in India had to be reimagined as something different than the mere blending of divergent communities into a singular whole. The best part to make India hospitable before all religious groups would therefore require Indian leaders of political thought [to] get rid of the idea of a unitary Indian nation based on something like a biological fusion of the communities.

Iqbal further corrected Nehru that it was not democracy that Indian Muslims feared, as the latter had insinuated in an earlier speech. What Muslims feared was 'communal [Hindu]

oligarchy in the garb of democracy'. Iqbal grimly predicted
that if Nehru continued to prop up nationalism as the catch-all
solution for India's communal and constitutional woes, 'the
country will have to be redistributed on the basis of religious
historical and cultural affinities'.[13]

Iqbal's prophecy turned out to be true. A vast number of Muslims
succumbed to this propaganda and put Islamic solidarity above
the imperative of submitting to a pluralistic, democratic free state
of India.

Today, the Congress leadership resurrects the dread associated
with Partition to warn against the possibility of 'RSS fascists'
declaring India a 'Hindu Rashtra', and subordinating Muslims
and other minorities to effect a second partition.[14]

Rahul Gandhi walked thousands of miles to highlight what
he claimed was the immediate need to unify a nation in the grip
of Hindutva supremacism.[15] Supporters of Rahul Gandhi's Bharat
Jodo campaign will, of course, never admit that even Savarkar, who
popularized the concept of a Hindu Rashtra—as recent scholarship
has shown and as has been cited at length in the previous chapter—
was more of an integrationist. While conscious of the difference
between the dharmic view of life and the Abrahamic way of life,
Savarkar was not an instinctive advocate of the two-nation theory.
Despite many attempts to suggest that Savarkar's Hindutva emerged
from a sense of racial supremacism and exclusivism,[16] the man who
gave shape to the Hindu Mahasabha political party took a broader
view of race and country. Vikram Sampath, who has written
arguably the most definitive two-part biography of Savarkar, quotes
his subject directly:

After all there is throughout the world, so far as man is
concerned, but a single race – the human race kept alive by

one common blood, the human blood. All other talk is at best provisional, a makeshift and only relatively true . . . to try to prevent the coming link of blood is to build on sand. Sexual attraction has proved more powerful than all the command of all the profits put together. Even as it is, not even the aborigines of the Andamans are without some sprinkling of the so-called Arian blood in their veins and vice versa.[17]

The last seventy-five years have decisively put paid to the scurrilous propaganda by the Congress camp. Savarkar was right. Hindus have turned out to be far more inclusive and far more accommodating than presumed. It is Islamic Pakistan and Bangladesh—not Hindu-majority India—where minorities are gasping for breath, choking as they are on the miasma of bigotry.

Not a 'Hindu Pakistan' but a Hindu Britain?

The innate Hindu tolerance for multiculturalism and various forms of theism is more akin to the temperament of Christians in several Christian-majority nations, like the United States, or even officially Christian nations, like England. Indeed, if anything, the recent history of independent India suggests that a putative Hindu Rashtra would have more in common with Britain than with Pakistan.

Britain has an official religion—Anglican Christianity.[18] It is curious that Britain, which nudged modern Indian constitutionalism towards the liberal idea of 'secularism', would itself continue with an arrangement that has been associated with a parochial conservatism. And it does so unapologetically.

England's national flag is based on the Saint George's Cross.[19] Saint George is venerated as a crusader who died defending the faith. In Britain's national anthem, 'God Save the King', there are six references to God, and there's little doubt which God.[20] As King Charles's coronation demonstrates, the sovereign is still the supreme governor of the Church of England and must be a member of it. The sovereign formally appoints all bishops, but in practice the appointments are made by the Crown Nominations Commission and approved by the prime minister.[21]

The most senior twenty-six Anglican bishops sit in the House of Lords, serving as 'Lords Spiritual' until they retire.[22] The state funds religious personnel to provide religious activities and services, such as prayer and counseling in the armed forces, prison services and the National Health Service.[23] The state also funds a number of 'faith schools' that must be 'in the main Christian, whilst taking account of the teaching and practices of the other principal religions represented in Great Britain'.[24]

In 2011, at a speech in Oxford on the 400th anniversary of the King James Bible, the then prime minister, David Cameron, called for a revival of traditional Christian values to counter Britain's 'moral collapse':[25]

> We are a Christian country and we should not be afraid to say so . . . Let me be clear: I am not in any way saying that to have another faith – or no faith – is somehow wrong. I know and fully respect that many people in this country do not have a religion. And I am also incredibly proud that Britain is home to many different faith communities, who do so much to make our country stronger. But what I am saying is that the Bible has helped to give Britain a set of values and morals which make Britain what it is today.[26]

Supplant the word 'Christian' with 'Hindu' and remove the reference to the Bible, and Cameron sounds, almost word for word, like RSS chief Mohan Bhagwat. Indeed, if state religiosity is considered an anathema to secularism by the British liberal establishment, why haven't they distanced the state from religion?

'Why? Because,' as David Cameron answers, 'the tolerance that Christianity demands of our society provides greater space for other religious faiths too.'[27]

The origins of this tolerance have been traced back to a period that some historians refer to as the Age of English Enlightenment. Ashley Walsh, who teaches early modern history at Cardiff University, in his book *Civil Religion and the Enlightenment in England, 1707–1800*, reveals how leading thinkers of that period argued that Christianity could evolve to be a 'civil' religion that allowed for tolerance without separating the church from state.[28]

In a sense, writes Walsh, this concept has undergone an evolution since the time of philosopher Jean-Jacques Rousseau, who advocated a civil religion and believed that Christians were intolerant and needed to adopt certain dogmas. As *Encyclopaedia Britannica* notes, 'They should affirm the afterlife, a God with divine perfection, the notion that the just will be happy and the wicked punished, and the sanctity of the social contract and the polity's laws. Civil religion should also condemn intolerance as a creedal matter.'[29] Significantly, Rousseau also argued for severe punishments for those who refused to obey the dogmas.[30]

Walsh writes, 'To develop a Christian civil religion, enlightened thinkers drew from a long anticlerical tradition of Christian thought. Priests, they argued, made Christianity uncivil with their "priestcraft" of superstition and intolerance. Civil religionists studied the efforts of Christian reformers in the medieval and early modern ages to strip Christianity back to the message of Jesus Christ in the primitive gospel . . . Pious Christians would tolerate if they understood that all they needed for their salvation was to profess the faith of Christ alone.'[31]

It is clear that the concept of civil religion solves the problem that besets thinkers in India—that pluralism and tolerance are not possible without a necessary separation of state and religion. If only liberal modernists in India had been like their British counterparts, who clearly were more trusting of and less condescending towards their God and their God's cultural–spiritual outlook.

Indeed, since British Christians, as David Cameron says, have 'confidence' in their 'Christian identity', it is much 'easier to be Jewish or Muslim here in Britain than it is [even] in a secular country like France'.[32]

In fact, a growing number of Britons today like to think of themselves as atheists.[33] The data published by the Office for National Statistics shows that the number of people identifying with 'no religion' jumped by over 8 million, from 25 per cent to 37 per cent, between 2011 and 2021.[34] Christians are now a minority in the census results for the first time, and in Wales Christians are outnumbered by the non-religious.

Many in Britain believe that the non-religious (non-practising) may even be far greater in number since the survey question used by the Office of National Statistics is biased.[35] It asks: 'What is your religion?' There's a presumption that those who tick 'Christian' 'do so only because they were christened or because their parents are or were Christian or because they went to a Christian school'.[36] Indeed, of those who selected their religion as Christian, 'less than half believe Jesus was a real person who was the son of God who died and came back to life'.[37]

Indian-origin Briton Rishi Sunak was picked by the British Conservative party, no less, to become prime minister of England in 2022. Not only is he the first person of colour to be PM in British history, but he is also a 'proud' practising Hindu.[38] He took oath as MP not on the Christian Bible but on the Bhagavad Gita, just as he had when he was appointed to the cabinet position of finance minister in 2017.[39] At that time Sunak described himself thus: 'I am now a citizen of Britain. But my religion is Hindu. My religious and cultural heritage is Indian. I proudly say that I am a Hindu and my identity is also a Hindu.'[40]

British constitutional expert Robert Hazell was a civil servant in the UK Home Office before pursuing a career in teaching at University College London.[41] To him, the role of the Church of England and that of the British monarch has evolved into assuming the mantle of being a spokesperson for spiritual values and, crucially, protecting the free practice of all religions in the UK.[42]

When we spoke to him for this book, he reminded us of a speech the late Queen Elizabeth had delivered at Lambeth Palace in 2012. She had said:

> The concept of our established church is occasionally misunderstood and, I believe, commonly under-appreciated. Its role is not to defend Anglicanism to the exclusion of other religions. Instead, the church has a duty to protect the free practice of all faiths in this country.
>
> It certainly provides an identity and spiritual dimension for its own many adherents. But also, gently and assuredly, the Church of England has created an environment for other faith communities and indeed people of no faith to live freely. Woven into the fabric of this country, the church has helped to build a better society – more and more in active co-operation for the common good with those of other faiths.[43]

This sentiment, Professor Hazell told us, has been reciprocated by members of other religious communities living in the United Kingdom who do not see the Church of England or the state's religious affiliation as an impediment to the practice of their respective faiths.[44]

Another distinguishing feature of the United Kingdom is how an individual's religious affiliation is almost a non-issue when it comes to voting in elections. 'Religion plays almost no part in our politics in this sense that although I'm very interested in politics, I could not tell you the religious affiliations of most of our leading politicians. It's just irrelevant,' Professor Hazell told us. 'And I think it's irrelevant to the political parties when selecting their candidates, certainly irrelevant to the public when voting. The public, like me, are generally blind. They are ignorant about whether a candidate is, I mean in Christian terms, a Catholic, Anglican or a Methodist, or [is from] some other branch of Christianity. If a candidate is of an ethnic minority, they're more likely to be able to guess what their religion might be. So, someone from the Indian subcontinent, they can guess, is probably a Hindu or a Muslim, although as you would know very well that there are some Christians and some Buddhists and some others [in that region]. Occasionally religion surfaces.

'When Tony Blair was prime minister he was known to be religious, and indeed you would know he converted and became a Catholic, but his press spokesman, Alastair Campbell, famously didn't want Blair's religion to be a factor. On one occasion he said, "We don't do God." He said that very firmly, and everyone understood what he meant. And he was making quite an important statement about the British political culture—that it didn't matter that Tony Blair was himself religious and that wasn't going to interfere with his politics. And everyone, I think, accepted Campbell's statement—both as a prescriptive statement, we are not going there, but also as a descriptive statement. This is what British politics is like—we don't do God.'[45]

This does not mean that the multiculturalism of 'Cool Britannia'[46] is destined to make the country any less Christian. The 'holidays' (a reference to the period between late November and early January) in the UK are a time when Christian festivities spill over into the public domain and are patronized by the state.[47] And, at least for the foreseeable future, the Church of England and the British state will noticeably overlap.

But if in Britain state patronage of a religion hasn't made life a nightmare for minorities, why should things be any different in India if the state was to officially embrace an inherently pluralistic dharmic philosophy?

Unlike Islam, Christianity had a Reformation. Over time, its evolution has made it more akin to Hinduism in that it is fundamentally more amenable to inquiry and new ideas, and more tolerant to new sects and traditions. And nowhere is Christianity more elastic than in the United States of America.

The American Example

According to political scientist Ahmet T. Kuru, America became the secular exemplar, notwithstanding the overwhelming Christianness of the early immigrants.[48] Generally, Christian refugees, who were chastened by the denominational conflicts in the lands they were leaving behind, were loath to subscribe to one 'hegemonic' Christian ethos. In his book *Secularism and State Policies towards Religion*, Kuru writes:

> The Republican elite did not perceive religion as an ally of an old monarchy. Instead, there was a diversity of competing Protestant denominations, none of which could claim a bare majority. Because of the intense religious diversity, many religious groups saw the church-state separation as a second-best choice and a guarantee to their religious freedom. Secular and religious elites had an ideational common ground based on John Locke's liberalism. The dominance of passive secularism

depended on an 'overlapping consensus' – an agreement
that secular and religious movements reached for different
purposes.[49]

As Allen Hertzke, who taught religion and politics at the University
of Oklahoma, told us, 'We were very diverse. Our colonies were
very diverse. You couldn't have an established national church
because you had too many different churches. In Pennsylvania,
you had Quakers. In New York, there were many Jews. Virginia
had Anglicans. Massachusetts had Congregationalists and
Puritans. So, when the constitution was written, there was one
clause that said there's no religious test for office, which some of
the colonies had. For instance, you had to believe in the Trinity
to hold office and so forth. All that ended.'[50]

While secular, America doesn't eschew Christian symbolism
altogether in the public domain. Kuru writes of the 1980
presidential campaign.[51] At that time, Republican presidential
nominee Ronald Reagan began to court the Christian Right. He
raised eyebrows and sparked a controversy when he accepted an
invitation to address evangelical Christians in Dallas, Texas. Kuru
cites Reagan, 'I know this group can't endorse me, but I want you
to know that I endorse you and what you are doing.'[52]

Reagan's outreach is widely commented upon as having
kick-started a new era in state–religion relations in the United
States.[53] But what was this cause that Reagan's outreach was
meant to endorse? Kuru writes that the Christian Right was
looking for an ally in the White House and had emerged as a
force after 'decade-long activism as a reaction to several court
decisions on issues such as the prohibition of Bible reading and
organised prayer in schools, the legalisation of abortions and
the removal of tax-exempt status of schools that practiced racial
discrimination'.[54]

Over the years, intense Christian activism has had a huge influence on legislation and policymaking in the avowedly secular United States. And this also extends to Supreme Court judgments in a country where judges in the highest court are appointed through a political process. In June 2022, the US Supreme Court reversed the landmark 'Roe vs Wade' judgment of 1973, which had accorded constitutional protection for abortion.[55] It was no coincidence that the judges who backed the majority view on the bench were appointed by Republican Presidents George H.W. Bush, George Bush and Donald Trump, and the dissenting judges were appointed by Presidents Bill Clinton and Barack Obama.[56] 'Secular' Americans viewed this as an assault on the separation of church and state, and lamented the interference by the 'Christian Right' into the reproductive rights of women.[57] The pro-life evangelicals hailed the verdict as a shield for millions of unborn children against the 'barbarity of abortion'.[58]

Unlike the Indian Constitution, the United States Constitution has an 'Establishment Clause'[59] in the First Amendment which states, 'Congress shall make no law respecting an establishment of religion.' And yet, the absence of a state religion has not allowed a complete divorce between religion and matters of the state. The American Pledge of Allegiance, a daily ritual in public schools as well as at many public gatherings, is a case in point. It reads, 'I pledge allegiance to the flag of the United States of America, and to the Republic for which it stands, one Nation under God, indivisible, with liberty and justice for all.'[60] The presence of 'God' in this text (the word was inserted in 1954),[61] in a country with no religious affiliation, has been a bone of contention between atheists and believers. In fact, in 2002 a US court ruled that this insertion was a violation of the Establishment Clause, but there was unanimity among the political class that this ruling was flawed, prompting the senate and the house to overturn the verdict.[62] The

Democrats went with the popular pulse on this issue and were just as keen not to alienate religious voters.

But there are areas where Christian activism has not managed to get its way. In the domain of religious instruction and prayer in public schools, the political consensus achieved in the case of the pledge has been absent in any deliberations to overturn Supreme Court verdicts that have upheld the wall of separation between religion and state.[63] Indeed, the extent of religious influence on matters of governance and law in the United States has been defined by a tussle between hard-line secularists and those who see religious, principally Christian, values as a guide to policymaking.[64] This is a debate that has resonance in India as well.

At a press conference in Ankara in 2009, the then US President, Barack Obama, was seated alongside the then Turkish President, Abdullah Gul. When specifically asked about the shared values between the two countries in their fight against terrorism, Obama emphasized a commitment to secularism. But his articulation would kick up a storm:

> I've said before that one of the great strengths of the United States is – although as I mentioned, we have a very large Christian population – we do not consider ourselves a Christian nation or a Jewish nation or a Muslim nation. We consider ourselves a nation of citizens who are bound by ideals and a set of values. I think Turkey was – modern Turkey was founded with a similar set of principles. And yet what we're seeing is in both countries that promise of a secular country that is respectful of religious freedom, respectful of rule of law, respectful of freedom, upholding these values and being willing to stand up for them in the international stage. If we are joined together in delivering that message, East and West . . . to the world, then I think that we can have an extraordinary impact.[65]

Those on the Christian Right saw this as a negation by Obama of America's foundational values that they believed were drawn from Christianity.[66] Perhaps Obama's own comments were a 'liberal' rebuttal to what his presidential rival John McCain had said in 2007 when asked if a Muslim candidate would make for a good President of the United States:[67] 'I just have to say in all candor that since this nation was founded primarily on Christian principles . . . personally, I prefer someone who I know who has a solid grounding in my faith. But that doesn't mean that I'm sure that someone who is Muslim would not make a good president. I would vote for a Muslim if he or she was the candidate best able to lead the country and defend our political values . . .' He went on to add, 'I would probably have to say yes, that the Constitution established the United States of America as a Christian nation. But I say that in the broadest sense. The lady that holds her lamp beside the golden door doesn't say, "I only welcome Christians." We welcome the poor, the tired, the huddled masses. But when they come here they know that they are in a nation founded on Christian principles.'[68]

However, Professor Hertzke drew our attention to the Treaty of Tripoli, signed in 1796[69] and brought into effect a year later, to illustrate why he believed that the conflation of religion with nation was problematic, all the more in an increasingly plural and diverse nation like the United States, where the free practice of religion was a cherished ideal.[70] The treaty was intended to prevent piracy against American ships trading in North Africa. As a gesture of friendship with the Muslim states in the region, Article 11 of the treaty read, 'As the government of the United States of America is not in any sense founded on the Christian Religion, as it has no character of enmity against the laws, religions or tranquility of Musselmen, and as the said States never entered into any war or act of hostility against any Mehomitan nation, it is declared by the parties that no pretext arising from religious opinions shall produce an interruption of the harmony existing between the two countries.'[71]

Like India, America constitutionally does not have a religious identity. But America is a Christian 'rashtra' to a significant proportion of its political class and their religious base, just as India is a Hindu Rashtra in a broader, cultural sense to many on the Hindu Right and their supporters. The secularists in both countries abhor this linking of the national character to values drawn from religious philosophy. And yet, John McCain, as a presidential hopeful, could openly propagate the idea of a Christian America, a 'Christian Rashtra', as part of his campaign.

Will the advocacy of a Hindu Rashtra ever become a poll issue for the BJP in a secular India?

Proud to Be Intolerantly Secular

It is quite clear that even America's Christian symbolism is not completely hidden by its appreciable commitment to secularism. It is almost impossible to imagine an Indian prime minister getting away with either taking oath of office on the Bhagavad Gita or openly attending a Dharam Sansad or endorsing the cause of their Hindu leadership. Indian liberals would be up in arms. Modi was, for instance, pilloried for attending the Ram Mandir temple consecration ceremony[72]—for 'betraying the ideals of secularism'.[73] Yet it is also true that these same secularists chafe at any talk of adopting the French model of secularism—*laïcité*.[74]

Secularism, as practised in France, is rebuked by the liberal torchbearers of multiculturalism and inter-faith accommodation in India as being intolerant.[75] Indeed, French secularism is incompatible with India's plural ethos. Manmohan Singh, Yogi Adityanath or Asaduddin Owaisi, if they were to ever join French politics, would be unable to enter the French National Assembly if they insisted on wearing their respective religious symbols.[76] Sikh students are not allowed to wear turbans to public schools[77] and Muslim women are not permitted to don the burqa in public spaces.[78] But French secularism is direct and unapologetic, and does not lend itself to the kind of appeasement that India's discriminatory secularism, as explained in earlier chapters, has become susceptible to.

Nothing captured this contrast more than the reaction of the two governments to perceived insults to Prophet Muhammad. On 16 October 2020, Samuel Paty, a secondary school teacher in Paris, was beheaded by an Islamist terrorist for showing a set of cartoons, published by *Charlie Hebdo* in 2012, that caricatured the Prophet.[79] On 26 May 2022, Nupur Sharma, a spokesperson of the Bharatiya Janata Party, on a television debate, made unpalatable references to the Prophet, claiming that these remarks were a response to the alleged insult of Lord Shiva by Muslim panellists.[80] Both countries have laws against hate speech. Yet each responded differently.

Emmanuel Macron, the French President, defended Paty's freedom of expression, posthumously honoured him with the *Légion d'honneur*—France's highest civilian award—and described Paty as the embodiment of the republic.[81] Macron talked about global Islam being in crisis and the necessity of 'liberating Islam in France from foreign influences'.[82] Macron was undeterred by the outrage his remarks evoked in Muslim countries.[83]

In India, the BJP suspended Nupur Sharma for hurting religious sentiments,[84] and the Central government labelled her a 'fringe element'.[85] Sharma was hounded; she received death threats[86] and was forced into hiding with police protection.[87] Two individuals who were said to have backed Sharma on social media—Kanhaiya Lal, a tailor from Udaipur in Rajasthan,[88] and

Umesh Kolhe, a pharmacist from Amravati in Maharashtra[89]—
were murdered by Islamist radicals. Violent protests were held by
Muslims against the 'defamation' of their Prophet;[90] open calls
to publicly hang Sharma were made, including by an elected
Muslim politician;[91] and even a Supreme Court judge, in his
oral observations, said she was 'single-handedly responsible' for
the turn of events, though the court eventually did provide her
protection from arrest.[92] Far from calling out Islamic countries
for interfering in India's internal matters, the Indian government
drew back in the wake of their criticism. Perhaps this was
motivated by a dependence on Middle Eastern oil; perhaps it was
to shield India's large diaspora in the Gulf from any reprisals; but
the Indian response was to backtrack under pressure.[93]

The Indian state has circumscribed speech and expression in
matters of religion.[94] Deliberately hurting religious sentiments
is already an offence—an inheritance of the colonial law, and
expected to be carried forward in the *Bharatiya Nyaya Sanhita*.[95]

French secularism, though, has been spared this
hypersensitivity, because of its roots in resistance to religious
authority. As Ahmed T. Kuru writes:

> Assertive secularism became the dominant ideology in France
> as a result of a long-lasting conflict between the anti-clerical
> secularists and conservative Catholics. These two forces
> regarded each other as enemies and perceived their struggle as
> a zero-sum game. They established either secular republics or
> Catholic monarchies through several back and forth regime
> changes from the French Revolution to the Fourth Republic.
> Throughout this conflict, the restoration of the ancient regime
> referring to the marriage of the monarchy and Catholic
> hegemony was a menace for the anticlerical republicans and an
> objective for the conservative Catholics.[96]

The 1905 French Law on the Separation of Church and State was an outcome of this arm-wrestle.[97]

Laïcité, however, also presents a problem for liberalism. For it is, according to Raphael Cohen-Almagor, a professor at the University of Hull in the United Kingdom, who spoke to us,[98] state-mandated coercion. He said. France's ban on the burqa (full veil) or the niqab (face veil) in public places—irrespective of what one may think of such an attire—works to discriminate against one religion. 'How does this stand in relation to the French motto, *Liberté, Egalité, Fraternité*? It doesn't,' Professor Cohen-Almagor says. 'If you prohibit such a thing, then, of course, there's no liberty, there's no equality. And where's the fraternity here? Other religions are able to get around such restrictions in public but not Muslims. Such an approach puts a higher stake on security and "public secularism", rejecting multiculturalism. There are other ways in which you can protect the republic than banning the burqa and niqab.'[99]

Assertive secularism of the French kind has few takers in India as well, but when secularists want to assert themselves here, their approach has been selective. There is outrage against Tulsidas's *Ramcharitmanas*, a sixteenth-century retelling of the Ramayana, over its 'insulting' references to the lower castes,[100] or against the 'patriarchy' of the *Manu Smriti*.[101] There is demand to delete 'derogatory' references in these texts. But there is rarely any criticism by the same set of people of any objectionable references in the holy texts of other faiths.

Interventionist secularism is welcomed when it is used to reform Hindu personal laws, but Muslim personal laws are accorded the luxury of evolving through consensus and internal deliberations. The uniform civil code, despite it being a constitutional prescription repeated multiple times by the courts, is viewed suspiciously[102] since the BJP is its sole political champion. State 'interference' in banning headscarves in Karnataka's public-school classrooms is frowned upon as anti-secular for regulating a religious practice[103] but direct state control over tens of thousands of Hindu places of worship is not.[104] The hypocrisy here is brazen.

Instead of acknowledging the inherent flaws embedded in India's secular superstructure that need to be addressed, its defenders choose to focus on the specter of a Hindu Rashtra that they believe hangs over their country, waiting to turn or convert her into a Hindu Pakistan.

Let us examine this trope a bit further.

Neither a Hindu Pakistan . . .

If India were ever to become a Hindu Pakistan, an outcome that Tharoor feared in his 2018 speech,[105] it would need to first mandate that only a Hindu could occupy the post of President. For Pakistan, when it officially became an Islamic republic in 1956, had added such a proviso, giving pride of place to Muslims and disqualifying non-Muslims on the grounds of their identity.[106] But this is unthinkable in a country like India, which has had five non-Hindu Presidents, including A.P.J. Abdul Kalam, who was backed by a so-called 'Hindu-nationalist' government led by the BJP in 2002.[107]

The next step towards a Hindu Pakistan would be to introduce a 'repugnancy' clause in the Constitution, like the Pakistanis did almost seven decades ago. It had then read: 'No law shall be enacted which is repugnant to the Injunctions of Islam as laid down in the Holy Quran and Sunnah, hereinafter referred to as Injunctions of Islam, and existing law shall be brought in conformity with such Injunctions.'[108] For this purpose, a Council of Islamic Ideology was formed to ensure consistency between Islamic and modern laws.[109]

The Hindu equivalent would have to be a 'Dharam Parishad' of sadhus, gurus and other Hindu religious experts who would have to examine every single law in our Constitution and penal code on the touchstone of conformity with Hindu sacred texts, of which there are numerous. This would be, to put it mildly, a cumbersome exercise—and not without disagreements, because there would first have to be consensus on which text, or collection of texts, to consider, with all their prescriptions, even contradictions, as a fundamental reference point. And, as established earlier, this is somewhat antithetical, given the flexibility of interpretation and tolerance of such scriptures within Hinduism.

But supposing, by a leap of faith, that such a consensus was to emerge over time, the next step towards being a 'Hindu Pakistan' would be to formalize Hinduism as a state religion, as the Pakistan Constitution of 1973 declared Pakistan an Islamic state.[110] Once this is done, a Hindu Pakistan would have to declare that not just the President but even the prime minister has to be a Hindu.[111]

After this, a Hindu Pakistan would have to start identifying 'heretics' within the Hindu fold and proceed to declare them as non-Hindus, just like the Pakistani parliament declared Ahmadiyyas as non-Muslims in 1974.[112] The situation grew worse for this community after the dictator Muhammad Zia-ul-Haq assumed power. As academic and scholar Madiha Afzal states in her book *Pakistan under Siege: Extremism, Society and the State*: 'It became illegal for Ahmadis to directly or indirectly pose as Muslim. They could no longer call themselves Muslims or their places of worship mosques; they could not recite the Azan, the

Muslim call for prayer; and could not refer to Mirza Ghulam Ahmad (their founder) with an Islamic honorific. They also could not "in any manner whatsoever outrage the religious feelings of Muslims.'"[113]

Attacks on Ahmadiyyas by agents of the state and hard-line Sunni fundamentalists continue.[114]

The othering of not just minorities but even sects within Islam to such an extreme is only possible in a country where all instruments of the state, not just the executive, collaborate in an exercise driven by collective prejudice. And can anyone be a heretic in Hinduism anyway? The twelfth-century philosopher Basavanna rejected the caste system as well as ritualistic worship.[115] His followers, the Lingayats, are a sect within the Hindu fold. While some among them have sought separation from Hinduism, demanding a separate status in the state of Karnataka,[116] advocates of Hindu unity have resisted this attempt.[117] So, far from excommunicating a sect from the Hindu faith for a divergence of views, a Hindu Republic of India would have to invest and engage with its own sects to prevent any divorce from Hinduism.

A Hindu Pakistan seems more than far-fetched.

Still, imagining the beast that a 'Hindu Rashtra' would have to become to mirror its neighbour underlines the vast distance it would have to travel to become a state predicated on prejudice. It would have to militate against its own proclamations of inclusivity and togetherness, overthrow its own constitutional structure, cast the dharmic as well as scriptural commitments to a diversity of views into the dustbin and render the judiciary impotent.

Such an exercise would have huge human and material costs—domestically and internationally.

So, if not a Hindu Pakistan, is a Hindu Bangladesh a more appropriate moniker for the dystopian state that our 'secular liberals' so fear?

. . . Nor a Hindu Bangladesh

On 11 August 1947, Dhirendranath Datta decided his family would stay back in Pakistan.[118] This was a decision taken at a moment of inspiration; he had heard Muhammad Ali Jinnah's pledge for a Pakistan, where distinctions between majorities and minorities would 'vanish' in a state centered on equality. Jinnah had said:

> We should begin to work in that spirit, and in the course of time all these singularities of the majority and minority communities, the Hindu community and the Muslim community . . . will vanish . . . You are free; you are free to go to your temples, you are free to go to your mosques or to any other place of worship in this state of Pakistan. You may belong to any religion or caste or creed – that has nothing to do with the business of the State . . . We are starting in the days where there is no discrimination, no distinction between one community and another, no discrimination between one caste or creed and another. We are starting with this fundamental principle, that we are all citizens, and equal citizens, of one state.[119]

But Datta, like millions of other Hindus and Sikhs who stayed behind in Pakistan, had been deceived. In Pakistan, Datta, as a lawmaker in the Constituent Assembly, would express outrage over the Bengali language being relegated to a subordinate status to Urdu, a sentiment his fellow Bengalis shared.[120] In 1964, Hindus were at the receiving end of a pogrom in East Pakistan following reports that a 'sacred lock' of Prophet Muhammad's hair had gone missing from the Hazratbal shrine in Srinagar.[121] Following the 1965 war, Hindus were again targeted with the introduction of the Enemy Property Act, whereby, in its implementation, 'the state identified Hindus with India' and proceeded to confiscate their assets.[122] This triggered an exodus of Hindus from East Pakistan to India.[123]

Datta raised his voice against these assaults on the Hindu identity by the Pakistani state. And the state would remember him for this. When Yahya Khan initiated Operation Searchlight on 25 March 1971[124]—the crackdown and genocide that would claim, as per some estimates, 3 million lives,[125] many of them Hindus, and set the stage for India's intervention following the biggest refugee crisis since Partition[126]—Datta was on the Pakistani hit list. He was picked up from Comilla, tortured in front of his family and shot. His body was 'thrown in a ditch', never to be found.[127] This was the man who had taken Jinnah at his word in 1947.

Manash Ghosh, who had covered the 1971 war for the *Statesman*, is also the author of *Bangladesh War: Reporting from Ground Zero*. In this book, he recounts how, during the height of the war that led to the creation of Bangladesh, Khondaker Mostaq Ahmad, senior leader of the Awami League and future President of his country, visited the camps of the Mukti Bahini.[128] This was the liberation force at the forefront of the movement for independence in East Pakistan, backed and trained by the Indian armed forces.

As Ahmad inspected the bunkers that the rebels were housed in, he noticed, much to his unease, symbols of Hinduism and Buddhism, along with those of Islam, adorning the walls of the small spaces they occupied.[129] He asked the soldiers to remove the non-Muslim symbols, advised them to chant slogans in praise of Allah,[130] notwithstanding the fact that there were many Hindus among their ranks as well. Even before the battle for a secular Bangladesh was won, Ahmad was sowing the seeds of Islamization in the liberation movement.

Though Bangladesh, under its founder Sheikh Mujibur Rahman, was originally committed to secularism,[131] the series of events that the likes of Ahmad had set in motion—including Mujib's assassination in 1975[132]—would ensure that secularism struggled for survival against the forces of Islamization. The word 'syncretic'[133] has often been used to describe Bengali nationalism in erstwhile East Pakistan, where the antipathy that the Punjabi-dominated West Pakistan felt for the Bengali was also to do with the Hindu influences that formed part of Bengali culture. Bangladesh may celebrate Durga Puja, revere Tagore, adopt 'Amar Sonar Bangla' as its national anthem, but not without ensuring that the country's identity was associated with Islam. This began with the amendment to the Bangladesh Constitution's Preamble in 1977, when the prayer 'Bismillah-ir-Rahman-ir-Rahim' (in the name of Allah, the most gracious and the most merciful) was inserted.[134] In 1988, Islam became the state religion.[135] In 2011, secularism was reintroduced as a 'fundamental principle of State Policy' in its constitution, but Islam remains the state religion[136] of Bangladesh.

Secularism in Bangladesh has not insulated Hindus living there from organized persecution. The successor to Pakistan's Enemy Property Act is the Vested Property Act,[137] which has continued to rob Hindus of their properties. Author and commentator Salil Tripathi spoke to Aroma Datta, granddaughter of Dhirendranath Datta, about the legal battle she has waged in Bangladesh to help Hindus recover these properties. In his book *The Colonel Who Would Not Repent: The Bangladesh War and Its Unquiet Legacy*, Tripathi has documented some of the findings of Datta's investigations. He writes: 'Their research found that in the 1990s through this Act, some two million acres of land, property and other resources were confiscated and that the 'total loss of assets by Hindus was estimated at Taka 1,505,204 million, which was about 88 percent of the prevailing GDP of Bangladesh. As many as 40 percent of Bangladeshi Hindu families were affected by that law. Hindus lost 1.64 million acres of land, which is nearly half of the total land Hindus had owned and nearly 5 percent of total land area of the country.'

The beneficiaries of this confiscation, Tripathi writes, were political parties: '44 per cent of the beneficiaries were from the Awami League, 31.7 per cent from the BNP, 5.8 per cent from the Jatiyo party, and 4.8 per cent from the Jamaat.'[138]

Tripathi also highlights another disturbing pattern from Datta's investigations: 'A rise in rape cases in villages where Hindus formed a sizeable minority, and the subsequent departure of Hindus from those villages, which enabled others to take over their property.'[139]

Abul Barkat, a professor of economics at Dhaka University, has been focusing on another serious problem: the vanishing Hindus of Bangladesh.[140] Hindus today form about 8.9 per cent of Bangladesh's population, but between 1964 and 2001, an estimated 8.1 million Hindus left Bangladesh (most of them moved to India).[141] According to Barkat's calculations, the Hindu outmigration per day between 1971 and 1981 was 521, between 1981 and 1991 it was 438, and between 1991 and 2011 it was 767. Not just incidents of violence, but the Vested Property Act and its consequences were among the reasons for this.[142]

Despite Bangladesh's attempts at adopting secularism, its subordination to Muslim interests has meant that non-Muslims, especially the Hindus, are constantly vulnerable to institutionalized discrimination.

The tragedy is that the approaches adopted by both Pakistan and Bangladesh are predicated on arrogance. The overwhelming numerical superiority of Muslims in these countries was reason enough for their leadership to ensure that their religion would occupy pride of place in the polity at the expense of others, instead of the state pursuing, if not secularism, tolerance to ensure equity and prosperity.

For this to happen in a Hindu Rashtra, the state would not only have to be prejudiced but embark upon a project to regularize discrimination on a mass scale—something that would require the complicity of all institutions of governance and justice in dismantling the system of checks and balances that our democracy offers. Not only does this militate against dharma, it's a self-defeating proposition that is a recipe for prolonged social and economic instability. A country poised to 'reclaim' its place in the world can ill afford undoing a hard-earned economic revival through any lurch towards an organized exclusion of minorities. The goings-on in India's own neighbourhood should serve as a deterrent.

10

'Yato Dharmastato Jayah'

The Judiciary's Bharat

'*Hindu Rashtra ki awadharna kahin galat nahi hai. Desh ki full bench ki Supreme Court ne iss par apna aadesh jaari kiya hai yeh. Hindutva koi mat, koi majhab ya upasana vidhi nahi hai. Balki,* it's a way of life [There is nothing wrong in the Hindu Rashtra concept. Hindutva does not mean religion or worship, but it's a way of life. A full bench of the Supreme Court has described it thus].'[1]

Yogi Adityanath, who said this in his first interview as chief minister of Uttar Pradesh in 2017, is not the first to latch on to the Supreme Court's broad endorsement allowing the terms 'Hinduism' and 'Hindutva' at the hustings,[2] despite the law disallowing direct appeals to one's religion for votes.[3] Nor will he be the last mainstream personality from the BJP or the Sangh Parivar to do so.

The Hindutva judgment will continue to trigger debate. One may ask that if Yogi Adityanath could use the Supreme Court's interpretation of Hindutva as a 'way of life of the Indian people', to make a case for a Hindu Rashtra, what is stopping the BJP's central leadership from doing the same in the near future?

Justice J.S. Verma's observations, in the *Prabhu vs Kunte* case in 1995[4], was celebrated by the BJP[5] for two reasons. First, they said the verdict affirmed that their idea of Hindu and Hindutva was inclusive and second, that they could now use it freely to appeal to a larger sense of Hindu solidarity.

It goes without saying that the Sangh Parivar's opponents, on the other hand, believe that the judgment upsets 'constitutional sanity'[6] in political discourse and jolts the secular applecart.

Is this so? While the judgment did divide opinion and turned out to be a watershed ruling in the Indian political context, what was Justice Verma's rationale for providing constitutional cover for the votaries of Hindutva?

Hindutva = 'A Way of Life of the Indian People'

In 1987, the Shiv Sena had firmly established itself in Maharashtra politics. Its leader, Bal Thackeray, was admired as much as he was feared. His 'son-of-the-soil' pitch would make Shiv Sena the party preferred by the Marathi voter in Mumbai. Through the potent mix of anti-Muslim venom in its speeches, the Shiv Sena, with its growing popularity, was mainstreaming what was once the language of the Hindu fringe.

As he strode towards the microphone in the Marathi middle-class suburb of Vile Parle to campaign for his party candidate Yeshwant Prabhu during an assembly by-election in November 1987, Thackeray knew his audience. 'All my Hindu brothers, sisters and mothers gathered here,' he began. 'Today, Dr Prabhu has been put up as candidate from Parle . . . But here one cannot do anything at any time about the snake in the form of Khalistan and Muslim . . . The entire country has been ruined and therefore

we took the stand of Hindutva and by taking the said stand we
will step in the Legislative Assembly.'[7]

Thackeray was just warming up. 'Who are [these] Muslims?
Who are these *lande* [a colloquial term used to derisively refer to
those who are circumcised]? Once Vasant Dada [Patil] had called
me when he was a chief minister. He told me that rest is okay. But
he asked me as to why I was calling them [Muslims] *lande*. But is
it correct if they call us *kafir* [non-believer]? Then we will certainly
call them *lande* . . . They should bear in mind that this country
is of Hindus, shall remain of Hindus . . . if Shiv Sena comes to
power and if the *morchas* [protests or rallies] come—first of all
[we] shall make them come. Everybody will have to take *diksha*
[initiation] of Hindu religion . . .'[8]

Thackeray would continue his invective during the campaign.
'It will do, if we do not get a vote from any Muslim. If anybody
from them is present here he should think for himself. I am not in
need of their votes. But I want your vote . . . You must send only
Dr Ramesh Prabhu of Shiv Sena, otherwise Hindus will be finished.
It will not take much take for Hindustan to become green.'[9]

Prabhu won the election by securing a vote share of 46.45
per cent and a victory margin of more than 10,000 votes.[10] His
opponent, Prabhakar Kunte of the Congress, challenged the
verdict on the grounds that the Sena's campaign speeches spewed
religious hate.[11]

The Bombay High Court held Thackeray and Prabhu guilty of
'corrupt practice' under the Representation of the People Act, and
Prabhu's election was overturned.[12] Prabhu challenged the verdict
in the Supreme Court, where the case was heard by a three-judge
bench led by Justice Verma.

The Supreme Court bench believed that Thackeray and
Prabhu had promoted ill will and enmity, and upheld the guilty
verdict of the Bombay High Court,[13] but it also chose to dwell

on the legality of using the phrases 'Hinduism' and 'Hindutva' on the stump.[14] The bench heard both sides but ultimately agreed with defence lawyer Ram Jethmalani that the phrases were more cultural in their connotation.[15]

Justice Verma began by citing precedent, referring to the first prominent instance of the Supreme Court attempting to define Hinduism. He began by citing Supreme Court justice P.B. Gajendragadkar, who, in 1966, had dismissed a petition by the Swaminarayan sect to be exempted from the purview of the Bombay Harijan Temple Entry Act, which had called on all Hindu temples to be thrown open to the scheduled castes.[16]

The sect claimed they were distinct from the Hindu community and that their temples could not be regarded as Hindu temples. It is in this case, known as 'Yagnapurushdasji vs Muldas', that the court first defined the Hindu religion as a 'way of life'.[17] To quote Justice Gajendragadkar: 'When we think of the Hindu religion, we find it difficult, if not impossible, to define [the] Hindu religion or even adequately describe it. Unlike other religions in the world, the Hindu religion does not claim any one God; it does not subscribe to any one dogma; it does not believe in any one philosophic concept; it does not follow any one set of religious rites . . . It does not appear to satisfy the narrow traditional features of any religion or creed. It may broadly be described as a way of life and nothing more.'[18]

None of the precedents cited by Justice Verma in 1995 dealt with defining Hindutva. So when Justice Verma began to look for a way to define Hindutva, he cited the material he had referenced.[19]

One such book was written by Maulana Wahiduddin Khan, an Islamic scholar. In his 1994 book, *Indian Muslims: The Need for a Private Outlook*, Khan equated Hindutva to a political concept. For him, Hindutva was a strategy that aimed at 'developing a uniform culture by obliterating the differences between all of the cultures coexisting in the country'.[20]

Despite citing Khan, Justice Verma went on to conclude that both Hinduism and Hindutva are at one in depicting the 'way of life of the Indian people'.[21] His judgment said:

> Thus, it cannot be doubted, particularly in view of the Constitution Bench decisions of this Court, that the words 'Hinduism' or 'Hindutva' are not necessarily to be understood and construed narrowly, confined only to the strict Hindu religious practices unrelated to the culture and ethos of the people of India, depicting the way of life of the Indian people. Unless the context of a speech indicates a contrary meaning or use, in the abstract these terms are indicative more of a way of life of the Indian people and are not confined merely to describe persons practising the Hindu religion as a faith.[22]
>
> Considering the terms 'Hinduism' or 'Hindutva' per se as depicting hostility, enmity or intolerance towards other religious faiths or professing communalism, proceeds to form an improper appreciation and perception of the true meaning of these expressions emerging from the detailed discussion in earlier authorities of this Court.[23]

Justice Verma delivered another judgment, on another Shiv Sena politician, Manohar Joshi, whose election had also been overturned after the Bombay High Court had ruled that his statement in 1990—that the 'first Hindu State will be established in Maharashtra'—was a violation of the Representative of the People Act.[24] Justice Verma reversed the Bombay High Court verdict, reasoning, 'In our opinion, a mere statement that the first Hindu State will be established in Maharashtra is by itself not an appeal for votes on the ground of his religion but the expression, at best, of such a hope. However despicable be such a statement, it cannot be said to amount to an appeal for votes on the ground of his religion.'[25]

Secular Outrage

Critics of these judgments point out that Justice Verma had erred in hyphenating Hinduism with Hindutva.[26] They accuse Justice Verma of ignoring Savarkar's views on Hindutva[27] and suggest that had he paid closer attention, he would have discovered that Savarkar had excluded Christians and Muslims from his definition of who is a Hindu.[28]

One of the most vocal critics was lawyer and political commentator A.G. Noorani, who, in an article in *Frontline*, decried Justice Verma for completely missing Maulana Wahiduddin Khan's point.[29] Noorani felt that Khan's phrase describing Hindutva as 'obliterating differences between all cultures' was really a criticism of Hindutva.[30] In other words, it was suggested that had Justice Verma not interpreted Khan's sentiments in the literal sense, he too would have thought twice before using the terms Hinduism (popularly understood as Hindu religion) and Hindutva (considered by some as a political ideology) interchangeably.[31]

Noorani lashed out at Justice Verma's verdict in the Manohar Joshi case too,[32] arguing that the judgment demolished the 'wall of separation between state and religion in a secular polity'.[33] It set a worrying precedent, he believed, because 'if this was law', any Sikh leader could demand a 'Khalsa state' in Punjab or a Muslim leader an 'Islamic state' in Kashmir.[34]

The Hindutva judgment by Justice Verma had also warned against the 'misuse' of terms such as Hinduism and Hindutva to 'promote communalism',[35] but that is precisely what the Opposition claims the BJP has been doing.[36] To the Congress and other parties on the Left, Hindutva is not a 'way of life' but a political project that thrives on othering minorities, particularly Muslims.[37]

Former prime minister Manmohan Singh said in 2018:

> This verdict had a decisive impact on the debate among political parties about the principles and practices of secularism in our Republic. The judgment ended up making our political discourse somewhat lopsided, and many believe there can be no doubt that the decision requires to be overruled . . . The judiciary as an institution needs never to lose sight of its primary duty to protect the secular spirit of the Constitution. This task has become much more demanding than before because the political disputes and electoral battles are increasingly getting laced with religious overtones, symbols, myths and prejudices.[38]

Two years before Manmohan Singh made this statement, petitions had been filed before the Supreme Court to undo the 'devastating consequences' of the 1995 judgment.[39] The petitioners, including the fierce Modi and BJP critic Teesta Setalvad, stated that Justice Verma's interpretation of Hindutva had led to 'demands of homogenisation and assimilation of minority communities and SC/ST (Scheduled Castes and Scheduled Tribes) in the Hindutva way of life', and that the judgment had caused Hindutva 'to become a mark of nationalism and citizenship'.[40]

The Supreme Court did not go into the matter.[41]

Hindutva vs Secularism and the Basic Structure Doctrine

Even though the bench in the 'Hindutva' judgment, on multiple occasions, underlined the need to protect secularism and 'promote the secular creed of the nation',[42] its critics have always seen it at odds with the 'basic structure doctrine'.[43]

Promulgated by the Supreme Court in the landmark 'Kesavananda Bharti vs State of Kerala' case in 1973, the basic structure entailed features of the Constitution that were 'inviolable' and that Parliament could not alter.[44] In a nutshell, these included fundamental rights, parliamentary democracy, unity and integrity of India, separation of powers, the 'secular' character of the Constitution and federalism.[45]

This fifty-year-old judgment preceded both Indira Gandhi's Emergency rule in 1975 and the insertion of the word 'secular' in the Preamble to the Indian Constitution a year later. The Supreme Court, in the Minerva Mills judgment in 1980,[46] backed the insertion and in 1994 went on to deliver a more pronounced endorsement of secularism's place in the basic structure in the S.R. Bommai judgment.[47] Justice A.M. Ahmadi wrote, 'Notwithstanding the fact that the words "Socialist" and "Secular" were added to the Preamble of the Constitution by the 42nd Amendment, the concept of secularism was very much embedded in our constitutional philosophy. The term "Secularism" has advisedly not been defined because it is a very elastic term not capable of precise definition and perhaps left best undefined. By this amendment, what was implicit was made explicit.'[48]

Justice Ahmadi's submission also summed up how the court itself could not arrive at a singular definition of secularism. Justices P.B. Sawant and Kuldip Singh, part of the nine-judge bench in the Bommai case, considered 'religious tolerance and equal treatment of all religious groups' as an 'essential part of secularism'. They added, 'The state's tolerance of religion or religions does not make it either a religious or a theocratic state. When the state allows citizens to practise or profess their religions, it does not either explicitly or implicitly allow them to introduce religion into non-religious or secular activities of the state.'[49]

Justice K. Ramaswamy saw secularism as 'essential for the unity of the country' and regarded the 'fundamentalism and communalization of politics as anti-secularism'.[50] Justice Jeevan Reddy thought it impossible that secularism could be removed from the Indian Constitution. 'We do not know how the Constitution can be amended so as to remove secularism from the basic structure of the Constitution. Nor do we know how the present Constitution can be replaced by another; it is enough for us to know that the Constitution does not provide for such a course that it does not provide for its own demise.'[51]

Many say the Kesavananda Bharti and S.R. Bommai cases, in their identification of secularism as part of the basic structure of the Constitution, are a shield against any future governments seeking to erase the word from the Constitution's Preamble.[52]

What these two judgments have stated has been reiterated in numerous verdicts, where matters of religion and state have been adjudicated. Indeed, these judgments have also been cited to school judges who are deemed to have crossed a line that separates secularism from a religious or a cultural identity.

In 2018, Justice S.R. Sen, of the Meghalaya High Court, after hearing a case involving the refusal of a domicile (residency) certificate to the petitioner, embarked on a retelling of the circumstances that had led to Partition and the treatment of religious minorities in Pakistan. He said, 'Pakistan declared themselves as an Islamic country and India, since it was divided on the basis of religion, should have also been declared as a Hindu country but it remained a secular country.'[53]

The response was swift: petitions were filed, and the Supreme Court issued a notice to the Meghalaya High Court,[54] which constituted a bench that would describe Justice Sen's judgment as 'legally flawed' and 'inconsistent with the constitutional principles, the observations made and directions passed therein are totally superfluous, therefore, is set aside in its entirety, as such shall be non-est'.[55]

Does a superfluous observation by the court in a judgment make it legally binding? Justice Verma's observations on Hindutva have been described by critics as 'irrelevant' and 'obiter',[56] but similar comments were made against the Supreme Court's resolute defence of the Places of Worship Act in the Ayodhya judgment[57] (discussed in an earlier chapter; the SC had hailed the Worship Act as an 'essential feature of our secular values'[58]). J. Sai Deepak, author and lawyer, argued in the *New Indian Express*, 'Given the non-application of the Places of Worship Act, and hence its irrelevance to the Ram Janmabhoomi case, the observations of the Constitution Bench must necessarily be treated as not legally binding.'[59] In a 2002 precedent, cited by Sai Deepak, the Supreme Court held, 'The statements of the Court on matters other than law like facts may have no binding force as the facts of the two cases may not be similar.'[60]

It does not take away from the fact that the Hindutva judgments of 1995 and the Ayodhya judgment's endorsement of the Places of Worship Act are quoted widely by supporters of these observations as a stamp of judicial approval to their points of view.[61] Now that the Places of Worship Act has been challenged in the Supreme Court on the grounds that it is unconstitutional,[62] how much importance the court places on its own endorsement of the act in the Ayodhya judgment remains to be seen.

As for the Hindutva judgments of 1995, Justice Verma may have endorsed Hindutva as a 'way of life of the Indian people', but there's nothing in that judgment that even remotely suggests that the term should be a basis for nationhood. Even as the bench gave relief to Manohar Joshi for his 'promise of a Hindu State in Maharashtra', it condemned these remarks as 'despicable'.[63] Moreover, as the reaction to the Meghalaya High Court judgment indicated, there is an aversion to ascribing a Hindu identity—whether religious or cultural—to our nationhood. So a judicial greenlight to a 'Hindu Rashtra' in the Preamble and the Constitution, for now, seems unlikely.

Is the 'Basic Structure' Unshakeable?

'In 1973 a wrong precedent began.'[64]

Vice President Jagdeep Dhankar added fuel to a proverbial fire that simmers underneath the public displays of cordiality between the judiciary and the government he represents.

'In 1973,' he went on, 'in the Kesavananda Bharati case, the Supreme Court gave the idea of basic structure saying Parliament can amend the Constitution but not its basic structure. With due respect to the judiciary, I cannot subscribe to this. Can parliament be allowed that its verdict will be subject to any authority . . . The executive has to follow laws and the judiciary cannot intervene in law-making. If any institution on any basis strikes down the law passed by Parliament then it will not be good for democracy and would be difficult to say are we a democratic nation.'[65]

Was Dhankar speaking as his own man, or was he conveying to the public the sentiments of the government he is a part of? Interestingly, Indira Gandhi's opposition to the basic structure doctrine formed the precursor to the autocratic rule she birthed with the Emergency.[66] Over the years, the basic structure doctrine has emerged as one of the key pillars of bipartisan consensus in a divided polity,[67] as well as a guarantor of protection of the rights of the people against any parliamentary impulse that might threaten them. Was Dhankar prescribing a change to the status quo?

Dhankar's comments were made in the context of the National Judicial Appointments Commission (NJAC), another reform that had bipartisan support in principle,[68] which sought to undo the opaque collegium system of judges appointing judges and replace it with a framework where the government would have a significant say.[69] But after it was passed by Parliament, the NJAC was struck down by the Supreme Court in 2015 as 'unconstitutional'.[70] It is likely to be the subject of more skirmishes between the judiciary and the government for some time to come. As of December 2022, the NDA had 'no proposal' to reintroduce the NJAC,[71] but should there be a rethink in the future, it may have implications for the composition of the judiciary.

But what if a system does emerge where the government has a greater say in the appointment of judges? And what if the judges of the future have sympathies for a Hindu Rashtra? What if a future Supreme Court feels 'secularism' is a misfit in our Constitution and its Preamble, and that the word 'plural' better captures our ethos? What if the court feels there is a need to review the basic structure doctrine as it stands today? Or if a Hindu Rashtra does become an election issue championed by a political party that goes on to win a massive mandate, can the judiciary stand in the way of the 'will of the people'? These are all valid questions, within the realm of possibility.

A Dharmic Rashtra

If not a Hindu Rashtra, will the judiciary back a Dharmic Rashtra?

One of the most elaborate expositions on dharma by the Supreme Court can be read in the 'Shri Narayana Deekshitulu vs State of Andhra Pradesh' judgment in 1996, pertaining to the constitutionality of certain sections of the Andhra Pradesh Charitable and Hindu Religious Institutions and Endowments

Act.[72] The bench, led by Justice K. Ramaswamy, who in the Bommai judgment had upheld secularism as part of the basic structure of the Constitution, delinked dharma from conventional religion.[73] The court said:

> The word 'Dharma' or 'Hindu Dharma' denotes upholding, supporting, nourishing that which upholds, nourishes or supports the stability of the society, maintaining social order and general well-being and progress of mankind; whatever conduces to the fulfillment of these objects is Dharma, it is Hindu Dharma and ultimately 'Sarva Dharma Sambhava'.
>
> In contra distinction, Dharma is that which approves oneself or good consciousness or springs from due deliberation for one's own happiness and also for welfare of all beings free from fear, desire, disease, cherishing good feelings and sense of brotherhood, unity and friendship for integration of Bharat. This is the core religion which the Constitution accords protection.[74]

It added, 'When Dharma is used in the context of duties of the individual and powers of the King (the State), it means constitutional law [Rajadharma]. Likewise when it is said that Dharmarajya is necessary for the peace and prosperity of the people and for establishing an egalitarian society, the word Dharma in the context of the word Rajya only means law, and Dharmarajya means Rule of Law and not rule of religion or a theocratic State.'[75]

The court cited the example of Dharmaraja Yudhishthira from the Mahabharata. The Pandava king explains his vision for a just society thus: '*Na Twaham Kamaye Rajyam Na Swargam Na Punarbhawam Kamye Dukh Taptanam Praninam Artnashnam* [I seek no kingdoms nor heavenly pleasure nor personal salvation, since to relieve humanity from its manifold pains and distresses is the supreme objective of mankind].'[76]

The court added: 'It is in this context that the phrase *Dharm Vijayah* (Victory of Dharma) could be understood, as employed by the Mauryan Emperor, Ashoka, in his rock edict at Kalsi which proclaimed his achievement in terms of moral and ethical imperatives of Dharma, and exemplified the ancient dictum *Yato Dharmastato Jayah* (where there is Law, there is Victory).'[77] This dictum also happens to be the precept of the Supreme Court engraved under its logo, the Dharma Chakra.[78]

Dharma, the Supreme Court said—while once again citing Justice Gajendragadkar—could even be invoked by the state to 'interfere in the interests of public good'[79] if certain religious practices 'impinged upon socioeconomic problems'.[80] This was the Supreme Court invoking dharma to make a case for an interventionist secularism.

The state and the courts have intervened directly in matters of religion. Throwing open temples to all classes and sections of Hindus, reforming Hindu laws, making a case for a uniform civil code, abolishing triple talaq in one sitting—all this is in a sense consistent with this understanding of dharma that does not hold back from interfering with religion to uphold a public good. The top court has also backed laws punishing illegal or induced conversions, ruling that the 'right to convert another person to one's own religion' is not a fundamental right.[81] Clearly, the court is also alive to the problem of unregulated proselytization and its socio-economic consequences.

The concept of dharma in India is a derivative of Hindu philosophy. Secularism, on the other hand, is a derivative of the conflict between the 'two swords' of human society in Europe[82]— the church, which regulated spiritual affairs, and the state, which was in charge of the temporal.

India's 'secularism', given its place in the Constitution, is worn as a badge of pride, never mind the word's Christian origins.

Indeed, there's nothing wrong about importing a Western concept and giving it an Indian flavour. But the concept of dharma is uniquely Indian, native to this land and, it could be argued, is as deserving of a constitutional expression as secularism, if not more.

So, if not a Hindu Rashtra, should the Supreme Court—given its own reverence for dharma—back a Dharmic Rashtra?

Conclusion

A few months into his first term in office, Prime Minister Modi, became the first Indian prime minister to visit Australia in twenty-eight years.[1] At a rally in Sydney attended by 20,000 people, mostly non-resident Indians, Modi spelt out his ambition for India. He wanted 'Mother India' to become a 'Vishwa Guru'. A teacher of the world.[2]

The desire to see India help shape a burgeoning humanity and strive towards Vishwa Guru status had been expressed by the towering spiritual master Swami Vivekananda. In his 1901 essay titled 'My Master', Vivekananda wrote that India should aspire to be a teacher to mankind:

> If you wish to be a true reformer, three things are necessary. The first is to feel. Do you really feel for your brothers? . . . Are you full of that idea of sympathy? . . . You must think next if you have found any remedy. The old ideas may be all superstition, but in and around these masses of superstition are nuggets of gold and truth. Have you discovered means by which to keep that gold alone, without any of the dross? If you have done

that . . . one more thing is necessary. What is your motive? Are
you sure that you are not actuated by greed of gold, by thirst
for fame or power? . . . Then you are a real reformer, you are a
teacher, a Master, a blessing to mankind.[3]

It is natural for nations to nurse grand ambitions. The United
States has long laid claim to global-superpower status, as had
many colonizing nations before it. The USA says it qualifies not
only because of its military might but also because it sees itself as
the custodian of Western civilization.[4]

Similarly, many have argued that India equally qualifies to
be the custodian of an ethical, uniquely Asian outlook. Vinay
Sahasrabuddhe says India is driven by a 'unique worldview'. It
is a 'spiritual democracy', founded on the concept of *ekam sat,
vipra bahuda vadanti* (the truth is one, but wise men describe
the same differently).[5] Readers will note that in prior chapters
this book has gone to great lengths to explain the roots of an
ancient pluralism that marks India out. And through the rough
and tumble of history, it has emerged today as the world's largest
democracy. India's liberal democratic credentials are its ticket to
Vishwa Guru status.

In his book *The India Way: Strategies for an Uncertain World*,
minister of external affairs S. Jaishankar states: 'What perhaps
distinguishes us from other traditions of statecraft is our approach
to governance and diplomacy. India's history shows that it does not
follow a "winner takes all" approach to contestations. Nor is there a
confident belief that the end justifies the means . . . That the reality
may not have always lived up to such a standard does not invalidate
these concepts. There is continuous reflection on both the goals and
the processes, sometimes to the point of self-doubt.'[6]

Jaishankar identifies India's collective ability to reflect as one
of its strongest assets. Let us not forget that the ability to ponder,

argue and shape policies and approaches can only exist in societies that are essentially open and tolerant.

He traces this unique trait to, among other sources, the influence of the Mahabharata. Analysing the epic, Jaishankar points to the Pandavas, who, in his view, are 'an excellent example of integration' achieved out of a willingness to work together: 'Born of different mothers and each with a complex paternal origin, they function very well as a team overcoming internal tensions. They have complementary skill sets that make the combination particularly effective. As a model, they should inspire greater deliberation on the difficulties of working together efficiently.'[7]

In short, India's evolution into a democracy is not merely because it adopted liberalism from the West but because its own long established philosophical and intellectual traditions exalted consensus, tolerance, openness and knowledge. It would only have been a matter of time before India had its own renaissance.

Jaishankar believes that this carefully nurtured self-image of India as an open society is by itself a powerful motivating factor. And certainly, it is critical in taking India towards realizing its stated ambition of emerging as a Vishwa Guru, which will allow it to submit an alternative model of rules-based governance to the world.

A start was made by Prime Minister Modi when he stated in December 2022: 'India's G20 presidency will work to promote this universal sense of oneness. Hence, India's theme—"One Earth, One Family, One Future".'[8]

The world today is beset with uncertainties. It is witnessing greater disruptions—both economic and ecological—deepening nationalisms and is seeing liberalism suffer a crisis of confidence. If India is to have its moment, it must be a source of stability—an insurance against volatility.

Jaishankar notes, 'As a civilisational power coming back on the global stage, it would be another powerful example of a return of history.'[9]

But as we decolonize our minds and celebrate our rich history and diverse traditions, we must eschew the temptation of becoming prisoners of our history, of pride for our legacy. Hubris, after all, is the blinding fatal flaw which has consumed many—nations and individuals alike.

In our immediate neighbourhood, Pakistan is a classic example of a nation beholden to this view and obsessed with avenging the past. In fact, unlike India, which evolved from a desire to embrace a future enriched by diversity and freedom, Pakistan was built to be an island of exclusivity.

Pakistan's inwardness, unsurprisingly, has caused it to embrace an insular ethnic nationalism. To paraphrase another revanchist, Germany's first chancellor, Otto von Bismarck, Pakistan thinks from its blood.[10] As did Germany under Adolph Hitler. And today, for instance, look where this kind of pride and parochialism has got Russia under President Vladimir Putin and Han-majority China under Xi Jinping.

India has been lucky to escape the fate of some of the countries cited above, despite the efforts of its leadership at different times.

Punjab was consumed by the hellfire of religious parochialism for nearly two decades at the end of the last century. The fires were lit by politicians who used cynical, identity-based political plays to whip up sentiment in their favour.

Sure, some politicians prospered momentarily, but the state itself was beggared. For nearly twenty years, Punjab's economy was in the pits. According to one study, Punjab's per capita income in 1979–80, at the onset of the insurgency, was twice that of the all-India average. By 1998–99, however, this figure had dropped to only 44.30 per cent higher than the all-India average.[11]

In terms of the human cost, ordinary Sikhs paid the highest price. The legendary super cop K.P.S. Gill, widely credited with breaking the backbone of the Khalistan movement in the late '80s and early '90s, noted that of the 11,694 people killed in Punjab by terrorists between 1981 and 1993, over 61 per cent were Sikhs.[12]

Punjab's return to normality has been a long, arduous journey, but separatism continues to rear its ugly head. Most recently, Amritpal Singh, a Dubai-returned Khalistan advocate and chief of Waris Punjab De (Heirs of Punjab), raised the banner of Sikh separatism.[13] In a short period of time his zealotry allowed him to acquire support, sparking concerns that Punjab could very easily once again descend into the quagmire of the 1980s. Fortunately, perhaps having learnt their lessons from the past, Punjabi politicians very quickly closed ranks behind the Indian state to shut out Amritpal Singh and his legionnaires.

India's North-east has been benighted by the curse of ethnic conflict too, as was most recently seen in Manipur.[14] Scores of mutinies have erupted, and violence has spread as one group put the other to the sword. Some of these groups have also directed their gaze at the Indian state in a violent campaign of secession. As in Punjab, restoring normality in the North-east is an ongoing process, delayed by politicians who have not been able to resist the temptation of playing the identity card.

This, of course, has come at a cost. The states in the North-east have missed out on the benefits of the 1991 liberalization of the Indian economy. According to one estimate, the combined share of the gross state domestic product of the eight north-eastern states in India's economy fell from 3.07 per cent in 1990–91 to 2.99 per cent in 2000–01 and 2.61 per cent in 2010–11.[15] In 2019–20, the figure (excluding Sikkim) stood at a marginally higher 2.8 per cent.[16]

Accommodation holds the key to the troubles in Kashmir too. But the Islamist extremists there refuse to resile from their maximalist world view. They simply will not accept the legitimacy of India's Constitution. Of late, their irridentism has taken on a particularly insidious edge. Targeted attacks on Hindu minorities in the Valley, with a view to driving them out of the state, threaten to undermine the green shoots of normality in post-Article 370 Kashmir.[17]

Of course, not all identity-based movements are born of a yearning for separateness. Some movements, articulated in the language of social justice, need to be encouraged. But history has taught us that even with regard to linguistic or caste-based movements, the line between activism and chauvinism is easily blurred.

India's leadership, mentored by time and schooled by experience—seventy-six years—is by now surely aware of the pitfalls of flirting with divisive populism. It must also be aware that, more than anyone else, Indians themselves have disincentivized demagoguery by voting it out of office.

Indira Gandhi was punished for imposing the Emergency that shook the edifice of democratic institutionalism in the 1970s. In the '90s, the BJP's shrill Hindutva campaign was severely dented by voters who refused to reward its saffron supremacism, forcing a course correction. The BJP-led NDA has won back-to-back mandates now, arguably because the public has largely bought into Modi's credo of *sabka saath, sabka vikas, sabka vishwas* and *sabka prayas* (unity and development for all).

The BJP today occupies the pole position in Indian politics and will likely remain there for some time to come, primarily because of its message that has allowed it to extend its appeal beyond upper-caste Hindus. As per a survey by the Centre for the Study of Developing Societies (CSDS), in the 2019 Lok Sabha election the

BJP was the preferred choice for several groups, including upper castes, almost 44 per cent of OBCs, 34 per cent of Hindu Dalits and 44 per cent of Hindu Adivasis, with the numbers in each category representing a significant jump from 2014.[18] Its appeal is growing even in Christian-majority Meghalaya and Nagaland in the North-east, where it has pragmatically stayed clear of using Hindutva to mobilize support.[19]

Today, with Opposition parties crumbling under the weight of the BJP's connect with the people and their own ideological contradictions, the saffron party leadership has little reason to stray from its philosophy of 'integral humanism'.[20]

Fortunately, the BJP's chiefs are, at least for now, walking the talk. Hotheads from within the BJP fold, who coarsened the narrative, have either been shunted out of the party or hauled up.[21] Taking no chances, the BJP refuses to assign spokespeople for primetime TV debates that may be dealing with sensitive communal issues.[22]

In the articles published in its own party mouthpiece, *Kamal Sandesh*, the BJP barely makes references to the words 'Hindu' or 'Mandir'.[23] In fact, according to the Narad Index, formulated by academics Nalin Mehta and Rishabh Srivastava, 'Modi', 'the BJP', 'development' and 'infrastructure' are the four most commonly referred to topics per 100 words across *Kamal Sandhesh*. The same index also reveals that in communiques to external audiences, the word 'Congress' appears most per 100 words—astonishingly, even more than the references to Modi or the BJP itself.[24]

Though Muslims remain a captive vote bank of the Opposition nationally, with just 8 per cent voting for the BJP in 2014 and 2019, according to a survey,[25] the BJP has not given up on them. It may not field Muslim candidates in the numbers that its opponents do, but at its national executive meeting in 2022, the BJP resolved to reach out actively to Pasmanda Muslims.[26]

They comprise more than 80 per cent of the Muslim population in India and trace their background to Hindus from the lower castes who had converted to Islam but continued to be denied equal opportunities for growth by the more privileged in their adopted community. The Modi government has also sought to emphasize that a large proportion of the beneficiaries (*labharthis*, as the BJP likes to call them)—more than a third—of some of its flagship welfare initiatives are 'minorities'.[27]

All this means that the party has not only seen a spurt in its vote share but also a huge jump in its membership. Today, the BJP's membership is growing impressively, even beyond the Hindi heartland, powered by the efforts of its cadres and two highly digitized and organized yearlong enrolment campaigns unleashed in November 2014 and July 2019.[28]

However, even though the BJP has adopted a mellower public stance, many observers of politics are still reluctant to fully accept that the party has entirely changed its spots.[29]

Some claim that the BJP has cleverly outsourced to its affiliates the task of deploying communal messaging as a tool to consolidate its Hindu base.[30] There might indeed be some truth to this. As a prominent party insider told us, 'The party won't be speaking on issues like love jihad, *gau hatya* (cow killing), and neither will its cadre be on the streets protesting. The Bajrang Dal is there for that.'[31]

In early 2023, on the back of the lynching of Muslims on the suspicion of illegally transporting cattle, the spotlight fell on alleged Bajrang Dal-linked vigilantes reported to have had connections with the state's law-and-order machinery in Haryana.[32] This tribe of self-styled *gau rakshaks*, who are often given a long rope, have already done much to undermine the PM's 'sabka saath' message. And reports indicate that saffron auxiliary groups like the Bajrang Dal are attracting members in record numbers.[33] This is problematic, as many Bajrang Dal members are not necessarily drawn from the relatively more apolitical ranks of the RSS.

Outfits like the Bajrang Dal may be useful now, but they threaten to unravel the BJP's carefully cultivated strategy of growing into a big-tent party with a pan-India appeal, grounded in the best that Hindu ethos has to offer.

In other instances, chilling hate speeches at a number of recent Dharam Sansads[34] have shown that the Sangh Parivar is finding it difficult to leash radicalized Hindus, who have been exposed to the less reasonable ideas of the Hindu Right.

Recently, however, there have been signs that the BJP is keen to curb this muscle-flexing. In early 2023, the Indian film industry breathed a sigh of relief when Prime Minister Modi asked his party workers to refrain from targeting actors and film-makers.[35] Modi was forced to speak up when many Bollywood notables appealed to first the prime minister and then UP chief minister, Yogi Adityanath, as saffron auxiliaries had begun to trend 'boycott Bollywood' hashtags, offended by what they chose to define as 'anti-Hindu' or 'pro-Muslim' content in films.[36]

Why we don't see more such immediate interventions remains a mystery. It is not as if reining in this base will cause the BJP to lose electoral support. For the BJP is in no danger of losing the Hindu voter to the Opposition. Many Hindus are suspicious of the motives of Opposition political parties, which, perhaps chastened by electoral humiliations, have begun to peddle a *chunavi* (opportunistic) Hindutva.[37]

Beyond politics, on the legal front, the courts too have not stood in the way of the BJP on its core objectives.

The Supreme Court ruled categorically in favour of Hindus in the title suit on Ram Janmabhoomi, has not blocked, or stayed, the government's move to nullify Article 370 and has, in fact, on multiple occasions criticized Parliament for not bringing in a uniform civil code (UCC).[38] The court has also agreed that adopting a UCC would be in consonance with the 'secular and democratic' values of our republic.

Moreover, even before the BJP came into being in 1980, the Supreme Court had upheld the validity of the 'anti-conversion' laws (officially called Freedom of Religion Act).[39] In 'Rev. Stanislaus vs State of Madhya Pradesh' in 1977, the apex court had ruled that the fundamental right to practise and propagate religion under Article 25 did not entail a fundamental right to convert.[40]

At least eight states in India, over time, have adopted legislation to regulate conversions. Some of their stringent provisions have been challenged, and stayed by the courts, but the laws themselves have survived judicial scrutiny.[41]

Even on the issue of state legislations banning cow slaughter, the court has deferred to Hindu sentiments.[42] As a result, today, at least sixteen states in India have anti-cow-slaughter laws.[43]

In 2022, the BJP government in Karnataka successfully defended its ban on the wearing of hijab in classrooms of government schools before the Karnataka High Court.[44] When the state government's order was challenged in the high court the state's counsel submitted that 'secularism is held to be the basic feature of the Constitution. Hence, while discharging the constitutional obligation of imparting education, the State must prescribe a secular/uniform dress for students.'[45] The petitioners appealed in the Supreme Court, which delivered a split verdict. As of today, while a Congress government has taken over in Karnataka, the restriction has not yet been formally overturned.[46]

Similarly, in 2022, the Gauhati High Court upheld the BJP-led Assam government's decision to convert state-funded madrasas and Sanskrit 'tolls'[47] imparting religious education into regular schools. The court agreed that religious instruction in an institution completely run on state funds was a violation of secularism.[48]

The courts have also backed the NDA's stance against *talaaq-e-biddat* or triple talaq (divorce) in one sitting.[49] The apex court ultimately agreed with the NDA's arguments that the practice undermined secularism.[50] The NDA asked the nation's top court to determine 'whether under a secular Constitution, Muslim women could be discriminated against, merely by virtue of their religious identity', and 'whether in a secular democracy, religion can be a reason to deny equal status and dignity to Muslim women'.[51]

It is apparent that the mission to evolve India into a 'Vishwa Guru' is there only for the party in power, currently the BJP, to squander. But it is also true that while the state must certainly do most of the heavy lifting, of creating an enabling environment, the people themselves must also do their bit to negotiate a lasting peace. Christianity, Islam and other minority denominations are safe, as is now visible, in a Hindu-majority India because of its dharma that has naturally stopped fanaticism from spreading beyond the fringes.

Constitutionalism is best served when all contenders submit to it willingly. As RSS chief Mohan Bhagwat said, those who are beyond the Hindu pale (and even those within) must 'abandon their boisterous rhetoric of supremacy'.[52]

A realistic starting point could begin with an agreement on the need for a uniform civil code. But as we have mentioned, so far members of the All India Muslim Personal Law Board—the self-proclaimed custodians of Muslim personal law—have sought to place Islamic customs beyond constitutional reach.[53] This exceptionalism is an obstacle to reform. Secularism is not a one-way street. If the UCC is to become the secular article of faith it is meant to be, then non-Hindus must be willing to effect a collective compromise to subject their personal codes to the will of the Constitution. Equally, the champions of a common civil code must steer clear of creating exceptions—for instance, leaving out tribals—and stay true to the idea of one set of civil laws for all Indians.

If Hindus have an obligation to address non-Hindu anxieties about 'majoritarian imposition', the non-Hindus are equally obligated to appreciate Hindu anxieties about conversion, whether forced or induced or through marriage.

Perhaps the time has come for non-Hindu faith leaders in India to publicly discourage conversions. In the corporate world, for instance, many rival corporations sometimes sign non-poaching agreements.[54] Perhaps a similar pact between faith leaders could go a long way in restoring confidence.

Also, the use of slurs like 'kafir', 'jihadi', 'lande', 'infidel' should invite stringent penal action. There is precedent. Hurling caste-based derogatory barbs already invites the prospect of severe punishment under the law.[55] In fact, the Supreme Court has gone a step further by chiming in and ordering states to suo moto prosecute hate speech and not wait for complaints to be registered.[56]

A third area where a common understanding should be evolved has to do with the imposition of an arbitrary statute of limitations upon demands arising from Hindu groups about being allowed to reclaim their places of worship. As of now, such demands fall foul of the Places of Worship Act, 1991.[57] This act, which primarily hurts Hindu interests, curbs any move to alter the status quo at places of worship that had been destroyed or occupied by another community prior to 1947. If not entirely junking the law altogether, then Muslims and other minorities must engage with Hindus to evolve a consensus over which places of worship should be exempted from the purview of the Places of Worship Act, 1991.

If some are committed to the perpetual expansion of an authority they deem superior to their country's Constitution, it will be difficult to sustain long spells of communal amity in India. This philosophy overrides earlier systems that defined humans by their birthright—an identity, by definition, we did not choose. Unfortunately, as we have seen, some of us have done more honour to this philosophy than to ourselves. When taken to the extreme, we have ended up achieving the precise opposite of the outcome we were hoping for. Today, in the name of protecting individual rights, the liberalism we have adopted has eroded community rights—especially Hindu rights. Indeed, some community rights have been privileged over others.

The idea of Bharat cannot be reduced to this deviation induced by the 'left-liberal' elite. Going forward, we will have to find a way of striking a better balance, of combining the spirit of liberty with our civilizational spirit—Sanatana Dharma.

India awaits a new 'tryst with destiny', when a second republic 'steps out from the old to the new'.

Notes

Introduction

1. Among those who did talk of such a possibility was M.V. Govindan of the CPI(M). See his interview with Rediff. com, 27 April 2023, https://www.rediff.com/news/ interview/m-v-govindan-idea-of-india-will-be-destroyed-in-2025/20230427.htm

2. Pratap Bhanu Mehta, 'The Delhi Darkness: Our Rulers Want an India That Thrives on Cruelty, Fear, Division, Violence', *Indian Express*, 29 February 2020, https://indianexpress. com/article/opinion/columns/delhi-violence-riots-police-caa-npr-6288323/

3. 'Indian Opposition Parties form "INDIA" Alliance', Reuters, 18 July 2023, https://www.reuters.com/world/india/indian-opposition-parties-form-alliance-called-india-2024-elections-2023-07-18/

4. Text of INDIA Joint Statement, https://www.inc.in/congress-sandesh/national/samuhik-sankalp-of-26-political-parties-belonging-to-i-n-d-i-a

5. Pratap Bhanu Mehta, interview with The Wire, 17 December 2021, https://thewire.in/rights/full-text-damage-to-indian-democracy-under-modi-is-lasting-pratap-bhanu-mehta

'"Attack on a Dream": Muslims In Fear As Indian Democracy Turns 75', Al Jazeera, 15 August 2022, https://www.aljazeera. com/news/2022/8/15/attack-on-a-dream-muslims-in-fear-as-india-democracy-turns-75

'On His Day Out in City, Tharoor Does Not Hold Back the Punches', *The Hindu*, 19 April 2018, https://www.thehindu. com/news/cities/mumbai/on-his-day-out-in-city-tharoor-does-not-hold-back-the-punches/article23591204.ece

6.   'BJP Not Winning a Single Seat in Kerala as Voters Are Educated, and Not "Andh Bhakt": Udit Raj', ANI, 20 May 2019, https://www.aninews.in/news/national/politics/bjp-not-winning-single-seat-in-kerala-as-voters-are-educated-and-not-andh-bhakt-udit-raj20190520184959/

Even Shashi Tharoor, a Congress MP, claimed he was accused of being a closet 'Sanghi' for merely expressing his condolences over the passing of an RSS veteran.

See Shashi Tharooor, 'Am I a Closet Sanghi for Mourning Demise of an RSS Man? Something's Terribly Wrong', The Print, 12 February 2020, https://theprint.in/opinion/ am-i-a-closet-sanghi-for-mourning-demise-of-an-rss-man-somethings-terribly-wrong-tharoor/363195/

7.   'Surjewala Sparks Row With "Demon" Jibe at BJP Supporters in Haryana, Khattar & Others Hit Back', The Print, 14 August 2023, https://theprint.in/politics/surjewala-sparks-row-with-demon-jibe-at-bjp-supporters-in-haryana-khattar-others-hit-back/1714129/

8.   Swati Goel Sharma, 'Meet Ajay Singh, The "Hindu Student Leader" at Aligarh Muslim University', *Swarajya*, 22 February 2019, https://swarajyamag.com/politics/meet-ajay-singh-the-hindu-student-leader-at-aligarh-muslim-university

Here's a twitter reference by Rachit Seth, who claims to have coined the term 'Musanghi' along with others, in response to a post critical of Congress leader Rahul Gandhi: https://twitter. com/rachitseth/status/1420594444277977090

9.   'Musanghi' has also been used to refer to the Muslim fringe. Dhruv Rathee: 'That's a lot of MuSanghis with their regressive mindsets, telling Irfan Pathan what his wife should and should

not do . . .', https://m.facebook.com/DhruvRatheePage/ photos/that's-a-lot-of-musanghis/1890653814532873/ Rohini Singh: 'And yes, regarding the term Musanghi – which means Muslim Sanghi – I think it's a pretty accurate description of some people on Twitter. Musanghis have the same attitude as sanghis when their arguments or facts are challenged', https://twitter.com/rohini_sgh/ status/1169232176480604173?lang=en

10. A phrase often used by American Presidents to refer to the USA. 'Full text of Obama Speech in Parliament', *India Today*, November 8, 2010, https://www.indiatoday.in/ obama-visit/latest-updates/story/full-text-of-obama-speech-in-parliament-85230-2010-11-07

11. *Time*, 10 September 2016, https://time.com/4486502/hillary-clinton-basket-of-deplorables-transcript/

12. Ibid.

13. 'Trump Releases New Ad Hitting Clinton for "Deplorables" Remark', Politico, 12 September 2016, https://www. politico.com/story/2016/09/clinton-deplorables-trump-ad-228018

14. 'Hillary Clinton Admits Her "Most Important" Blunder That Swayed the 2016 Presidential Election', ABC News, 10 September 2017, https://abcnews.go.com/Politics/hillary-clinton-admits-important-blunder-swayed-2016-presidential/ story?id=49740865

15. Ibid.

16. Congress Sandesh, Bharat Jodo Yatra, 23 August 2022, https:// www.inc.in/congress-sandesh/report/bharat-jodo-yatra

17. 'Bharat Jodo Yatra against Fear, Hatred Being Spread', PTI, 8 January 2023, https://timesofindia.indiatimes.com/india/ bharat-jodo-yatra-against-fear-hatred-being-spread-rahul-gandhi/articleshow/96830118.cms
'Bharat Jodo Yatra Target: "Hate Project of RSS"', *Telegraph*, 1 November 2022, https://www.telegraphindia.com/india/ bharat-jodo-yatra-target-hate-project-of-rss/cid/1895381
'Appeal to All Indians to Maintain Brotherhood: Rahul Gandhi', *Times of India*, 2 August 2023, https://timesofindia.indiatimes.

com/india/appeal-to-all-indians-maintain-brotherhood-rahul-gandhi/articleshow/102362946.cms?from=mdr

'"India is Not in A Good Place, BJP Has Spread Kerosene All over the Country": Rahul Gandhi At London Event', ABP News, 21 May 2022, https://news.abplive.com/news/india/rahul-gandhi-on-bjp-s-polarisation-at-london-event-india-not-in-a-good-place-bjp-has-spread-kerosene-all-over-the-country-1532866

18. 'Undertook Yatra Not for Self or Congress but for People: Rahul Gandhi', PTI, 31 January 2023, https://www.outlookindia.com/national/undertook-yatra-not-for-self-or-congress-but-for-people-rahul-gandhi-news-258150

19. Rahul Gandhi vs Purnesh Ishwarbhai Modi, judgment by the Gujarat High Court, 7 July 2023, p. 102. Operative portion: 'Now, "Modi" surname holder and member of "Modi Community" are certainly identifiable / well defined class. Further, "Modi" people are a fraction of Ganchi / Taili / Modhvanik Ghnyati, as per the evidence and thus, again a well-defined identifiable / suable class.'

20. 'Supreme Court Stays Rahul Gandhi's Conviction in "Modi Surname" Remark Criminal Defamation Case', *The Hindu*, 4 August 2023, https://www.thehindu.com/news/national/sc-stays-rahul-gandhis-conviction-in-modi-surname-remark-criminal-defamation-case/article67157567.ece

21. Lok Sabha Secretariat Revokes Disqualification, Reinstates Rahul Gandhi as MP, *Hindustan Times*, 7 August 2023, https://www.hindustantimes.com/india-news/congress-leader-rahul-gandhi-s-lok-sabha-membership-restored-after-disqualification-revoked-by-house-secretariat-101691385081724.html

22. 'India Is a Country of Hindus, not Hindutvawadis: Rahul Gandhi', *Hindustan Times*, 12 December 2021, https://www.hindustantimes.com/india-news/india-a-country-of-hindus-not-hindutvavadis-rahul-gandhi-101639333504046.html

'Kerala CM Accuses Sangh Parivar of Treating Minorities as "Enemies"; BJP Hits Back', *Times of India*, 26 January 2023, https://timesofindia.indiatimes.com/india/kerala-cm-accuses-sangh-parivar-of-treating-minorities-as-enemies-bjp-hits-back/articleshow/97358890.cms?from=mdr

Ashutosh Varshney, 'Jim Crow Hindutva', *Indian Express*, 20 October 2021, https://indianexpress.com/article/opinion/columns/jim-crow-hindutva-7577159/

'Shashi Tharoor: A "Hindu Pakistan" Wouldn't Be Hindu at All, but a Sanghi Hindutva State', The Print, 13 July 2018, https://theprint.in/opinion/shashi-tharoor-hindu-pakistan-wouldnt-be-hindu-but-sanghi-hindutva-state/82782/

'Fight in India Is between Hindus and Hindutvawadis, Says Rahul', PTI, 18 December 2021, https://www.theweek.in/news/india/2021/12/18/fight-in-india-is-between-hindus-and-hindutvawadis-says-rahul0.html

23. M.V. Govindan (CPI[M]), interview with Rediff.com, 27 April 2023, https://www.rediff.com/news/interview/m-v-govindan-idea-of-india-will-be-destroyed-in-2025/20230427.htm

24. 'Abrogating Article 370 Aimed At Changing Demography of J&K: CPM', PTI, 22 August 2019, https://timesofindia.indiatimes.com/india/abrogating-article-370-aimed-at-changing-demography-of-jk-cpm/articleshow/70790890.cms

25. 'CAA, NRC Part of Their Agenda for Hindu Rashtra: P. Chidambaram', *Outlook*, 28 December 2019, https://www.outlookindia.com/magazine/story/india-news-caa-nrc-part-of-their-agenda-for-hindu-rashtra-p-chidambaram/302560

26. 'Congress Objects to Introduction of Private Member's Bill Seeking Repeal of Places of Worship Act', PTI, 4 February 2023, https://www.outlookindia.com/national/congress-objects-to-introduction-of-private-member-s-bill-seeking-repeal-of-places-of-worship-act-news-259314

27. 'Move to Introduce Uniform Civil Code a Bluff Linked to Hindu Rashtra, Says Nobel-Winning Economist Amartya Sen', *The Hindu*, 6 July 2023, https://www.thehindu.com/news/national/move-to-introduce-ucc-a-bluff-linked-to-hindu-rashtra-amartya-sen/article67046309.ece

28. 'BJP Shares Manmohan's 2003 Video to Target Cong over CAA', *Hindustan Times*, 20 December 2019, https://www.hindustantimes.com/india-news/bjp-shares-manmohan-s-2003-video-to-target-cong-over-caa/story-3KmfNRtoakSiSWvuXHVgaJ.htmlThe video: https://twitter.com/BJP4India/status/1207542398282162177

Additional references: In 1954, the Congress government in Madhya Pradesh had set up the Niyogi Committee to look into Christian missionary activities in the state. Details can be read here: Arun Anand, '1956 Niyogi Panel and Meenakshipuram 1981: Defining Moments of Religious Conversions Debate', The Print, https://theprint.in/india/1956-niyogi-panel-and-meenakshipuram-1981-defining-moments-of-religious-conversions-debate/689898/ This article in *Frontline* refers to the Congress government's unsuccessful attempts in Madhya Pradesh in 1958 and 1963 to introduce the Freedom of Religion Bills to regulate conversions: Anando Bhakto, 'Madhya Pradesh Government's Anti-Love Jehad Bill to Curb Interfaith Marriages by "Forced Conversion"', *Frontline*, 1 December 2020, https://frontline.thehindu.com/cover-story/madhya-pradesh-government-anti-love-jihad-bill-to-curb-interfaith-marriages-by-forced-conversion/article33214010.ece

29. 'Temporary Provisions with Respect to the State of Jammu and Kashmir', Constitution of India, 1949, Article 370 https://indiankanoon.org/doc/666119/

30. 'Government Brings Resolution to Repeal Article 370 of the Constitution; Ministry of Home Affairs', PIB release, 5 August 2019, https://pib.gov.in/newsite/PrintRelease.aspx?relid=192487 Full text of President's order on Article 370: https://egazette.gov.in/WriteReadData/2019/210049.pdf

31. 'Special Status to J&K Is Temporary, Even Nehru Said Ye Ghiste Ghiste Ghis Jaayegi: MoS Jitendra Singh', *India Today*, 29 June 2019, https://www.indiatoday.in/india/story/special-status-j-k-temporary-nehru-ghiste-ghiste-mos-jitendra-singh-1558366-2019-06-29 'Constitution Meant for Article 370 to Be 'Temporary' Provision: Amit Shah', PTI, 15 May 2023, https://www.ndtv.com/india-news/constitution-meant-for-article-370-to-be-temporary-provision-amit-shah-4035848 'Amit Shah Says Congress Amended Article 370 Twice in the Past', ANI, 5 August 2019, https://www.indiatoday.in/india/story/j-k-article-370-amit-shah-congress-1577402-2019-08-05

Additionally, as this article mentions, forty-seven Presidential orders had been issued 1947 onwards to make most articles of the Constitution and subjects in the Union list applicable to Jammu and Kashmir: Yogesh Vajpeyi, 'The Rise and Fall of Article 370', *New Indian Express*, 25 August 2019, https://www.newindianexpress.com/magazine/voices/2019/aug/25/the-rise-and-fall-of-article-370-2022858.html

32.   Several references to 'pseudo secularism', Presidential speeches, L.K. Advani, https://library.bjp.org/jspui/bitstream/123456789/247/1/Lal%20Krishna%20Advani.pdf

33.   Lok Sabha Debates, 6 February 2020
      Sangeeta Barooah Pisharothy, 'Defending CAA, Did Modi Cite Same Nehru-Bordoloi Letter Which BJP Used to Slam Congress With?', The Wire, 6 February 2020, https://thewire.in/politics/narendra-modi-caa-jawaharlal-nehru-bordoloi
      'Liaquat Pact, Letter to Bordoloi, CAA — the 24 Times PM Modi Mentioned Nehru in Parliament', The Print, 7 February 2020, https://theprint.in/politics/liaquat-pact-letter-to-bordoloi-caa-the-24-times-pm-modi-mentioned-nehru-in-parliament/361370/

34.   Ibid.

35.   Ibid.

36.   'Ram Mandir to Be Ready by Jan 1, 2024 Ahead of Lok Sabha Elections: Amit Shah', *India Today*, 5 January 2023, https://www.indiatoday.in/india/story/ram-mandir-to-be-ready-by-jan-1-2024-ahead-of-lok-sabha-elections-amit-shah-2317944-2023-01-05
      'BJP Polarising People on Communal Lines before 2024 Polls: Sitaram Yechury', IANS, 11 January 2023, https://www.mid-day.com/news/india-news/article/bjp-polarising-people-on-communal-lines-before-2024-polls-sitaram-yechury-23264986

37.   Pratap Bhanu Mehta, 'Ayodhya's Ram Temple Is First Real Colonisation of Hinduism by Political Power', *Indian Express*, 5 August 2020, https://indianexpress.com/article/opinion/columns/ayodhya-temple-ram-i-will-not-find-you-there-6539473/

38.   'Construction of Ram Temple in Ayodhya Begins', ANI, 20 August 2020, https://www.ndtv.com/india-news/

construction-of-ram-mandir-in-ayodhya-begins-2282554
Judgment of Supreme Court resolving the Ayodhya
land dispute, 9 November 2019, Part Q, Reliefs and
Directions, p. 925, https://main.sci.gov.in/supremecourt/
2010/36350/36350_2010_1_1502_18205_Judgement_09-
Nov-2019.pdf

39. 'Govt Forms 15-Member Trust for Building Ram
Mandir', *India Today*, 6 February 2020, https://www.
indiatoday.in/mail-today/story/govt-forms-15-member-
trust-for-building-ram-mandir-1643677-2020-02-06
Ibid., SC Ayodhya judgment, p. 926.

40. Pavan K. Varma, *The Great Hindu Civilisation: Achievement,
Neglect, Bias and the Way Forward*, Westland, 2021, pp. 4,

41. 'Kashi Vishwanath Dham Is a Symbol of the Sanatan Culture
of India: PM Modi', 13 December 2021, https://www.
narendramodi.in/text-to-prime-minister-narendra-modi-
s-speech-at-inauguration-of-kashi-vishwanath-dham-in-
varanasi-uttar-pradesh-558897

42. '"Temple Reclamation": RSS, BJP Seek Legal Resolution in
New Stance', *Hindustan Times*, 20 May 2022, https://www.
hindustantimes.com/india-news/temple-reclamation-rss-bjp-
seek-legal-resolution-in-new-stance-101652985889784.html

43. A term broadly used to define advocates of an unequal
secularism. Authors Harsh Madhusudan and Rajeev Mantri
define it thus in their book *New Idea of India*: 'Hence Nehruvian
secularism is like the erstwhile Ottoman system where different
communities had their own laws and ghettos, even though
the Ottoman State was explicitly Islamic. But when it comes
to economic redistribution and the welfare state, the ghettos
disappear for the Nehruvian worldview and we all become
Indians once again, rather conveniently.' Harsh Madhusudan
and Rajeev Mantri, *A New Idea of India: Individual Rights in a
Civilisational State*, Westland, 2020, pp. 16–17.

44. Pavan K. Varma, *The Great Hindu Civilisation*, p. 296.
Relevant excerpt from Varma's book was also published in The
Print: 'India's Textbooks Were Written with Nehru in Mind.
It Rejected the Past', 9 Aug 2021, https://theprint.in/opinion/

secularism-language-religion-ayodhya-bhoomi-pujan-ram-
mandir-kashmir/475307/

45. Lord Ram's photo from the original copy of the Constitution,
Times of India, 5 August 2020, https://timesofindia.
indiatimes.com/india/heres-lord-rams-photo-from-
original-copy-of-constitution/articleshow/77367241.cms
Also read: Justice R.S. Chauhan (retd), 'Artwork in the
Constitution – Myriad Interpretations', The Leaflet, 12 February
2023, https://theleaflet.in/artwork-in-the-constitution-myriad-
interpretations/
Vandana Kalra, 'The Handcrafted Constitution Is
a Work of Art', *Indian Express*, 27 January 2020,
https://indianexpress.com/article/express-sunday-
eye/handcrafted-constitution-india-6233517/
Shatavisha Mustafi, 'Decoding the Images in the Handcrafted
Edition of the Indian Constitution', Sahapedia, November
2021, https://map.sahapedia.org/search/article/Decoding%20
the%20Images%20in%20the%20Handcrafted%20
Edition%20of%20the%20Indian%20Constitution/11541

46. Rakesh Sinha, 'With Central Vista, Bose Statue, Narendra Modi
Is Decolonising Indian Mind', *Indian Express*, 15 September
2022, https://indianexpress.com/article/opinion/columns/
narendra-modi-decolonising-indian-mind-central-vista-bose-
statue-rakesh-sinha-8150168/

47. 'The Panch Pran of Amrit Kaal, goal of developed India, to
remove any trace of colonial mindset, take pride in our roots,
unity and sense of duty among citizens.' Prime Minister's
Office PIB release, 15 August 2022, https://pib.gov.in/
PressReleasePage.aspx?PRID=1852024

48. Ibid., point 30.

49. These will be discussed in subsequent chapters, but the
initiatives and measures include the virtual abrogation of
Article 370, the ongoing consultations with states on minority
status for Hindus, the Law Commission examining the
Uniform Civil Code, legislative assemblies adopting laws to
regulate conversions, the courts hearing petitions challenging
state control of temples, as well as the Places of Worship

(Special Provisions) Act, 1991, and seeking the government's response, among other measures.

50. It's difficult to define 'dharma' in precise terms, but in the context of inclusivity, we will rely on how the Supreme Court defined dharma in A.S. Narayana Deekshitulu vs State of Andhra Pradesh and Others, 19 March 1996. It said, 'The word "Dharma" or "Hindu Dharma" denotes upholding, supporting, nourishing that which upholds, nourishes or supports the stability of the society, maintaining social order and general well-being and progress of mankind; whatever conduces to the fulfilment of these objects is Dharma, it is Hindu Dharma and ultimately "Sarva Dharma Sambhava". In contra distinction, Dharma is that which approves oneself or good consciousness or springs from due deliberation for one's own happiness and also for welfare of all beings free from fear, desire, disease, cherishing good feelings and sense of brotherhood, unity and friendship for integration of Bharat.'

51. '"President of Bharat": G20 Dinner Invite Sparks Row', NDTV, 6 September 2023, https://www.ndtv.com/india-news/president-draupadi-murmus-g20-dinner-invite-sparks-buzz-republic-of-bharat-4360671

52. 'PM Modi's Plaque at G20 Summit says "Bharat"', *Economic Times*, 9 September 2023, https://economictimes.indiatimes.com/news/india/pm-modi-plaque-at-g20-summit-says-bharat/articleshow/103526983.cms?from=mdr

53. 'What Is Bharat Mandapam, the Venue of G20 Summit in New Delhi? Details', *Hindustan Times*, 9 September 2023, https://www.hindustantimes.com/india-news/g20-summit-updates-what-is-bharat-mandapam-pragati-maidan-venue-in-new-delhi-details-101693996059937.html

54. S. Gurumurthy: 'Recalling the Pre-March 24, 1940 Idea of India', *New Indian Express*, 22 June 1940, https://www.newindianexpress.com/opinions/columns/s-gurumurthy/2023/jun/22/recalling-the-pre-march-24-1940-idea-of-india-2587442.html

55. 'If BJP Wins in 2019, India Will Become "Hindu Pakistan": Shashi Tharoor', NDTV, 12 Jul 2018, https://www.ndtv.com/

india-news/shashi-tharoor-if-bjp-wins-2019-polls-india-will-become-hindu-pakistan-1881846

Chapter 1: A Pledge to Bharat Redeemed

1. 'Kashmir Turmoil: Mobile Internet Services Snapped in Jammu and Kashmir; Security Tightened', *India Today*, 5 August 2019, https://www.indiatoday.in/india/story/jammu-and-kashmir-turmoil-live-updates-1576967-2019-08-04

2. 'Restrictions, Night Curfews Imposed in Several Parts of Jammu and Kashmir', PTI, 5 August 2019, https://www.theweek.in/news/india/2019/08/05/Restrictions-night-curfews-imposed-in-several-parts-of-J-K.html

3. 'Restoration of Internet Services in Jammu and Kashmir: A Timeline', *Indian Express*, 5 February 2021, https://indianexpress.com/article/india/jk-4g-internet-mobile-timeline-7176408/

4. 'The Silencing of Kashmir: Arundhati Roy on India, Modi, and Fascism', The Intercept, 3 October 2019, https://theintercept.com/2019/10/03/deconstructed-podcast-kashmir-india-arundhati-roy/

5. 'Pakistan Army Landmine, Cache of Arms Recovered along Amarnath Yatra Route: Army', *Outlook*, 2 August 2019, https://www.outlookindia.com/website/story/pakistan-and-pakistan-army-disrupting-peace-in-kashmir-valley-indian-army/335373

6. Security Advisory, Government of Jammu and Kashmir, Governemnt Order No. Home 881 of 2019, 2 August 2019.

7. Ibid.

8. 'Pakistan Army Landmine, Cache of Arms Recovered along Amarnath Yatra Route: Army', *Outlook*.

9. 'Amarnath Yatra Curtailed after Fear of Terror Attack; Panic in Valley', *Economic Times*, 3 August 2019, https://economictimes.indiatimes.com/news/politics-and-nation/govt-curtails-amarnath-yatra-due-to-terror-threat-asks-tourists-yatri-to-leave-the-valley-immediately/articleshow/70497614.cms?from=mdr

10. 'Leave Kashmir ASAP: J&K Govt Issues Advisory for Amarnath Yatra Pilgrims and Tourists', *India Today*, 2 August 2019,

https://www.indiatoday.in/india/story/leave-kashmir-j-k-administration-issues-security-advisory-for-amarnath-pilgrims-1576494-2019-08-02

11. 'Omar Abdullah, Mehbooba Mufti Placed under House Arrest; Section 144 Imposed in Srinagar', *The Hindu*, 5 August 2019, https://www.thehindu.com/news/national/omar-abdullah-mehbooba-mufti-placed-under-house-arrest-section-144-imposed-in-srinagar/article61587802.ece

12. 'Jaleel Muzamil, Masood Bashaarat, Akhzer Adil, Kashmir Valley Has Seen Many a Lockdown but Why This Time It Is So Different', *Indian Express*, 7 August 2019, https://indianexpress.com/article/india/valley-has-seen-many-a-lockdown-but-why-this-time-it-is-so-different-article-370-kashmir-amit-shah-5884129/

13. Lt Gen. K.J.S. 'Tiny' Dhillon (retd), *Kitne Ghazi Aaye Kitne Ghazi Gaye: My Life Story*, Penguin Veer, pp. 237–39.

14. Ibid., p. 239.

15. 'Lockdown in Kashmir: 400 Politicians, Aides, Separatist under Arrest as Valley Turns into Massive Prison', *India Today*, 7 August 2019, https://www.indiatoday.in/india/story/lockdown-in-kashmir-400-politicians-aides-separatist-under-arrest-valley-prison-1578055-2019-08-06

16. 'The Amit Shah Photo That Grabbed Attention After Article 370 Announcement', NDTV, 5 August 2019, https://www.ndtv.com/india-news/the-amit-shah-photo-that-grabbed-attention-after-article-370-announcement-on-jammu-and-kashmir-2080547

17. 'This Amit Shah Photo Reveals Modi Govt's Top Secret Plan on Article 370', *Economic Times*, 5 August 2019, https://economictimes.indiatimes.com/news/politics-and-nation/revealed-this-amit-shah-photo-reveals-modi-govts-top-secret-plan-on-article-370/articleshow/70535131.cms?from=mdr

18. Ibid.

19. Ibid.

20. Ibid.

21. 'Government brings Resolution to Repeal Article 370 of the Constitution', Ministry of Home Affairs, PIB release,

5 August 2019, https://pib.gov.in/PressReleseDetailm. aspx?PRID=1581308

22. 'Modi Can't Repeal Article 370 Even If He becomes PM for 10 Terms: Farooq Abdullah', *India Today*, 3 December 2013, https://www.indiatoday.in/india/north/story/narendra-modi-article-370-jammu-farooq-abdullah-modi-cant-be-pm-219462-2013-12-02

23. The Constitution (Application to Jammu and Kashmir) Order, 2019, https://egazette.nic.in/WriteReadData/2019/210049.pdf

24. Reference to Jawaharlal Nehru's speech 'Tryst with Destiny' at the Constituent Assembly, 1947.

25. Interview conducted in Delhi in November 2022.

26. Ibid.

27. 'BJP President Amit Shah Takes Charge as Home Minister', NDTV, 1 July 2019, https://www.ndtv.com/india-news/bjp-president-amit-shah-takes-charge-as-home-minister-2046378

28. 'Amit Shah Writes: An Election in 1987 and Decoding the Modi Strategy of Winning', News18, 12 May 2022, https://www.news18.com/news/opinion/amit-shah-writes-an-election-in-1987-and-decoding-the-modi-strategy-of-winning-5162371.html

29. Ibid.

30. 'During Cong-Led UPA regime, CBI Was "Putting Pressure" on Me to "Frame" Modi, says Amit Shah', PTI, 30 March 2023, https://indianexpress.com/article/india/cong-upa-cbi-pressure-me-frame-modi-amit-shah-8527327/
'UPA Govt Falsely Jailed Amit Shah, Tried to Destroy Gujarat: PM Modi', *Hindustan Times*, 17 April 2019, https://www.hindustantimes.com/india-news/upa-govt-falsely-jailed-amit-shah-tried-to-destroy-gujarat-pm-modi/story-LJyI1Urd2ok3WUPGnTVW5N.html

31. 'Amit Shah Invokes Rajiv Gandhi to Blunt Congress Criticism of Assam NRC', *India Today*, 31 July 2018, https://www.indiatoday.in/india/story/parliament-disrupted-after-govt-opposition-face-off-over-assam-nrc-1301108-2018-07-31

32. 'Pressure Groups Stalled Effort for J&K's Equitable Growth: Shah', *Times of India*, 21 June 2018, https://timesofindia.

indiatimes.com/india/govt-to-treat-agri-derivatives-trading-as-non-speculative/articleshow/64672895.cms

33. 'Nehru's Mistake of Taking Kashmir Issue to UN Bigger than Himalayas: Amit Shah', *India Today*, 9 February 2022, https://www.indiatoday.in/india/story/amit-shah-jawaharlal-nehru-kashmir-mistake-un-bigger-than-himalayas-article-370-1604467-2019-09-29

34. 'Full Text of Amit Shah's Speech in Parliament, Laying Out Classic RSS/BJP View on Kashmir', The Print, 29 June 2019, https://theprint.in/india/full-text-of-amit-shahs-first-speech-as-home-minister-in-lok-sabha-on-28-june/256034/

35. Lok Sabha Debates, Friday, 28 June 2019.

36. Ibid.

37. 'Amit Shah Moves Resolution to Extend President's Rule in Jammu & Kashmir for 6 Months', Times of India, 28 June 2019, https://timesofindia.indiatimes.com/india/amit-shah-movesresolution-to-extend-presidents-rule-in-jammu-kashmir-for-6-months/articleshow/69987017.cms

38. 'Article 370 Only a Temporary Provision, Not Permanent: Amit Shah', Livemint, 28 June 2019, https://www.livemint.com/politics/news/article-370-only-a-temporary-provision-not-permanent-amit-shah-1561710130555.html

39. Gazette notification (G.S.R. 551[E]), Ministry of Law and Justice, 5 August 2019, https://egazette.gov.in/WriteReadData/2019/210049.pdf

40. 'How Erasing Article 370 Became an Article of Faith for RSS and BJP', The Print, 5 August 2019, https://theprint.in/india/how-erasing-article-370-became-an-article-of-faith-for-rss-and-bjp/272688/

41. 'Don't Lose Focus on Core Values, RSS Tells Cadres', *Hindustan Times*, 1 May 2018, https://www.hindustantimes.com/india-news/don-t-lose-focus-on-core-values-rss-tells-cadres/story-OTmwphoOiknfcTrF1O11dL.html
'PM Modi Has Gone Back on Ram Temple, Art 370 Promise: Pravin Togadia', PTI, 21 September 2018, https://www.thestatesman.com/india/pm-modi-has-gone-back-on-ram-temple-art-370-promise-pravin-togadia-1502687563.html

Shivam Sarkar Singh, 'Four Years of Narendra Modi Have Not Just Failed India's Middle Class but Also the RSS', The Print, 26 July 2018, https://theprint.in/opinion/four-years-of-narendra-modi-have-not-just-failed-indias-middle-class-but-also-the-rss/88630/

42. 'Saffron Cadre Upset over Centre Abandoning Stance on Article 370', *Tribune*, 19 June 2018, https://www.tribuneindia.com/news/archive/nation/chinks-in-pdp-bjp-alliance-cadres-upset-but-alliance-may-continue-for-now-607636

43. Ibid.

44. 'Full Text: Common Minimum Programme of PDP-BJP Government in J&K', News18, 2 March 2018, https://www.news18.com/news/india/full-text-common-minimum-progamme-of-pdp-bjp-government-in-jk-970414.html

45. 'Mehbooba Mufti Invites Separatists for Talks with All Party Delegation in Kashmir', PTI, 3 September 2016, https://indianexpress.com/article/india/india-news-india/kashmir-mehbooba-mufti-invites-separatists-for-talks-with-all-party-team-3011963/

46. 'JK Govt Approves Withdrawal of Cases against Stone Pelters', *Deccan Herald*, 29 November 2017, https://www.deccanherald.com/content/645431/jk-govt-approves-withdrawal-cases.html

47. 'BJP Pulls the Plug on Alliance with PDP, Governor's Rule in the Offing', *Business Today*, 19 June 2018, https://www.businesstoday.in/latest/economy-politics/story/jammu-kashmir-governor-rule-bjp-pdp-alliance-mehbooba-mufti-148578-2018-06-19 'Jammu-Kashmir: BJP Ends Its Alliance with PDP, Cites National Interest, Security Slide', *Indian Express*, 20 June 2018, https://indianexpress.com/article/india/jammu-kashmir-bjp-pdp-alliance-break-up-narendra-modi-mehbooba-mufti-amit-shah-5224904/

48. 'Article 370: Revisiting Election Manifestos, BJP's push and Congress's Silence', *India Today*, 5 August 2019, https://www.indiatoday.in/diu/story/jammu-and-kashmir-article-370-revisiting-election-manifestos-bjp-push-and-congress-silence-1577579-2019-08-05

49. 'How Mookerjee's Push against Art 370 Became an Article
    of Faith for BJP', *Times of India*, 6 August 2019, https://
    timesofindia.indiatimes.com/india/how-mookerjees-
    push-against-art-370-became-an-article-of-faith-for-bjp/
    articleshow/70545310.cms
50. Interview with an NDA insider conducted in Delhi in
    November 2022.
51. Ibid.
52. Ibid.
    Additional reference: On 1 December 2013, at a rally in Jammu,
    Modi had called for an open debate on whether Article 370 had
    benefited the people of J&K. He said that the path that Dr Syama
    Prasad Mukherjee had advocated for Jammu and Kashmir had
    been proven to be the right one and that Nehru had ignored
    Mookerjee's advice. He also said, 'Article 370 has become a shield
    and is being used as one. It has been armoured with communal
    jewels and just because of this, a valid discussion on it is not
    happening. I want the experts of the Constitution to discuss it.'
    Full text of Modi's speech at Lalkaar Rally, Jammu,
    Narendramodi.in, 1 December 2013, https://www.
    narendramodi.in/ma/full-text-of-shri-modis-speech-at-lalkaar-
    rally-jammu-2806
    Additionally: 'Had Sardar Patel Been First PM, Entire Kashmir
    Would Have Been Ours: PM Modi in Lok Sabha', PTI, 7
    February 2018, https://www.indiatoday.in/politics/story/had-
    sardar-patel-been-first-pm-entire-kashmir-would-have-been-
    ours-pm-modi-in-lok-sabha-1162756-2018-02-07
    'Nehru Taking Kashmir to UN Was a Himalayan Blunder:
    Amit Shah', NDTV, 30 September 2019, https://www.
    ndtv.com/india-news/jawaharlal-nehru-taking-kashmir-
    to-un-was-a-himalayan-blunder-amit-shah-2109219
    Kiren Rijiju, 'Nehru's 5 Blunders on Kashmir – The Real
    Story', News 18, https://www.news18.com/news/opinion/
    opinion-union-law-minister-kiren-rijiju-writes-nehrus-
    5-blunders-on-kashmir-the-real-story-6377083.html
    For a view on Nehru's decision to go to the UN on Kashmir,
    read this excerpt from Rajiv Dogra's book *India's World:*

How Prime Ministers Shaped Foreign Policy, Rupa, published in The Print on 27 August 2020: https://theprint.in/pageturner/excerpt/nehru-going-to-un-on-kashmir-was-an-error/490062/

53. Ibid. Additionally, see 'Legal Work behind Scrapping of Article 370 Began before Lok Sabha Polls', *Economic Times*, 7 August 2019, https://economictimes.indiatimes.com/news/politics-and-nation/legal-work-began-before-lok-sabha-polls/articleshow/70561234.cms?from=mdr

54. Ibid.

55. 'Government Brings Resolution to Repeal Article 370 of the Constitution Ministry of Home Affairs', PIB release, 5 August 2019, https://pib.gov.in/newsite/PrintRelease.aspx?relid=192487

'Explained: President's Order Scraps Its Predecessor and Amends Article 370', *The Hindu*, 5 August 2019, https://www.thehindu.com/news/national/explained-presidents-order-scraps-its-predecessor-and-amends-article-370/article61587647.ece

56. Ibid.

57. Arghya Sengupta, Jinaly Dani, Kevin James and Pranay Modi, *Hamin Ast?: A Biography of Article 370*, Navi Books, 2022, Chapter VI: 'Collapse', p. 72.

58. 'Abrogation of Article 370 Unconstitutional, People of J&K Bypassed: Petitioners to SC', PTI, 10 December 2019, https://economictimes.indiatimes.com/news/politics-and-nation/sc-commences-hearing-on-pleas-challenging-abrogation-of-article-370/articleshow/72454345.cms?from=mdr

'Power to Abrogate Cannot Be Exercised When Constituent Assembly Has Ceased to Exist, Submits Sr Adv Dinesh Dwivedi', Livelaw, 21 January 2020, https://www.livelaw.in/top-stories/art-370-hearing-day-1-power-to-abrogate-cannot-be-exercised-when-constituent-assembly-has-ceased-to-exist-submits-sr-adv-dinesh-dwivedi-151871

'The Proposal to Alter Article 370 Must Emanate from the People of Jammu and Kashmir, Submits Raju Ramachandran', Livelaw, 10 December 2019, https://www.livelaw.in/top-stories/article-370-day-1the-people-of-jammu-and-kashmir-raju-ramachandran-150667 'Revocation of Article 370 Biggest Betrayal of J&K, Won't Stand Test of Law', interview of former J&K law minister Abdul Rahim Rather in The Wire, 14 August 2019, https://thewire.in/politics/abdul-rahim-rather-national-conference-interview-article-370-kashmir

59. 'Hearing Commences in SC on Batch of Petitions Challenging Abrogation of Article 370', *Times of India*, 2 August 2023, https://timesofindia.indiatimes.com/india/sc-begins-hearing-on-batch-of-petitions-challenging-abrogation-of-article-370/articleshow/102336566.cms?from=mdr
'Supreme Court Reserves Verdict in Article 370 Abrogation Challenge', *The Hindu*, 5 September 2019, https://www.thehindu.com/news/national/supreme-court-reserves-verdict-in-article-370-abrogation-challenge/article67274228.ece#:~:text=A%20Constitution%20Bench%20headed%20by,privileges%20to%20Jammu%20and%20Kashmir

60. 'Maps of Newly Formed Union Territories of Jammu Kashmir and Ladakh, with the Map of India', Ministry of Home Affairs, PIB release 2 Nov 2019, https://pib.gov.in/PressReleasePage.aspx?PRID=1590112#:~:text=Under%20the%20leadership%20of%20Prime,on%2031st%20October%202019.
The Jammu and Kashmir Reorganisation Act, 2019, https://egazette.gov.in/WriteReadData/2019/210407.pdf

61. 'Trifurcate J&K, Reiterates RSS', PTI, 25 July 2002, https://timesofindia.indiatimes.com/india/trifurcate-jk-reiterates-rss/articleshow/17094733.cms

62. 'BJP Rules Out RSS's Demand for Trifurcation of J&K', PTI, 27 July 2002, https://timesofindia.indiatimes.com/india/bjp-rules-out-rsss-demand-for-trifurcation-of-jk/articleshow/17270408.cms

63. 'Seek "Complete Autonomy": Leh, Kargil Pass Resolution for Separate Division for Ladakh Region', *Indian Express*, 8 December 2018, https://indianexpress.com/article/india/seek-complete-autonomy-leh-kargil-pass-resolution-for-separate-division-for-ladakh-region-5483926/

64. 'Why Ladakh Demanded Autonomy Since India's Independence', *Mint Lounge*, 19 October 2021, https://lifestyle.livemint.com/news/big-story/why-ladakh-demanded-autonomy-since-india-s-independence-111635480768700.html
Excerpt from Venkataraghavan Subha Srinivasan's book *The Origin Story of India's States*, Penguin Ebury Press, 2021.

65. 'Justice Desai to Head J&K Delimitation Panel', *Tribune*, 6 March 2020, https://www.tribuneindia.com/news/j-k/justice-desai-to-head-jk-delimitation-panel-52193

66. 'Delimitation Commission Finalizes the Delimitation Order Today, Election Commission of India', Press Note, 5 May 2022, https://eci.gov.in/files/file/14156-delimitation-commission-finalises-the-delimitation-order-today/

67. 'Article 370 Scrapped: Jammu Celebrates, Calls It a "Historic Day"', *Outlook*, 5 August 2019, https://www.outlookindia.com/website/story/india-news-article-370-scrapped-jammu-celebrates-calls-it-a-historic-day/335616
'Pandits in Jammu Camps Hail Revocation of Article 370', *India Today*, 8 August 2019, https://www.indiatoday.in/mail-today/story/pandits-jammu-s-camps-hail-revocation-article-370-1578455-2019-08-08

68. 'Ladakhis Ecstatic after Government Proposes Union Territory Status', *Hindustan Times*, 10 June 2020, https://www.hindustantimes.com/india-news/ladakhis-ecstatic-after-government-proposes-union-territory-status/story-nnizyj4AaqjE3dPkOHhXXM.html

69. Sant Kumar Sharma, 'Empowering the Region: The Jammu Viewpoint', India Foundation, 30 October 2020, https://indiafoundation.in/articles-and-commentaries/empowering-the-region-the-jammu-viewpoint/
Ram Madhav, 'The Significance of Delimitation in J&K', *Hindustan Times*, 10 January 2022, https://www.hindustantimes.com/opinion/the-significance-of-delimitation-in-jk-101641827540924.html
'Ladakhis Ecstatic after Government Proposes Union Territory Status', *Hindustan Times*, 10 June 2020, https://www.hindustantimes.com/india-news/ladakhis-ecstatic-

after-government-proposes-union-territory-status/story-nnizyj4AaqjE3dPkOHhXXM.html

70. Interview with Ram Madhav, 2022.
    'India's Most Influential Think-Tanks', *Hindustan Times*, 16 August 2015, https://www.hindustantimes.com/india/india-s-most-influential-think-tanks/story-emb0db2lmqltL8pKeYuZiL.html

71. P. Vaidyanathan Iyer, 'BJP-PDP Alliance in J&K: How Two Men Worked Out the Deal and Became Friends', *Indian Express*, 16 March 2015, https://indianexpress.com/article/political-pulse/the-alliance-that-almost-wasnt/

72. Interview with Ram Madhav, 2022.

73. 'Sharada of Kashmir: The Goddess That Is India', *Swarajya*, 22 March 2023, https://swarajyamag.com/culture/sharada-of-kashmir-the-goddess-that-is-india

74. Thomas Watters MRAS, *On Yuan Chwang's Travels in India, 629-645 AD*, London Royal Asiatic Society, 1904, Chapter VIII, 'Kashmir to Rajapur', p. 261, https://www.rarebooksocietyofindia.org/book_archive/196174216674_10153425489631675.pdf

75. Vikram Sampath, *Bravehearts of Bharat: Vignettes from Indian History*, Penguin Random House, 2022, Chapter 1: 'Lalitaditya Muktapida of Kashmir', p. 5.

76. Ibid.

77. Ibid., p. 7.

78. Ibid., p. 28.

79. Sanjay Nahar, 'Understanding Kashmir's Rich and Long History Is Imperative in These Times', *Indian Express*, 26 August 2019, https://indianexpress.com/article/opinion/columns/jammu-kashmir-culture-history-article-370-bjp-5936232/

80. Vikram Sampath, *Bravehearts of Bharat: Vignettes from Indian History*, p. 16.

81. Professor Upendra Kaul, 'Shankaracharya Temple: History on a Hill', *Greater Kashmir*, 1 May 2022, https://www.greaterkashmir.com/todays-paper/editorial-page/shankaracharya-temple-history-on-a-hill

82. Devdutt Patnaik, 'A Reminder on the Border', 31 October 2016, https://devdutt.com/articles/a-reminder-on-the-border/

83. 'Tracing Adi Shankara's Trail: Journeys of Faith and Unity', *Swarajya*, 7 November 2021, https://swarajyamag.com/culture/tracing-adi-shankaras-trail-journeys-of-faith-and-unity Devdutt Patnaik, 'How Adi Shankaracharya United a Fragmented Land with Philosophy, Poetry and Pilgrimage', Scroll.in, 19 September 2016, https://scroll.in/article/816610/how-adi-shankaracharya-united-a-fragmented-land-with-philosophy-poetry-and-pilgrimage

84. Anirban Ganguly, 'Why Kashmir Is More Than Just a Land for India', *Daily Guardian*, 11 August 2020, https://thedailyguardian.com/why-kashmir-is-more-than-just-a-land-for-india/

85. 'Scrapping of Article 370 Was Step towards Achieving Dream of Akhand Bharat: Fadnavis', PTI, 10 August 2020, https://theprint.in/india/scrapping-of-article-370-was-step-towards-achieving-dream-of-akhand-bharat-fadnavis/1076393/

86. Interview with Rakesh Sinha, 2022.

87. Ashok Malik, 'Art 370 Killed Because Hindu Jammu, Buddhist Ladakh & Muslim Kashmir Only Benefitted Pakistan', The Print, 8 August 2019, https://theprint.in/opinion/art-370-killed-because-hindu-jammu-buddhist-ladakh-muslim-kashmir-only-benefitted-pakistan/273915/

88. Monideepa Banerjie, 'How BJP Paid Its Debt to Founder Syama Prasad Mookerjee with Kashmir Move', NDTV, 5 August 2019, https://www.ndtv.com/india-news/article-370-scrapped-how-bjp-paid-its-debt-to-founder-syama-prasad-mookerjee-with-kashmir-move-2080682

89. 'Shyama Prasad Mukherjee, the Barrister Who Founded Bharatiya Janta Party', *India Today*, 23 June 2020, https://www.indiatoday.in/education-today/gk-current-affairs/story/remembering-shyama-prasad-mukherjee-the-founder-of-bharatiya-jana-sangh-that-later-became-bharatiya-janta-party-1563356-2019-07-06

90. Tathagata Roy, *Syama Prasad Mookerjee: Life and Times*, Penguin, 2018, p. 330.

91. Article 370 in the Constitution of India, 1949, https://indiankanoon.org/doc/666119/

Abhinav Chandrachud, 'The Spirit of Article 370', BQ Prime, 21 August 2019, https://www.bqprime.com/opinion/the-spirit-of-article-370-by-abhinav-chandrachud
Arghya Sengupta, Jinaly Dani, Kevin James and Pranay Modi, *Hamin Ast?: A Biography of Article 370*, p. 19.

92. 'Explained: Syama Prasad Mookerjee and the BJP's "Emotional connect" with Kashmir', *Indian Express*, 5 August 2019, https://indianexpress.com/article/explained/explained-syama-prasad-mookerjee-and-the-bjps-emotional-connect-with-kashmir-5879168/

93. S. Gopal, *Selected Works of Jawaharlal Nehru*, JNMF/OUP India, 1997, 5 February letter of Nehru to Shyama Prasad Mookerjee, Series 2, Volume 21, January1953–March 1953, pp. 228–29.

94. Ibid.

95. Ibid., Pledge to Build a New India, Series 2, Volume 17, November 1951–March 1952, pp. 102–3.

96. Bharatiya Jana Sangh, Party Documents, Manifesto 1951, p. 49.

97. Eminent Parliamentarians monograph series, *Dr Syama Prasad Mookerjee*, Lok Sabha Secretariat 1990, *Dr Mookerjee and Kashmir* by Professor Balraj Madhok, pp. 18–20, https://eparlib.nic.in/bitstream/123456789/58670/1/Eminent_Parliamentarians_Series_Syama_Prasad_Mookerjee.pdf

98. Ibid., p. 20.

99. Ibid.

100. Syama Prasad Mukherjee, Lok Sabha debate on 26 June 1952, pp. 2570–84, https://eparlib.nic.in/bitstream/123456789/55051/1/lsd_01_01_26-06-1952.pdf

101. Constituent Assembly Debates, 27 May 1949, Part I, https://indiankanoon.org/doc/283368/

102. 'Revisiting 27 May, 1949 – To Understand Nehru and His Kashmir Policy', *Swarajya*, 18 June 2016, https://swarajyamag.com/politics/revisiting-27-may-1949-to-understand-nehru-and-his-kashmir-policy

103. Constituent Assembly Debates on 27 May 1949, Part I, https://indiankanoon.org/doc/283368/

Ram Madhav, 'Correcting a Historic Blunder', *Indian Express*, 6 August 2019, https://indianexpress.com/article/opinion/columns/kashmir-article-370-scrapped-correcting-a-historic-blunder-5880790/

104. Ibid.
105. Constituent Assembly Debates on 27 May 1949, Part I, https://indiankanoon.org/doc/283368/
106. Ibid.
107. Ibid.
108. Ibid.
109. 'Revisiting 27 May, 1949 - To Understand Nehru and His Kashmir Policy, *Swarajya*.
110. Constituent Assembly Debates, Official Report, Lok Sabha Secretariat, Volune X, 17 October 1949, p. 424, https://eparlib.nic.in/bitstream/123456789/763271/1/cad_17-10-1949.pdf
111. Ibid.
112. Ibid.
113. Arghya Sengupta, Jinaly Dani, Kevin James, Pranay Modi, *Hamin Ast?: A Biography of Article 370*, p. 6.
114. Hindol Sengupta, *The Man Who Saved India: Sardar Patel and the Idea of India*, Penguin Books, 2018, pp. 383–84.
115. Ibid., pp. 394–95.
116. Constitution of India, Part XXI, Temporary, Transitional and Special Provisions, https://www.mea.gov.in/Images/pdf1/Part21.pdf
'In Constitution, a Range of "Special Provisions" for States Other Than J&K, Too', *Indian Express*, 6 September 2017, https://indianexpress.com/article/explained/simply-put-in-constitution-a-range-of-special-provisions-for-states-other-than-jammu-kashmir-too-4830520/
117. 'How Syama Prasad Mookerjee Launched First Nationwide Campaign on J&K and Paid with His Life', The Print, 23 June 2020, https://theprint.in/india/how-syama-prasad-mookerjee-launched-first-nationwide-campaign-on-jk-and-paid-with-his-life/446397/
118. Tathagata Roy, *Syama Prasad Mookerjee: Life and Times*, Penguin, 2018, pp. 348–50.

119. Article 35A of the Constitution, Lok Sabha Secretariat, https://parliamentlibraryindia.nic.in/writereaddata/Library/Reference%20Notes/Article%2035A%20of%20the%20Constitution-%20An%20overview.pdf
BJP Lok Sabha Election Manifesto 2019, p. 12, https://library.bjp.org/jspui/bitstream/123456789/2988/1/BJP-Election-english-2019.pdf

120. Rahul Shivshankar, 'What Binds J&K to India? It's Kashmiriyat. Article 370 Merely Set up an Architecture of Otherness, Thankfully Annulled', *Times of India*, 7 August 2019, https://timesofindia.indiatimes.com/blogs/beyond-the-headline/what-binds-jk-to-india-its-kashmiriyat-article-370-merely-set-up-an-architecture-of-otherness-thankfully-annulled/

121. 'BJP Committed to Bringing Uniform Civil Code after Following All Processes: Amit Shah', *Indian Express*, 25 November 2022, https://indianexpress.com/article/india/bjp-committed-to-bringing-uniform-civil-code-after-following-all-processes-bjp-amit-shah-8288334/

122. 'BJP Welcomes Gyanvapi Order, UP Deputy CM Says Mathura, Kashi Churning', *Indian Express*, 13 September 2022, https://indianexpress.com/article/political-pulse/bjp-welcomes-gyanvapi-order-up-deputy-cm-says-mathura-kashi-churning-8147230/
'"Temple Reclamation": RSS, BJP Seek Legal Resolution in New Stance', *Hindustan Times*, 20 May 2022, https://www.hindustantimes.com/india-news/temple-reclamation-rss-bjp-seek-legal-resolution-in-new-stance-101652985889784.html

123. 'Centre Justifies Article 370 Decision in Supreme Court', PTI, 11 November 2019, https://www.livemint.com/news/india/centre-justifies-article-370-decision-in-supreme-court-11573485747301.html

124. Article 370(3) in the Constitution of India 1949, https://indiankanoon.org/doc/1577416/

125. 'How Kashmir Changed on August 5', *India Today*, 6 August 2019, https://www.indiatoday.in/india-today-insight/story/how-kashmir-changed-on-august-5-1577706-2019-08-06

126. Ibid.

127. 'Harish Salve on Why the Supreme Court Is Unlikely to Void Article 370 Move', The Wire, 22 October 2019, https://thewire.in/law/harish-salve-supreme-court-article-370-kashmir

128. Ibid.

129. Counter Affidavit on Behalf of Union of India, p. 24, 9 November 2019.

130. 'Special Status to J&K Is Temporary, Even Nehru Said Ye Ghiste Ghiste Ghis Jaayegi: MOS Jitendra Singh', *India Today*, 29 June 2019, https://www.indiatoday.in/india/story/special-status-j-k-temporary-nehru-ghiste-ghiste-mos-jitendra-singh-1558366-2019-06-29

131. Ram Madhav, 'Are Gupkaris Listening?', Greater Kashmir, 7 September 2020, https://www.greaterkashmir.com/todays-paper/are-gupkaris-listening?amp

132. Abhay K., 'How India Can Popularise "Vasudhaiva Kutumbakam" like Its Yoga and Diwali', Daily O, 28 January 2018, https://www.dailyo.in/arts/vedas-upanishads-ancient-india-narendra-modi-vasudhaiva-kutumbakam-united-nations-22026

133. '"Kashmiriyat" Exemplifies India's Cultural-Religious Pluralism: Scholars Deliberate at JKPJF Seminar in Srinagar', ANI, 5 February 2023, https://www.aninews.in/news/national/politics/kashmiriyat-exemplifies-indias-cultural-religious-pluralism-scholars-deliberate-at-jkpjf-seminar-in-srinagar20230205182335/

134. Guru Nanak's Blessed Trail: The Sacred Sites across Punjab, Department of Tourism and Cultural Affairs, Government of Punjab, Lonely Planet Global Limited, 2019, p. 11.

135. Sumantra Bose, 'Sufi Mystics from 1370s Changed Kashmir's Identity. But Orthodoxy of 1970s Is a Challenge', Excerpt from *Kashmir at the Crossroads: Inside a 21st-Century Conflict*, Pan Macmillan India, published in The Print, 2 January 2022, https://theprint.in/pageturner/excerpt/sufi-mystics-from-1370s-changed-kashmirs-identity-but-orthodoxy-of-1970s-is-the-challenge/793297/

136. Hazratbal Shrine, Times Travel, 7 October 2016, https://timesofindia.indiatimes.com/travel/Srinagar/Hazratbal-Shrine/ps51718080.cms;

'Shankaracharya Temple: History on a Hill', Greater Kashmir, 1 May 2022, https://www.greaterkashmir.com/todays-paper/editorial-page/shankaracharya-temple-history-on-a-hill

137. 'Full Text of Document on Govt's Rationale behind Removal of Special Status to J&K', *The Hindu*, 6 August 2019, https://www.thehindu.com/news/national/full-text-of-document-on-govts-rationale-behind-removal-of-special-status-to-jk/article28821368.ece

'Article 35A of the Constitution – An Overview', Lok Sabha Secretariat, October 2017, https://parliamentlibraryindia.nic.in/writereaddata/Library/Reference%20Notes/Article%2035A%20of%20the%20Constitution-%20An%20overview.pdf

138. 'Article 370 and Article 35-A: Discriminatory in Nature', *Hindustan Times*, https://www.hindustantimes.com/static/ht2019/8/Final%20booklet%20on%20Article%20370%20&%20article%2035-A.pdf

Ashok Malik, 'Jammu-Kashmir and Ladakh: Exploring a New Paradigm', Observer Research Foundation Special Report, August 2019, https://www.orfonline.org/wp-content/uploads/2019/08/ORF_SpecialReport_94_Kashmir_NEW.pdf

139. Counter Affidavit on Behalf of Union of India, p. 26, 9 November 2019.

'Kashmir Article 370: Women Cheer Equal Property Rights', *India Today*, 6 August 2019, https://www.indiatoday.in/mailtoday/story/kashmir-article-370-women-cheer-equal-property-rights-1577637-2019-08-05

140. 'Full Text of Document on Govt's Rationale behind Removal of Special Status to J&K', *The Hindu*, 6 August 2019, https://www.thehindu.com/news/national/full-text-of-document-on-govts-rationale-behind-removal-of-special-status-to-jk/article28821368.ece

'Article 35A of the Constitution – An Overview', Lok Sabha Secretariat, October 2017, https://parliamentlibraryindia.nic.in/writereaddata/Library/Reference%20Notes/Article%2035A%20of%20the%20Constitution-%20An%20overview.pdf

'West Pakistan Refugees in J&K Move SC Challenging Article 35A', PTI, 10 September 2017, https://indianexpress.

com/article/india/west-pakistan-refugees-in-jk-move-sc-challenging-article-35a-4836667/

141. 'Punjab's Valmikis in Jammu and Kashmir Move Supreme Court against Article 35A', *Times of India*, 11 April 2019, https://timesofindia.indiatimes.com/city/chandigarh/punjabs-valmikis-in-jammu-and-kashmir-move-sc-against-article-35a/articleshow/68827731.cms

142. Video of the BJP press conference on 23 April 2019: https://www.youtube.com/watch?v=Z__6E5hPbHg

143. The Citizenship (Amendment) Act, 2019, https://egazette.gov.in/WriteReadData/2019/214646.pdf

144. 'Parliament Passes the Citizenship (Amendment) Bill 2019', Ministry of Home Affairs, PIB release, 11 December 2019, https://pib.gov.in/newsite/PrintRelease.aspx?relid=195783

145. Sanjeev Nayyar, 'Long Read: NRC across India is What We Need to Stem the Tide of Illegal Immigration from Bangladesh', *Swarajya*, 22 October 2019, https://swarajyamag.com/politics/long-read-nrc-across-india-is-what-we-need-to-stem-the-tide-of-illegal-immigration-from-bangladesh MHA Advisory to States, Identification of Illegal Immigrations and Monitoring Thereof–Regarding, 8 August 2017, https://www.mha.gov.in/sites/default/files/advisoryonillegalmigrant_10092017_2.PDF

146. Irena Akbar, 'Why I Protest as a Muslim', *Indian Express*, 3 January 2020, https://indianexpress.com/article/opinion/columns/why-i-protest-as-a-muslim-citizenship-act-lucknow-6197041/ Harsh Mander, 'Citizenship Amendment Bill Will Result in Untold Fear and Dislocation of Muslim Citizens', *Indian Express*, 3 October 2019, https://indianexpress.com/article/opinion/columns/citizenship-amendment-bill-nrc-india-6049329/

147. Video of the BJP press conference on 23 April 2019: https://www.youtube.com/watch?v=Z__6E5hPbHg

148. 'Amit Shah Relates TMC to Tushtikaran-Mafia-Chit Fund', IANS, 11 April 2019, https://www.business-standard.com/article/news-ians/amit-shah-relates-tmc-to-tushtikaran-mafia-chit-fund-119041101069_1.html

149. 'Two Crore Bangladeshi Immigrants Illegally Staying in India, Centre Informs Rajya Sabha', *Times of India*, 17 November 2016, https://timesofindia.indiatimes.com/india/two-crore-bangladeshi-immigrants-illegally-staying-in-india-centre-informs-rajya-sabha/articleshow/55457903.cms

150. The Citizenship (Amendment) Act, 2019, https://egazette.nic.in/WriteReadData/2019/214646.pdf

151. Ibid.

152. 'What RSS Chief Bhagwat Really Meant When He Said "Akhand Bharat" Could Be Reality in 10-15 Years', The Print, 23 May 2022, https://theprint.in/india/what-rss-chief-bhagwat-really-meant-when-he-said-akhand-bharat-could-be-reality-in-10-15-yrs/963004/

153. 'PM Modi, Amit Shah Pitch for Citizenship Bill, NRC on Campaign Trail in Assam and Bengal', PTI, 11 April 2019, https://timesofindia.indiatimes.com/elections/news/pm-modi-amit-shah-pitch-for-vexed-cab-nrc-on-campaign-trail-in-assam-and-bengal/articleshow/68837271.cms

154. Partition on the Basis of Religion Was a Historical Mistake: Amit Shah Blames Nehru for Problems in J-K', ANI, 28 June 2019, https://www.business-standard.com/article/news-ani/partition-on-basis-of-religion-was-a-historical-mistake-amit-shah-blames-nehru-for-problems-in-j-k-119062800837_1.html

155. Video of the BJP press conference on 23 Apr 2019: https://www.youtube.com/watch?v=Z__6E5hPbHg

156. 'What Is NRC: All You Need to Know about National Register of Citizens', *India Today*, 18 December 2019, https://www.indiatoday.in/india/story/what-is-nrc-all-you-need-to-know-about-national-register-of-citizens-1629195-2019-12-18

157. 'CAA an Attempt to Convert India into Hindu Rashtra: Activist in Mangaluru Rally', *Times of India*, 15 January 2020, https://timesofindia.indiatimes.com/city/mangaluru/caa-an-attempt-to-convert-india-into-hindu-rashtra-activist-in-mangaluru-rally/articleshow/73279755.cms 'CAA, NRC Part of Their Agenda for Hindu Rashtra: P Chidambaram', *Outlook*, 28 December 2019, https://www.

outlookindia.com/magazine/story/india-news-caa-nrc-part-of-their-agenda-for-hindu-rashtra-p-chidambaram/302560

158. Video of the BJP press conference on 23 April 2019: https://www.youtube.com/watch?v=Z__6E5hPbHg
'Amit Shah Relates TMC to Tushtikaran-Mafia-Chit Fund', IANS, 11 April 2019, https://www.business-standard.com/article/news-ians/amit-shah-relates-tmc-to-tushtikaran-mafia-chit-fund-119041101069_1.html

159. P. Chidambaram's comments on Twitter (now X) on CAA, 22 March 2021, https://twitter.com/PChidambaram_IN/status/1373840587036631042?ref_src=twsrc%5Etfw

160. 'Why Rohingya, Ahmadiyya Muslims Not Covered Under CAA? Karat Asks', *Economic Times*, 18 February 2020, https://economictimes.indiatimes.com/news/politics-and-nation/why-rohingya-ahmadiyya-muslims-not-covered-under-caa-karat-asks/articleshow/74186741.cms?from=mdr

161. '8 Die in 2 Days as Anti-CAA Protests Rage across Country', *India Today*, 20 December 2019, https://www.indiatoday.in/india/story/anti-citizenship-amendment-act-protest-violence-deaths-karnataka-up-1630188-2019-12-20

162. 'PM Narendra Modi: No Talk of NRC at All, Lies Being Spread about Detention Centres', *Indian Express*, 23 December 2019, https://indianexpress.com/article/india/pm-narendra-modi-citizenship-amendment-law-nrc-bjp-campaign-delhi-6179940/

163. 'Kerala Challenges Citizenship Act in Supreme Court, First State to Do So', NDTV, 14 January 2020, https://www.ndtv.com/india-news/kerala-government-challenges-citizenship-act-in-supreme-court-first-state-to-do-so-2163600

164. 'Preliminary Counter Affidavit on Behalf of the Union of India', March 2020, p. 80. Mahesh Jethmalani, 'Besieged by Sophistry: The CAA Is Constitutionally Sound and Is Unfairly Picked Apart by Its Enemies', *Times of India*, 16 January 2020, https://timesofindia.indiatimes.com/blogs/toi-edit-page/besieged-by-sophistry-the-caa-is-constitutionally-sound-and-is-unfairly-picked-apart-by-its-enemies/

165. Interview, November 2022.

166. Ibid.

167. Ibid.

168. Karimbil Kunhikoman vs State of Kerala on 5 December 1961, 1962 AIR 723, 1962 SCR Supl. (1) 829.

169. Preliminary Counter-Affidavit on Behalf of Union of India, March 2020.

170. 'Pakistan Paradox: Ahmadis Are Anti-National but Those Who Opposed the Country's Creation Are Not', Scroll.in, 6 May 2017, https://scroll.in/article/836580/how-ahmadis-became-anti-pakistan-and-those-who-opposed-its-creation-came-to-define-nationalism

171. Lautenberg Program Fact Sheet, US Committee for Refugees and Immigrants, 7 September 2022, https://refugees.org/lautenberg-program-fact-sheet/ 'CAA Has Corollary in US Lautenberg Amendment', *Economic Times*, 18 January 2020, https://economictimes.indiatimes.com/news/politics-and-nation/caa-has-corollary-in-us-lautenberg-amendment/articleshow/73347361.cms?from=mdr

172. Press Information Bureau, FAQ on Citizenship Amendment Act, 18 December 2019, https://pibindia.wordpress.com/2019/12/18/citizenship-amendment-act-2019/

173. 'Modi Govt Gave Citizenship to 600 Muslims from Pakistan, Afghanistan, Bangladesh: Amit Shah', *India Today*, 18 December 2021, https://www.indiatoday.in/india/story/amit-shah-modi-government-muslims-citizenship-pakistan-afghanistan-bangladesh-1629134-2019-12-17 'Sitharaman: In last 6 Yrs, 2838 Pak Refugees, Including Muslims, Were Given Citizenship', *Indian Express*, 19 January 2020, https://indianexpress.com/article/india/adnan-sami-citizenship-nirmala-sitharaman-chennai-6224379/

174. 'Pakistan Must Repeal Its Discriminatory Measures Leading to Persecution of Ahmadis, Say UN Experts', United Nations Human Rights Office of the High Commissioner, 25 July 2018, https://www.ohchr.org/en/press-releases/2018/07/pakistan-must-repeal-discriminatory-measures-leading-persecution-ahmadis-say 'Deep Dive: Plight of Pakistan's Ahmadiyyas and Demands

for Their Inclusion in CAA', *India Today*, 7 January 2020, https://www.indiatoday.in/india/story/caa-pakistan-ahmadiyya-muslims-1634592-2020-01-07

175. '"No Citizenship for Ahmadiyas, They Took up Arms to Establish Pakistan": BJP Leader', *Outlook*, 25 December 2019, https://www.outlookindia.com/website/story/india-news-no-citizenship-for-ahmadiyas-they-took-up-arms-to-establish-pakistan-bjp-leader/344673

176. Abhinav Chandachud, 'Secularism and The Citizenship Amendment Act', SSRN, 4 January 2020, https://ssrn.com/abstract=3513828 or http://dx.doi.org/10.2139/ssrn.3513828

Chapter 2: The Hindu Ethos and the Calumny of Communalism

1. 'Ram Mandir: First Phase of Construction Complete, Darshan of Lord Ram in Garbhagriha from Dec 2023', *Swarajya*, 16 October 2021, https://swarajyamag.com/insta/ram-mandir-first-phase-of-construction-complete-darshan-of-lord-ram-in-garbhagriha-from-dec-2023

2. 'Ayodhya Verdict: Understanding the Supreme Court Judgement', *Hindustan Times*, 28 July 2020, https://www.hindustantimes.com/india-news/ayodhya-verdict-understanding-the-supreme-court-judgment/story-G7mzXfBFEDJ88PmuLj8CpL.html

3. 'PM Modi Performs "Bhoomi Pujan" for Ram Temple in Ayodhya', PTI, 5 August 2020, https://timesofindia.indiatimes.com/india/pm-modi-performs-bhoomi-pujan-for-ram-temple-in-ayodhya/articleshow/77368168.cms

4. Sharat Pradhan, 'At Ayodhya Bhoomi Pujan, Modi Became All-in-One; Proper Rituals Not Followed, Allege Pundits', The Wire, 7 August 2020, https://thewire.in/politics/ayodhya-bhoomi-pujan-narendra-modi-priests-pundits

5. Ibid.

6. Ibid.

7. Nalin Mehta, *The New BJP: Modi and the Making of the World's Largest Political Party*, Westland, 2022, p. 548.

8. 'PM Performs Bhoomi Pujan at "Shree Ram Janmabhoomi Mandir"', website of Prime Minister Narendra Modi, 5 August 2020, https://www.narendramodi.in/prime-minister-narendra-modi-performs-bhoomi-pujan-of-ram-mandir-in-ayodhya-550820

9. 'Ram Mandir Bhumi Pujan: Full text of PM Narendra Modi's Speech in Ayodhya', *Indian Express*, 5 August 2020, https://indianexpress.com/article/india/ram-mandir-bhumi-pujan-full-text-of-pm-narendra-modis-speech-in-ayodhya/

10. Ibid.

11. Sumit Kaul, 'Gandhi's "Ram Rajya" – What the Mahatma Meant by the Term, and Its Significance Today', Times Now, 1 October 2019, https://www.timesnownews.com/india/article/gandhi-s-ram-rajya-what-the-mahatma-meant-by-the-term-and-its-significance-today/498343
    References to 'Ramrajya' by Gandhi: https://www.mkgandhi.org/momgandhi/chap67.htm

12. 'Excerpt: How (and Why) the "Ramayana" TV Serial Brought Much of India to a Standstill in the 1980s', Scroll.in, 30 March 2020, https://scroll.in/reel/957548/excerpt-how-and-why-the-ramayana-tv-serial-brought-much-of-india-to-a-standstill-in-the-1980s; excerpted with permission from Amrita Shah, Telly-Guillotined: How Television Changed India, Sage Publications/Yoda Press, 2019.

13. 'Woman Touches Feet of Ramayan Fame Arun Govil at the Airport; Netizens Say, "People Still See Lord Ram in Him"', Entertainment Times, 1 October 2022, https://timesofindia.indiatimes.com/tv/news/hindi/woman-touches-feet-of-ramayan-fame-arun-govil-at-the-airport-netizens-say-people-still-see-lord-ram-in-him/articleshow/94586772.cms

14. 'Ramayan Actor Arun Govil: People Don't Call Me by My Name, They Call Me Ram', PTI, 15 May 2020, https://indianexpress.com/article/entertainment/television/people-dont-call-me-arun-govil-they-call-me-ram-ramayan-star-6337266/

15. '30 years of DD's Ramayana: The Back Story of the Show That Changed Indian TV Forever', *Hindustan Times*, 13 January 2018, https://www.hindustantimes.com/tv/30-years-of-dd-s-

ramayana-the-back-story-of-the-show-that-changed-indian-tv-forever/story-og0vbfSYwK75Zl7mQmdsjN.html

16. Suhas Palshikar, 'At Ayodhya, We Will See Dismantling of the Old, and the Bhoomi Pujan of the New Republic', *Indian Express*, 4 August 2020, https://indianexpress.com/article/opinion/ayodhya-ram-temple-bhoomi-pujan-pm-narendra-modi-6537822/

17. Ibid.

18. Ibid.

19. Pratap Bhanu Mehta, 'Ayodhya's Ram Temple Is First Real Colonisation of Hinduism by Political Power', *Indian Express*, 5 August 2020, https://indianexpress.com/article/opinion/columns/ayodhya-temple-ram-i-will-not-find-you-there-6539473/

20. Ibid.

21. Ibid.

22. Suhas Palshikar, 'At Ayodhya, We Will See Dismantling of the Old, and the Bhoomi Pujan of the New Republic', *Indian Express*.

23. 'Babri Demolition Badly Dented BJP's Credibility, Says Advani', *Indian Express*, 14 March 2011, http://archive.indianexpress.com/news/babri-demolition-badly-dented-bjp-s-credibility-says-advani/762059/

24. L.K. Advani, *My Country My Life*, Rupa, 2008, p. 407.

25. Ibid., p. 408.

26. 'Post Supreme Court Verdict, Ram Temple May Not Be a Vote Catcher for BJP', *Economic Times*, 13 November 2019, https://economictimes.indiatimes.com/news/politics-and-nation/view-post-supreme-court-verdict-ram-temple-may-not-be-a-vote-catcher-for-bjp/articleshow/72035256.cms?from=mdr

27. Vinod Sharma, 'Not Really a Swan Song for Advani', *Hindustan Times*, 20 December 2009, https://www.hindustantimes.com/india/not-really-a-swan-song-for-advani/story-2Qs2nCtT6vfCwPBwpOBDRP.html

28. 'Tempered by Power, BJP's Shift Away from 1989 Palampur Resolution on Temple Rows', *Indian Express*, 24 May 2022, https://indianexpress.com/article/political-pulse/gyanvapi-mosque-temple-row-bjp-palampur-resolution-7932478/

29. BJP   Political   Resolutions,   https://library.bjp.org/jspui/
    bitstream/123456789/264/1/Untitled-2.pdf
30. 'Ayodhya: Genuine Mediation Is Welcome', *Sunday Guardian*,
    4 May 2019, https://sundayguardianlive.com/news/ayodhya-
    genuine-mediation-welcome
31. Advani, *My Country My Life*, p. 408.
32. Ibid.
33. Ibid., pp. 408–9.
34. Pavan K. Varma, *The Great Hindu Civilisation: Achievement,
    Neglect, Bias and the Way* Forward, Westland, 2021, p. 4.
35. Ibid., p. 6.
36. Ibid.
37. Excerpts from the Times of India interview from 18 July 1993,
    accessed from: http://www.hvk.org/2020/0820/19.html
38. L.K. Advani referring to Girilal Jain's book *The Hindu
    Phenomenon* (1994), Advani, *My Country My Life*, p. 409.
39. Pratap Bhanu Mehta, 'Ayodhya's Ram Temple Is First Real
    Colonisation of Hinduism by Political Power', *Indian Express*.
40. M. Siddiq (D) Thr Lrs vs Mahant Suresh Das & Ors, judgment
    dated 9 November 2019, (923 Para 801), https://www.sci.gov.
    in/pdf/JUD_2.pdf
41. Ibid.
42. 'New Book Documents How Hindus Saved Idols and Rebuilt
    Temples Destroyed by Islamic Iconoclasm', R. Jagannathan's
    review of Meenakshi Jain's *Flight of Deities and Rebirth of
    Temples*, *Swarajya*, 5 March 2019, https://swarajyamag.com/
    books/new-book-documents-how-hindus-saved-idols-and-
    rebuilt-temples-destroyed-by-islamic-iconoclasm
    Abhinav Prakash Singh, 'Where Did the Temples Go?', *Open*,
    15 November 2019, https://openthemagazine.com/cover-
    stories/where-did-the-temples-go/
43. 'Hindu Society Has Been at War for over 1000 Years. It Is
    Natural for People Those at War to Be Aggressive', interview with
    Sarsanghchalak Mohan Bhagwat, *Organiser*, 10 January 2023,
    https://organiser.org/2023/01/10/104033/rss-news/hindu-
    society-has-been-at-war-for-over-1000-years-it-is-natural-for-
    people-those-at-war-to-be-aggressive/

44. '"Retaining the Core Essence & Direction of Sangh during the Favourable Times Is the Biggest Test": Dr Mohan Bhagwat', *Organiser*, 9 January 2023, https://organiser.org/2023/01/09/103855/bharat/retaining-the-core-essence-direction-of-sangh-during-the-favourable-times-is-the-biggest-test/

45. Ibid.

46. Pratap Bhanu Mehta, 'Ayodhya's Ram Temple Is First Real Colonisation of Hinduism by Political Power', *Indian Express*.

47. M. Siddiq (D) Thr Lrs vs Mahant Suresh Das & Ors, judgment of Supreme Court dated 9 November 2019, 913, para 788 (XVII), https://www.sci.gov.in/pdf/JUD_2.pdf

48. Ibid.; 922, 923, para 800.

49. 'Finally, Ayodhya Mosque Trust Gets Tax Exemption for Donations after 9 Months', *Times of India*, 29 May 2021, https://timesofindia.indiatimes.com/city/lucknow/finally-ayodhya-mosque-trust-gets-tax-exemption-for-donations-after-9-months/articleshow/83049741.cms

50. 'Mosque Complex in Ayodhya gets Hindus' Backing', *Hindustan Times*, 13 August 2020, https://www.hindustantimes.com/india-news/mosque-complex-in-ayodhya-gets-hindus-backing/story-IJzQ3A19Hz1ELnhsHiYtXI.html
Reference to article on the ABP website about 40 per cent of donations for the construction of a mosque in Ayodhya coming from Hindus, 13 November 2022, https://www.abplive.com/states/up-uk/ayodhya-uttar-pradesh-hindus-contributed-40-percent-of-total-donations-for-construction-of-dhannipur-mosque-ann-2258379

51. Kenan Malik, 'Mezquita and Hagia Sophia: Two Sacred Symbols and the Culture Wars That Belie Their Complex History', *Guardian*, 14 March 2023, https://www.theguardian.com/commentisfree/2023/mar/04/mezquita-hagia-sophia-two-sacred-symbols-culture-wars-belie-complex-history
Aatish Taseer, 'In Search of a Lost Spain', *New York Times Style Magazine*, 3 November 2022, https://www.nytimes.com/2022/11/03/t-magazine/spain-islamic-history.html

52. 'Turkey Converts Istanbul's Iconic Hagia Sophia Back into a Mosque', NPR, 10 July 2020, https://www.npr.org/2020/07/10/889691777/turkish-court-ruling-clears-way-for-hagia-sophia-to-be-converted-to-a-mosque

53. Purnima Tripathi, 'Justice and the Babri Masjid', The Citizen, 3 October 2020, https://www.thecitizen.in/index.php/en/NewsDetail/index/9/19447/Justice-and-the-Babri-Masjid 'Babri Masjid Demolition Verdict: All 32 Accused Acquitted', *Hindustan Times*, 30 September 2020, https://www.hindustantimes.com/india-news/babri-masjid-demolition-verdict-all-32-accused-acquitted/story-pEH3vJXWUCxhkfZ44kCnaI.html

54. M. Siddiq (D) Thr Lrs vs Mahant Suresh Das & Ors, judgment of Supreme Court dated 9 November 2019; 913 para 788 (XVII), https://www.sci.gov.in/pdf/JUD_2.pdf

55. Ibid., p. 123, para 82.

56. The Place of Worship (Special Provisions) Act, 1991, 18 September 1991, https://www.mha.gov.in/sites/default/files/PlaceWorshipAct1991.pdf

57. M. Siddiq (D) Thr Lrs vs Mahant Suresh Das & Ors, 124 para 83, https://www.sci.gov.in/pdf/JUD_2.pdf

58. Petition filed by Ashwini Kumar Upadhyay in Supreme Court. It can be accessed here: https://www.scobserver.in/wp-content/uploads/2021/10/Places_of_Worship_Act_WP.pdf

59. A.J. Philip, 'Varanasi and Mathura, New Ayodhya in the Making', The Leaflet, 18 April 2021, https://theleaflet.in/varanasi-and-mathura-new-ayodhya-in-the-making/ Mohammad Wasim, 'The Challenge to the Places of Worship (Special Provisions) Act, 1991 Is Misconceived', The Leaflet, 12 September 2022, https://theleaflet.in/the-challenge-to-places-of-worship-special-provisions-act-1991-is-misconceived/

60. 'Mohan Bhagwat: No More Andolan . . . Why Look for Shivling in Every Mosque?', *Indian Express*, 3 June 2022, https://indianexpress.com/article/cities/mumbai/rss-chief-mohan-bhagwat-no-more-andolan-shivling-mosque-7949964/

61. 'Congress Objects to Introduction of Bill Seeking Repeal of Places of Worship Act', PTI, 3 February 2023,

https://www.indiatoday.in/india/story/congress-objects-
introduction-of-bill-seeking-repeal-of-places-of-worship-
act-2330262-2023-02-03
'"Blatant Violation of Places of Worship Act": Asaduddin
Owaisi on Gyanvapi Mosque Order', The Wire, 13 May
2022, https://thewire.in/politics/blatant-violation-of-places-of-
worship-act-asaduddin-owaisi-on-gyanvapi-mosque-order

Chapter 3: They Took the Hindu Out of the Indian

1. 'Honduras v El Salvador: The Football Match That Kicked
    Off a War', BBC, 27 June 2019, https://www.bbc.com/news/
    world-latin-america-48673853
2. '"Vande Mataram" Penned in Bengali, Says TN, and Candidate
    Gets One Mark', *Times of India*, 14 June 2017, https://
    timesofindia.indiatimes.com/city/chennai/vande-mataram-
    penned-in-bengali-says-tn-and-candidate-gets-one-mark/
    articleshow/59588206.cms
3. Ibid.
4. Ibid.
5. Ibid.
6. 'Vande Mataram First Written in Bengali or Sanskrit, Man Asks
    Madras Court', NDTV, 8 July 2017, https://www.ndtv.com/
    tamil-nadu-news/national-song-vande-mataram-first-written-
    in-bengali-or-sanskrit-man-asks-madras-court-1722103
7. 'Vande Mataram of Sanskrit Origin, But Written
    in Bengali: Tamil Nadu Advocate General', *Indian
    Express*, 13 July 2017, https://indianexpress.com/article/
    india/vande-mataram-of-sanskrit-origin-but-written-
    in-bengali-tamil-nadu-advocate-general-4749236/
    'Vande Mataram Was Written in Bengali, TN Govt Tells
    Madras HC', *Times of India*, 13 July 2017, https://timesofindia.
    indiatimes.com/city/chennai/vande-mataram-was-written-in-
    bengali-tn-govt-tells-madras-hc/articleshow/59576411.cms
8. K. Veeramani vs the Chairman on 25 July 2017, Madras
    High Court Order, 25 July 2017, https://indiankanoon.org/
    doc/123111536/

9.   Ibid.
10.   Ibid.
11.   Ibid.
12.   'Vande Mataram Fiat Riles Muslim Outfit', *The Hindu*, 26 July 2017, https://www.thehindu.com/news/national/tamil-nadu/vande-mataram-fiat-riles-muslim-outfit/article19360475.ece 'Controversy over Vande Mataram in Maharashtra Yet Again', *India Today*, 17 July 2017, https://www.indiatoday.in/india/story/controversy-vande-mataram-maharashtra-1026724-2017-07-27
13.   A. Faizur Rehman, 'Why Muslims Reject Vande Mataram', *Hindustan Times*, 30 August 2006, https://www.hindustantimes.com/india/why-muslims-reject-vande-mataram/story-rRNDm0d1waQ3FCfew9IhxJ.html
14.   Ibid.
       Shirk in Islam, Britannica, https://www.britannica.com/topic/shirk
15.   Doctrines of the Qu'ran, Britannica, https://www.britannica.com/topic/Islam/Doctrines-of-the-Qur-an A. Faizur Rahman, 'Why Muslims Reject Vande Mataram', *Hindustan Times*, 30 August 2006, https://www.hindustantimes.com/india/why-muslims-reject-vande-mataram/story-rRNDm0d1waQ3FCfew9IhxJ.html
16.   Ibid.
       'Love India, But Only One God in Islam: Deoband's Fatwa against Bharat Mata Ki Jai', *India Today*, 1 April 2016, https://www.indiatoday.in/india/story/love-india-but-only-one-god-in-islam-deobands-fatwa-against-bharat-mata-ki-jai-315794-2016-04-01
17.   'Love India, But Only One God in Islam: Deoband's Fatwa against Bharat Mata Ki Jai', *India Today*, 1 April 2016, https://www.indiatoday.in/india/story/love-india-but-only-one-god-in-islam-deobands-fatwa-against-bharat-mata-ki-jai-315794-2016-04-01
18.   'A history of the Origins of the Vande Mataram and Its Journey Thereafter', *Indian Express*, 27 July 2017, https://indianexpress.com/article/research/a-history-of-the-origins-of-the-vande-mataram-and-its-journey-thereafter/

19. Sabyasachi Bhattacharya, 'Vande Mataram: In Rewind Mode', *Frontline*, 4 December 2009, https://frontline.thehindu.com/the-nation/article30185996.ece

20. Radhika Iyengar, 'A History of the Origins of the Vande Mataram and Its Journey Thereafter', *Indian Express*, 27 July 2017, https://indianexpress.com/article/research/a-history-of-the-origins-of-the-vande-mataram-and-its-journey-thereafter/.

21. Ibid.

22. Ibid.

23. Ibid.
    A. Faizur Rahman, 'Why Muslims Reject Vande Mataram'.

24. Prabash K. Dutta, 'How Bharat Mata Came to Personify India', *Times of India*, 11 August 2022, https://timesofindia.indiatimes.com/india/how-bharat-mata-came-to-personify-india/articleshow/93451355.cms

25. 'Kerala Governor Accuses CMO of "Patronising Smuggling": Meet Arif Mohammed Khan, Known for Candour and Controversy', *Indian Express*, 4 November 2022, https://indianexpress.com/article/explained/who-is-kerala-governor-arif-mohammed-khan-8247428/

26. 'Unnecessary and Irrelevant', *Outlook*, 3 February 2022 https://www.outlookindia.com/website/story/unnecessary-and-irrelevant/232420 (piece written by Arif Mohammad Khan, first published in Pioneer).

27. Ibid.

28. Ibid.

29. Ibid.

30. Ibid.

31. 'Vande Mataram Fiat Riles Muslim Outfit, *The Hindu*. 'Madras High Court Order on Compulsory Singing of Vande Mataram Sparks Row', PTI, 28 July 2017, https://economictimes.indiatimes.com/news/politics-and-nation/madras-high-court-order-on-compulsory-singing-of-vande-mataram-sparks-row/articleshow/59803662.cms?from=mdr 'Judicial Over-reach', editorial in Statesman, 27 July 2017, https://www.thestatesman.com/opinion/judicial-overreach-1501186789.html

S.A. Aiyar, 'Nobody Should Be Forced to Sing Vande Mataram', *Times of India*, 29 July 2017, https://timesofindia.indiatimes. com/blogs/Swaminomics/nobody-should-be-forced-to-sing-vande-mataram/

32. 'Here Is a Breakdown of Laws in 47 States That Require Reciting the Pledge of Allegiance', The Hill, 2 April 2022, https:// thehill.com/homenews/3256719-47-states-require-the-pledge-of-allegiance-be-recited-in-schools-here-is-a-breakdown-of-each-states-laws/

33. 'Expression of Support for the Pledge of Allegiance', Congressional Record Volume 148, Number 87, 26 June 2002, pp. S6105–S6112, from the Congressional Record Online through the Government Publishing Office, www.gpo. gov, https://www.govinfo.gov/content/pkg/CREC-2002-06-26/html/CREC-2002-06-26-pt2-PgS6105.htm

34. Pavan K. Varma, *The Great Hindu Civilisation: Achievement, Neglect, Bias and the Way* Forward, Westland, 2021, p. 6.

35. The authors here refer to recent works, such as Pavan K. Varma's *The Great Hindu Civilisation* and Meenakshi Jain's *The Hindus of Hindustan: A Civilizational Journey* (Aryan Books International, 2023), among others. More details in Chapter 6 as well.

36. K.E. Radhakrishna, 'Gandhiji's Rama Unified India', *Deccan Herald*, 14 August 2021, https://www.deccanherald.com/opinion/main-article/gandhiji-s-rama-unified-india-1019587.html

37. Girilal Jain, 'Advani Is Nehru's Successor', The Daily, 7 April 1991, https://www.girilaljainarchive.net/1991/04/advani-is-nehrus-successor-girilal-jain/

38. Pavan K. Varma, *The Great Hindu Civilisation*, pp. 11–12.

39. A reference used to suggest an integration of Hindu and Muslim cultural influences, among others.

40. Virendra Kumar, *Committees and Commissions in India*, vol. 7, 1966, Concept Publishing Company, p. 328.

41. 'Lenin on Party Organisation and Party Literature', sourced from *Lenin's Collected Works*, Progress Publishers, 1905, https://www.marxists.org/archive/lenin/works/1905/nov/13.htm

Reference to Girilal Jain's reference to Lenin in Girilal Jain, *The Hindu Phenomenon*, UBS Publishers Distributors Ltd, 1994, p. 114.

42. Another reference to 'composite culture', a syncretism of Hindu and Islamic cultural influences.

43. Pavan K. Varma, *The Great Hindu Civilisation*, pp. 13–14.

44. 'Sengol Signified "Transfer of Power" Says Tamil Nadu HRCE Ministry's 2021-22 Policy Note', *Swarajya*, 27 May 2023, https://swarajyamag.com/news-brief/sengol-signified-transfer-of-power-says-tamil-nadu-hrce-ministrys-2021-22-policy-note
'At the Inauguration of the New Parliament House, PM Modi Will Establish the Historical and Sacred "Sengol" in the Parliament House', PIB, MHA, 24 May 2023, https://pib.gov.in/PressReleasePage.aspx?PRID=1926883
'All You Need to Know about the History and Significance of the Sengol to Be Placed in the New Parliament Complex', *Swarajya*, 24 May 2023, https://swarajyamag.com/culture/all-you-need-to-know-about-the-history-and-significance-of-the-sengol-to-be-placed-in-the-new-parliament-complex
The 2021-22 Policy Note of Hindu Religious and Charitable Endowments: https://hrce.tn.gov.in/resources/docs/actrule/4/149/document_1.pdf

45. Aravindan Neelakandan, 'Sengol: Not Symbol of Power but Dharma over Power', *Swarajya*, 25 May 2023, https://swarajyamag.com/politics/sengol-not-symbol-of-power-but-dharma-over-power

46. N. Sai Charan, 'The Sengol - A Historic Sceptre with a Deep Tamil Nadu Connection', *The Hindu*, 24 May 2023, https://www.thehindu.com/news/national/tamil-nadu/sengol-a-historic-sceptre-with-a-deep-tamil-nadu-connection/article66888264.ece

47. 'India: Oh Lovely Dawn', *Time*, 25 August 1947, https://content.time.com/time/subscriber/article/0,33009,798062,00.html

48. Dominique Lapierre and Larry Collins, *Freedom at Midnight*, Avon, 1976, pp. 282–83.

49. Girilal Jain, *The Hindu Phenomenon*, UBS Publishers Distributors Ltd, 1994, p. 115.

50. Romila Thapar, 'Imagined Religious Communities?', excerpt from *The Historian and her Craft: Collected Essays and Lectures of Romila Thapar*, Oxford University Press, republished in Newsclick, 26 December 2017, https://www.newsclick.in/imagined-religious-communities

51. Romila Thapar, *The Penguin History of Early India: From the Origins to AD 1300*, Penguin India, 2003, p. 19. Pavan K. Varma, *The Great Hindu Civilisation*, p. 21.

52. Ashwin Sanghi, 'Want to Preserve Secularism in India? Well, Preserve the Hindu Ethos First', *Swarajya*, 8 August 2020, https://swarajyamag.com/ideas/want-to-preserve-secularism-in-india-well-preserve-the-hindu-ethos-first

53. Constituent Assembly Debates on 6 December 1948, Part I, https://indiankanoon.org/doc/1933556/

54. Ram Madhav, *The Hindutva Paradigm: Integral Humanism and Quest for a Non-Western Worldview*, Westland, 2021, p. 117.

55. Ibid.

56. Ibid.

57. Ibid.

58. 'Hindu Spiritual Leaders to Seek Exit of Govts from Temple Management', *Indian Express*, 4 April 2023, https://indianexpress.com/article/cities/ahmedabad/hindu-spiritual-leaders-to-seek-exit-of-govts-from-temple-management-8536267/
'VHP Announces Month-Long Nationwide Campaign to Raise Awareness on "Love-Jihad", Demands Anti-Conversion Laws', *Outlook*, 1 December 2022, https://www.outlookindia.com/national/vhp-announces-month-long-nationwide-campaign-to-raise-awareness-on-love-jihad-demands-anti-conversion-laws-news-241652

59. Vinay Sitapati, *Jugalbandi: The BJP before Modi*, Penguin, 2020, p. 139.

60. 'NCERT Syllabus Rationalisation Gives Rise to Fresh Row: Topics Removed and Why the Syllabus Was Cut Down', *India*

Today, 7 April 2023, https://www.indiatoday.in/education-today/news/story/ncert-syllabus-rationalisation-gives-rise-to-fresh-row-topics-removed-and-why-the-syllabus-was-cut-down-2356572-2023-04-06

61. 'NCERT Textbook Revision: Why It Happens Every Few Years & What Makes It Controversial', *Indian Express*, 7 April 2023, https://indianexpress.com/article/explained/revising-school-textbooks-ncert-8543190/

62. 'Express Investigation–Part 3: Textbook Revision Slashes Portion in History on Islamic Rulers of India', *Indian Express*, 20 June 2022. 'NCERT Syllabus Rationalisation Gives Rise to Fresh Row: Topics Removed and Why the Syllabus Was Cut Down', *India Today*, 7 April 2023, https://www.indiatoday.in/education-today/news/story/ncert-syllabus-rationalisation-gives-rise-to-fresh-row-topics-removed-and-why-the-syllabus-was-cut-down-2356572-2023-04-06

63. 'Maulana Azad Reference Omitted in NCERT Textbook', *The Hindu*, 12 April 2023, https://www.thehindu.com/news/national/deleted-from-ncert-text-maulana-azads-name-autonomy-condition-for-jk-accession/article66729738.ece

64. Dinesh Saklani's interview to Times Now, 4 April 2023. Also see, '"It's a Lie, Chapters on Mughals Have Not Been Dropped": NCERT Chief Dinesh Saklani Clarifies', ANI, 5 April 2023, https://timesofindia.indiatimes.com/videos/news/its-a-lie-chapters-on-mughals-have-not-been-dropped-ncert-chief-dinesh-prasad-saklani-clarifies/videoshow/99256532.cms

65. Ibid.

66. 'Concerted Attempt to "Re-Write" History, Pass on "Distorted Legacy": Congress on Removal of Maulana Azad References from NCERT Textbook', *Indian Express*, 13 April 2023, https://indianexpress.com/article/india/removal-of-maulana-azad-references-from-ncert-textbook-congress-8554984/

67. Subject: Newspaper item on Azad reference omitted in NCERT textbook regarding, NCERT, 13 April 2023, https://ncert.nic.in/pdf/Rationalisation-of-textbook/Response_on_Maulana_Azad_in_NCERT_textbook.pdf

68. Lakshmi Iyer and Ashok Malik, 'NCERT Censors Politically Inconvenient Textbooks, but Banality in History Teaching Remains', *India Today*, 10 December 2001, https://www.indiatoday.in/magazine/nation/story/20011210-ncert-censors-politically-inconvenient-textbooks-but-banality-in-history-teaching-remains-774900-2001-12-09

69. Ibid.

70. Aravindan Neelakandan, 'Why Meenakshi Jain's New Book Is a Correction Indian Historiography Desperately Needed', *Swarajya*, 17 March 2023, https://swarajyamag.com/books/pioneering-history-text-a-journey-into-the-early-millennia-of-hindu-civilisation

71. Interview conducted in April 2023.

72. Ibid.

73. Interviews conducted in April and May 2023.

74. 'Citing Overlap, NCERT Removes Portions on 2002 Gujarat Riots, Emergency, Mughal Courts from Class 12 Books', *The Hindu*, 17 June 2022, https://www.thehindu.com/education/overlapping-ncert-portions-2002-gujarat-riots-emergency-mughal-courts-class-12-books/article65537166.ece
Also see: 'Express Investigation: Part 1: From Emergency to Gujarat riots, Lessons of Past Deleted from Textbooks of Future', *Indian Express*, 18 June 2022, https://indianexpress.com/article/express-exclusive/express-investigation-part-1-from-emergency-to-gujarat-riots-lessons-of-past-deleted-from-textbooks-of-future-7976207/

75. 'Full Transcript of LK Advani's Interview', *India Today*, 20 June 2015, https://www.indiatoday.in/india/story/lk-advani-interview-with-karan-thappar-to-the-point-258566-2015-06-19

76. Converse interview with S. Gurumurthy on Times Now, 15 April 2023, https://www.youtube.com/watch?v=tuPZRfpcopk

77. Ibid.

78. Ibid.

79. Ibid.

80. Ibid.

81. Ibid.

82. Ibid.
83. 'Will Win 2024 Polls under PM Modi's Leadership: Gadkari', IANS, 3 June 2023, https://morungexpress.com/will-win-2024-polls-under-pm-modis-leadership-gadkari
84. '2024 Polls, G20 Focus of PM's Message to BJP Colleagues', *Hindustan Times*, 6 December 2022, https://www.hindustantimes.com/india-news/2024-polls-g20-focus-of-pm-s-message-to-bjp-colleagues-101670263937091.html

Chapter 4: Whither Ganga–Jamuni Tehzeeb?

1. Maḥmūd King of Ghazna, Encyclopedia Britannica; https://www.britannica.com/biography/Mahmud-king-of-Ghazna
2. Ibid.
3. Ibid.
4. M.J. Akbar, *The Shade of Swords: Jihad and the Conflict between Islam and Christianity*, Roli Books, 2003, Chapter 8, 'Jihad in the East: A Crescent over Delhi', loc. 2018 (on Kindle).
   Meenakshi Jain, *The Hindus of Hindustan: A Civilizational Journey*, Aryan Books International 2023, pp. 215–16.
5. Maḥmūd King of Ghazna, Britannica; https://www.britannica.com/biography/Mahmud-king-of-Ghazna
6. Ibid.
7. M.J. Akbar, *The Shade of Swords*, loc. 2024.
8. Ibid., loc. 2035.
   B.R. Ambedkar, *Pakistan or Partition of India*, p. 43.
   Abraham Eraly, *The Age of Wrath: A History of the Delhi Sultanate*, pp 40-49
9. Makarand Paranjape, 'And Thus Fell Nalanda', *Swarajya*, 9 March 2018, https://swarajyamag.com/magazine/and-thus-fell-nalandaa
10. Pavan K. Varma, *The Great Hindu Civilisation*, pp. 193–94.
11. Ibid., pp. 194–96.
12. Ibid., p. 196.
13. Ibid.
14. Ibid.
15. Ibid.

16. Donald Eugene Smith, *India as a Secular State*, Princeton University Press, 1963, p. 63.

17. Ibid.

18. Pavan K. Varma, *The Great Hindu Civilisation*, p. 200.

19. Ibid.

20. Ibid.
     Also read: Ayush Kaushik, 'Secularism or Faith: The Ethos of India', *Times of India*, 27 October 2020, https://timesofindia.indiatimes.com/blogs/voices/secularism-or-faith-the-ethos-of-india/

21. Donald Eugene Smith, *India as a Secular State*, p. 63.

22. Ibid., pp. 64–65.

23. Ibid., p. 61.

24. Vikram Sampath, *Bravehearts of Bharat: Vignettes from Indian History*, Penguin Random House India, 2022, p. 103.

25. Abraham Eraly, *Emperors of the Peacock Throne: The Saga of the Great Mughals*, Penguin India, 2007, pp. 401–2.

26. Ibid., pp. 406–7.

27. Ibid., pp. 398–99.

28. Heather Souvaine Horn, 'Facing up to the Past, German-Style', *New Republic*, 31 October 2019, https://newrepublic.com/article/155546/facing-past-german-style
     Lizzie Widdicombe, 'What Can We Learn from the Germans about Confronting Our History?', *New Yorker*, 21 October 2019, https://www.newyorker.com/culture/cultural-comment/what-can-we-learn-from-the-germans-about-confronting-our-history

29. Ibid.

30. '"A New Star Rises": Jawaharlal Nehru's Speech on the Birth of Independent India', *Hindustan Times*, 12 August 2018, https://www.hindustantimes.com/india-news/a-new-star-rises-jawaharlal-nehru-s-speech-on-the-birth-of-independent-india/story-fT9JIPYpMnz2OkRUgGNIZP.html

31. Report of the University Education Commission (December 1948 – August 1949), vol. 1, Ministry of Education, Government of India, 1962, para 53, p. 51.

32. Ibid.

33. Virendra Kumar, *Committees and Commissions in India*, vol. 7, 1966, Concept Publishing Company, p. 328.

34. Ibid.
35. B.R. Ambedkar, *Pakistan or the Partition of India*, p. 21.
36. Ibid.
37. Ibid.
38. Ibid.
39. Ibid., p. 24.
40. Ibid.
41. Mubarak Ali, 'Past Present: When the Empire Crumbled', *Dawn*, 25 August 2013, https://www.dawn.com/news/1038270
    Also read: Rohit Sahasrabudhe, '261 Years Since Panipat: How a Sufi Preacher Reached Out to Abdali and Asked Him to Restore Islamic Supremacy in India', *Swarajya*, 14 January 2022, https://swarajyamag.com/culture/panipat-a-failed-attempt-to-revive-islamic-supremacy-in-india
42. J. Sai Deepak, *India, Bharat and Pakistan: The Constitutional Journey of a Sandwiched Civilisation*, Bloomsbury, 2022.
43. Ibid., pp. 37–38.
44. Ibid., p. 42.
45. Ibid. p. 58.
    Also read: Ghulam Rasool Dehlvi, 'Syed Ahmad Rai Barelvi and the 18th Century Mujahidin Movement in the Indian Subcontinent', Firstpost, 22 May 2016, https://www.firstpost.com/india/syed-ahmad-rai-barelvi-and-the-18th-century-mujahidin-movement-in-the-indian-subcontinent-2790982.html
46. Ibid., pp. 58–60.
    Also read: Uday Mahurkar, 'Steeped in Extremism: Balakot Has Been a Hub of Wahabi Ideology and Radical Islam for Far Too Long', DailyO, 28 February 2019, https://www.dailyo.in/voices/balakot-wahabi-islam-jaish-e-mohammad-jem-masood-azhar-hafiz-saeed-lashkar-e-taiba-iaf-air-strike-iaf-mig-21-29687
47. 'Balakot Was Epicentre of Jihad in South Asia', IANS, 26 February 2019, https://www.business-standard.com/article/news-ians/balakot-was-epicentre-of-jihad-in-south-asia-119022601242_1.html

48. 'Balakot Camp Blown up by IAF Was Jaish's Preferred Training Spot for 18 Yrs', *Hindustan Times*, 16 June 2020, https://www.hindustantimes.com/india-news/terror-breeding-ground-brought-down/story-KuJuIOQLsLmsBmocZbTRYK.html

49. 'Jaish Terrorists Attack CRPF Convoy in Kashmir, Kill at Least 40 Personnel', PTI, 16 February 2019, https://timesofindia.indiatimes.com/india/37-crpf-jawans-martyred-in-ied-blast-in-jks-pulwama/articleshow/67992189.cms

50. 'Rahul Gandhi Says He Isn't Savarkar, Won't Apologise', *Economic Times*, 27 March 2023, https://economictimes.indiatimes.com/news/politics-and-nation/rahul-gandhi-says-he-isnt-savarkar-wont-apologise/articleshow/98991209.cms 'VD Savarkar Had Sown Seed of Partition: Chhattisgarh CM; Slams BJP-RSS on "Akhand Bharat"', PTI, 14 August 2022, https://theprint.in/india/v-d-savarkar-had-sown-seed-of-partition-chhattisgarh-cm-slams-bjp-rss-on-akhand-bharat/1082585/

51. T.C.A. Raghavan, 'The Softer Savarkar', *Open*, 21 December 2017, https://openthemagazine.com/new-year-2018-double-issue/the-softer-savarkar/

52. Ibid.

53. Ibid.

54. J. Sai Deepak, *India, Bharat and Pakistan*, pp. 109–10.

55. 'The Founder of a "Mini-India"', *The Hindu*, 18 October 2021, https://www.thehindu.com/opinion/op-ed/the-founder-of-a-mini-india/article37044994.ece

56. J. Sai Deepak, *India, Bharat and Pakistan*, p. 130.

57. Ibid., pp. 133–35.

58. Ibid., Deepak citing historian R.C. Majumdar, p. 153.

59. Ibid., p. 155.

60. Ibid.

61. James Sherwood, 'Hall of Fame, Muhammad Ali Jinnah, Henry Poole & Co', https://henrypoole.com/individual/muhammad-ali-jinnah/

62. Ishtiaq Ahmed, *Jinnah: His Successes, Failures and Role in History*, Viking, pp. 294–95.

63. 'The Venkat Dhulipala Interview: "On Partition Issue, Jinnah and Ambedkar Were on the Same Page"', Scroll.in, 28 June

2016, https://scroll.in/article/810132/the-venkat-dhulipala-interview-on-the-partition-issue-jinnah-and-ambedkar-were-on-the-same-page

64. Ishtiaq Ahmed, *Jinnah: His Successes, Failures and Role in History*, pp. 309–10.
Also read: 'The Elections of 1946 and the Road to Partition', News18, 11 February 2023, https://www.news18.com/news/opinion/the-elections-of-1946-and-the-road-to-partition-7056181.html

65. 'The Venkat Dhulipala Interview: "On Partition Issue, Jinnah and Ambedkar Were on the Same Page"', Scroll.in.

66. Ibid.

67. Ibid.

68. Ibid.

69. Shamsul Islam, 'India's First War of Independence, and the Legacy of Hindu-Muslim Unity', *Indian Express*, 12 May 2020, https://indianexpress.com/article/opinion/columns/1857-india-war-of-independence-hindu-muslim-6405053/
Also read: Vikram Sampath, *Bravehearts of Bharat*, p. 305.

70. Hasan Suroor, 'Why Owaisi Is Wrong that Muslim Freedom Fighters Have Been Written Out of History', Firstpost, 8 September 2022, https://www.firstpost.com/opinion-news-expert-views-news-analysis-firstpost-viewpoint/why-owaisi-is-wrong-that-muslim-freedom-fighters-have-been-written-out-of-history-11206141.html

71. Kamaldeep Singh Brar, 'A Tribute to Struggle for Independence in Undivided Punjab', *Indian Express*, 15 August 2020, https://indianexpress.com/article/india/a-tribute-to-struggle-for-independence-in-undivided-punjab-6555763/

72. 'Role of Muslims in India's Freedom Struggle', Newsclick, 7 August 2022, https://www.newsclick.in/role-muslims-indias-freedom-struggle

73. Sanjeev Sanyal, *Revolutionaries: The Other Story of How India Won Its Freedom*, HarperCollins, 2023, p. 280.
Anirban Mitra, 'Freedom on the Waves: The Story of the 1946 Indian Naval Mutiny', The Wire, 24 January 2022, https://thewire.in/history/freedom-on-the-waves-the-indian-naval-mutiny-70-years-later

74. Adrija Roychowdhury, 'Why a Majority of Muslims Opposed Jinnah's Idea of Partition and Stayed on in India', *Indian Express*, 15 August 2022, https://indianexpress.com/article/research/why-a-majority-of-muslims-opposed-jinnahs-idea-of-partition-and-stayed-on-in-india-8090835/

75. Mushirul Hasan, 'In Search of Integration and Identity: Indian Muslims Since Independence', *Economic and Political Weekly*, vol. 23, no. 45/47, November 1988, pp. 2467–2778.

76. Ibid.

77. Ibid.

78. Ibid.

Chapter 5: A Discriminatory Secularism

1. 'Karnataka Polls: Bharat Jodo Impact – Rahul Gandhi Rise & Victory Trail', *Times of India*, 14 May 2023, https://timesofindia.indiatimes.com/elections/assembly-elections/karnataka/news/karnataka-result-congress-wins-37/51-on-jodo-route/articleshow/100219297.cms

2. Yogendra Yadav's tweet, 27 October 2022, https://twitter.com/_YogendraYadav/status/1585618745455775746

3. Amnesty International, India, 2022, https://www.amnesty.org/en/location/asia-and-the-pacific/south-asia/india/report-india/ Jeffrey Gettleman, Kai Schultz, Suhasini Raj and Hari Kumar, 'Under Modi, a Hindu Nationalist Surge Has Further Divided India', *New York Times*, 11 April 2019, https://www.nytimes.com/2019/04/11/world/asia/modi-india-elections.html

4. '"Denounce Insult of Religious Personalities": BJP Removes Spokespersons', NDTV, 5 June 2022, https://www.ndtv.com/india-news/bjp-suspends-spokespersons-nupur-sharma-naveen-jindal-over-controversial-comments-news-agency-ani-3040000.

5. '"Pasmanda Muslims Treated as Untouchables": PM Modi Leads Outreach to Marginalized Muslim Community in Poll-Bound MP', *Swarajya*, 27 June 2023, https://swarajyamag.com/politics/pasmanda-muslims-treated-as-untouchables-pm-modi-leads-outreach-to-marginalized-muslim-community-in-poll-bound-mp

6. 'BJP Candidate List for UP Civic Polls Shows Outreach to Pasmanda Muslims', *The Hindu*, 1 May 2023, https://www.thehindu.com/news/cities/Delhi/bjp-candidate-list-for-up-civic-polls-shows-outreach-to-pasmanda-muslims/article66801133.ece

7. Read Section 195 (1) (a) of the Bharatiya Nyaya Sanhita, 2023, accessed from PRS Legislative Research, https://prsindia.org/files/bills_acts/bills_parliament/2023/Bharatiya_Nyaya_Sanhita,_2023.pdf

8. 'Unveiling of the Logo, Theme and Website of India's G20 Presidency', Prime Minister's Office press release, 8 November 2022, https://pib.gov.in/PressReleasePage.aspx?PRID=1874524

9. 'English Rendering of PM's Reply to the Motion of Thanks to President's Address in Rajya Sabha', Prime Minister's Office press release, 9 February 2023, https://www.pib.gov.in/PressReleseDetailm.aspx?PRID=1897766

10. 'Secularism Constitutional Commitment of BJP; "Pseudo Secularists" Misused It for Votes: Naqvi', PTI, 12 February 2022, https://theprint.in/india/secularism-constitutional-commitment-of-bjp-pseudo-secularists-misused-it-for-votes-naqvi/828796/

11. 'Full Text of Modi's First Speech after Historic Election Victory', *Business Insider*, 26 May 2019, https://www.businessinsider.in/full-text-of-modi-speech-lok-sabha-election-2019/articleshow/69467611.cms

12. 'Objectives under ARTICLE II of the BJP Constitution provide that - The Party shall bear true faith and allegiance to the Constitution of India as by law established and to the principles of socialism, secularism and democracy and would uphold the sovereignty, unity and integrity of India', https://eci.gov.in/files/file/4929-bharatiya-janata-party-constitution/

13. Pledge under the BJP constitution includes, 'I subscribe to the concept of a Secular State and Nation not based on religion', https://eci.gov.in/files/file/4929-bharatiya-janata-party-constitution/

14. 'Antony Panel Report Lists out Reasons for LS Poll Rout', *Hindustan Times*, 17 August 2014, https://www.hindustantimes.

com/india/antony-panel-report-lists-out-reasons-for-ls-poll-rout/story-Qlg82GBxRBua7k3TwgSa3M.html

15. Constituent Assembly debates on 27 August 1947, Part Ii, Sardar Vallabhbhai Patel, https://indiankanoon.org/doc/522288/

16. Ibid.

17. Constituent Assembly debates on 25 May 1949, Part Ii, https://indiankanoon.org/doc/790979/

18. Abhinav Chandrachud, *Republic of Religion: The Rise and Fall of Colonial Secularism in India*, Penguin, 2020, p. 87.

19. Ibid.

20. Ibid.
    Also see: Christina George, 'Begum Aizaz Rasul: The Only Muslim Woman to Oppose Minority Reservations in the Constituent Assembly', *Indian Express*, 14 February 2018, https://indianexpress.com/article/gender/begum-aizaz-rasul-the-only-muslim-woman-to-oppose-minority-reservations-in-the-constituent-assembly-5057096/

21. Ibid.
    Also see: Constituent Assembly debates on 25 May 1949, Part Ii, https://indiankanoon.org/doc/790979/

22. Ibid.
    Also see: Constituent Assembly debates on 25 May 1949, Part Ii, https://indiankanoon.org/doc/790979/

23. Fatima Khan, 'Sardar Hukam Singh, a Minority Rights Champion in Constituent Assembly', The Print, 13 October 2018, https://theprint.in/forgotten-founders/sardar-hukam-singh-a-minority-rights-champion-in-constituent-assembly/132147/
    Constituent Assembly of India debates on 4 January 1949, https://loksabha.nic.in/writereaddata/cadebatefiles/C04011949.html

24. Facts about the Constituent Assembly, https://loksabha.nic.in/constituent/facts.html

25. Constituent Assembly debates, 11 October 1949, read H.V. Kamath's reference to separate electorates, https://loksabha.nic.in/writereaddata/cadebatefiles/C11101949.html

26. Constituent Assembly debates on 25 May 1949, Part I, https://indiankanoon.org/doc/1067214/

27. 'Report That Central Government Likely to Scrap Ministry of Minority Affairs Is False and Contrary to Facts', Ministry of Minority Affairs press release, 3 October 2022, https://pib.gov. in/Pressreleaseshare.aspx?PRID=1864782

28. Ibid.

29. Bharatiya Janata Party, Election Manifesto 1998, https:// library.bjp.org/jspui/bitstream/123456789/241/1/BJP%20 ELECTION%20MANIFESTO%201998.pdf

30. National Commission for Minorities Ministry of Minority Affairs, Government of India,https://www.ncm.nic.in/homepage/about_ ministry.php

31. Ibid.

32. Article 30 in the Constitution of India 1949, Right of Minorities to Establish and Administer Educational Institutions, https:// indiankanoon.org/doc/1983234/

33. Article 29 in the Constitution of India 1949, Protection of Interests of Minorities, https://indiankanoon.org/doc/ 1888152/

34. P.R. Kumarswamy, 'Time Is Right to Upgrade the Minorities Commission', *Swarajya*, 15 June 2016, https://swarajyamag. com/politics/time-is-right-to-upgrade-the-minorities-commission
Read reference to MHA resolution on 12 January 1978 about aims to set up Minorities Commission, p. 106, https://www.minorityaffairs.gov.in/WriteReadData/ RTF1984/1658830363.pdf

35. The National Commission for Minorities Act, 1992, 17 May 1992, https://www.minorityaffairs.gov.in/WriteReadData/ RTF1984/1658314068.pdf 'Minority Report', editorial in *Times of India*, 6 December 2004, https://timesofindia. indiatimes.com/edit-page/todays-editorial-minority-report/ articleshow/947222.cms

36. 'Development of Minority Communities', Ministry of Minority Affairs press release, 28 July 2022, https://www.pib. gov.in/PressReleseDetailm.aspx?PRID=1845932

37. 'PIL in Supreme Court Seeks Minority Status for Hindus in These 8 States', *Outlook*, 31 October 2017, https://www. outlookindia.com/website/story/pil-in-supreme-court-

seeks-minority-status-for-hindus-in-these-8-states/303726
Petitioner Ashwini Kumar Upadhyay has made the following
claim in the Supreme Court: 'Hindus are merely 1% in Laddakh,
2.75% in Mizoram, 2.77% in Lakshadweep, 4% in Kashmir,
8.74% in Nagaland, 11.52% in Meghalaya, 29% in Arunachal
Pradesh, 38.49% in Punjab, 41.29% in Manipur but Centre
has not declared them 'minority', thus Hindus are not protected
Articles 29-30 and cannot establish & administer educational
institution of their choice.' Affidavit can be accessed here through
the Supreme Court Observer website: https://www.scobserver.in/
wp-content/uploads/2021/10/State_Wise_Minority_WP.pdf
Also see: 'These Are the 7 States, 1 UT Where a PIL Wants
Hindus to Be Declared as Minorities', *Indian Express*, 1
November 2017, https://indianexpress.com/article/research/
these-are-the-7-states-1-ut-where-a-pil-wants-hindus-to-be-
declared-as-minorities-4916788/

38. 'T.M.A. Pai Foundation & Ors vs State Of Karnataka & Ors',
writ petition (civil) 317, 1993, judgment dated 31 October
2022, https://indiankanoon.org/doc/512761/

39. 'Affidavit in Supreme Court: States Too Can Define Minority
Status, Says Centre', *Indian Express*, 28 March 2022, https://
indianexpress.com/article/india/affidavit-in-supreme-court-
states-too-can-define-minority-status-says-centre-7839550/
'Should States or Union Notify Who's a Minority? No
Consensus among States, Modi Govt Tells SC', The Print,
13 January 2023, https://theprint.in/judiciary/should-states-
or-union-notify-whos-a-minority-no-consensus-among-states-
modi-govt-tells-sc/1312669/

40. 'Affidavit in Supreme Court: States Too Can Define Minority
Status, Says Centre', *Indian Express*. Also see: 'States Can Give
Minority Status if They're in Minority There; Minority Welfare
Schemes Not Unconstitutional, Centre Tells Supreme Court',
Live Law, 27 March 2022, https://www.livelaw.in/top-stories/
hindus-minority-status-in-states-where-they-are-in-minority-
centre-tells-supreme-court-195122?infinitescroll=1

41. Ibid.

42. Ibid.

43. 'Minority Status for Hindus: Far-Reaching Ramifications, Need Time, Says Centre', *Indian Express*, 10 May 2022, https://indianexpress.com/article/india/far-reaching-ramifications-need-time-centre-7909013/ Also read: Minority status for Hindus too? What changed Centre's approach to this question, *India Today* 10 May 2022, https://www.indiatoday.in/news-analysis/story/minority-status-hindus-centre-approach-1947725-2022-05-10

44. 'Identification of Minorities: SC Gives 6 Weeks to Raj, T'gana, J-K for Reply', PTI, 10 April 2023, https://www.rediff.com/news/report/identification-of-minorities-sc-gives-6-weeks-to-raj-tgana-j-k-for-reply/20230410.htm
'Identification of Minorities at State Level: "Why Isn't Your Own Regime Responding to Your Query?" SC Asks Centre', *Indian Express*, 18 January 2023, https://indianexpress.com/article/india/identification-minorities-state-respond-query-sc-asks-centre-8387372/
'Should States or Union Notify Who's a Minority? No Consensus among States, Modi Govt Tells SC', The Print, 13 January 2023, https://theprint.in/judiciary/should-states-or-union-notify-whos-a-minority-no-consensus-among-states-modi-govt-tells-sc/1312669/
Reference note in Lok Sabha Secretariat: https://loksabhadocs.nic.in/Refinput/New_Reference_Notes/English/14072022_161133_1021205175.pdf

45. Shivkumar Jolad, 'What Our Constituent Assembly Debates Reveal of a Vital Process', Livemint, 25 November 2021, https://www.livemint.com/opinion/online-views/what-our-constituent-assembly-debates-reveal-of-a-vital-process-11637857451306.html

46. Ibid.

47. Ronojoy Sen, *Articles of Faith: Religion, Secularism, and the Indian Supreme Court*, Oxford India Paperbacks, 2012, p. xxiii.

48. Constituent Assembly debates on 3 December 1948, https://indiankanoon.org/doc/607985/

49. Sucheta Sarkar, 'One Part to Guide Them All: Preamble - The Constitution's "Adi- Vakya"', SCC Online, 25 January 2023,

https://www.scconline.com/blog/post/2023/01/25/one-part-to-guide-them-all-preamble-the-constitutions-adi-vakya/

50. Ronojoy Sen, *Articles of Faith*, p. xxiii.
    Also see: Suhrith Parthasarathy, 'Understanding Secularism in the Indian Context', *The Hindu*, 2 January 2018, https://www.thehindu.com/opinion/lead/the-secular-condition/article22347527.ece

51. Abhinav Chandrachud, *Republic of Religion: The Rise and Fall of Colonial Secularism in India*, Penguin, 2020, p. 105.

52. Ibid.

53. Ibid., p. 106.

54. Ibid.

55. Article 25 in the Constitution of India 1949, Freedom of Conscience and Free Profession, Practice and Propagation of Religion (Clause 1), https://indiankanoon.org/doc/631708/

56. Ibid., Clause 2a.

57. Ibid., Clause 2b.

58. Article 17: Abolition of Untouchability, https://indiankanoon.org/doc/1987997/
    '1947: Madras Devadasis (Prevention of Dedication) Act Passed', *Frontline*, 10 August 2022, https://frontline.thehindu.com/arts-and-culture/india-at-75-epochal-moments-1947-madras-devadasis-prevention-of-dedication-act/article65720943.ece

59. Article 26 in the Constitution of India 1949, Freedom to Manage Religious Affairs Subject to Public Order, Morality and Health, Every Religious Denomination or Any Section Thereof Shall Have the Right, https://indiankanoon.org/doc/1858991/

60. 'Great Hypocrisy of "Secular" Indian State: It Controls Only Temples; We Must Take Them Back', *Swarajya*, 6 November 2017, https://swarajyamag.com/magazine/great-hypocrisy-of-secular-indian-state-it-controls-only-temples-we-must-take-them-back
    'Temple Ownership and State's Interference with Article 25 and 26', *Times of India*, 14 November 2021, https://timesofindia.indiatimes.com/readersblog/rise/temple-ownership-and-states-interference-with-article-25-and-26-38972/

J. Sai Deepak, 'Severing the State from the Temple', *Swarajya*, 6 November 2017, https://swarajyamag.com/magazine/this-model-legislation-will-take-the-government-out-of-our-temples

61. 'BJP Leader Files Plea in SC Seeking Uniform Code for Religious, Charitable Endowments', PTI, 22 July 2021, https://theprint.in/judiciary/bjp-leader-files-plea-in-sc-seeking-uniform-code-for-religious-charitable-endowments/700979/ (According to petitioner Upadhyay's estimate, the number of temples under state control stands at 4 lakh. The court has asked him to furnish relevant details.) In Karnataka alone, there are 34,563 temples under the Endowments Department, https://itms.kar.nic.in/hrcehome/hrce_aboutus.phpIn Tamil Nadu, the number stands at 46,020 Hindu and Jain temples, https://hrce.tn.gov.in/hrcehome/hrce_temple.php

62. Abhinav Chandrachud, *Republic of Religion*, pp. 94–95.

63. Ibid.

64. Ibid., p. 104.

65. Ibid., p. 109. (Until 1960, Assam, West Bengal, Punjab and Uttar Pradesh did not have laws governing Hindu temples.)

66. Andhra Pradesh Charitable and Hindu Religious Institutions And Endowments Act, 1987, Section 29 (e), https://www.indiacode.nic.in/bitstream/123456789/16889/1/act_no_30_of_1987.pdf

67. 'The Commissioner, Hindu Religious Endowments, Madras vs. Respondent: Sri Lakshmindra Thirtha Swamiar of Sri Shirur Mutt', Supreme Court of India, date of judgment 16 April 1954, https://main.sci.gov.in/jonew/judis/933.pdf
Also read petition filed in the Supreme Court challenging the TN HRCE Act by SRI SUBRAMANYASWAMIKOIL SWATHANTHRA PARIPALANA STHALATHARGAL SABHAI AND OTHERS vs State of Tamil Nadu, can be accessed here: https://www.indiccollective.org/wp-content/uploads/2020/01/Writ-Petition-for-Tiruchendur.pdf

68. Ibid.

69. Donald Eugene Smith, *India as a Secular State*, Princeton University Press, 1963, p. 246.

70. Ibid., p. 247.
   Article 25 (2)(a): 'Nothing in this article shall affect the operation of any existing law or prevent the State from making any law, regulating or restricting any economic, financial, political or other secular activity which may be associated with religious practice', https://indiankanoon.org/doc/631708/

71. Donald Eugene Smith, *India as a Secular State*, p. 247.
   Also read: Petition filed in the Supreme Court challenging the TN HRCE Act by Sri Subramanyaswamikoil Swathanthra Paripalana Sthalathargal Sabhai and Others vs State of Tamil Nadu, can be accessed here: https://www.indiccollective.org/wp-content/uploads/2020/01/Writ-Petition-for-Tiruchendur.pdf

72. 'The Commissioner, Hindu Religious Endowments, Madras vs Respondent: Sri Lakshmindra Thirtha Swamiar of Sri Shirur Mutt', Supreme Court of India, date of judgment 16 April 1954, https://main.sci.gov.in/jonew/judis/933.pdf
   Also: Donald Eugene Smith, *India as a Secular State*, pp. 247–48.

73. Ibid., p. 50 (the reference here is to an editorial in *The Hindu* published after the 1959 bill was brought in).

74. Petition filed in the Supreme Court challenging the TN HRCE Act by Sri Subramanyaswamikoil Swathanthra Paripalana Sthalathargal Sabhai and Others vs State of Tamil Nadu, can be accessed here: https://www.indiccollective.org/wp-content/uploads/2020/01/Writ-Petition-for-Tiruchendur.pdf

75. Ibid.

76. Ibid., para 26.

77. Ibid., para 28.

78. Ibid., para 28 (c).

79. Ibid., para 28 (h) (iv).

80. Total Immovable Waqf Properties in India as of June 2022, Waqf Management System of India, https://wamsi.nic.in/wamsi/progress/WAMSI_MPR_JUN2022.pdf
   Also Read: Abhinav Chandrachud, *Republic of Religion*, pp. 116–17.

81. The Waqf Act 1995, https://centralwaqfcouncil.gov.in/sites/default/files/The%20Waqf%20Act%201995.pdf

82. Ibid., Sections 63, 64.
Abhinav Chandrachud, *Republic of Religion*, pp. 116–17.
83. Ibid., Section 14 (4).
84. Ibid., Section 32 (2)(e).
85. The Tamil Nadu Hindu Religious and Charitable Endowments Act, 1959, Section 36 (B), https://www.indiacode.nic.in/bitstream/123456789/13275/1/TNHR%26CE%20ACT%2C%201959%20-%20revised%20and%20updated.pdf
86. Sri Subramanyaswamikoil Swathanthra Paripalana Sthalathargal Sabhai And Others Versus State Of Tamil Nadu, 166, Para BBB, https://www.indiccollective.org/wp-content/uploads/2020/01/Writ-Petition-for-Tiruchendur.pdf
87. Hindu Religious Institutions and Charitable Endowments Department, https://itms.kar.nic.in/hrcehome/hrce_aboutus.php
88. 'Karnataka Government Notifies Order Prohibiting Use of Temple Funds for Non-Hindu Religious Institutions', *Swarajya*, 31 July 2021, https://swarajyamag.com/news-brief/karnataka-government-notifies-order-prohibiting-use-of-temple-funds-for-non-hindu-religious-institutions
89. 'Uttarakhand Withdraws Char Dham Act Ahead of Polls', *Hindustan Times*, 30 November 2011, https://www.hindustantimes.com/india-news/uttarakhand-announces-repeal-of-char-dham-devasthanam-management-act-101638259292095.html
'Explained: Why Was Trivendra Singh Rawat Asked to Resign as Uttarakhand CM?', *The Hindu*, 10 March 2021, https://www.thehindu.com/news/national/why-was-trivendra-singh-rawat-asked-to-resign-as-uttarakhand-cm/article34034388.ece
90. Manuraj Shanmugasundaram, 'A Case for State Control of Hindu Temples', *The Hindu*, 6 January 2023, https://www.thehindu.com/opinion/op-ed/a-case-for-state-control-of-hindu-temples/article66313240.ece
91. Interview with Ashwini Upadhyay, April 2023.
92. 'Founder Member, Three Others from AAP Join BJP', *Times of India*, 26 November 2014, https://timesofindia.indiatimes.com/city/delhi/founder-member-three-others-from-aap-join-bjp/articleshow/45277048.cms

93. Ibid.
94. 'Ashwini Kumar Upadhyay versus Union of India & Ors.', Writ Petition (Civil) No. 190, 2023, judgment dated 27 February 2023, https://main.sci.gov.in/supremecourt/2023/6310/6310_2023_3_23_42310_Judgement_27-Feb-2023.pdf
95. Ibid., 2 Para 3.
96. '"You Want to Keep Country on the Boil?" SC Asks Petitioner Seeking to Rename Historical Places', *India Today*, 27 February 2023, https://www.indiatoday.in/law/story/you-want-to-keep-country-on-the-boil-sc-asks-petitioner-seeking-rename-historical-places-2340276-2023-02-27
97. Interview with Ashwini Upadhyay, April 2023.
98. 'Notification of Minorities: Centre Submits Views of 24 States to Supreme Court', *The Hindu*, 13 January 2023, https://www.thehindu.com/news/national/centre-submits-views-of-24-states-to-sc-on-notification-of-minorities/article66371099.ece
99. 'Supreme Court to Hear Petition Challenging Places of Worship Act in July', ANI, 5 April 2023, https://www.ndtv.com/india-news/supreme-court-to-hear-petition-challenging-places-of-worship-act-in-july-3922850
100. 'Delhi HC Seeks RBI Stand on PIL Seeking Uniform Banking Code for Foreign Exchange Transactions', ANI, 5 December 2022, https://theprint.in/india/delhi-hc-seeks-rbi-stand-on-pil-seeking-uniform-banking-code-for-foreign-exchange-transactions/1249301/
101. Ibid.
102. Interview with Ashwini Upadhyay, April 2023.
103. 'Supreme Court Dismisses PILs Seeking Uniform Religion & Gender Neutral Laws on Divorce, Adoption & Maintenance', Live Law, 29 March 2023, https://www.livelaw.in/news-updates/supreme-court-dismisses-pils-seeking-uniform-religion-gender-neutral-laws-on-divorce-adoption-maintenance-225112#:~:text=The%20Supreme%20Court%20on%20Wednesday,and%20maintenance%20across%20the%20country.

104. 'SC Closes Petitions on Uniform Civil Code, Leaves Issue for Parliament to Consider', *Hindustan Times*, 29 March 2023, https://www.hindustantimes.com/india-news/sc-closes-petitions-on-uniform-civil-code-leaves-issue-for-parliament-to-consider-101680103381069.html

105. '"Uniform Civil Code Is Public Policy Matter, No Direction Can Be Issued to Parliament": Centre to Delhi High Court', Live Law, 7 January 2022, https://www.livelaw.in/news-updates/uniform-civil-code-public-policy-matter-delhi-high-court-cant-issue-direction-to-parliament-189029

106. Article 44, https://indiankanoon.org/doc/1406604/ 'Explained | The Uniform Civil Code', *The Hindu*, 6 November 2022, https://www.thehindu.com/news/national/explained-the-uniform-civil-code/article66105351.ece

107. 'Uniform Civil Code in BJP Manifestos over the Years', News 18, 13 October 2016, https://www.news18.com/news/india/uniform-civil-code-in-bjp-manifestos-over-the-years-1301339.html

108. 'BJP Pledges Uniform Civil Code for Karnataka: What's the Status of Its Promise in Other States', *India Today*, 1 May 2023, https://www.indiatoday.in/india/story/bjp-pledges-implement-ucc-karnataka-look-at-status-in-other-states-2367015-2023-05-01

109. 'BJP Committed to Bring UCC Once Democratic Discussions Are Over: Amit Shah', PTI, 24 November 2022, https://economictimes.indiatimes.com/news/politics-and-nation/bjp-committed-to-bring-ucc-once-democratic-discussions-are-over-amit-shah/articleshow/95735796.cms

110. Arghya Sengupta, 'How Secularism Lost Face after Rajiv's Shah Bano Volte-Face', *Times of India*, 11 August 2022, https://timesofindia.indiatimes.com/india/how-secularism-lost-face-after-rajivs-shah-bano-volte-face/articleshow/86747159.cms

111. 'Mohd. Ahmed Khan vs Shah Bano Begum and Ors', 23 April 1985; equivalent citations: 1985 AIR 945, 1985 SCR (3) 844, https://indiankanoon.org/doc/823221/

112. Ibid.

113. Ibid.

114. Ibid.

115. Ibid.
116. Ibid.
117. All India Muslim Personal Law Board, https://aimplboard.org/index_html.html
     Ali Mirza, 'The Curse of the Muslim Personal Law Board', *Swarajya*, 2 October 2014, https://swarajyamag.com/commentary/the-curse-of-the-muslim-personal-law-board
118. 'Angry over Stand on Triple Talaq, Board Slams Govt: Uniform Code to Create Discord', *Indian Express*, 14 October 2016, https://indianexpress.com/article/india/india-news-india/angry-over-stand-on-triple-talaq-board-slams-govt-uniform-code-to-create-discord-3081210/
119. Ali Mirza, 'The Curse of the Muslim Personal Law Board', *Swarajya*, 2 October 2014, https://swarajyamag.com/commentary/the-curse-of-the-muslim-personal-law-board
     Also read: 'AIMPLB Opposes Plea against Polygamy, Nikah Halala, Moves Supreme Court', *Indian Express*, 28 January 2020, https://indianexpress.com/article/india/aimplb-opposes-plea-against-polygamy-nikah-halala-moves-supreme-court-6238496/
120. 'Mohd. Ahmed Khan vs Shah Bano Begum and Ors', 23 April 1985; equivalent citations: 1985 AIR 945, 1985 SCR (3) 844, https://indiankanoon.org/doc/823221/
121. Ibid.
122. Ibid.
123. Ibid.
124. '1985: Shah Bano Case', *Frontline*, 15 August 2022, https://frontline.thehindu.com/the-nation/india-at-75-epochal-moments-1985-shah-bano-case/article65730545.ece
125. The Muslim Women (Protection of Rights on Divorce) Act, 1986, https://www.indiacode.nic.in/bitstream/123456789/15353/1/muslim_women_%28protection_of_rights_on_divorce%29_act%2C_1986.pdf
126. Neerja Chowdhury, *How Prime Ministers Decide*, Aleph, 2023, pp 129–30.
127. Ibid., p. 118.
128. Ibid., p. 128.

129. Ramachandra Guha, *India after Gandhi*, HarperCollins, 2007, pp. 574–75.

130. Ibid.

131. Ibid.
    'Shah Bano Makes a Dramatic Turnaround, Requests Supreme Court to Withdraw Its Judgement', *India Today*, 15 December 1985, https://www.indiatoday.in/magazine/religion/story/19851215-shah-bano-makes-a-dramatic-turnaround-requests-supreme-court-to-withdraw-its-judgement-802240-2014-01-21

132. 'My Faith Is Progressive: Arif Mohammed Khan', *India Today*, 15 September 2014 (first published in 1986), https://www.indiatoday.in/magazine/from-the-archives/story/20140915-arif-mohammed-khan-my-faith-is-progressive-805190-2014-09-08

133. 'Arif Mohammad Khan on Shah Bano Case: "Najma Heptullah Was Key Influence on Rajiv Gandhi"', Scroll.in, 30 May 2015, https://scroll.in/article/730642/arif-mohammad-khan-on-shah-bano-case-najma-heptullah-was-key-influence-on-rajiv-gandhi

134. Ibid.

135. Ajay Kumar, 'Muslim Women's Bill Sparks off Heated Debate, Puts Rajiv Gandhi Govt in a Tight Corner', *India Today*, 31 March 1986, https://www.indiatoday.in/magazine/indiascope/story/19860331-muslim-women-protection-of-rights-on-divorce-bill-raises-too-many-shackles-800736-1986-03-30

136. Neerja Chowdhury, *How Prime Ministers Decide*, Aleph, 2023, p. 128.

137. Lok Sabha Debates, 5 May 1986, Parliament of India, Lok Sabha Digital Library, https://eparlib.nic.in/bitstream/123456789/1364/1/lsd_08_05_05-05-1986.pdf, Page 516-517

138. Ibid.

139. 'Centre Changed Personal Laws of Only Hindus: SC', *Times of India*, 9 February 2011, https://timesofindia.indiatimes.com/india/centre-changed-personal-laws-of-only-hindus-sc/articleshow/7456761.cms

140. One such precedent is: 'Smt Sarla Mudgal, President, Kalyani and ORS vs Union of India', equivalent citations: 1995 AIR 1531, 1995 SCC (3) 635, May 10, 1995, https://indiankanoon. org/doc/733037/

141. '"UCC Is Long Due; Can't Be Made Voluntary": Allahabad HC Calls upon Central Govt to Implement the Mandate of Article 44', Live Law, 18 November 2021, https://www.livelaw. in/news-updates/ucc-long-due-allahabad-high-court-central-govt-implement-mandate-article-44-constitution-185845

142. Lok Sabha Debates, 5 May 1986, Parliament of India, Lok Sabha Digital Library, https://eparlib.nic.in/ bitstream/123456789/1364/1/lsd_08_05_05-05-1986.pdf, Page 436-438

143. Ibid.

144. Ibid.

145. Ramachandra Guha, *India after Gandhi*, pp. 237–40.

146. Ibid.
'Nehru and the Hindu Code Bill', *Outlook*, 3 February 2022, https://www.outlookindia.com/website/story/nehru-and-the-hindu-code-bill/221000

147. Interview, December 2022.

148. Eminent Parliamentarians Monograph series, *Dr Syama Prasad Mookerjee*, Lok Sabha Secretariat New Delhi, 1990, 83, https://eparlib.nic.in/bitstream/123456789/58670/1/ Eminent_Parliamentarians_Series_Syama_Prasad_Mookerjee.pdf

149. Ramachandra Guha, *India after Gandhi*, p. 247.

150. Abhinav Chandrachud, *Republic of Religion*, pp. 146–48.

151. Ibid., p. 148.

152. Ibid., pp. 149–50.

153. Ibid.

154. The Muslim Personal Law (Shariat) Application Act, 1937, https://indiankanoon.org/doc/1325952/

155. Abhinav Chandrachud, *Republic of Religion*, p. 152.

156. The first being the Constituent Assembly, and the second being the reformation of Hindu personal law in the 1950s.

157. Instances where the courts have intervened in Hindu and Christian personal law:

'Landmark Ruling. Supreme Court Removes 6-Month Waiting Period for Divorce', *Business Today*, 1 May 2023, https://www.businesstoday.in/latest/in-focus/story/landmark-ruling-supreme-court-removes-6-month-waiting-period-for-divorce-379583-2023-05-01 '[Christian Divorce] Kerala High Court Strikes Down 10A of Divorce Act, 1869, One Year Waiting Period for Filing Divorce Petition by Mutual Consent Declared Unconstitutional', Live Law, 9 December 2022, https://www.livelaw.in/top-stories/kerala-high-court-christian-divorce-strikes-down10a-divorce-act-1869-one-year-waiting-period-filing-divorce-petition-mutual-consent-216281 'Supreme Court Gives Equal Inheritance Right to Daughters from 1956', *Times of India*, 12 August 2020, https://timesofindia.indiatimes.com/india/sc-gives-equal-inheritance-right-to-daughters-from-1956/articleshow/77493244.cms 'The Landmark Mary Roy Case in SC, Which Gave Syrian Christian Women Equal Right to Property', *Indian Express*, 1 September 2022, https://indianexpress.com/article/explained/mary-roy-case-syrian-christian-women-equal-property-case-sc-explained-8125339/

158. 'Uniform Civil Code against the Spirit of Constitution, Say AIMPLB', *The Hindu*, 5 February 2023, https://www.thehindu.com/news/national/aimplb-opposes-ucc-urges-implementation-of-places-of-worship-act/article66474939.ece

159. Ibn Khaldun Bharati, 'Muslim Personal Law Is an Embarrassment. Adapt It to Modern Life—Marriage, Divorce, Adoption', The Print, 4 April 2023, https://theprint.in/opinion/muslim-personal-law-is-an-embarrassment-adapt-it-to-modern-life-marriage-divorce-adoption/1494440/ 'Uniform Civil Code: Who Is Afraid of UCC?', *India Today*, 29 April 2022, https://www.indiatoday.in/magazine/the-big-story/story/20220509-uniform-civil-code-who-is-afraid-of-a-ucc-1943159-2022-04-29

160. 'Shayara Bano versus Union of India and Others', Writ Petition (C) No. 118 of 2016, Supreme Court of India, judgment

dated 22 August 2017, https://www.scobserver.in/wp-content/
uploads/2021/10/Supreme-Court-of-India-Judgment-WPC-
No.118-of-2016-Triple-Talaq.pdf

161. Ibid.
162. Ibid.
163. Ibid., paras 84, 93.
164. Ibid., 400 para 57.
165. 'Bill Criminalising Instant Triple Talaq Passed in Parliament', PTI,
30 July 2019, https://timesofindia.indiatimes.com/india/triple-
talaq-bill-passed-in-rajya-sabha/articleshow/70452299.cms
The Muslim (Protection of Rights on Marriage) Bill, 2019,
PRS Legislative Research, https://prsindia.org/billtrack/the-
muslim-women-protection-of-rights-on-marriage-bill-2019
166. 'BJP Marks Anniversary of Passage of Triple Talaq Law as
Muslim Women's Rights Day, Union Ministers Hail PM Modi',
Hindustan Times, 31 July 2020, https://www.hindustantimes.
com/india-news/bjp-marks-anniversary-of-passage-of-triple-
talaq-law-as-muslim-women-s-rights-day-union-ministers-
hail-pm-modi/story-0ro4MBT23QUiYpkQAla8IK.html
167. 'Polygamy, "Nikah Halala" Hearing: Supreme Court to Set
New 5-Judge Bench', PTI, 20 January 2023, https://www.ndtv.
com/india-news/polygamy-nikah-halala-hearing-supreme-
court-to-set-new-5-judge-bench-3708833
168. 'Triple Talaq: Your Faith Is Faith, Mine Is Not? Asks Owaisi',
Indian Express, 28 December 2018, https://indianexpress.com/
article/india/lok-sabha-passes-triple-talaq-your-faith-is-faith-
mine-is-not-asks-owaisi-5512624/
169. 'Law Panel Tables Consultation Paper on Reform of Family
Law', Livemint, 31 August 2018, https://www.livemint.
com/Politics/EeanqCFBypfMMyCititzHI/Panel-tables-
consultation-paper-on-common-personal-laws.html
170. Government of India Law Commission of India Consultation
Paper on Reform of Family Law, 31 Aug 2018, p. 7, para
1.15, https://archive.pib.gov.in/documents/rlink/2018/aug/
p201883101.pdf
171. Ibid.

172. 'Nagaland Assembly Unanimously Adopts Resolution Seeking Exemption from Uniform Civil Code', The Wire, 13 September 2023, https://thewire.in/government/nagaland-assembly-adopts-resolution-seeking-exemption-from-uniform-civil-code
'Uniform Civil Code Goes Against Idea of India: Meghalaya Chief Minister Conrad Sangma', India Today, 1 July 2023, https://www.indiatoday.in/india/story/uniform-civil-code-goes-against-idea-of-india-meghalaya-cm-conrad-sangma-2400359-2023-07-01
'Tribals in Odisha Hold Protest Against Uniform Civil Code', Outlook, 4 July 2023, https://www.outlookindia.com/national/tribals-in-odisha-hold-protest-against-ucc-news-300169
'Chhattisgarh Tribal Body Terms Uniform Civil Code as Threat to Existence of Tribals', PTI, 4 July 2023, https://www.telegraphindia.com/india/chhattisgarh-tribal-body-terms-uniform-civil-code-as-threat-to-existence-of-tribals/cid/1949729
'Use Special Powers to Exempt Jharkhand Tribals from Uniform Civil Code: Adivasi Bodies to Governor Radhakrishnan', The Hindu, 5 July 2023, https://www.thehindu.com/news/national/other-states/use-special-powers-to-exempt-jharkhand-tribals-from-uniform-civil-code-adivasi-bodies-to-governor-radhakrishnan/article67044728.ece

173. 'Uniform Civil Code: Law Commission Says It Received over 75 Lakh Responses from Public', India Today, 28 July 2023, https://www.indiatoday.in/law/story/uniform-civil-code-law-commission-received-over-75-lakh-public-feedback-2413073-2023-07-28

174. 'PM Inaugurates Shri Kashi Vishwanath Dham in Varanasi', PIB, 13 December 2021, https://www.pib.gov.in/PressReleasePage.aspx?PRID=1780884

175. Uttar Pradesh District Gazetteers, Varanasi, 1965, pp. 56–57. Vivek Gumaste, 'Gyanvapi Mosque Row: Time for Enlightened Community Leaders to Choose the Path of Discussion and Reconciliation', Firstpost, 8 June 2022, https://www.firstpost.com/opinion/gyanvapi-mosque-row-time-for-enlightened-community-leaders-to-choose-the-path-of-discussion-and-reconciliation-10770151.html,

Alok Kumar, 'Gyanvapi Complex: History of Kashi Vishwanath Temple, Its Present and Future', *Outlook*, 12 September 2022, https://www.outlookindia.com/magazine/national/gyanvapi-complex-history-of-kashi-vishwanath-temple-its-present-and-future-magazine-198538

176. 'Gyanvapi Land Title Dispute Pending in HC – Why Varanasi Court's ASI Order Is a Big Surprise', The Print, 12 April 2021, https://theprint.in/judiciary/gyanvapi-land-title-dispute-pending-in-hc-why-varanasi-courts-asi-order-is-a-big-surprise/637669/

177. '"Vishweshwar Jyotirlinga" Is Situated below Gyanvapi Mosque Which Is Self Manifested: Lord's Next Friend Argues in Allahabad HC', Live Law, 20 May 2022, https://www.livelaw.in/news-updates/vishweshwar-jyotirlinga-is-situated-below-gyanvapi-mosque-which-is-self-manifested-lords-next-friend-argues-in-allahabad-hc-199695

178. The Places of Worship (Special Provisions) Act, 1991, https://www.mha.gov.in/sites/default/files/PlaceWorshipAct1991.pdf Note that the Hindu petitioners in the Gyanvapi case have argued that their suit does not come under the purview of the Places of Worship Act. Read: 'Gyanvapi Not a Mosque; Property Continues to Vest in Deity; Places of Worship Act Not Applicable: Hindu Plaintiffs to Supreme Court', Live Law, 20 May 2022, https://www.livelaw.in/top-stories/gyanvapi-not-a-mosque-property-continues-to-vest-with-deity-places-of-worship-act-not-applicable-hindu-plaintiffs-to-supreme-court-199609 The Muslim side, however, has invoked the Places of Worship Act in suits in this case. Read: 'Gyanvapi Mosque Survey an Attempt to Disrupt Communal Harmony, Violates Places of Worship Act: Mosque Committee Tells Supreme Court', Live Law, 15 May 2022, https://www.livelaw.in/top-stories/gyanvapi-mosque-survey-disrupt-communal-harmony-violates-places-of-worship-act-mosque-committee-supreme-court-199171

179. Places of Worship Act 1991; Section 5. Act not to apply to Ram Janma Bhumi-Babri Masjid, https://www.mha.gov.in/sites/default/files/PlaceWorshipAct1991.pdf

180. '3-Judge Supreme Court Bench to Hear Places of Worship Act Pleas', *Indian Express*, 6 April 2023, https://indianexpress.com/

article/india/sc-centre-reply-pleas-challenging-validity-1991-law-religious-places-8540600/

181. Parliamentary debates, Places of Worship, 9 September 1991, 679, https://eparlib.nic.in/bitstream/123456789/7926/1/10_I_09091991_p342_p387_t276.pdf

182. Ibid., 684.

183. Ibid., 684–85.

184. Ibid, 686.

185. Ibid, 686–87.

186. Ibid., 707.

187. Mani Shankar Aiyar, *Confessions of a Secular Fundamentalist*, Penguin India, 2006.

188. Parliamentary debates, Places of Worship, 9 September 1991, 707, 708, https://eparlib.nic.in/bitstream/123456789/7926/1/10_I_09091991_p342_p387_t276.pdf

189. Ibid., 709.

190. Ibid., 710.

191. Parliamentary debates, Places of Worship Bill, 9 September 1991, 711, 712, https://eparlib.nic.in/bitstream/123456789/7926/1/10_I_09091991_p342_p387_t276.pdf

192. Ibid., 712–13.

193. Ibid., 714, 715.

194. Parliamentary debate, Places of Worship Bill, 10 September 1991, https://eparlib.nic.in/bitstream/123456789/8847/1/10_I_10091991_p180_p247_t260.pdf

195. Parliamentary debates, Places of Worship Bill, 9 September 1991, 725, https://eparlib.nic.in/bitstream/123456789/7926/1/10_I_09091991_p342_p387_t276.pdf

196. Parliamentary debate, Places of Worship Bill, 10 September 1991, https://eparlib.nic.in/bitstream/123456789/8847/1/10_I_10091991_p180_p247_t260.pdf

197. Shishir Tripathi, 'How Places of Worship Act Infringes Basic Human and Constitutional Right of Seeking Justice', Firstpost, 20 May 2022, https://www.firstpost.com/opinion/how-places-

of-worship-act-infringes-basic-human-and-constitutional-right-of-seeking-justice-10696611.html

198. In a statement issued by the MHA on 22 March 2019, the word 'genocide' was used to describe the killings and exodus of Kashmiri Pandits. Strong Action against Terrorism in Jammu and Kashmir, Ministry of Home Affairs, PIB release, 22 Mar 2019, https://pib.gov.in/PressReleasePage.aspx?PRID=1569293

199. 'Kashmiri Pandits Observed January 19 as "Holocaust Day"', PTI, 19 January 2022, https://theprint.in/india/kashmiri-pandits-observed-january-19-as-holocaust-day/807813/

200. 'Centre Seeks More Time to Clarify Stand on Validity of Places of Worship Act', *The Hindu*, 9 January 2023, https://www.thehindu.com/news/national/centre-seeks-more-time-to-clarify-stand-on-validity-of-places-of-worship-act/article66357990.ece '3-Judge Supreme Court Bench to Hear Places of Worship Act Pleas', *Indian Express*, 6 April 2023, https://indianexpress.com/article/india/sc-centre-reply-pleas-challenging-validity-1991-law-religious-places-8540600/

201. Interview conducted in January 2023.

202. Interview with Uday Mahurkar, chief information commissioner, March 2023.

203. Ibid.

204. Interviews, January–March 2023.

205. L.K. Advani, *My Country My Life*, p. 346.

206. Swami Vivekananda, *Complete Works*, Lectures from Colombo to Almora, 'The Future of India', Kindle loc. 17389–17400. Sudheendra Kulkarni, 'From Somnath to Ayodhya', *Indian Express*, 3 October 2010, https://indianexpress.com/article/opinion/columns/from-somnath-to-ayodhya/

207. Parliamentary debates, Places of Worship, 9 September 1991, 735, https://eparlib.nic.in/bitstream/123456789/7926/1/10_I_09091991_p342_p387_t276.pdf

208. Ibid., 736.

209. 'RSS Interpretation of Hindutva Does Not Exclude Muslims: Mohan Bhagwat', The Print, 18 September 2018, https://theprint.in/politics/rss-interpretation-of-hindutva-does-not-exclude-muslims-mohan-bhagwat/120751/

Chapter 6: Hindu Raj: A Study of Inclusivity

1. For a retelling of this story, see Bibek Debroy's translation of the Mahabharata, Vol. 3 (Sections 33 to 44), Penguin, 2015, loc. 2574–2633.
2. Ibid.
3. Ibid.
4. Devdutt Pattanaik, 'Of Weight and Value: The Human Mind Has Power to Create Value and Also Strip Value', *Economic Times*, 11 June 2021, https://economictimes.indiatimes.com/news/company/corporate-trends/of-weight-and-value-the-human-mind-has-power-to-create-value-and-also-strip-value/articleshow/83425698.cms?from=mdr
5. Devdutt Pattanaik, 'Who Is a Hindu? How "Dharma" Manifests in Vedas and Puranas', *Mumbai Mirror*, 29 March 2020, https://mumbaimirror.indiatimes.com/others/sunday-read/who-is-a-hindu-how-dharma-manifests-in-vedas-and-puranas/articleshow/74869736.cms
6. Ibid.
7. Makarand R. Paranjape, 'Dharma Is Not the Same as Religion', *New Indian Express*, 24 July 2021, https://www.newindianexpress.com/opinions/columns/2021/jul/24/dharma-is-not-the-same-as-religion-2334479.html
8. '"It Served the British to Paint Indian Rajahs as Clueless, Despotic Idiots," Says Author Manu Pillai', *Times of India*, 17 October 2021, https://timesofindia.indiatimes.com/home/sunday-times/it-served-the-british-to-paint-indian-rajahs-as-clueless-despotic-idiots-says-author-manu-pillai/articleshow/87065085.cms
9. 'Read Book Review: How Historians and Intellectuals Justified the British Empire's Conquest', Rudrangshu Mukherjee reviews Priya Satia's *Time's Monster: History, Conscience and Britain's Empire*, The Wire, 31 January 2021, https://thewire.in/books/book-review-times-empire-priya-satia-british-empire
10. Devdutt Pattanaik, 'Who Is a Hindu? How "Dharma" Manifests in Vedas and Puranas', *Mumbai Mirror*, 29 March 2020, https://mumbaimirror.indiatimes.com/others/sunday-read/who-is-a-hindu-how-dharma-

manifests-in-vedas-and-puranas/articleshow/74869736.cms
Pavan K. Varma, *The Great Hindu Civilisation*, p. 150.

11. *The Great Hindu Civilisation*, pp. 149–50.
12. Ibid., p. 150.
13. Ibid., pp. 150–51.
14. Ibid., p. 180.
15. Radhakrishnan Pillai, 'Chanakya's Raj Dharma: Enlightened Governance', Speakingtree.in, 15 February 2017, https://www.speakingtree.in/article/chanakya-s-raj-dharma-enlightened-governance
16. Ibid.
17. Pavan K. Varma, 'How Govt's Own Credo of Accountability Got Violated', *Deccan Chronicle*, 16 May 2021, https://www.deccanchronicle.com/opinion/columnists/160521/pavan-varma-how-govts-own-credo-of-accountability-got-violated.html
18. Pavan K. Varma, *The Great Hindu Civilisation*, pp. 176–77.
19. Ibid., p. 178.
20. Ibid.
21. Ram Madhav, *The Hindutva Paradigm: Integral Humanism and the Quest for a Non-Western Worldview*, Westland Publications Private Limited, 2021, p. 68.
22. Ibid., p. 69.
23. Charles Allen, Ashoka: *The Search for India's Lost Emperor*, Abacus, 2013, p. 190.
24. Ibid., pp. ix–xi.
25. Rupert Gethin, 'A Lesson in Religious Tolerance from Ancient India', *Guardian*, 24 April 2019, https://www.theguardian.com/world/2019/apr/24/a-lesson-in-religious-tolerance-from-ancient-india
26. Ibid.
27. Prakash Bajpai, 'Ekam Sat Vipra Bahuda Vadanti', Speakingtree.in, 19 August 2012, https://www.speakingtree.in/blog/ekam-sat-vipra-bahuda-vadanti
28. G.S. Chawla, 'Holy Words and Thoughts of Great Men', Speakingtree.in, 20 May 2014, https://www.speakingtree.in/blog/holy-words-thoughts-of-great-men
29. Interview with historian and author Meenakshi Jain, January 2023.

30. Ibid.
31. Christopher Bayly, *Origins of Nationality in South Asia*, Oxford University Press, 2001, p. 219.
32. Email interview with historian and author Meenakshi Jain, January 2023. Jain also cited Christopher Bayly for the Shivaji example.
33. Ibid.
34. Ibid.
35. Constable's Oriental Miscellany of Original and Selected Publications, vol. 4, Letters from a Mahratta Camp during the Year 1809: Descriptive of the Character Manners Domestic Habits and Religious Ceremonies of the Mahrattas by Thomas Duer Broughton, p. 257, https://ir.nbu.ac.in/bitstream/123456789/2307/1/25990.pdf Full text of 'Letters from a Maratha Camp: During the Year 1809', Indian Council for Historical Research, 1977, https://archive.org/stream/lettersfromamara025327mbp/lettersfromamara025327mbp_djvu.txt
36. Ibid.
37. Ibid., p. 51.
38. Ibid.
39. Akhilesh Pillalamarri, 'The Truth behind the Maratha Empire in India', Diplomat, 5 January 2016, https://thediplomat.com/2016/01/the-truth-behind-the-maratha-empire-in-india/
40. Simon Jenkins, *A Short History of Europe: From Pericles to Putin*, Penguin, 2019, p. 108.
41. Meenakshi Jain, *Parallel Pathways: Essays on Hindu-Muslim Relations 1707-1857*, Konark Publishers, 2010, p. 96. Christopher Bayly, *Origins of Nationality in South Asia*, Oxford University Press, 2001, pp. 219–20. H.R. Gupta, *History of the Sikhs Vol. 5*, Munshiram Manoharlal Publishers Pvt. Ltd, 2008, pp. 425–28.
42. Ibid.
43. Email Interview with historian and author Meenakshi Jain, January 2023. Baqir Muhammad, *Lahore: Past and Present*, BR Publishing Corporation, 1985, pp. 357–58.
44. Ibid.

45. Gottlieb Wilhelm Leitner, *History of Indigenous Education in Punjab*, Archive.org, https://archive.org/stream/dli. ernet.469581/469581-History%20Of%20Indigenous%20 Education%20In%20The%20Punjab_djvu.txt

46. Charles Masson, *Narrative of Various Journeys in Baluchistan, Afghanistan, and the Panjab*, Archive.org, https://archive.org/ stream/in.ernet.dli.2015.132092/2015.132092.Narrative-Of-Virous-Journeys-In-Balochistan-Afghnistan-And-The-Punjab_ djvu.txt

47. Email interview with historian and author Meenakshi Jain, January 2023.
Baron Charles Hugel, *Travels in Kashmir and the Panjab*, John Petheram, 1845, p. 387.

48. Charles Masson, *Narrative of Various Journeys in Baluchistan, Afghanistan, and the Panjab*.

49. Email interview with historian and author Meenakshi Jain, January 2023.

Chapter 7: Faith in Dharma

1. Himani Datar, 'Faith, Belief and Worship', *The Hindu*, 5 December 2021, https://www.thehindu.com/opinion/open-page/faith-belief-and-worship/article37838783.ece

2. Rajiv Malhotra, 'Dharma Is Not the Same as Religion', Huffpost, 13 June 2011, https://www.huffpost.com/entry/ dharma-religion_b_875314
Makarand R. Paranjape, 'Dharma Is Not the Same as Religion', *New Indian Express*, 24 July 2021, https://www. newindianexpress.com/opinions/columns/2021/jul/24/ dharma-is-not-the-same-as-religion-2334479.html

3. Shriman Narayan (ed.), *The Selected Works of Mahatma Gandhi, vol. 5, The Voice of Truth*, Navajivan Publishing House, p. 214.

4. Bharatan Kumarappa (ed.), *Mahatma Gandhi: My Religion*, Navajivan Publishing House, 1955, p. 7.

5. Rajiv Malhotra, 'Dharma Is Not the Same as Religion', Huff Post 13 Jun 2011.

6. Ibid.

7. Ibid.
8. The foundations of Jewish law can be traced to the Torah. The foundations of Islamic law can be traced to the Quran.
I. Yu. Kozlikhin, V.V. Pugachev, *Jewish and Islamic Law: A Comparative Analysis*, St Petersburg State University, 2017.
9. Rajiv Malhotra, Dharma Is Not the Same as Religion, Huff Post.
10. Himanshu Roy, 'Western Secularism and Colonial Legacy in India', *Economic and Political Weekly*, vol. 41, issue no. 2, 14 January 2006, https://www.epw.in/journal/2006/02/special-articles/western-secularism-and-colonial-legacy-india.html
11. Constituent Assembly debates on 6 December 1948, Part I, https://indiankanoon.org/doc/1933556/
12. Ibid.
13. Ibid.
14. Ibid.
15. Vinay Sahasrabuddhe: 'Hindutva Is a Philosophy with Spiritual Democracy at Its Core', *Outlook*, 3 December 2018, https://www.outlookindia.com/website/story/hindutva-is-a-philosophy-with-spiritual-democracy-at-its-core-vinay-sahasrabuddhe/321144
16. 'India Moving towards Ram Rajya: Rajnath Singh', PTI, 4 April 2023, https://timesofindia.indiatimes.com/india/india-moving-towards-ram-rajya-rajnath-singh/articleshow/99247647.cms?from=mdr
'BJP Governments Living up to Concept of Ram Rajya, Says Yogi Adityanath', ANI, 26 October 2019, https://www.livemint.com/news/india/bjp-governments-living-up-to-concept-of-ram-rajya-says-yogi-adityanath-11572107975860.html
17. Interview with Vinay Sahasrabuddhe, April 2023.
18. Ibid.
19. Ibid.
20. Ibid.
21. Constituent Assembly debates, 12 August 1949, Part I, https://indiankanoon.org/doc/215406/
Constituent Assembly debates, 15 November 1948, https://indiankanoon.org/doc/163623/

22. Ibid.

23. Anand Ranganathan citing Ian Copland in 'The Great Secularism Debate', Newslaundry, 30 January 2015, https://www.newslaundry.com/2015/01/30/the-great-secularism-debate Ian Copland, Ian Mabbett, Asim Roy, , Kate Brittlebank and Adam Bowes, A History of State and Religion in India, Routledge, 2012, p. 230.

24. Adrija Roychowdhury, 'Secularism: Why Nehru Dropped and Indira Inserted the S-Word in the Constitution', *Indian Express*, 27 December 2017, https://indianexpress.com/article/research/anant-kumar-hegde-secularism-constitution-india-bjp-jawaharlal-nehru-indira-gandhi-5001085/

25. Ibid.

26. 'Cow Protection Was a Sensitive Subject in India Even When the Constitution Was Being Framed', Scroll.in, 7 July 2021, https://scroll.in/article/998735/cow-protection-was-a-sensitive-subject-in-india-even-when-the-constitution-was-being-framed

27. Article 48 of the Constitution: The State shall endeavour to organise agriculture and animal husbandry on modern and scientific lines and shall, in particular, take steps for preserving and improving the breeds, and prohibiting the slaughter, of cows and calves and other milch and draught cattle.

28. Adrija Roychowdhury, 'Secularism: Why Nehru Dropped and Indira Inserted the S-Word in the Constitution', *Indian Express*.

29. Ashok Malik, 'Dharma and Drama', Observer Research Foundation, 14 December 2015, https://www.orfonline.org/research/dharma-and-drama/, provided to Asian Age, 28 November 2015.

30. Ibid.

31. Lalit Mohan, 'What Secular Means', *Times of India*, 18 March 2008, https://timesofindia.indiatimes.com/edit-page/sotto-voce-what-secular-means/articleshow/2875443.cms

32. 'Oppn Slams BJP over "Hindu Rashtra" Tweet with Fadnavis Photo', *Indian Express*, 14 April 2023, https://indianexpress.com/article/cities/mumbai/oppn-slams-bjp-over-hindu-rashtra-tweet-with-fadnavis-photo-8555365/

33. Rajiv Malhotra, 'Dharma Is Not the Same as Religion', Huff Post.
34. Himanshi Dahiya, '"Didn't Let Us Study, Wear Good Clothes": Dalits in Delhi Convert to Buddhism', The Quint, 5 October 2022, https://www.thequint.com/news/india/dalits-in-delhi-convert-to-buddhism-mission-jai-bheem-aam-aadmi-party#read-more
35. Ibid.
36. Ibid.
37. 'AAP Minister Rajendra Pal Gautam Resigns after Dalit-Buddhist Conversion Row', The Quint, 9 October 2022, https://www.thequint.com/news/politics/aap-minister-rajendra-pal-gautam-resign-dalit-buddhist-conversion
'Who Is Rajendra Pal Gautam, AAP Minister in Eye of Storm?', Indian Express, 8 October 2022, https://indianexpress.com/article/cities/delhi/who-is-rajendra-pal-gautam-aap-minister-in-eye-of-storm-8196389/
'"Anti-Hindu comments": BJP Seeks Action against Former AAP Minister Gautam', Indian Express, 30 March 2023, https://indianexpress.com/article/cities/delhi/anti-hindu-comments-bjp-seeks-action-against-former-aap-minister-gautam-8526958/
38. 'Ambedkar's 22 Vows: Why Babasaheb Made the Pledge at the Centre of BJP-AAP Row', Indian Express, 10 October 2022, https://indianexpress.com/article/explained/explained-politics/ambedkars-22-vows-why-centre-of-bjp-aap-row-8197971/
39. Ibid.
40. Abhishek Dey, 'Ambedkar to AAP—Mass Conversions Still Bristle Indian Politics. Delhi Event Is Nothing New', The Print, 15 October 2022, https://theprint.in/opinion/newsmaker-of-the-week/ambedkar-to-aap-mass-conversions-still-bristle-indian-politics-delhi-event-is-nothing-new/1168947/
41. Veda B., Chapter 11, Purusha Suktam, National Institute of Open Schooling, https://nios.ac.in/media/documents/OBE_indian_knowledge_tradition/Level_B/Veda_B/VBCh-11.pdf
Pavan K. Varma, The Great Hindu Civilisation, p. 180.
42. The Great Hindu Civilisation, p. 180.
43. Ibid.

44. Ibid., p. 182.

45. Pavan K. Varma, *Adi Shankaracharya: Hinduism's Greatest Thinker*, Tranquebar Press, Westland Books, 2022, pp. 143–46. Neepa Sarkar, 'Speaking Her Mind', *History Today*, vol. 69, issue 5, 5 May 2019, https://www.historytoday.com/history-matters/speaking-her-mind'Why a 12th Century Bhakti Saint Is Key for BJP in Karnataka', *Indian Express*, 15 May 2017, https://indianexpress.com/article/explained/why-a-12th-century-bhakti-saint-is-key-for-bjp-in-karnataka-4655880/
    Neepa Sarkar, 'Speaking Her Mind', *History Today*.

46. Vinay Nalwa, 'Veer Savarkar's Crusade against Caste Discrimination Remains Under-Appreciated', *Indian Express*, 29 May 2019, https://indianexpress.com/article/opinion/columns/vinayak-damodar-savarkar-the-reformer-5753369/

47. Ibid.

48. Vikram Sampath, *Savarkar: Echoes from a Forgotten Past 1883–1924*, Penguin Random House India, 2019, p. xvi.

49. Ibid., p. 414.

50. Ibid., p. 335.

51. Vikram Sampath, Savarkar: *A Contested Legacy 1924–1966*, Penguin Viking, p. 12.

52. Ibid., p. 11.

53. Ibid, p. 17.
    Read Sampath's reproduction of the transcript of the reported meeting between Maulana Shaukat Ali of the Khilafat movement and Savarkar. This meeting had been reported, as Sampath writes, on 25 February 1925, in the special issues of *Lokmanya* and *Mahratta*.
    Ibid., p. 36.

54. Ibid., p. 25. Read Sampath's reference to *Times of India*'s reportage on atrocities during the Moplah riots. Additionally, read: B.R. Ambedkar, *Thoughts on Pakistan*, Thacker and Company Limited, 1941, p. 159.

55. 'Decoding Dr BR Ambedkar's Conversion to Buddhism', The Quint, 13 April 2021, https://www.thequint.com/news/india/br-ambedkar-conversion-to-buddhism

Pragyanshu Gautam, 'Why Ambedkar Converted to Buddhism', *Outlook*, 15 April 2022, https://www.outlookindia.com/national/why-ambedkar-converted-to-buddhism-news-191616

56. *Dr. Babasaheb Ambedkar Writings and Speeches*, vol. 1, compiled by Vasant Moon, 69, XXI.

57. Ibid.

58. Ashok Gopal, 'The Myth of Ambedkar's Support for Savarkar, Hindu Mahasabha's Social Reform', *Indian Express*, 15 April 2023, https://indianexpress.com/article/opinion/columns/ashok-gopal-new-book-ambedkar-savarkar-hindu-mahasabha-8555885/

59. Ibid.

60. Rajiv Malhotra and Vijaya Vishwanathan, *Varna Jati Caste: A Primer on Indian Social Structures*, p. 21.

61. Ibid., p. 31.

62. Ibid., p. 32.

63. Ibid.

64. 'Udhyanidhi Stalin Alleges Sanatan Dharma "Against Social Justice, Must Be Destroyed"', PTI, 3 September 2023, https://www.telegraphindia.com/india/udhayanidhi-stalin-alleges-sanatana-dharma-against-social-justice-must-be-destroyed/cid/1963516

65. https://twitter.com/Udhaystalin/status/1698032382077800748?lang=en

66. 'I.N.D.I.A Bloc Can Become Anti-Hindu For Votes: BJP's Ravi Shankar on Udhyanidhi Stalin's Remark on "Sanatan Dharma"', Firstpost, 4 September 2023, https://www.firstpost.com/politics/i-n-d-i-a-bloc-can-become-anti-hindu-for-votes-bjps-ravi-shankar-on-udhayanidhi-stalins-remark-on-sanatan-dharma-13074852.html

67. 'Opposition Wants to Crush Sanatan, Attack Us across Country, Need to Stop Them: PM', *Indian Express*, 15 September 2023, https://indianexpress.com/article/political-pulse/pm-modi-madhya-pradesh-chhattisgarh-bjp-polls-8939487/

68. Article 16(4): Nothing in this article shall prevent the State from making any provision for the reservation of appointments or posts in favor of any backward class of citizens which, in

the opinion of the State, is not adequately represented in the services under the State, https://indiankanoon.org/doc/211089/

69. Arun Anand, 'Right Word | How RSS Deals with Caste Conundrum', Firstpost, 7 February 2023, https://www.firstpost.com/opinion/right-word-how-rss-deals-with-caste-conundrum-12117102.html

70. Rakesh Chandra, 'The Rise and Rise of Narendra Modi', *India Today*, 14 September 2013, https://www.indiatoday.in/featured/story/narendra-modi-modi-as-pm-bjp-gujarat-210885-2013-09-12
'PM Modi's "Janata Curfew" Finds Echo in a 1973 Movement He Took Part In', The Print, 20 March 2020, https://theprint.in/india/pm-modis-janata-curfew-finds-echo-in-a-1973-gujarat-movement-he-took-part-in/384840/

71. Anil Baluni, 'Towards Babasaheb's India', *Indian Express*, 14 April 2018, https://indianexpress.com/article/opinion/columns/b-r-ambedkar-birth-anniversary-dalit-atrocities-babasahebs-teachings-5136553/
'RSS Chief Favours Caste-Less Society', *Times of India*, 5 October 2017, https://timesofindia.indiatimes.com/city/patna/rss-chief-favours-caste-less-society/articleshow/60944794.cms

72. Nalin Mehta, 'Three Reasons Why Experts Got It So Wrong on BJP in UP', News 18, 14 March 2022, https://www.news18.com/news/opinion/nalin-mehta-writes-three-reasons-why-experts-got-it-so-wrong-on-bjp-in-up-4873370.html

73. Nalin Mehta, The New BJP: Modi and the Making of the World's Largest Political Party, Westland, 2022, pp. 62–80.
'BJP banks on Labharthi Factor in UP but Past Losses Show It Has Its Limits', *India Today*, 17 February 2022, https://www.indiatoday.in/elections/uttar-pradesh-assembly-polls-2022/story/bjp-banks-on-labharthi-factor-up-polls-1914260-2022-02-17

74. Ibid., p. 31.

75. Mirza Asmer Beg, Shashikant Pandey and Shreyas Sardesai, 'The BJP's Rock Solid Social Coalition', *The Hindu*, 12 March 2022, https://www.thehindu.com/elections/uttar-pradesh-assembly/the-bjps-rock-solid-coalition/article65215484.ece

76. Interview with Professor Badri Narayan, April 2023.

77. 'SP's Swami Prasad Maurya Seeks Deletion of "Casteist Insults" in Ramcharitmanas', ANI, 22 January 2023, https://theprint.in/politics/sps-swami-prasad-maurya-seeks-deletion-of-casteist-insults-in-ramcharitmanas/1329315/

78. 'Pages from Ramcharitmanas Burned in Vrindavan in Support of SP Leader Swami Prasad Maurya', PTI, 29 January 2023, https://www.news18.com/news/politics/pages-from-ramcharitmanas-burned-in-vrindavan-in-support-of-sp-leader-swami-prasad-maurya-6946129.html

79. Interview with Professor Badri Narayan, April 2023.

80. 'SC status to Converted Community Members Will Open "Floodgates" for Religious Conversions: VHP', PTI, 17 October 2022, https://economictimes.indiatimes.com/news/india/sc-status-to-converted-community-members-will-open-floodgates-for-religious-conversions-vhp/articleshow/94924918.cms?from=mdr

81. Interview with Professor Badri Narayan, 2021 and April 2023.

82. Interview with Professor Badri Narayan, April 2023.
'Rs 15 Crore Nishadraj Park in Prayagraj to Be Icon of Caste Unity', *Times of India*, 8 January 2021, https://timesofindia.indiatimes.com/city/allahabad/rs-15cr-nishadraj-park-in-prayagraj-to-be-icon-of-caste-unity/articleshow/80161227.cms

83. 'UP CM Yogi Adityanath Woos Nishads with Ramayana Recall', *Times of India*, 18 December 2021, https://timesofindia.indiatimes.com/city/lucknow/up-cm-yogi-adityanath-woos-nishads-with-ramayana-recall/articleshow/88350458.cms

84. 'Six-Decade-Long Battle for Citizenship Comes to an End as Valmikis Get Domicile Certificates in Jammu and Kashmir', PTI, 31 July 2020, https://www.thehindu.com/news/national/other-states/six-decade-long-battle-of-citizenship-comes-to-an-end-as-valmikis-get-domicile-certificates-in-jammu-and-kashmir/article32239828.ece
'Can Now Dare to Dream: J&K's Valmiki Community Rejoices End of Article 370', *India Today*, 8 August 2019, https://www.indiatoday.in/india/story/can-now-dare-to-

dream-j-k-s-valmiki-community-rejoices-end-of-article-370-1578908-2019-08-08

85. 'Devaraj Urs Did it 4 Decades Ago. Now, Siddaramaiah Aims for This Karnataka Feat', *Hindustan Times*, 7 May 2018, https://www.hindustantimes.com/india-news/devaraja-urs-did-it-3-decades-ago-now-siddaramaiah-aims-for-this-karnataka-feat/story-hZqodm3CLFlcqhgavFTTjN.html

86. 'BJP Woos Karnataka's Powerful Castes with Reservation Sop Ahead of Assembly Election', *Frontline*, 18 February 2023, https://frontline.thehindu.com/politics/bjp-woos-karnatakas-powerful-castes-with-reservation-sop-ahead-of-assembly-election/article66525254.ece

    'Following UP-Bihar Playbook, Karnataka BJP Seeks to Trump Cong's Social Calculus, Guns for Siddaramaiah', *Indian Express*, 12 April 2023, https://indianexpress.com/article/political-pulse/up-bihar-karnataka-bjp-trump-congress-social-calculus-siddaramaiah-8549756/

87. 'The Ahinda Advantage for the Congress', *The Hindu*, 15 May 2023, https://www.thehindu.com/elections/karnataka-assembly/lokniti-csds-survey-the-ahinda-advantage-for-the-congress/article66851101.ece

88. 'Karnataka Govt. Scraps Muslim Quota of 4%, Increases Quota of Lingayats and Vokkaligas by 2% Each', *The Hindu*, 24 March 2023, https://www.thehindu.com/news/national/karnataka/state-govt-scraps-muslims-quota-of-4-increases-quota-of-lingayats-and-vokkaligas-by-2-each/article66658455.ece

89. 'Owaisi Slams BJP for Scrapping 4% Quota for Muslims in Karnataka', *India Today*, 17 March 2023, https://www.indiatoday.in/india/story/asaduddin-owaisi-slams-bjp-for-scrapping-quota-for-muslims-in-karnataka-2351820-2023-03-27

90. '"Religion-Based Reservation Unconstitutional": Karnataka On Muslim Quota', NDTV, 26 April 2023, https://www.ndtv.com/karnataka-news/karnataka-government-on-muslim-quota-religion-based-reservation-unconstitutional-3982231

91. 'Shivasundar: Denying OBC reservation to Muslims is Unconstitutional and Communal', The Wire, 4 April 2023, https://thewire.in/communalism/obc-reservation-muslims-karnataka

92. For a perspective on the divide within the BJP over the Mandal report, read Vinay Sitapati, *Jugalbandi: The BJP Before Modi*, Penguin, 2020, p. 205.

93. Interview with Vinay Sahasrabuddhe, April 2023.

94. Ibid.

95. Ibid.

96. 'Varna and Caste System Should Be Discarded, Says RSS Chief Mohan Bhagwat', PTI, 8 October 2022, https://www.thehindu.com/news/national/varna-and-caste-system-should-be-discarded-says-rss-chief-mohan-bhagwat/article65982475.ece

97. 'RSS Chief Mohan Bhagwat: Caste in Politics Because Voting Is on Caste', *Indian Express*, 26 January 2018, https://indianexpress.com/article/india/rss-chief-mohan-bhagwat-caste-in-politics-because-voting-is-on-caste-5039615/

Chapter 8: Imagining a Hindu Rashtra

1. 'Ramasamy Udayar vs the District Collector, Perambalur District & Ors', W.A. nos 743 and 2064 of 2019, High Court of Madras, order dated 30 April 2021.

2. Ibid.

3. Ibid.

4. 'Nuh Violence: 312 People Arrested, 142 FIRs Lodged; Bus Services Resume', *India Today*, 8 August 2023, https://www.indiatoday.in/india/story/haryana-nuh-communal-violence-bus-services-resume-curfew-relaxed-2417946-2023-08-08
   Priyadarshi Dutta, 'Nuh Violence: How the Scars of "Meostan" Haunt Haryana', Firstpost, 3 August 2023, https://www.firstpost.com/opinion/nuh-violence-how-the-scars-of-meostan-haunts-haryana-12955152.html
   'Police in Assam, Uttar Pradesh Flag Concerns at Demographic Changes in Districts Bordering Bangladesh, Nepal', *The Hindu*, 31 July 2022, https://www.thehindu.com/news/

national/police-in-assam-uttar-pradesh-flag-concerns-at-demographic-changes-in-districts-bordering-bangladesh-nepal/article65707221.ece

M.J. Akbar, 'An East Bengal in West Bengal', *Open*, 12 March 2021, https://openthemagazine.com/cover-stories/an-east-bengal-in-west-bengal/'Demography Watch: Two-Thirds of Karnataka's Muslims Are Urban', *Swarajya*, 18 July 2016, https://swarajyamag.com/politics/demography-watch-two-thirds-of-karnatakas-muslims-are-urban 'Muslim Population in Border Districts Rising, Need to Strengthen Intelligence, Says CM Himanta', News 18, 4 August 2022, https://www.news18.com/news/politics/assam-muslim-population-in-border-districts-rising-need-to-stregthen-intelligence-says-cm-himanta-5690071.html 'RSS National Meeting Upshot: Conversion, Infiltration Causing Population Imbalance, Says Top Leader', *Indian Express*, 20 October 2022, https://indianexpress.com/article/cities/lucknow/conversion-infiltration-are-leading-to-population-imbalance-says-dattatreya-hosabale-8219619/ 'The Continuing Decline of Hindus in Kerala', *Swarajya*, 25 April 2016, https://swarajyamag.com/politics/the-continuing-decline-of-hindus-in-kerala

5.   'Percentage of Adivasis Declining in J'khand under Soren Govt: Shah', PTI, 4 February 2023, https://www.outlookindia.com/national/percentage-of-adivasis-declining-in-j-khand-under-soren-govt-shah-news-259557

6.   'What's behind Declining Adivasi Population in Jharkhand?', *Outlook*, 12 May 2023, https://www.outlookindia.com/national/cause-and-effect-magazine-284928 'Influx of Bangladesh-Origin Muslims Causes Demographic Change in Jharkhand, Tribals under Grave Threat', *Swarajya*, 10 February 2023, https://swarajyamag.com/commentary/influx-of-bangladesh-origin-muslims-causes-demographic-change-in-jharkhand-tribals-under-grave-threat

7.   'Percentage of Adivasis Declining in J'khand under Soren Govt: Shah', PTI, 4 February 2023, https://www.outlookindia.com/national/percentage-of-adivasis-declining-in-j-khand-under-soren-govt-shah-news-259557

8.   Jaideep Mazumdar, 'Influx of Bangladesh-Origin Muslims Causes Demographic Change in Jharkhand, Tribals Under Grave Threat', *Swarajya*, 10 February 2023, https://swarajyamag.com/commentary/influx-of-bangladesh-origin-muslims-causes-demographic-change-in-jharkhand-tribals-under-grave-threat

9.   Ibid.

10. 'Why the BJP Is Wooing Tribal Voters in Jharkhand', *India Today*, 9 June 2022, https://www.indiatoday.in/india-today-insight/story/why-the-bjp-is-wooing-tribal-voters-in-jharkhand-1960336-2022-06-09
     Kunal Shahdeo, 'Will Adivasis Be Able to Stave off Attempts to Saffronise Them?', *Outlook*, 24 November 2022, https://www.outlookindia.com/national/will-adivasis-be-able-to-stave-off-attempts-to-saffronise-them--magazine-239473

11. Jaideep Mazumdar, 'Influx of Bangladesh-Origin Muslims Causes Demographic Change in Jharkhand, Tribals Under Grave Threat', *Swarajya*.

12. Snigdhendu Bhattacharya, 'The Politics of Demography in Assam and West Bengal', *Outlook*, 12 May 2023, https://www.outlookindia.com/national/politicising-demography-magazine-284973
     Snigdhendu Bhattacharya, 'Bengal Election: How BJP and TMC Are Using Old Census Data to Fuel Identity-Based Politics', Scroll.in, 29 March 2021, https://scroll.in/article/990780/bengal-election-how-bjp-and-tmc-are-using-old-census-data-to-fuel-identity-based-politics

13. Ibid.

14. 'Bengal Beats India in Muslim Growth Rate', *Times of India*, 26 August 2018, https://timesofindia.indiatimes.com/india/bengal-beats-india-in-muslim-growth-rate/articleshow/48675987.cms
     Census 2011, Assam data: https://www.census2011.co.in/data/religion/state/18-assam.htmlCensus 2011, West Bengal data: https://www.census2011.co.in/data/religion/state/19-west-bengal.html

15. 'Total Fertility Rate Down across All Communities', *Times of India*, 8 May 2022, https://timesofindia.indiatimes.com/

india/total-fertility-rate-down-across-all-communities/
articleshow/91407169.cms

'Fertility Rate below Replacement Level for All but Hindus and
Muslims', *Times of India*, 12 January 2018, https://timesofindia.
indiatimes.com/india/fertility-rate-below-replacement-level-
for-all-but-hindus-muslims/articleshow/62465588.cms

'Growth of Muslim Population a Matter of Concern:
VHP', *Times of India*, 28 August 2015, https://timesofindia.
indiatimes.com/india/growth-of-muslim-population-a-matter-
of-concern-vhp/articleshow/48704022.cms

16. 'Theory That Muslims Can Exceed Hindus in India Is
    Propaganda: Ex-CEC SY Quraishi', The Quint, 29 March
    2022,   https://www.thequint.com/news/india/former-chief-
    election-commissioner-sy-quraishi-muslims-overtaking-hindu-
    population-propaganda

    'Fact vs Fiction: National Family Health Survey Busts Some
    Myths about Muslims in India', The Print, 23 May 2022,
    https://theprint.in/india/fact-vs-fiction-national-family-health-
    survey-busts-some-myths-about-muslims-in-india/966513/
    Arfa Khanum Sherwani, 'As Muslims See Sharpest Drop in
    Fertility Rate, Hindutva Propaganda Falls Flat', The Wire, 10
    May 2022, https://thewire.in/government/watch-as-muslims-
    see-sharpest-drop-in-fertility-rate-hindutva-propaganda-falls-flat

17. R. Jagannathan, 'It's Not Just About Muslim TFR; Hindus
    Need to Articulate Their Demographic Concerns Better',
    Swarajya, 11 May 2022, https://swarajyamag.com/politics/
    its-not-just-about-muslim-tfr-hindus-need-to-articulate-their-
    demographic-concerns-better

18. National Family Health Survey (NFHS-5), 2019–21 India
    Report, p. 124, https://dhsprogram.com/pubs/pdf/FR375/
    FR375.pdf

19. R. Jagannathan, *Dharmic Nation: Freeing Bharat, Remaking
    India*, Rupa Publications, 2023, pp. 119–21.

20. Ibid.

21. 'German Court Convicts Ex-IS Member of Murder, Role
    in Yazidi Genocide', VOA News, 30 November 2021,
    https://www.voanews.com/a/german-court-convicts-ex-is-

member-of-murder-role-in-yazidi-genocide/6333801.html
'German Court Tries Daesh Terrorist over Yazidi Genocide,
Child Murder', *Daily Sabah*, 24 April 2020, https://www.
dailysabah.com/world/german-court-tries-daesh-terrorist-over-
yazidi-genocide-child-murder/news

22. 'Yazidi Genocide: IS Member Found Guilty in German
Landmark Trial', BBC, 30 November 2021, https://www.bbc.
com/news/world-europe-59474616
23. Sanjeev Sanyal, 'The Last Pagans of Iraq', Project Syndicate, 8
August 2014, https://www.project-syndicate.org/commentary/
sanjeev-sanyal-on-the-worsening-plight-of-the-yezidi-minority
24. Ibid.
25. Ibid.
26. Ibid.
27. Catherine Nixey, *The Darkening Age: The Christian Destruction
of the Classical World, Pan Books*, 2017, Kindle edition, loc. 304.
28. Ibid., loc. 303.
29. Ibid., p. 166.
30. George Thundiparambil, 'Reawakening of Pagan India and
the Challenge It Can Pose to Abrahamic Worldviews: Part
II', *Swarajya*, 14 September 2020, https://swarajyamag.com/
politics/reawakening-of-pagan-india-and-the-challenge-it-can-
pose-to-abrahamic-worldviews-part-ii
31. Centre for Policy Studies, 'The Christianisation of the Northeast:
It All Began on the Eve of Independence', https://cpsindia.org/
wp-content/uploads/2023/06/Blog-28-Northeast-Web.pdf
Also read: Aadrita Chakravorty, 'Khasi Society and Its Pagan
Resemblance', *Shillong Times*, 3 September 2018, https://
theshillongtimes.com/2018/09/03/khasi-society-and-its-
pagan-resemblance/
32. 'Kashmiri Pandits Observe "Holocaust Day" to Mark 30 Years
of Mass Exodus from Valley', *Indian Express*, 19 January 2020,
https://indianexpress.com/article/india/kashmiri-pandits-
observe-holocaust-day-to-mark-30-years-of-mass-
exodus-6224739/
'The Kashmir Killings: Jihadis Continue to Murder Innocent
Civilians; Bihar Migrant 9th Victim Since May 1', News 18,

2 June 2022, https://www.news18.com/news/india/kashmiri-hindu-teachers-killing-puts-focus-back-on-targeted-attacks-on-civilians-as-at-least-12-killed-since-2021-heres-a-list-5286487.html

33. Aakar Patel, 'If India Turns into a Hindu Rashtra, What Will It Mean', *Deccan Chronicle*, 26 April 2022, https://www.deccanchronicle.com/opinion/columnists/260422/aakar-patel-if-india-turns-into-a-hindu-rashtra-what-will-it-mean.html

34. Raju Rajagopal, 'How the Exclusionary Hindu Rashtra Project Threatens the Foundations of Indian Democracy', Scroll.in, 12 May 2023, https://scroll.in/article/1047597/how-the-exclusionary-hindu-rashtra-project-threatens-the-foundations-of-indian-democracy

35. 'Hinduism Different from Hindutva; RSS-BJP Ideology Has Overshadowed Congress: Rahul Gandhi', *Economic Times*, 13 November 2021, https://economictimes.indiatimes.com/news/politics-and-nation/hinduism-different-from-hindutva-rss-bjp-ideology-has-overshadowed-congress-rahul-gandhi/articleshow/87677199.cms?from=mdr

36. Supreme Court in Dr Ramesh Yeshwant Prabhoo v Shri Prabhakar Kashinath Kunte, 11 December 1995, https://indiankanoon.org/doc/925631/
'Hindu, Hinduism and Hindutva, as Understood by Supreme Court', *Times of India*, 24 January 2022, https://timesofindia.indiatimes.com/india/hindu-hinduism-and-hindutva-as-understood-by-supreme-court/articleshow/89081806.cms

37. Hasan Suroor, 'RIP Secularism. Let's Try a Hindu Democratic Republic of India (T&C Apply)', *Times of India*, 29 May 2022, https://timesofindia.indiatimes.com/blogs/voices/rip-secularism-lets-try-a-hindu-democratic-republic-of-india-tc-apply/

38. Ibid.

39. Ibid.

40. 'President Ignores Oppn, Unveils Savarkar Portrait', *Economic Times*, 27 February 2003, https://economictimes.indiatimes.com/president-ignores-oppn-unveils-savarkar-portrait/articleshow/38698461.cms?from=mdr

41. Ibid.

'Divided over Savarkar: Once upon a Time, CPI MPs, Feroze Gandhi Spoke up for Him', *Indian Express*, 1 April 2023, https://indianexpress.com/article/political-pulse/savarkar-row-cpi-mp-feroze-gandhi-spoke-up-for-him-8532389/

42. Shashi Tharoor, 'VD Savarkar: The Man Credited with Creating Hindutva Didn't Want It Restricted to Hindus', The Print, 26 February 2018, https://theprint.in/pageturner/excerpt/veer-savarkar-hindutva-india/38073/

43. Vikram Sampath, 'Read This before Deciding Whether Savarkar Was a British Stooge or Strategic Nationalist', The Print, 20 November 2018, https://theprint.in/opinion/read-this-before-deciding-whether-savarkar-was-a-british-stooge-or-strategic-nationalist/151667/

44. Vikram Sampath, *Savarkar: A Contested Legacy 1924–1966*, Penguin Random House, 2021, pp. 30–1.

45. Ibid., p. 94.

46. Ibid., p. 205.

47. Ibid., p. 24.

48. Ibid., pp. 93–4.

49. Ibid., p. 88.

50. Ibid., p. xvi.

51. Ibid., p. 413.

52. V.D. Savarkar, *Essentials of Hindutva*, 44i, https://savarkar.org/en/encyc/2017/5/23/2_12_12_04_essentials_of_hindutva.v001.pdf_1.pdf

53. Ibid., pp. 42–3.

54. Ibid., 42.

55. Ibid., pp. 49, 50.

56. *Swatantryaveer Vinayak Damodar Savarkar*, Lok Sabha Secretariat New Delhi, February 2003, Parliament Digital Library, 4, https://eparlib.nic.in/bitstream/123456789/56237/1/Swatantryaveer_VDSavarkar.English.pdf

57. Ibid., pp. 4, 5.

58. Vikram Sampath, *Savarkar: A Contested Legacy 1924–1966*, pp. 394–99.

59. Ibid., p. 398.

60. Ram Madhav, *The Hindutva Paradigm: Integral Humanism and the Quest for a Non-Western Worldview*, Westland, 2021, p. 2.

61. 'Mohan Bhagwat Distances RSS from Former Chief Golwalkar's Views on Muslims', *Business Standard*, 20 September 2018, https://www.business-standard.com/article/politics/ahead-of-poll-season-mohan-bhagwat-presents-moderate-face-of-rss-118091901306_1.html

62. 'All Indians Share the Same DNA, Cannot Be Differentiated on Basis of Worship, Says RSS Chief', *The Hindu*, 4 July 2021, https://www.thehindu.com/news/national/all-indians-share-the-same-dna-cannot-be-differentiated-on-basis-of-worship-says-rss-chief/article35136818.ece

63. M.S. Golwalkar, *We or Our Nationhood Defined*, Bharat Publications, 1939, pp. 64–5.

64. Ibid., pp. 104, 105.

65. 'RSS Officially Disowns Golwalkar's Book', *Times of India*, 9 March 2006, https://timesofindia.indiatimes.com/india/rss-officially-disowns-golwalkars-book/articleshow/1443606.cms

66. Ibid.

67. Ibid.

68. M.S. Gowalkar, *Bunch of Thoughts*, Rashtrotthana Sahitya, 2000, p. 111, https://www.thehinducentre.com/multimedia/archive/02486/Bunch_of_Thoughts_2486072a.pdf

69. Ibid., p. 114.

70. Ibid.

71. Mohan Bhagwat, *Future Bharat: An RSS Perspective* (compilation of lectures held at Vigyan Bhawan, New Delhi on 17, 18, 19 September 2018), Vimarsh Prakashan, p. 89.

72. Ibid.

73. Walter K. Andersen and Shridhar D. Damle, *The RSS: A View to the Inside*, Penguin Books, 2018, p. 120.

74. Ibid.

75. 'RSS Kick Starts Future of Bharat', *India Today*, 18 September 2018, https://www.indiatoday.in/mail-today/story/rss-kick-starts-future-of-bharat-1342595-2018-09-18
Mohan Bhagwat, *Future Bharat: An RSS Perspective*.

76. Ram Madhav, 'Glasnost in RSS', *Indian Express*, 25 September 2018, https://indianexpress.com/article/opinion/columns/mohan-bhagwat-rss-event-glasnost-in-rss-hindu-rashtra-muslims-5372558/

77. Mohan Bhagwat, *Future Bharat: An RSS Perspective*, p. 56.

78. Ibid., p. 57.

79. Ibid.

80. Ibid., p. 58.

81. Ibid.

82. Ibid., p. 88.

83. Sunil Ambekar, *The RSS: Roadmaps for the 21st Century*, Rupa Publications, 2019, loc. 1506.

84. 'RSS Chief Mohan Bhagwat Visits Mosque, Top Cleric Calls Him "Rashtra Pita"', NDTV, 22 September 2022, https://www.ndtv.com/india-news/rss-chief-mohan-bhagwats-mosque-visit-in-delhi-amid-outreach-to-muslim-leaders-3367035

85. Ibid.

86. S.Y. Quraishi, 'Why We Met the RSS Chief', *Indian Express*, 26 September 2022, https://indianexpress.com/article/opinion/columns/why-we-met-the-rss-chief-muslim-community-members-dialogue-8172702/

87. Ibid.

88. Javed M. Ansari, 'As a Muslim, What Mohan Bhagwat's Outreach Means to Me', NDTV, 24 September 2022, https://www.ndtv.com/opinion/as-a-muslim-what-mohan-bhagwats-outreach-means-to-me-3369348

89. Mohan Bhagwat, *Future Bharat: An RSS Perspective*, p. 88.

90. 'Constitution and Rules, as Amended by the National Council at Delhi on 6th February 2004', Bharatiya Janata Party, 18, https://eci.gov.in/files/file/4929-bharatiya-janata-party-constitution/ The Indian National Congress Constitution, https://cdn.inc.in/constitutions/inc_constitution_files/000/000/001/original/Congress-Constitution.pdf?1505640610 The BJP's constitution mentions the words 'secular' or 'secularism' five times, the Congress's three times.

91. 'Secularism Biggest Threat to India's Tradition on Global Stage, Says Yogi Adityanath', *India Today*, 8 March 2021, https://www.indiatoday.in/india/story/yogi-adityanath-

secularism-biggest-threat-to-india-tradition-on-global-stage-1776752-2021-03-08

92. 'Constitution and Rules, as Amended by the National Council at Delhi on 6th February 2004', Bharatiya Janata Party, 18, https://eci.gov.in/files/file/4929-bharatiya-janata-party-constitution/

93. Shashi Tharoor, 'Secularism Is Just a Word, but Opposition Will Resist BJP Bid to Drop It from Constitution', The Print, 15 March 2018, https://theprint.in/opinion/secularism-word-opposition-will-still-resist-bjps-bid-to-drop-it-from-constitution/41917/

94. Vinay Sitapati, *Jugalbandi: The BJP Before Modi*, pp. 149–50.

95. 'Govt under Fire for Using Old Version of Constitution Preamble without "Secular" Word', *Indian Express*, 28 January 2015, https://indianexpress.com/article/india/india-others/ad-shows-constitution-without-socialist-or-secular-creates-furore/ 'CPI Opposes Dropping of "Secular" Word from Preamble', PTI, 31 January 2015, https://indianexpress.com/article/india/india-others/cpi-opposes-dropping-of-secular-word-from-preamble/

96. '"Committed to Secularism; Wouldn't Remove the Word": Venkaiah Naidu', PTI, 30 January 2015, https://economictimes.indiatimes.com/news/politics-and-nation/committed-to-secularism-wouldnt-remove-the-word-venkaiah-naidu/articleshow/46055757.cms?from=mdr

97. Amit Shah at Agenda Aaj Tak, 28 December 2019, the video of his interview can be accessed here: https://www.indiatoday.in/india/video/we-do-not-see-india-as-a-hindu-rashtra-says-amit-shah-1629187-2019-12-17 (Amit Shah's response to a question about Hindu Rashtra is in the thirty-first minute). 'BJP Does Not See India as Hindu Rashtra: Amit Shah', *India Today*, 18 December 2019, https://www.indiatoday.in/india/story/bjp-does-not-see-india-as-hindu-rashtra-amit-shah-1629164-2019-12-17

98. Rajya Sabha party-wise seat strength as on September 2023, https://sansad.in/rs/members

99. Prime Minister Narendra Modi's speech on 6 February 2020 in the Lok Sabha can be accessed here: https://eparlib.nic.in/

bitstream/123456789/789218/1/lsd_17_03_06-02-2020.pdf (operative excerpt on p. 185).

'PM Modi on CAA: Nehru Was in Favour of Protecting Pak Minorities, Did He Want a Hindu Rashtra?', *Indian Express*, 6 February 2020, https://indianexpress.com/article/india/prime-minister-narendra-modi-lok-sabha-speech-motion-of-thanks-kashmir-caa-protests-congress-left-6254096/

100. Ibid.

101. '"Muslims in India . . .": Nirmala Sitharaman on Negative Western "perception"', *Hindustan Times*, 11 April 2023, https://www.hindustantimes.com/india-news/muslims-in-india-nirmala-sitharaman-on-negative-western-perception-101681171340854.html

102. Interview with Rajeev Mantri, March 2023.

9: Can India Be Tolerant without Being 'Secular'?

1. 'The Future of World Religions: Population Growth Projections, 2010–2050', Pew Research Center, 2 April 2015, https://www.pewresearch.org/religion/2015/04/02/religious-projections-2010-2050/

2. Sadanand Dhume, 'India Needs to Find a Sane Way to Discuss Relative Decline in Hindu Population', *Economic Times*, 24 April 2015, https://economictimes.indiatimes.com/blogs/et-commentary/india-needs-to-find-a-sane-way-to-discuss-relative-decline-in-hindu-population/

3. '6 Facts about South Korea's Growing Christian Population', Pew Research Center, 12 August 2014, pewresearch.org/short-reads/2014/08/12/6-facts-about-christianity-in-south-korea/

4. 'Zen No More: Japan Shuns Buddhist Traditions as Temples Close', *Guardian*, 6 November 2015, https://www.theguardian.com/world/2015/nov/06/zen-no-more-japan-shuns-its-buddhist-traditions-as-temples-close

'Japan's Shinto Shrines in Crisis Despite Abe Pushing Religion', Bloomberg, 24 May 2016, https://www.bloomberg.com/news/articles/2016-05-23/abe-shines-spotlight-on-japan-s-shinto-shrines-in-grip-of-crisis#xj4y7vzkg

5.   'This Pew Research Article Projects That in 2050, 90% of Thailand's Population Will Still Remain Buddhist', Pew Research Center, 2 April 2015, https://www.pewresearch.org/religion/2015/04/02/buddhists/

6.   See Sections 3 and 67 of the Thai Constitution: https://www.ilo.org/dyn/natlex/docs/ELECTRONIC/103607/132859/F-1348511433/THA103607%202019.pdf

7.   Article 25 in the Constitution of India 1949, Freedom of Conscience and Free Profession, Practice and Propagation of Religion, https://indiankanoon.org/doc/631708/

8.   'Shashi Tharoor Kicks up Row with "Hindu Pakistan" Jibe', *The Hindu*, 12 July 2018, https://www.thehindu.com/news/national/shashi-tharoor-kicks-up-row-with-hindu-pakistan-jibe/article24399540.ece

9.   Ibid.

10. Tripurdaman Singh and Adeel Hussain, *Nehru: The Debates That Defined India*, Fourth Estate, 2021, pp. 3–4.

11. Ibid., p. 4.

12. Ibid.

13. Ibid.

14. 'Triumph of Hindutva Movement Would Mark End of "Indian idea": Tharoor', PTI, 31 October 2020, https://www.thehindu.com/news/national/triumph-of-hindutva-movement-would-mark-end-of-indian-idea-tharoor/article32990160.ece 'Congress Leaders Accuse BJP, RSS of Turning India into a Neo-Fascist State', PTI, 9 April 2016, https://economictimes.indiatimes.com/news/politics-and-nation/congress-leaders-accuse-bjp-rss-of-turning-india-into-neo-fascist-state/articleshow/51756189.cms?from=mdr

15. 'Rahul Launches Yatra: Tricolour under Attack, BJP Wants to Divide Country on Religious Lines', *Indian Express*, 8 September 2022, https://indianexpress.com/article/political-pulse/congress-rahul-gandhi-launch-bharat-jodo-yatra-8137068/

16. Ajay Skaria, 'Why Hindutva Is a Racist Supremacism – Not Merely Communalism or Majoritarianism', The Wire, 10 September 2021, https://thewire.in/politics/why-hindutva-is-a-racist-supremacism-not-a-communalism-or-majoritarianism

17. Vikram Sampath, Savarkar: *Echoes from a Forgotten Past 1883–1924*, Penguin Random House, 2019, p. 411.

18. David Torrance, 'The Relationship between Church and State in the United Kingdom', House of Commons Library, 25 January 2023, https://researchbriefings.files.parliament.uk/documents/CBP-8886/CBP-8886.pdf

19. Encyclopedia Brittanica, Flag of England, https://www.britannica.com/topic/flag-of-England

20. National Anthem, the Royal Family, https://www.royal.uk/encyclopedia/national-anthem

21. David Torrance, 'The Relationship between Church and State in the United Kingdom', House of Commons Library.
    Crown Nominations Commission, Functions, The Church of England, https://www.churchofengland.org/sites/default/files/2020-06/CNC%20General%20Synod%20Amendments%20to%20Standing%20Orders%20136-141%20July%202019.pdf

22. The Church of England in Parliament, https://churchinparliament.org/about-the-lords-spiritual/

23. UK Prisons Act: https://www.legislation.gov.uk/ukpga/Geo6and1Eliz2/15-16/52/crossheading/prison-officers/ enacted 'The Spirit of Healthcare: The NHS's 25m Pound Brigade of Chaplains', *Guardian*, 22 February 2016, https://www.theguardian.com/society/2016/feb/22/spirit-of-healthcare-the-nhs-chaplains-religion Royal Army Chaplains' Department: https://www.army.mod.uk/who-we-are/corps-regiments-and-units/royal-army-chaplains-department/

24. Robert Long and Shadi Danechi, 'Faith Schools in England: FAQ', House of Commons Library, https://researchbriefings.files.parliament.uk/documents/SN06972/SN06972.pdf Education Act, 1996: https://www.legislation.gov.uk/ukpga/1996/56/section/375?view=plain

25. 'David Cameron Says the UK Is a Christian Country', BBC, 16 December 2011, https://www.bbc.com/news/uk-politics-16224394

26. Ibid.

27. Ibid.

28. Ashley Walsh, 'Civil Religion and the Enlightenment in England, 1707-1800', blog on Boydell and Brewer about his book *Civil Religion and the Enlightenment in England, 1707–1800*, 5 February 2020, https://boydellandbrewer.com/blog/early-modern-and-modern-history/civil-religion-and-the-enlightenment-in-england-1707-1800/

29. Ibid.
    See: Encyclopaedia Britannica, Civil Religion, https://www.britannica.com/topic/civil-religion

30. Jean Jacques Rousseau, Stanford Encyclopedia of Philosophy, 27 September 2010, https://plato.stanford.edu/entries/rousseau/

31. Ashley Walsh, 'Civil Religion and the Enlightenment in England, 1707-1800'.

32. 'David Cameron Says the UK Is a Christian Country', BBC, 16 December 2011, https://www.bbc.com/news/uk-politics-16224394

33. 'UK Secularism on Rise as More Than Half Say They Have No Religion', *Guardian*, 11 July 2019, https://www.theguardian.com/world/2019/jul/11/uk-secularism-on-rise-as-more-than-half-say-they-have-no-religion

34. Religion, England and Wales: Census 2021, Office for National Statistics, https://www.ons.gov.uk/peoplepopulationandcommunity/culturalidentity/religion/bulletins/religionenglandandwales/census2021

35. 2021 'Census: More Non-Religious Than Christians among Those under 67', Humanists UK, 30 January 2023, https://humanists.uk/2023/01/30/2021-census-more-non-religious-than-christians-among-those-under-67/

36. Ibid.

37. Ibid.

38. 'Hindu and Proud: How Britain's Prime Minister Rishi Sunak Has Always Worn His Religion on His Sleeve', Firstpost, 27 October 2022, https://www.firstpost.com/explainers/hindu-and-proud-how-britains-prime-minister-rishi-sunak-has-always-worn-his-religion-on-his-sleeve-11521981.html

39. 'Rishi Sunak Is a "Proud Hindu", Has Taken Oath at House of Commons on Bhagavad Gita Since 2017', Firstpost, 25 October 2022, https://www.firstpost.com/world/rishi-sunak-is-a-proud-hindu-has-taken-oath-at-house-of-commons-on-bhagavad-gita-since-2017-11507291.html

40. Ibid.

41. Profile of Professor Robert Hazell, https://www.ucl.ac.uk/constitution-unit/about-us/people/professor-robert-hazell

42. Interview with Professor Robert Hazell, April 2023.

43. A speech by the Queen at Lambeth Palace, 2012, The Royal Family, 15 February 2012, https://www.royal.uk/queens-speech-lambeth-palace-15-february-2012

44. Interview with Professor Robert Hazell, April 2023.

45. Ibid.

46. Dan Balz, '"Cool Britannia" Becomes '90s Anthem', Washington Post, 9 December 1997, https://www.washingtonpost.com/archive/politics/1997/12/09/cool-britannia-becomes-90s-anthem/d0c228ea-e951-40db-9adb-2f71c6f1ccdc/

47. 'These UK Towns and Cities Spend the Most on Christmas Lights and Decorations', Yorkshire Evening Post, 12 November 2020, https://www.yorkshireeveningpost.co.uk/lifestyle/christmas/these-uk-towns-and-cities-spend-the-most-on-christmas-lights-and-decorations-3033904

48. Ahmed T. Kuru, Secularism and State Policies towards Religion: The United States, France, and Turkey, Cambridge University Press, 2009, pp. 79–84.

49. Ibid., pp. 28–29.

50. Interview with Professor Allen Hertzke, April 2023.

51. Ahmed T. Kuru, Secularism and State Policies towards Religion, p. 41.

52. Ibid.

53. Ibid.
    Also read: Juan Williams, 'The Religious Merges with the Political in Reagan's Campaign', Washington Post, 6 March 1984, https://www.washingtonpost.com/archive/politics/1984/03/06/the-religious-merges-with-the-

political-in-reagans-campaign/0ecb1b15-fe06-4704-9b56-ba1124be7fd2/

54. Ibid.
55. 'Supreme Court Overturns Roe v. Wade, Ending Right to Abortion Upheld for Decades', NPR, 24 June 2022, https://www.npr.org/2022/06/24/1102305878/supreme-court-abortion-roe-v-wade-decision-overturn Copy of the judgement: https://www.supremecourt.gov/opinions/21pdf/19-1392_6j37.pdf
56. Michael Drummond, 'Roe v Wade: Who Are the US Supreme Court Justices and What Did They Say about Abortion and Other Civil Rights?', Sky News, 24 June 2022, https://news.sky.com/story/roe-v-wade-who-are-the-us-supreme-court-justices-and-what-did-they-say-about-abortion-and-other-civil-rights-12639860
57. Katherine Stewart, 'How the Christian Right Took over the Judiciary and Changed America', *Guardian*, 25 June 2022, https://www.theguardian.com/world/2022/jun/25/roe-v-wade-abortion-christian-right-america Sarah Posner, 'Overturning Roe Is the Crowning Achievement of Christian Nationalism', Nation, 9 May 2022, https://www.thenation.com/article/society/dobbs-christian-right/
58. 'Faith Leaders React with Joy, Anger to Roe's Reversal', PBS Newshour, 24 June 2022, https://www.pbs.org/newshour/politics/faith-leaders-react-with-joy-anger-to-roes-reversal 'For Conservative Christians, the End of Roe Was a Spiritual Victory', New York Times, 25 June 2022, https://www.nytimes.com/2022/06/25/us/conservative-christians-roe-wade-abortion.html
59. Constitution of the United States, Amendment 1 (1791), p. 29, https://www.senate.gov/civics/resources/pdf/US_Constitution-Senate_Publication_103-21.pdf
60. Pledge of allegiance to the flag, US Government Publishing Office, https://www.govinfo.gov/content/pkg/USCODE-2018-title4/html/USCODE-2018-title4-chap1-sec4.htm
61. Ahmed T. Kuru, *Secularism and State Policies towards Religion*, p. 43.

62. Ibid., pp. 42–43.
    'Judges Ban Pledge of Allegiance from Schools, Citing "Under God"', *New York Times*, 27 June 2002
    Pledge of Allegiance Resources, Pew Research Center, Fact Sheet, 19 March 2004, https://www.pewresearch.org/religion/2004/03/19/publicationpage-aspxid643/
    Statement of Attorney General John Ashcroft Regarding the Pledge of Allegiance Case, Department of Justice, 30 Apr 2003, https://www.justice.gov/archive/opa/pr/2003/April/03_ag_265.htm

63. Ahmed T. Kuru, *Secularism and State Policies towards Religion*, pp. 46–73.

64. Ibid.

65. The President's News Conference with President Abdullah Gul of Turkey in Ankara, Turkey, University of California, Santa Barbara, 6 April 2009, https://www.presidency.ucsb.edu/documents/the-presidents-news-conference-with-president-abdullah-gul-turkey-ankara-turkey

66. J. Randy Forbes, 'Obama Is Wrong When He Says We're Not a Judeo-Christian Nation', US News, 7 May 2009, https://www.usnews.com/opinion/articles/2009/05/07/obama-is-wrong-when-he-says-were-not-a-judeo-christian-nation

67. 'Constitution Based in Christian Principles, McCain Says', *New York Times*, 29 September 2007, https://www.nytimes.com/2007/09/29/us/politics/29cnd-mccain.html

68. Ibid.

69. Treaty of Peace and Friendship, Signed at Tripoli, 4 November 1796, Yale Law School, https://avalon.law.yale.edu/18th_century/bar1796t.asp

70. Interview with Professor Allen Hertzke, April 2023.

71. Treaty of Peace and Friendship, Signed at Tripoli, 4 November 1796, Yale Law School, https://avalon.law.yale.edu/18th_century/bar1796t.asp

72. 'Bhoomi Pujan: Over 300 Concerned Citizens Make "Last Appeal" to PM Modi to Not Attend', The Wire, 4 August 2020, https://thewire.in/communalism/ayodhya-bhoomi-pujan-modi-ram-temple-nfiw-last-appeal

73. 'PM Modi Shouldn't Attend "Bhoomi Pujan" of Ram Temple as Prime Minister, Says Owaisi', PTI, 28 July 2020, https://theprint.in/india/pm-modi-shouldnt-attend-bhoomi-pujan-of-ram-temple-as-prime-minister-says-owaisi/469889/

74. '"India Is Not France," Says Activists Fighting to Wear the Hijab in Schools', TRT World, https://www.trtworld.com/magazine/india-is-not-france-say-activists-fighting-to-wear-the-hijab-in-schools-54410

75. Abdul Khaliq, 'A Dirge for Secularism in India', *Indian Express*, 24 January 2022, https://indianexpress.com/article/opinion/columns/a-dirge-for-secularism-in-india-7738338/
    M. Sihabudheen, 'What the Opposition to the Hijab Says about Indian Secularism and the Sidelining of Muslim Identity', Scroll.in, 8 March 2023, https://scroll.in/article/1044738/what-the-opposition-to-the-hijab-says-about-indian-secularism-and-the-sidelining-of-muslim-identity

76. 'French Lawmakers Banned from Wearing Religious . . .and Football Shirts in Parliament', Local/AFP, 25 January 2018, https://www.thelocal.fr/20180125/no-football-shirts-french-mps-must-adhere-to-dress-code-in-parliament

77. 'French Assembly Votes to Ban Religious Symbols in Schools', *New York Times*, 11 Febuary 2004, https://www.nytimes.com/2004/02/11/world/french-assembly-votes-to-ban-religious-symbols-in-schools.html

78. 'Explained: France's Problem with the Burqa', *Indian Express*, 22 October 2019, https://indianexpress.com/article/explained/france-problem-with-the-burqa-ban-islam-muslims-islamophobia-6080468/

79. 'France Teacher Attack: Seven Charged over Samuel Paty's Killing', BBC, 22 October 2020, https://www.bbc.com/news/world-europe-54632353

80. 'FIR against Nupur Sharma for Her Remarks on Prophet Mohammad', Times Now, 29 May 2022, https://www.timesnownews.com/india/maharashtra-fir-against-bjps-nupur-sharma-for-her-remarks-on-prophet-muhammad-article-91864377

81. 'Samuel Paty Posthumously Awarded French Légion d'honneur', *Guardian*, 21 October 2020, https://www.theguardian.com/world/2020/oct/21/samuel-paty-attack-two-pupils-among-seven-facing-terror-charges 'France Pays Homage to Slain Teacher Samuel Paty at Sorbonne Ceremony', France 24, 21 October 2020, https://www.france24.com/en/europe/20201021-france-to-pay-respects-to-beheaded-teacher-with-ceremony-at-sorbonne

82. 'President Macron Says Islam "in Crisis All over the World", Prompting Backlash', Independent, 2 October 2020, https://www.independent.co.uk/news/world/europe/macron-france-islam-speech-seperatism-religion-b746835.html

83. 'Anger Spreads in Islamic World after Macron's Backing for Muhammad Cartoons', *Guardian*, 26 October 2020, https://www.theguardian.com/world/2020/oct/26/france-islamic-end-boycott-french-goods-macron-muhammad-cartoons

84. 'Amid Global Outrage, BJP Acts against Leaders for Hate Remarks', *The Hindu*, 5 June 2022, https://www.thehindu.com/news/national/bjp-suspends-spokespersons-nupur-sharma-and-naveen-kumar-from-primary-membership/article65496840.ece

85. '"Views of Fringe Elements": India on Qatar's Response to Comments on Prophet', *Hindustan Times*, 5 June 2022, https://www.hindustantimes.com/india-news/views-of-fringe-elements-india-on-qatar-s-response-to-comments-on-prophet-101654435692243.html

86. 'Nupur Sharma Complains of Death Threat', *The Hindu*, 6 June 2022, https://www.thehindu.com/news/cities/Delhi/nupur-sharma-claims-receiving-threats-police-probe-on/article65500726.ece

87. 'Rape, Death Threats: Delhi Police Provide Security to Former BJP Spokesperson Nupur Sharma', *Indian Express*, 7 June 2022, https://indianexpress.com/article/cities/delhi/rape-death-threats-delhi-police-provide-security-to-former-nupur-sharma-7956677/

88. 'Udaipur Tailor Beheaded for Post Backing Ex-BJP Spokesperson Nupur Sharma, Two Arrested', *Times of India*,

29   June   2022,   https://timesofindia.indiatimes.com/city/
udaipur/udaipur-tailor-beheaded-for-post-backing-nupur-two-
held/articleshow/92531046.cms

89. 'Umesh Kolhe Murder: NIA Files Chargesheet Against 11
     Accused', *Indian Express*, 16 December 2022

90. '2 Gruesome Murders, Nationwide Protests: India Reels
     under Violence over Prophet Remarks', *India Today*,
     3   July   2022,   https://www.indiatoday.in/india/story/
     prophet-row-bjp-nupur-sharma-udaipur-amravati-killing-
     protests-1969593-2022-07-03

91. '"Nupur Sharma Should Be Hanged on This Very Square of
     Aurangabad": AIMIM MP Imtiaz Jaleel', Times Now, 11
     June   2022,   https://economictimes.indiatimes.com/news/
     politics-and-nation/nupur-sharma-should-be-hanged-on-
     this-very-square-of-aurangabad-aimim-mp-imtiaz-jaleel/
     videoshow/92149686.cms?from=mdr

92. '"Nupur Sharma Single-Handedly Responsible for What Is
     Happening in the Country": Supreme Court on Her Comments
     on Prophet Mohammed', Live Law, 1 July 2022, https://www.
     livelaw.in/top-stories/supreme-court-nupur-sharma-remarks-
     prophet-mohammed-provocation-islam-202722
     'SC Protects Nupur Sharma from Arrest in Blasphemy FIRs',
     Times of India, 20 July 2022, https://timesofindia.indiatimes.
     com/india/sc-protects-ex-bjp-spokesperson-nupur-from-arrest-
     in-firs-over-prophet-remarks/articleshow/92990513.cms

93. 'List of Countries Attacking India Rises, but Their Track
     Record on Religion Questionable', Firstpost, 7 June 2022,
     https://www.firstpost.com/india/the-14-nations-which-
     have-condemned-remarks-on-the-prophet-10767571.html
     '"Views of Fringe Elements": India on Qatar's response to
     Comments on Prophet', *Hindustan Times*, 5 June 2022,
     https://www.hindustantimes.com/india-news/views-of-
     fringe-elements-india-on-qatar-s-response-to-comments-on-
     prophet-101654435692243.html
     India did, however, describe the OIC's views as 'narrow-
     minded': '"Narrow-minded": India's Response to Islamic
     Nations' Group after Row over BJP Leader's Prophet Remarks',

India Today, 6 June 2022, https://www.indiatoday.in/india/story/narrow-minded-india-response-islamic-nations-group-oic-nupur-sharma-prophet-remarks-1958887-2022-06-06

94. Section 153A carries punishment for promoting enmity between groups; Section 295A is a penal offence for offending religious sentiments.Section 153A: https://indiankanoon.org/doc/811548/Section 295A: https://indiankanoon.org/doc/1803184/

95. Section 295A in the Indian Penal Code, deliberate and malicious acts, intended to outrage religious feelings of any class by insulting its religion or religious beliefs, https://indiankanoon.org/doc/1803184/
    Also read: The Proposed Section 297 in the Bharatiya Nyaya Sanhita:'297. Whoever, with deliberate and malicious intention of outraging the religious feelings of any class of citizens of India, by words, either spoken or written, or by signs or by visible representations or through electronic means or otherwise, insults or attempts to insult the religion or the religious beliefs of that class, shall be punished with imprisonment of either description for a term which may extend to three years, or with fine, or with both.'
    PRS Legislative Research: https://prsindia.org/files/bills_acts/bills_parliament/2023/Bharatiya_Nyaya_Sanhita,_2023.pdf

96. Ahmed T. Kuru, *Secularism and State Policies towards Religion*, p. 157.

97. Ibid., p. 150.
    It must also be noted, however, that, as Kuru writes, 'since the Law of 1905, the French state and local governments have owned and funded the maintenance of a grand majority of forty—five thousand Catholic churches, in addition to half of the Protestant churches and a tenth of the synagogues. The central and local governments have allowed Catholics, Protestants, and Jews to use these buildings. These and other policies can be better understood by a detailed analysis of the struggles between the assertive and passive secularists.'

98. Interview with Professor Raphael Cohen-Almagor, April 2023.

99. Ibid.

100. 'Portions of Ramcharitmanas Insult Large Section of Society on Basis of Caste: SP Leader', *Outlook*, 22 January 2023, https://www.outlookindia.com/national/portions-of-ramcharitmanas-insult-large-section-of-society-on-basis-of-caste-sp-leader-news-255847

101. Kavita Krishnan, 'One Cannot Be a Feminist in India If You Are Not Fighting the Manusmriti', *Indian Express*, 27 October 2020, https://indianexpress.com/article/opinion/columns/periyar-and-feminism-manusmriti-on-women-manu-dharma-feminism-6887237/

102. 'UCC Will Destroy India's Diversity, Pluralism, Says Asaduddin Owaisi', *Deccan Chronicle*, 14 October 2016, https://www.deccanchronicle.com/nation/politics/141016/uniform-civil-code-will-destroy-indias-diversity-pluralism-asaduddin-owaisi.html

103. 'Sangh Parivar Conspiring to Deny Education to Muslim Girls: Siddaramaiah', *Indian Express*, 18 February 2022, https://indianexpress.com/article/cities/bangalore/sangh-parivar-deny-education-muslim-girls-siddaramaiah-7780349/

104. '"Historic Blunder": Karnataka Congress on Plan to Free Hindu Temples from State Control', PTI, 30 December 2021, https://www.ndtv.com/india-news/historic-blunder-congress-on-karnataka-bjp-plan-to-free-hindu-temples-from-state-control-2679616

105. 'Shashi Tharoor Kicks up Row with "Hindu Pakistan" Jibe', *The Hindu*, 12 July 2018, https://www.thehindu.com/news/national/shashi-tharoor-kicks-up-row-with-hindu-pakistan-jibe/article24399540.ece

106. 1956 Constitution of Pakistan, See Article 32(2), https://ocd.lcwu.edu.pk/cfiles/Pakistan%20Studies/Maj/pak-st-301/Constitution_of_Pakistan_1956.pdf

107. Former Presidents of India, https://presidentofindia.nic.in/former-presidents

108. Madiha Afzal, *Pakistan Under Siege: Extremism, Society and the State*, Penguin Books, 2018, pp. 56–57.
See Articles 197 and 198, 1956 Constitution of Pakistan, and Article 32(2), https://ocd.lcwu.edu.pk/cfiles/Pakistan%20Studies/Maj/pak-st-301/Constitution_of_Pakistan_1956.pdf

109. Ibid., p. 59.
110. Ibid.
    See Pakistan's 1973 Constitution, Preamble and Article 1: https://na.gov.pk/uploads/documents/1549886415_632.pdf
111. Ibid.
    See Pakistan's 1973 Constitution, See Article 91(3): https://na.gov.pk/uploads/documents/1549886415_632.pdf
112. Ibid., pp. 60–62.
113. Ibid., p. 62.
114. 'Persecution of Ahmadiyya Community Continues in Pakistan, PML-Q Issues New Eviction Diktat', ANI, 1 August 2022, https://theprint.in/world/persecution-of-ahmadiyya-community-continues-in-pakistan-pml-q-issues-new-eviction-diktat/1064856/
115. Rajmohan Gandhi, *Modern South India: A History from the 17th Century to Our Times*, Aleph Book Company, 2018, loc. 2816–2842.
    Adrija Roychowdhury, 'The Lingayat Sect: Why Hindu and Why Not Hindu?', *Indian Express*, 12 May 2018, https://indianexpress.com/article/research/lingayat-karnataka-hinduism-basava-veerashaivism-4982608/
116. 'Karnataka: Lingayats Demand Separate Religion Status, Threaten Stir', *Hindustan Times*, 12 February 2023, https://www.hindustantimes.com/india-news/karntaka-lingayats-demand-separate-religion-status-threaten-stir-101676208774379.html
117. 'RSS Publicly Criticises Demand for Religion Status for Lingayats', *The Hindu*, 2 October 2017, https://www.thehindu.com/news/national/karnataka/rss-publicly-criticises-demand-for-religion-status-for-lingayats/article19786856.ece
    '"Won't Allow Divide": Amit Shah's Telling Comment on Lingayat Proposal', NDTV, 4 April 2018, https://www.ndtv.com/karnataka-news/wont-allow-divide-amit-shahs-telling-comment-on-congresss-lingayat-move-in-karnataka-1832677
118. Salil Tripathi, *The Colonel Who Would Not Repent: The Bangladesh War and Its Unquiet Legacy*, Aleph Book Company, 2014, loc. 950.
    Mohammad Afzalur Rahman, 'Dhirendranath Dutta: Portrait of a Patriot', *Daily Star*, 8 November 2021, https://www.

thedailystar.net/views/in-focus/news/dhirendranath-dutta-portrait-patriot-2224291

119. Muhammad Ali Jinnah's first Presidential Address to the Constituent Assembly of Pakistan, 11 August 1947, http://www.columbia.edu/itc/mealac/pritchett/00islamlinks/txt_jinnah_assembly_1947.html

120. Salil Tripathi, *The Colonel Who Would Not Repent*, loc. 906–928.

121. Ibid., loc. 1153.
     '"I Want to Go Back": When Ex-CBI Officer Left Bangladesh in 1964 for His Safety, Regrets "Betraying" His People', News 18, 3 November 2021, https://www.news18.com/news/india/want-to-go-back-when-ex-cbi-officer-left-bdesh-in-1964-for-his-safety-regrets-betraying-his-people-4395692.html

122. Ibid.
     Sushmita Sharmin Preeth, 'Protecting Whose Vested Interests?', *Daily Star*, 23 September 2011, https://www.thedailystar.net/magazine/2011/09/03/human.htm

123. Ibid.

124. Ibid., loc. 2002–2078.

125. Jayant Prasad, 'March 25, 1971: When the Indian Subcontinent Changed', *Hindustan Times*, 24 March 2021, https://www.hindustantimes.com/opinion/march-25-1971-when-the-indian-subcontinent-changed-101616593040387.html

126. Lt Gen. (retd) Subrata Saha, 'And Thus a Desh Was Born', *Outlook*, 17 December 2021, https://www.outlookindia.com/magazine/story/india-news-and-thus-a-desh-was-born/304092

127. Salil Tripathi, *The Colonel Who Would Not Repent*, loc. 2002–2078.

128. Interview with Manas Ghosh in April 2022. Manash Ghosh covered the Bangladesh War and is the author of the book *Bangladesh War: Report from Ground Zero*, Niyogi Books, 2021. The interview can be accessed here: https://www.timesnownews.com/videos/times-now/india/turning-the-page-reporting-the-bangladesh-war-video-91027610

129. Ibid.

130. Ibid.

131. Salil Tripathi, *The Colonel Who Would Not Repent*, loc. 1567.
132. Manash Ghosh, *Bangladesh War: Report from Ground Zero*, Niyogi Books, 2021, pp 125–26.
133. Salil Tripathi, *The Colonel Who Would Not Repent*, loc. 1088.
134. Salil Tripathi, *The Colonel Who Would Not Repent*, loc. 5261. Also see: The Bangladesh Constitution: http://bdlaws.minlaw. gov.bd/act-367.html
135. Ibid., loc. 5367. Also see: the Bangladesh Constitution: http://bdlaws.minlaw. gov.bd/act-367.html
136. Ahrar Ahmad, 'Secularism in Bangladesh: The Troubled Biography of a Constitutional Pillar', *Daily Star*, 16 December 2020, https://www.thedailystar.net/supplements/news/secularism-bangladesh-the-troubled-biography-constitutional-pillar-2011933
137. Salil Tripathi, *The Colonel Who Would Not Repent*, loc. 5625–5669.
138. Ibid.
139. Ibid., loc 5669–5680.
140. 'In 30 Years, There Would Be No Hindus in Bangladesh', *Times of India*, 6 June 2022, https://timesofindia.indiatimes.com/india/in-30-years-there-would-be-no-hindus-in-bangladesh/articleshow/92017468.cms
141. Ibid.
142. Ibid.

Chapter 10: 'Yato Dharmastato Jayah'

1. 'Yogi Adityanath Says Nothing Wrong with Hindu Rashtra Concept, BJP Defends Him', *Hindustan Times*, 6 April 2017, https://www.hindustantimes.com/india-news/up-cm-yogi-adityanath-says-there-s-nothing-wrong-with-hindu-rashtra-concept-bjp-defends-him/story-aJcX0rQV7bpclddfm80P8I.html
2. Dr Ramesh Yeshwant Prabhoo vs Shri Prabhakar Kashinath Kunte & . . ., 11 December 1995, equivalent citations: 1996 AIR 1113, 1996 SCC (1) 130, Supreme Court of India, https://indiankanoon.org/doc/925631/

3. 'Seeking Votes In the Name of Religion Corrupt Practice: SC Constitution Bench [Read Judgment]', Live Law, 2 January 2017, https://www.livelaw.in/seeking-votes-name-religion-corrupt-practice-sc-constitution-bench/

4. Dr Ramesh Yeshwant Prabhoo vs Shri Prabhakar Kashinath Kunte & . . ., on 11 December 1995, equivalent citations: 1996 AIR 1113, 1996 SCC (1) 130, Supreme Court of India, https://indiankanoon.org/doc/925631/

5. Presidential Speeches, Shri L.K. Advani, Bharatiya Janata Party, National Executive, 23 December 1995, p. 403, https://library.bjp.org/jspui/bitstream/123456789/247/1/Lal%20Krishna%20Advani.pdf
    Also: This clip shows L.K. Advani welcoming the observations of the Supreme Court in 1995: https://www.youtube.com/watch?v=zz2cYUWr-ds 'Endorsing Hindutva', *Outlook*, 6 February 2022 (the article carries reactions to the 1995 judgments), https://www.outlookindia.com/magazine/story/endorsing-hindutva/200472

6. 'What Manmohan Singh Said on "Hindutva Is a Way of Life" Judgement', NDTV, 26 September 2018, https://www.ndtv.com/india-news/what-manmohan-singh-said-on-hindutva-is-a-way-of-life-judgement-1922254

7. Dr Ramesh Yeshwant Prabhoo vs Shri Prabhakar Kashinath Kunte & . . .m on 11 December 1995, equivalent citations: 1996 AIR 1113, 1996 SCC (1) 130, Supreme Court of India, https://indiankanoon.org/doc/925631/

8. Ibid.

9. Ibid.

10. 'Results of the 1987 Vile Parle Bypoll', Indiavotes.com, https://www.indiavotes.com/ac/byeDetail/1355

11. Rakshit Sonawane, 'Vile Parle Flashback in Times of CDs', *Indian Express*, 19 April 2007, http://archive.indianexpress.com/news/vile-parle-flashback-in-times-of-cds/28785/

12. Ibid.

13. Dr Ramesh Yeshwant Prabhoo vs Shri Prabhakar Kashinath Kunte & . . ., on 11 December 1995, equivalent citations:

1996 AIR 1113, 1996 SCC (1) 130, Supreme Court of India, https://indiankanoon.org/doc/925631/

14. Ibid.
15. Ibid.
16. Ibid.
17. Sastri Yagnapurushadji and . . .vs Muldas Brudardas Vaishya and . . ., 14 January 1966, equivalent citations: 1966 AIR 1119, 1966 SCR (3) 242, Supreme Court of India, https://indiankanoon.org/doc/145565/
18. Ibid.
19. Dr Ramesh Yeshwant Prabhoo vs Shri Prabhakar Kashinath Kunte & . . ., on 11 December 1995, equivalent citations: 1996 AIR 1113, 1996 SCC (1) 130, Supreme Court of India, https://indiankanoon.org/doc/925631/
20. Ibid.
21. Ibid.
22. Ibid.
23. Ibid.
24. Manohar Joshi vs Nitin Bhaurao Patil & Anr, 11 December 1995, equivalent citations: 1996 AIR 796, 1996 SCC (1) 169, Supreme Court of India, https://indiankanoon.org/doc/1215497/
25. Ibid.
26. A.G. Noorani, 'A Sad Betrayal', *Frontline*, 18 January 2017, https://frontline.thehindu.com/the-nation/a-sad-betrayal/article9486946.ece
    Also read: Ronojoy Sen, *Articles of Faith: Religion, Secularism, and the Indian Supreme Court*, Oxford University Press, 2010, pp. 28–30.
27. Ibid.
28. Ibid.
29. Ibid.
30. Ibid.
31. Ibid.
32. Ibid.
33. Ibid.
34. Ibid.

35. Dr Ramesh Yeshwant Prabhoo vs Shri Prabhakar Kashinath Kunte & . . ., 11 December 1995, equivalent citations: 1996 AIR 1113, 1996 SCC (1) 130, Supreme Court of India, https:// indiankanoon.org/doc/925631/

36. 'Endorsing Hindutva', *Outlook*, 6 February 2022 (this article carries reactions to the 1995 judgments), https://www. outlookindia.com/magazine/story/endorsing-hindutva/200472 'Voting BJP Means Promoting Communalism: CPM', PTI, 9 February 2014, https://www.hindustantimes.com/india/ voting-bjp-means-promoting-communalism-cpm/story- usgQTcMRM1icBqK7bGHzIO.html

37. '"Hinduism different from Hindutva: RSS-BJP Ideology Has Overshadowed Congress": Rahul Gandhi', *Economic Times*, 13 November 2021, https://economictimes.indiatimes.com/ news/politics-and-nation/hinduism-different-from-hindutva- rss-bjp-ideology-has-overshadowed-congress-rahul-gandhi/ articleshow/87677199.cms?from=mdr

38. Manmohan Singh, 'Judiciary's Primary Duty to Save Secular Spirit of Constitution', *Indian Express*, 26 September 2018, https://indianexpress.com/article/india/manmohan- singh-judiciarys-primary-duty-to-save-secular-spirit-of- constitution-5374481/

39. Ibid.

40. 'Ban Use of "Hindutva" in Polls: Teesta', *Times of India*, 21 October 2016, https://timesofindia.indiatimes.com/india/ban- use-of-hindutva-in-polls-teesta/articleshow/54968047.cms

41. 'SupremeCourtSaysItWon'tReconsider1995JudgmentDefining Hindutva as "Way of life"', *Times of India*, 25 October 2016, https://timesofindia.indiatimes.com/india/supreme-court- says-it-wont-reconsider-1995-judgment-defining-hindutva-as- way-of-life/articleshow/55045616.cms

42. Dr Ramesh Yeshwant Prabhoo vs Shri Prabhakar Kashinath Kunte & . . ., on 11 December 1995, equivalent citations: 1996 AIR 1113, 1996 SCC (1) 130, Supreme Court of India, https://indiankanoon.org/doc/925631/

43. Suhrith Parthasarathy, 'Hindutva at the Hustings', *The Hindu*, 4 December 2021, https://www.thehindu.com/opinion/

lead/Hindutva-at-the-hustings/article62114402.ece
'Ban Use of "Hindutva" in Polls: Teesta', *Times of India*, 21 October 2016, https://timesofindia.indiatimes.com/india/ban-use-of-hindutva-in-polls-teesta/articleshow/54968047.cms

44. Kesavananda Bharati . . .vs State of Kerala and Anr, Supreme Court of India, 24 April 1973, https://indiankanoon.org/doc/257876/

45. Ibid.

46. Minerva Mills Ltd. & Ors vs Union Of India & Ors, 31 July 1980, Supreme Court of India, equivalent citations: 1980 AIR 1789, 1981 SCR (1) 206, https://indiankanoon.org/doc/1939993/ Also read: The Constitution (Forty-Second Amendment) Act, 1976, https://www.india.gov.in/my-government/constitution-india/amendments/constitution-india-forty-second-amendment-act-1976

47. S.R. Bommai vs Union of India, 11 March 1994, Supreme Court of India, equivalent citations: 1994 AIR 1918, 1994 SCC (3) 1; https://indiankanoon.org/doc/60799/

48. Ibid., para 29.

49. Ibid., para 148.
Also read: Ronojoy Sen, *Articles of Faith: Religion, Secularism, and the Indian Supreme Court*, pp. xxviii–xxix.

50. Ibid., para 197.

51. Ibid., para 310.
Also read: Ronojoy Sen, *Articles of Faith: Religion, Secularism, and the Indian Supreme Court*, pp. xxviii–xxix.

52. Sanjay Hegde, 'Secular in Spirit and in Letter', *The Hindu*, 7 December 2015, https://www.thehindu.com/opinion/lead/secularism-and-the-provision-for-it-in-the-constitution/article7955211.ece

53. 'Based on Religion India Should Have Been Declared a Hindu Country: Meghalaya HC [Read Judgement]', Live Law, 12 December 2018, https://www.livelaw.in/based-on-religion-india-should-have-been-declared-a-hindu-country-meghalaya-hc-read-judgement/ Also read: '"Nothing Against Secularism": Meghalaya Judge on "Hindu Country" Comment', NDTV, 15 December

2018, https://www.ndtv.com/india-news/meghalaya-high-court-judge-sudip-ranjan-sen-clarifies-on-hindu-country-comment-1963092

54. 'SC Issues Notice on Plea Seeking Removal of Hindu Rashtra Comments from Meghalaya HC Judgement', Live Law, 25 February 2019, https://www.livelaw.in/top-stories/sc-issues-notice-in-plea-seeking-removal-of-hindu-rashtra-comments-from-meghalaya-hc-judgment-143146

55. '"Offends Secular Colour of Country": Meghalaya HC DB Sets Aside Judgement with "Hindu Rashtra" Remarks (Read Judgement)', Live Law, 24 May 2019, https://www.livelaw.in/top-stories/breaking-meghalaya-hc-db-sets-aside-hindu-rashtra-judgment-145247

56. A.G. Noorani, 'A Sad Betrayal', *Frontline*, 18 January 2017, https://frontline.thehindu.com/the-nation/a-sad-betrayal/article9486946.ece

57. 'Places of Worship Act: Validity of Act "May Not Be Covered" by SC Opinion in Ayodhya Case, Says Solicitor General', *Indian Express*, 13 October 2022, https://indianexpress.com/article/delhi/places-of-worship-act-sc-opinion-in-ayodhya-case-may-not-cover-validity-of-act-says-solicitor-general-8204386/

58. M. Siddiq (D) Thr Lrs vs Mahant Suresh Das & Ors, judgment of Supreme Court dated 9 November 2019 (923 para 801) https://www.sci.gov.in/pdf/JUD_2.pdf; 122, para 82.

59. J. Sai Deepak, 'Ayodhya Verdict and the Places of Worship Act', *New Indian Express*, 3 June 2020, https://www.newindianexpress.com/opinions/2020/jun/03/ayodhya-verdict-and-the-places-of-worship-act-2151505.html

60. Dir. of Settlements, A.P. & Ors vs M.R. Apparao & Anr, 20 March 2002, Supreme Court of India, appeal (civil) 2517 of 1999, https://indiankanoon.org/doc/703650/ Also read: '"Not Everything Said in a Judgement Constitutes a Precedent": Supreme Court Explains Distinction between Obiter Dicta and Ratio Decidendi', Live Law, 2 May 2023, https://www.livelaw.in/supreme-court/supreme-court-obiter-dicta-ratio-decidendi-distinction-career-institute-educational-society-vs-om-shree-thakurji-educational-society-227739

61. '"Blatant Violation of Places of Worship Act": Asaduddin Owaisi on Gyanvapi Mosque Order', The Wire, 13 May 2022, https://thewire.in/politics/blatant-violation-of-places-of-worship-act-asaduddin-owaisi-on-gyanvapi-mosque-order Presidential Speeches, Shri L.K. Advani, Bharatiya Janata Party, National Executive, 23 December 1995, p. 403, https://library.bjp.org/jspui/bitstream/123456789/247/1/Lal%20Krishna%20Advani.pdf

    Also: This clip shows L.K. Advani welcoming the observations of the Supreme Court in 1995: https://www.youtube.com/watch?v=zz2cYUWr-ds 'Endorsing Hindutva', Outlook, 6 February 2022 (the article carries reactions to the 1995 judgments), https://www.outlookindia.com/magazine/story/endorsing-hindutva/200472

62. 'Supreme Court to Hear Petition Challenging Places of Worship Act in July', NDTV, 5 April 2023, https://www.ndtv.com/india-news/supreme-court-to-hear-pleas-against-places-of-worship-act-on-october-11-3330261

63. Manohar Joshi vs Nitin Bhaurao Patil & Anr, 11 December 1995, equivalent citations: 1996 AIR 796, 1996 SCC (1) 169, Supreme Court of India, https://indiankanoon.org/doc/1215497/

64. 'Watch Vice President Jagdeep Dhankar's Address at the 83rd All India Presiding Officers' Conference', Sansad TV, 11 January 2023, operative portions from the twenty-ninth minute onwards, https://www.youtube.com/watch?v=2RygIjSF7G8

    'Dhankar Questions "Basic Structure" Doctrine, Says Parliament's Sovereignty Cannot Be Compromised by Judiciary', Outlook, 11 January 2023, https://www.outlookindia.com/national/dhankar-questions-basic-structure-doctrine-says-parliament-s-sovereignty-cannot-be-compromised-by-judiciary-news-252815

    'Keshvananda Bharati Case Judgment Was a Bad Precedent, I Don't Subscribe to It: Jagdeep Dhankhar', Times of India, 11 January 2023, https://timesofindia.indiatimes.com/india/keshvananda-bharati-case-judgment-was-a-bad-precedent-i-dont-subscribe-to-it-jagdeep-dhankhar/articleshow/96906884.cms

65. 'Dhankar Questions "Basic Structure" Doctrine, Says Parliament's Sovereignty Cannot Be Compromised by Judiciary', PTI, 11 January 2023, https://www.outlookindia.com/national/dhankar-questions-basic-structure-doctrine-says-parliament-s-sovereignty-cannot-be-compromised-by-judiciary-news-252815

66. 'Jagdeep Dhankhar's Criticism of the Basic Structure Doctrine Should Ring Alarm Bells', *Indian Express*, 13 January 2023, https://indianexpress.com/article/opinion/editorials/jagdeep-dhankhars-criticism-of-the-basic-structure-doctrine-should-ring-alarm-bells-8378697/ Sangeeta Barooah Pisharoty, 'History Warns That Altering a Constitution's Basic Structure Leads Down a Dark Path', The Wire, 17 January 2023, https://thewire.in/rights/constitution-basic-structure-nazi-germany-jagdeep-dhankhar

67. 'As VP Dhankar Criticises Basic Structure, Recalling What BJP Margdarshak LK Advani Once Wrote: "One of Law's Greatest Ever Triumphs"', Indian Express publishes an excerpt from L.K. Advani's *My Country My Life* (Rupa, 2008), https://indianexpress.com/article/opinion/columns/v-p-dhankhar-criticises-basic-structure-bjp-margdarshak-l-k-advani-greatest-ever-triumphs-8380445/
Also read: L.K. Advani, Rediff, 1998, 'Those who say the present government seeks to undo the good work done by Dr Ambedkar would do well to study his own views in this regard', https://www.rediff.com/news/1998/may/27cons1.htm '"Constitution Is Supreme . . .": P Chidambaram Dismisses Vice President's Remarks', *Hindustan Times*, 12 January 2023, https://www.hindustantimes.com/india-news/constitution-is-supreme-p-chidambaram-dismisses-vice-president-s-remarks-101673498456077.html

68. 'All Got Together to Pass NJAC, Now Oppn Rethink: "Need to Protect Judiciary"', *Indian Express*, 16 December 2022, https://indianexpress.com/article/political-pulse/njac-parliament-opposition-protect-judiciary-8327352/

69. The Constitution (Ninety-Ninth Amendment) Act, 2014, https://prsindia.org/files/bills_acts/acts_parliament/2014/the-constitution-(99th-amendment)-act,-2014.pdf

70. 'SC Bench Strikes Down NJAC Act as "Unconstitutional and Void"', *The Hindu*, 17 October 2015, https://www.thehindu.com/news/national/Supreme-Court-verdict-on-NJAC-and-Collegium-system/article60384480.ece

71. 'No Proposal at Present to Reintroduce NJAC: Govt in RS', PTI, 8 December 2022, https://economictimes.indiatimes.com/news/india/no-proposal-at-present-to-reintroduce-njac-govt-in-rs/articleshow/96090866.cms

72. Shri A.S. Narayana Deekshitulu vs State of Andhra Pradesh & Ors, 19 March 1996, Supreme Court of India, equivalent citations: 1996 AIR 1765, JT 1996 (3) 482, https://indiankanoon.org/doc/49052391/

73. Ibid.

74. Ibid.

75. Ibid.

76. Ibid.

77. Ibid.

78. Dharma Chakra Logo of Supreme Court, 7, https://main.sci.gov.in/pdf/Museum/m2.pdf

79. Shri A.S. Narayana Deekshitulu vs State of Andhra Pradesh & Ors, 19 March 1996, Supreme Court of India, equivalent citations: 1996 AIR 1765, JT 1996 (3) 482, https://indiankanoon.org/doc/49052391/

80. Ibid.

81. Rev Stanislaus vs State of Madhya Pradesh and Ors, 17 January 1977, Supreme Court of India, equivalent citations: 1977 AIR 908, 1977 SCR (2) 611, https://indiankanoon.org/doc/1308071/

82. A background to the term: Catholic Dictionary, Catholic Culture, https://www.catholicculture.org/culture/library/dictionary/index.cfm?id=36967

Conclusion

1. 'After a Gap of 28 Years: PM Narendra Modi's Australia Trip to Boost Trade, Investment, Energy and Security Partnership', *Economic Times*, 13 November 2014, https://economictimes.indiatimes.com/news/politics-and-nation/

after-a-gap-of-28-years-pm-narendra-modis-australia-trip-to-boost-trade-investment-energy-and-security-partnership/articleshow/45129851.cms

2. 'Prime Minister Narendra Modi's Speech in Sydney: Full Transcript', *India Today*, 17 November 2014, https://www.indiatoday.in/india/story/narendra-modi-sydney-pm-in-oz-australia-visit-allphones-arena-227519-2014-11-17

3. Swami Vivekananda, My Master, pp. 19, 20, 21, http://www.vivekananda.net/PDFBooks/My_Master.pdf

4. 'End of the Soviet Union; Text of Bush's Address to Nation on Gorbachev's Resignation', *New York Times*, 26 December 1991, https://www.nytimes.com/1991/12/26/world/end-soviet-union-text-bush-s-address-nation-gorbachev-s-resignation.html George H.W. Bush, 'A Whole Europe, a Free Europe', Voices of Democracy, 31 May 1989, https://voicesofdemocracy.umd.edu/bush-a-whole-europe-speech-text/

5. Vinay Sahasrabuddhe, 'Vishwa Guru India: The Why and the How', *New Indian Express*, 22 June 2022, https://www.newindianexpress.com/opinions/2022/jun/22/vishwa-guru-india-the-why-and-the-how-2468181.html

6. S. Jaishankar, *The India Way: Strategies for an Uncertain World*, HarperCollins Publishers India, 2020, pp. 55–6.

7. Ibid., p. 75.

8. 'G-20 and India's Presidency', Ministry of External Affairs, PIB release, 9 December 2022, https://pib.gov.in/PressReleaseIframePage.aspx?PRID=1882356

9. S. Jaishankar, *The India Way: Strategies for an Uncertain World*, p. 221.

10. Otto von Bismarck, 'Excerpt of Otto von Bismarck's "Blood and Iron" Speech', 19th & 20th Century Europe, https://europeanhistory.omeka.net/items/show/54

11. Prakarsh Singh, 'Economics of Civil Conflict: Evidence from the Punjab Insurgency', November 2016, p. 6, https://docs.iza.org/dp10390.pdf

12. Punjab: The Knights of Falsehood IV, Psalms Of Terror, South Asia Terrorism Portal, https://www.satp.org/satporgtp/publication/nightsoffalsehood/falsehood4.htm

13. Rishab Sharma, 'From Dubai to Ajnala: Amritpal Singh's Transformation into a Radical Leader', *India Today*, 23 April 2023, https://www.indiatoday.in/india/story/amritpal-singh-detained-jalandhar-khalistan-waris-punjab-de-dubai-ajnala-2348454-2023-03-18
'On the Run for Over a Month, Amritpal Singh Arrested, Sent to Jail in Assam', *Indian Express*, 24 April 2023, https://indianexpress.com/article/cities/chandigarh/waris-de-punjab-amritpal-singh-arrested-say-police-8570954/

14. 'Manipur Violence: Death Toll Touches 175 Mark, Few Stolen Weapons Recovered, Say Police', *Hindustan Times*, 15 September 2023, https://www.hindustantimes.com/india-news/manipur-toll-175-few-stolen-weapons-recovered-police-101694716778763.html

15. Rakhee Bhattacharya, 'Other Side of the Growth Story', *Statesman*, 6 September 2021, https://www.thestatesman.com/northeast/side-growth-story-1503003406.html

16. Varun Kumar Das and Vikash Vaibhav, 'Northeast Needs to Boost Its Economy. Even Assam Has Failed to Participate in India's Growth', The Print, 13 December 2021, https://theprint.in/opinion/northeast-needs-to-boost-its-economy-even-assam-has-failed-to-participate-in-indias-growth/780676/

17. 'Kashmiri Pandit out to Buy Groceries Shot in Year's 1st Targeted Killing', *Times of India*, 27 February 2023, https://timesofindia.indiatimes.com/city/srinagar/bank-guard-killed-in-first-fatal-attack-on-kashmiri-pandits-since-october/articleshow/98256032.cms?from=mdr
'Analysing Violence in the Kashmir Valley over the Years', *The Hindu*, 8 March 2023, https://www.thehindu.com/data/data-analysing-violence-in-the-kashmir-valley-over-the-years/article66591257.ece

18. 'Post-Poll Survey: The 2019 Verdict Is a Manifestation of the Deepening Religious Divide in India', *The Hindu* CSDS-Lokniti Post-Poll Survey, *The Hindu*, 30 May 2019, https://www.thehindu.com/elections/lok-sabha-2019/the-verdict-is-a-manifestation-of-the-deepening-religious-divide-in-india/article27297239.ece?art=package

19. P.K. Balachandran, 'How Did BJP Win Christian-Dominated North-East?', Citizen, 4 March 2023.
    Rakhi Bose and Syeda Ambia Zahan, 'How BJP–RSS Kept Hindutva on the Back Burner in Poll-Bound Northeastern States', *Outlook*.

20. Ram Madhav, *The Hindutva Paradigm: Integral Humanism and the Quest for a Non-Western Worldview*, Westland, 2021, p. 54.
    Pulakesh Upadhyaya, 'Integral Humanism and the BJP', *Swarajya*, 8 December 2012, https://swarajyamag.com/commentary/integral-humanism-and-the-bjp

21. 'BJP Suspends Telangana MLA Raja Singh', *The Hindu*, 23 August 2022, https://www.thehindu.com/news/national/telangana/bjp-suspends-telangana-mla-raja-singh/article65801110.ece

22. 'No Comments on Religion, BJP Advises Its Spokespersons', *Hindustan Times*, 8 June 2022, https://www.hindustantimes.com/india-news/no-comments-on-religion-bjp-advises-its-spokespersons-101654628889889.html

23. Shishir Tripathi, 'What's behind the Rise of "The New BJP"? Nalin Mehta's "NARAD" Provides Significant Clue', India.com, 6 April 2022, https://www.india.com/opinion/whats-behind-the-rise-of-the-new-bjp-nalin-mehtas-narad-provides-significant-clue-5323383/

24. Nalin Mehta, The New BJP, pp. 110–11.

25. 'Post-Poll Survey: The 2019 Verdict Is a Manifestation of the Deepening Religious Divide in India', *The Hindu* CSDS-Lokniti Post-Poll Survey, *The Hindu*, 30 May 2019, https://www.thehindu.com/elections/lok-sabha-2019/the-verdict-is-a-manifestation-of-the-deepening-religious-divide-in-india/article27297239.ece?art=package

26. 'BJP Woos Pasmanda Muslims at the Behest of Narendra Modi', *The Hindu*, 27 August 2022, https://frontline.thehindu.com/politics/bjp-woos-pasmanda-muslims-at-the-behest-of-narendra-modi/article65787301.ece
    Swaminathan S. Anklesaria Aiyar, 'What Victory of Its Muslim Candidates in UP Says about BJP', *Times of India*, 3 June 2023, https://timesofindia.indiatimes.

com/india/what-victory-of-its-muslims-candidates-in-up-says-about-bjp/articleshow/100732015.cms
Dr Prashant Prabhakar Deshpande, 'A Peep into the Pasmanda Outreach of Modi & RSS – Part I', *Times of India*, 30 January 2023, https://timesofindia.indiatimes.com/blogs/truth-lies-and-politics/a-peep-into-the-pasmanda-outreach-of-modi-rss-part-i/ Prashant Prabhakar Deshpande, 'A Peep into the Pasmanda Outreach of Modi & RSS – Part II', *Times of India*, 1 February 2023, https://timesofindia.indiatimes.com/blogs/truth-lies-and-politics/a-peep-into-the-pasmanda-outreach-of-modi-rss-part-ii/

27. 'Welfare of Minorities without Appeasement, Discrimination Mantra of Modi Govt: Naqvi', *Economic Times*, 24 March 2022, https://economictimes.indiatimes.com/news/india/welfare-of-minorities-without-appeasement-discrimination-mantra-of-modi-govt-naqvi/articleshow/90415812.cms?from=mdr

28. 'BJP Membership Near 18 Crore, Only Seven Countries Have More Population: JP Nadda', *Times of India*, 29 August 2019, https://timesofindia.indiatimes.com/india/bjp-membership-near-18-crore-only-seven-countries-have-more-population-jp-nadda/articleshow/70897742.cms
     Nalin Mehta, *The New BJP*, pp. 168–82.

29. 'Pasmanda Muslims Want "Sammaan", Not "Sneh", Says Former MP Ali Anwar Ansari in Open Letter to PM', *Indian Express*, 22 July 2022, https://indianexpress.com/article/political-pulse/pasmanda-muslims-mp-ali-anwar-ansari-open-letter-modi-8042760

30. Dhirendra Jha, 'Shadow Armies: Reporting on Fringe Organisations and Foot Soldiers of Hindutva', Firstpost, 23 April 2017, https://www.firstpost.com/india/shadow-armiesreporting-on-the-fringe-organisations-and-foot-soldiers-of-hindutva-3399788.html
     Also read: Christophe Jaffrelot, 'Bajrang Dal and Making of the Deeper State', *Indian Express*, 5 June 2023, https://indianexpress.com/article/opinion/columns/karnataka-election-result-poll-campaign-congress-bjp-8645595/

31. Interview conducted in February 2023.
32. 'Rajasthan: Two Muslim Men Found Charred Inside Car; 5 Bajrang Dal Workers Named in FIR, One Arrested', News 18, 17 February 2023, https://www.news18.com/news/india/rajasthan-two-muslim-men-found-charred-inside-car-bajrang-dal-workers-named-in-fir-one-arrested-7109179.html Rao Jaswant Singh and Bhaskar Mukherjee, 'How Cow Vigilantism Thrives Here with Police Help', *Times of India*, 23 February 2023, https://timesofindia.indiatimes.com/india/how-cow-vigilantism-thrives-here-with-police-help/articleshow/98144950.cms 'Muslim Men's Killing: 3 Accused Had Worked as Haryana Police Informers', NDTV, 21 February 2023, https://www.ndtv.com/india-news/muslim-mens-killing-accused-had-worked-as-haryana-police-informers-3800644
33. 'Who Runs Bajrang Dal? Here Are the Men Who Power "Moral Policing and Vigilante" Hindutva Group', The Print, 6 December 2021, https://theprint.in/india/who-runs-bajrang-dal-here-are-the-men-who-power-moral-policing-vigilante-hindutva-group/776452/ '3 lakh from 5 States Have Joined Us on First Day of Membership Drive: Bajrang Dal', *Times of India*, 20 November 2017, https://timesofindia.indiatimes.com/india/3-lakh-from-5-states-have-joined-us-on-first-day-of-membership-drive-bajrang-dal/articleshow/61728544.cms
34. 'Hindutva Leaders at Haridwar Event Call for Muslim Genocide', The Wire, 22 December 2021, https://thewire.in/communalism/hindutva-leaders-dharma-sansad-muslim-genocide '"Spoiling the Whole Atmosphere," Says SC on Haridwar Dharam Sansad Hate Speech', *Hindustan Times*, 13 May 2022, https://www.hindustantimes.com/india-news/haridwar-hate-speech-spoiling-atmosphere-in-country-supreme-court-101652381097960.html 'Taking U-turn, Delhi Police Registers FIR in Dharam Sansad Hate Speech Case', *India Today*, 9 May 2022, https://www.indiatoday.in/india/delhi/story/u-turn-delhi-police-registers-fir-in-dharam-sansad-hate-speech-case-1947033-2022-05-09

35. 'PM Modi Asks BJP Leaders to Not Make "Unnecessary Remarks" on Films', *The Hindu*, 18 January 2023, https://www.thehindu.com/news/national/pm-modi-asks-bjp-leaders-to-not-make-unnecessary-remarks-on-films/article66396136.ece

36. 'Suniel Shetty Asks UP CM Yogi Adityanath to Help Stop #BoycottBollywood Trend: "We Are Doing Good Work, Don't Take Drugs"', *Indian Express*, 5 January 2023, https://indianexpress.com/article/entertainment/bollywood/suniel-shetty-asks-up-cm-yogi-adityanath-to-help-stop-boycottbollywood-trend-8363897/
'Bajrang Dal Workers Tear Pathaan Posters at Ahmedabad Mall', *Indian Express*, 5 January 2023, https://indianexpress.com/article/cities/ahmedabad/bajrang-dal-workers-pathaan-posters-ahmedabad-mall-8361891/
Abhilash Malik and Kritika, 'The Booming "Boycott Bollywood" Trend: Who are the Players Behind It?', The Quint, 7 October 2022, https://www.thequint.com/news/webqoof/people-behind-the-boycott-bollywood-trend-analysis

37. '"Chunavi Hindu": BJP Links Rahul Gandhi's Mahakal Temple Visit to Gujarat Polls', *India Today*, 30 November 2022, https://www.indiatoday.in/india/story/chunavi-hindu-bjp-links-rahul-gandhi-mahakal-temple-visit-to-gujarat-polls-2303724-2022-11-30

38. 'Government Has Failed to Bring in Uniform Civil Code, Says Supreme Court', *The Hindu*, 14 September 2019, https://www.thehindu.com/news/national/government-has-failed-to-bring-in-uniform-civil-code-says-supreme-court/article29412592.ece
Smt Sarla Mudgal, President . . .vs Union of India and Ors, 10 May 1995, Supreme Court of India, equivalent citations: 1995 AIR 1531, 1995 SCC (3) 635, https://indiankanoon.org/doc/733037/

39. Anando Bhakto, 'Madhya Pradesh Government's Anti-Love Jehad Bill to Curb Interfaith Marriages by "Forced Conversion"', *Frontline*, 1 December 2020, https://frontline.thehindu.com/cover-story/madhya-pradesh-government-anti-love-jihad-bill-to-curb-interfaith-marriages-by-forced-conversion/article33214010.ece

40. Rev. Stainislaus vs State of Madhya Pradesh & Ors, 17 January 1977, Supreme Court of India, equivalent citations: 1977

AIR 908, 1977 SCR (2) 611, https://main.sci.gov.in/jonew/judis/5403.pdf

41. 'Anti-Conversion Laws in India: How States Deal with Religious Conversion', *India Today*, 23 December 2020, https://www.indiatoday.in/news-analysis/story/anti-conversion-laws-in-india-states-religious-conversion-1752402-2020-12-23 '"All Conversions Can't Be Said to Be Illegal": Supreme Court Refuses to Stay MP HC Order Against Declaration before DM to Change Religion', Live Law, 3 January 2023, https://www.livelaw.in/top-stories/supreme-court-conversion-madhya-pradesh-freedom-of-religion-act-2021-217951

42. Mohd Hanif Quareshi & Others vs the State of Bihar (and Connected . . .), 23 April 1958, Supreme Court of India, equivalent citations: 1958 AIR 731, 1959 SCR 629, https://indiankanoon.org/doc/93885/

43. ANNEX II (8) Gist of State Legislations on Cow Slaughter, Department of Animal Husbandry and Dairying, https://dahd.nic.in/hi/related-links/annex-ii-8-gist-state-legislations-cow-slaughter

44. 'Karnataka High Court Upholds Hijab Ban in Class: Not Essential to Islam', *Indian Express*, 16 March 2022, https://indianexpress.com/article/cities/bangalore/karnataka-high-court-upholds-hijab-ban-in-class-not-essential-to-islam-7821592/ Ayesha Hajeera Almas vs Chief Secretary, 15 March 2022, Karnataka High Court, https://indiankanoon.org/doc/140390250/

45. Para 16, pp. 26–27 of the Karnataka government's affidavit in the Karnataka High Court, 7 February 2022.

46. 'Karnataka Hijab Ban Case: Supreme Court Delivers Split Verdict', *Hindustan Times*, 14 October 2022, https://www.hindustantimes.com/india-news/karnataka-hijab-ban-case-supreme-court-delivers-split-verdict-101665640868155.html '"Can't Change Govt Order on Hijab Just like That": Karnataka Minister Madhu Bangarappa', *Indian Express*, 2 June 2023, https://indianexpress.com/article/education/cant-change-govt-order-on-hijab-just-like-that-karnataka-education-minister-8639188/

Aishat Shaifa v State of Karnataka and Ors, 13 October 2022, https://main.sci.gov.in/supremecourt/ 2022/8344/8344_2022_6_1501_38867_Judgement_13-Oct-2022.pdf

47. 'Madrassas Run on State-Funds Can't Impart Religious Instructions: Gauhati High Court Upholds Assam Law', Live Law, 4 February 2022, https://www.livelaw.in/top-stories/ madrassas-state-funds-cant-impart-religious-instructions-gauhati-high-court-upholds-assam-law-provincialised-madrasas-191182

48. Gauhati High Court, WP(C)/3038/2021 on 4 February 2022, https://indiankanoon.org/doc/32113545/

49. Supreme Court Observer, Case Description and Documents, https://www.scobserver.in/cases/shayara-bano-union-india-triple-talaq-case-background/
Supreme Court Observer, link to 2017 judgment: https://www.scobserver.in/wp-content/uploads/2021/10/Supreme-Court-of-India-Judgment-WPC-No.118-of-2016-Triple-Talaq.pdf

50. Supreme Court Observer, written submission on behalf of the Union of India, https://www.scobserver.in/wp-content/ uploads/2021/10/WS_by_UOI.pdf

51. Ibid.

52. 'Population Is an Asset, but It Can Be a Burden Too; It's Essential to Frame Long-Term Population Policy: Dr Mohan Bhagwat', *Organiser*, 20 April 2023, https://organiser.org/2023/04/20/104146/rss-news/muslims-have-nothing-to-fear-in-india-but-they-must-abandon-the-boisterous-rhetoric-of-supremacy/

53. 'Muslim Personal Law Board Passes Resolution Against Uniform Civil Code, Calls It "Irrelevant"', *Swarajya*, 6 February 2023, https://swarajyamag.com/news-brief/muslim-personal-law-board-passes-resolution-against-uniform-civil-code-calls-it-irrelevant

54. 'India's Top Companies Are Getting into Informal No-Poach Pacts', Mint, 30 June 2022, https://www.livemint.com/ companies/news/nopoaching-pacts-on-the-rise-as-cos-guard-top-talent-11656528361751.html

55. Several sub-sections applicable under Section 3 of the Scheduled Castes and Scheduled Tribes (Prevention of Atrocities) Act, 1989, https://socialjustice.gov.in/writereaddata/UploadFile/The%20Scheduled%20Castes%20and%20Scheduled%20Tribes.pdf
Additionally, refer to: R. Jagannathan, *Dharmic Nation: Freeing Bharat, Remaking India*, Rupa Publications, 2023, p. 196.

56. 'SC Orders All States & UTs to Act Against Hate Speech Suo Moto, Warns of Contempt if Directions Not Followed', The Print, 28 April 2023, https://theprint.in/judiciary/sc-orders-all-states-uts-to-act-against-hate-speech-suo-motu-warns-of-contempt-if-directions-not-followed/1544735/

57. 'Supreme Court to Hear Petition Challenging Places of Worship Act in July', NDTV, 5 April 2023, https://www.ndtv.com/india-news/supreme-court-to-hear-petition-challenging-places-of-worship-act-in-july-3922850

Scan QR code to access the
Penguin Random House India website